GHOST
EMPIRE

GHOST EMPIRE

A Journey to the Legendary Constantinople

RICHARD FIDLER

PEGASUS BOOKS
NEW YORK LONDON

GHOST EMPIRE

Pegasus Books Ltd
148 West 37th Street, 13th Floor
New York, NY 10018

First Pegasus Books hardcover edition September 2017

ISBN: 978-1-68177-511-1

10 9 8 7 6 5 4 3 2 1

Printed in the United States of America
Distributed by W. W. Norton & Company, Inc.

For Emma and Khym, with love.

*I believe that what we become depends on what our
fathers teach us at odd moments, when they aren't trying
to teach us. We are formed by little scraps of wisdom.*

Umberto Eco, *Foucault's Pendulum*

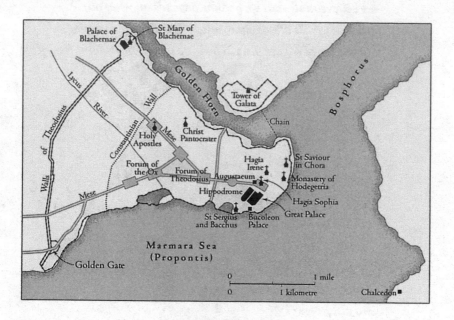

Constantinople

Contents

Author's Note

I LEARNT NOTHING about Byzantium in school. For a long while all I had were images: flashes of lapis lazuli, golden mosaic tiles, gloomy icons. Byzantium was like an undiscovered continent that I planned to get around to exploring one day. My first encounter with the Romans of Constantinople came in my mid-twenties, when I bought the first of John Julius Norwich's three-volume history of Byzantium. I can recall thinking, as I plunged into the spectacularly colourful thousand-year story, *why have I not heard about this before? Why don't more people know about this?* I've heard my friends, after I've regaled them with some of the tales that follow in this book, ask the same question.

Following the thread of Byzantine history, I arrived at the tale of the Fourth Crusade and the sack of Constantinople by the Crusaders in 1204, which was, surely, one of the greatest debacles in the history of the world: a perfect storm of bad planning, low cunning and greed masked as high principle. The story was so rich, I wondered if it could possibly be true. Fortunately we have no shortage of first-hand narratives. Some of them are unintentionally and blackly funny, written by earnest Crusader knights who twist themselves into some very awkward moral contortions to justify the taking of something that does not belong to them, and the desecration of the most beautiful city they had ever seen.

One of those French knights, Geoffrey de Villehardouin, wrote a vivid account of his voyage to Constantinople on that infamous Crusade, the greatest adventure of his life. At the end, Villehardouin describes how, after three days of looting, the Crusaders agreed to pool the plundered wealth of Constantinople and divide it among themselves. As I read this I pictured the Frankish and Venetian soldiers coming and going, depositing barrowloads and sackfuls of treasure into glittering heaps, enough to fill three churches. Villehardouin describes his astonishment in such a way you can almost feel the pen trembling in his hand:

> *The booty gained was so great that none could tell you the end of it: gold and silver, and vessels and precious stones, and samite, and cloth of silk, and robes fair and grey, and ermine, and every choicest thing found upon the earth ... Never, since the world was created, had so much booty been won in any city.*

I have often felt like one of those Crusaders, staring open-mouthed at this treasure heap of stories from the lost world of Constantinople. Professional historians approach such stories with great caution, knowing there will certainly be many fake baubles in the pile. Some accounts will be almost entirely untrue. All will be somewhat distorted according to the prejudices of the author and the political requirements of the moment. Different accounts must be weighed against each other, as well as the documentary evidence and the archaeological record. Sometimes the surviving records are scant and confusing.

Historians are also obliged to discard supernatural explanations for natural phenomena, which is difficult here, because the people of Constantinople were quick to see the hand of God or an angel or a demon in almost everything that happened to them. A modern reader might be inclined to attribute the victory against the Arabs' siege of 718 to Roman technological ingenuity, the brilliant deployment of Greek fire and the cunning exploitation of their complex network of land walls. But in their own accounts they were eager to credit the defeat of the Saracens to the divine intercession of the Virgin Mary, whose presence was seen hovering over the city walls.

The Dutch historian Johan Huizinga wrote of the extreme 'excitability' of the medieval soul. Tales of angels and devils intruding into the lives of everyday people were commonplace in Constantinople. The line between the physical and the metaphysical was blurry, if it existed at all. Demons, goblins and witches were as real as the house next door. God's will could be discerned from the clouds in the sky, and the Devil's presence could be sensed within a raking shadow in the street, in the maw of a rabid dog or within the psychotic words of a madman.

As someone who is more of a history enthusiast than an historian, I chose to take some of these stories at face value, to place myself in the thought-worlds of the medieval men and women who saw a kind of cosmic resonance in everything around them. Their myths and phantasms tell something of their obsessions, anxieties and secret longings.

Myth and fabrication are often intertwined with the concrete and the real. There are wild stories attached to real people, like the insufferably virtuous St Irene, the floating nun. There's the story of Theodora, the bear-keeper's daughter turned prostitute and comedian, who became a powerful empress. Our understanding of her has been somewhat skewed by a secret history written by Procopius, Justinian's bitchy court historian, who wrote at length, and in great detail, about her participation in preposterous and lurid public sex acts. Roman histories often portray talented and powerful women as whores and poisoners. Are the stories of Theodora an exaggeration or a slanderous lie? Could they possibly be true? We don't know.

There are stories surrounding world-transformative figures like Constantine the Great, who became a Christian, it was said, after receiving an electrifying vision on the eve of battle. Should we interpret that as a dream, or a vague apprehension or a psychotic episode, or should we discard the whole story as a convenient fabrication? And what are we to make of emperors with exotic nicknames such as 'Justinian the Slit-Nose', a man cruelly disfigured by a soldier's knife, and Constantine V, known to history as 'Constantine the Shit-Named', after an unpleasant accident at his christening where he allegedly befouled the baptismal font?

Some of the most improbable and fabulous tales are tangibly truthful, woven into the fabric of the city and available for all to see: the construction of the Hagia Sophia, the most beautiful church in the world, and the mighty Theodosian Walls, the massive land fortifications that sealed the city for a thousand years. These are places we can see and touch today. If we had nothing but an accurate written description of the Hagia Sophia to go on, we might easily think it was little more than Christian propaganda, or even a myth, like the Tower of Babel. But there it is, still squatting in the ancient heart of Istanbul, as real as the Pyramids or the Sydney Opera House.

It's fair to assume that if a story seems too good to be true, then it probably isn't. Ongoing historical research sometimes requires us to accept that certain events, no matter how compellingly told, simply could not have happened, or were written by impostors. Sometimes I have chosen to tell the story anyway, but have noted its false provenance. On the other hand, research can transform a wildly improbable tale into something altogether more plausible: in 1993, a NASA scientist came forward with new research that offers a compelling explanation for the strange phenomena witnessed in Constantinople in the week before its fall in 1453.

The use of Latin in Constantinople fell away almost completely by the seventh century, overtaken by Greek. Nonetheless I have preferred the Latin spelling for names over their Greek versions – I write of Alexius Comnenus, for example, instead of Alexios Komnenos – mainly to emphasise the 'Roman-ness' of this world, even though, in time, these Romans would travel a very long way from their ancient origins on the Tiber. The slow evolution of the Romans of the east brings to mind the paradox of the ship of Theseus: over time, every plank on the ship was repaired and replaced, so that eventually, nothing of the original ship remained. If so, can it still be called the ship of Theseus? The medieval Roman empire presents a similar conundrum: can we still call these people Romans if there are no temples, no Latin, no togas and no Rome? I call them Romans because that's what they called themselves, and because it stresses the long strands of continuity they were proud to share with their ancient forebears. Theseus was, after all, pretty sure it was still his damn boat.

I wish Byzantine names were easier to follow, that it were easier to distinguish between Constantine Monomachus, Constantine Porphyrogenitus and Constantine Paleologus. I wish the emperors had snappier names like 'Sven Forkbeard' or 'Ethelred the Unready', but they don't. I have tried to simplify and contract them wherever I could.

I have no Latin, Greek or Arabic, and so I have had to read the original narratives in translation. For a brief shining moment, I was able to fool my son that I speak fluent Turkish, but I have no Turkish words to offer you, dear reader, other than this helpful phrase of hospitality, gleaned from a cheap guidebook: *Güle güle kullanin*, which means, 'May you use this smiling'.

Timeline

657 BC   Byzantium is founded by Greek settlers.

27 BC   Augustus becomes the first Roman emperor.

73 AD   Byzantium is fully incorporated into the Roman empire under Vespasian.

203   Emperor Septimius Severus orders construction of the Hippodrome in Byzantium.

312   Battle of the Milvian Bridge. Constantine adopts Christianity.

324   Constantine becomes sole ruler of the Roman empire.

330   Byzantium is re-inaugurated as the new Roman capital by Constantine, and is renamed Constantinople.

380   An edict from Emperor Theodosius proclaims Christianity as the official religion of the empire.

395   The empire divides in half; the western portion is ruled from Ravenna in Italy, the eastern from Constantinople.

410   Rome is sacked by the Visigoths, the first time in eight centuries that Rome has fallen to an enemy.

413   Construction of the Theodosian Walls is completed.

447   The Theodosian Walls partially collapse after an earthquake. The walls are repaired and reinforced just in time to thwart an attack from Attila the Hun.

726	Leo the Isaurian bans the veneration of icons. Widespread destruction of religious images across the city.
800	Charlemagne crowned as holy Roman emperor in Rome.
843	Use of icons is restored. The empire regains some territories and enters a revival.
976	Basil II, 'the Bulgar Slayer', takes the throne. The empire regains control of Syria and Greece.
1054	The great schism begins as the Latin Roman church and the Orthodox church excommunicate each other.
1071	The Battle of Manzikert: the empire enters its long, final decline.
1095	Emperor Alexius Comnenus appeals to Pope Urban II for help against the Seljuk Turks. The First Crusade is proclaimed at the Council of Clermont.
1096	The First Crusade arrives and then passes through Constantinople.
1148	Anna Comnena writes the *Alexiad*.
1198	Pope Innocent III calls for a new Crusade to reclaim the Holy Land.
1204	Sack of Constantinople by Fourth Crusade. Latin empire of Constantinople declared.
1261	Byzantine empire restored under Michael VIII Palaeologus.
1347	The Black Death returns to Constantinople. The plague kills half the population of Europe.
1451	Sultan of the Ottoman Turks Murad II dies, succeeded by his son Mehmed II.

1452	Mehmed orders construction of the Throat Cutter fortress on the Bosphorus.
1453	Constantinople falls to the Ottoman Turks and is renamed Istanbul. The Roman empire ceases to exist.

Introduction

*If the Earth were a single state, Constantinople
would be its capital. – Napoleon*

ON THE OUTSKIRTS of Istanbul's Fatih district is a pedestrian
underpass that runs underneath a major traffic artery. My son
Joe and I follow the steps down into the underpass and we see a large,
brightly coloured mural fixed to the tiled wall. In the foreground, a
turbaned figure sits astride a white horse. Behind him, a bannered
army surges forward. In the centre of the picture a team of oxen
hauls the muzzle of a great bronze cannon.

I step up close to inspect the mural, but Joe stands back to take in
the whole scene. Joe is fourteen. He's thin, with hair like mine, wavy
to the point of curly. Joe wishes it were straight. He likes history and
he's always asking questions.

'So,' he ventures, 'the guy with the turban – that would be Mehmed the Conqueror?'

'That's him alright.'

I pause for a moment to consult my map, and then I look around.

'It's funny, but this painting marks the spot, more or less, where the Roman empire died in 1453. Somewhere above our heads'.

'What's the story here?' he asks.

So I tell him.

ON 6 APRIL 1453, the young sultan of the Ottoman Turks came to the walls of this city, which was then known as Constantinople. His name was Mehmed, and he had brought with him an army of 200,000 men and the biggest bronze cannon in the world. Mehmed had longed to possess this city since childhood. Taking it would make his empire whole, and allow him to claim the mantle of the Caesars of Rome.

Mehmed's soldiers had marched for many days down the old Roman road from their capital of Edirne. They came to a halt a quarter-mile from Constantinople's formidable land walls, where they assembled thousands of tents and positioned their artillery. A group of workers constructed a palisade fence. An Ottoman observer marvelled at the spreading mass of soldiers that flowed like 'a river of steel' and were 'as numerous as the stars'. Mehmed's luxurious red-and-gold tent was placed in the front and centre of the Ottoman line, so he might observe the firing of the massive cannon that had been hauled all the way from Edirne.

That night the Turks lit hundreds of bonfires. High up on the walls, the defenders looked on in wonder and terror at the long line of camps, extending as far as they could see along the entire length of the three-mile land walls.

CONSTANTINOPLE WAS AN OLD and exhausted city. It had served as the capital of the eastern Roman empire for eleven hundred years, but by 1453 this was an empire in name only. The Romans of Constantinople were like threadbare aristocrats eking out a living on a dilapidated estate, surrounded by lands that no longer belonged to them. Even so, something of the glory of the Roman name still clung to this sad and shrunken city founded eleven centuries earlier by Constantine the Great. It was still seen as the seat of world power, the second Rome. The Muslim warriors at the gates were fired by the words of a prophecy, uttered by Muhammad himself: *Surely, Constantinople will be conquered; how blessed the commander who will conquer it, and how blessed his army.*

CONSTANTINOPLE WAS THE CAPITAL of what historians now call 'Byzantium' or 'the Byzantine Empire'. But 'Byzantine' is just a name of convenience, coined after the empire had ceased to exist. The 'Byzantines' themselves never used such a term – they called themselves Romans, and they were the inheritors of the incomparably great civilisation that once had dominion of all the lands from the north of England to the Syrian desert, from the Pillars of Hercules to the Danube River. Emperors of Constantinople were proud to trace the line of their predecessors all the way back to Augustus.

In Augustus's time, the city of Rome was indisputably the heart of the empire it had given its name. But as centuries rolled on, the Eternal City became less and less relevant, too far from the action

3

and the money. So in 330 AD, the emperor now known as Constantine the Great rebooted the whole imperial project and shifted the Roman capital to the east. Constantine cast about for an ideal site and found it in the small Greek city of Byzantium, at the crossroads of Europe and Asia. The site was on a promontory, surrounded by water on three sides, so its location was both defensible and spectacularly beautiful. Here Constantine could re-found the empire and Christianise it, away from the traditionalists in Rome. The city's first name was simply *Nova Roma* – 'New Rome' – but it soon adopted the name of its founder and became Constantinople, the city of Constantine. In time, the Romans came to build a city so large, powerful and beautiful that people from all over the world would describe it as a mirror of heaven.

THIS LOST WORLD of the eastern Romans was somehow forgotten by the west. I was taught in school that the Roman empire sputtered out in 476, when the boy-emperor Romulus Augustulus was ordered off his throne by a German chieftain and sent into a very early retirement. But as the memory of Roman rule faded in the west, the Roman empire in the east, based in Constantinople, endured for another *thousand years*. The arc of its lifespan is an awesome thing, touching the ancient world at one end and the Age of Discovery at the other. While western Europe struggled through the miseries of the Dark Ages, Constantinople blazed with light as a bastion of Roman law, Greek culture and Christian spiritualism.

The city was protected by the most elaborate defensive fortifications in the world. Constantinople projected into the Sea of Marmara and the Bosphorus Strait like a stubby thumb. Two-thirds of its perimeter was surrounded by water. A hostile land army could therefore attack the city from one direction, and one direction only: the stretch of land on its western side. But here the invaders would be rebuffed by the legendary land walls of Theodosius: a massive, triple-layered defensive network of thick stone and brick walls and towers that were a wonder of the medieval world.

SAFE BEHIND THEIR IMPREGNABLE walls, the Romans of Constantinople changed beyond recognition, like sea creatures that had evolved to walk on land. By 1453 they bore little resemblance to the Romans of the ancient world. The use of Latin evaporated, replaced by the Greek patois that was much more widely used across the eastern Mediterranean. Worship of the old pagan gods of Jupiter, Diana and Saturn had been long since rooted out and expunged; the Romans were now devout Christians who could be drawn into tiresome infighting over the most intricate points of theology. But the Romans of Constantinople saw no rupture with their glorious ancestors, only a renovation; the strong links of continuity with the Roman past were more meaningful to them than the differences. They called themselves *Romaioi*, and the lands under their dominion 'Romania'.* To their minds, 'Roman-ness' was a shared set of ideas and traditions that had little to do with geography, much the same way that modern Australians consider themselves westerners, while living south of East Asia.

But by the fifteenth century Constantinople had lived too long, seen too much and done too much; its glory and greatness had dissipated, its treasures stolen and scattered across western Europe. The capital of the Roman empire was little more than a broken Christian city-state, with much of its population melted away. Whole neighbourhoods were destroyed and then abandoned; fields and orchards sprung up within the city walls to replace them.

---

* Not to be confused with the modern eastern European nation of the same name, which the Romans knew as the troublesome province of Dacia.

By the time Mehmed and his army showed up at the gates in 1453, the Ottoman Turks were already in possession of all the lands around the city; Constantinople had become a conspicuously Christian island in an Islamic sea. But, shrivelled as it was, Constantinople glimmered dimly with the aura of the Roman name. It was a truism, still uttered throughout the Christian and the Muslim worlds, that 'he who becomes the emperor of the Romans, becomes the emperor of the whole world'. Mehmed had made his plans to seize that world-throne for himself.

Alone and almost friendless, Constantinople could summon only six thousand men to defend it. Women, children, nuns, priests and the elderly were called to the walls to help.

THE IMPERIAL PALACE OF BLACHERNAE sat high above the north-west corner of the land walls. On that spring day in 1453, the emperor watched from a tower window as the Turkish forces fanned out along the full length of the walls. Then he left the palace with his retinue of advisors and set up a command outpost close to the most vulnerable section of the walls at the Romanus Gate. His name was Constantine XI Palaeologus and it fell to him to be the very last emperor of the Romans. He was forty-eight years old.

Constantine XI and his court were operating under a different cloud of prophecies and predictions. The most famous of these was attributed to Methodius, a church founder who foresaw that the destruction of Constantinople would trigger nothing less than the end of the world. In this apocalypse, the last emperor of the Romans was to play a critical role. As the end of days approached, he said, the armies of Gog and Magog, who had been held behind iron gates for thousands of years at the edge of the world, would be unleashed. The unclean hordes would swarm towards the city, but the last emperor would stand firm and defeat them in a cataclysmic battle. Then the last emperor would travel to Jerusalem, to the hill of Golgotha. There he would place his crown on the Holy Cross, and then fall down and die, as the cross and crown would be gathered up into heaven.

The prophecy was widely known and accepted among the people of Constantinople. As the Ottoman threat began to loom over the city, monks and priests clustered on street corners to remind the Romans of their long-foretold doom. In these final weeks, with Gog and Magog evidently at the gate, the people of Constantinople believed themselves to be the central actors in a drama in which the fate of the cosmos hung in the balance.

ALTHOUGH THE CITY'S DEFENDERS were badly outnumbered, Constantine had not succumbed to apocalyptic despair; he was busily preparing to fight to the death. Even as reports came to him of the enemy's overwhelming numbers, the emperor had reason to hope he might prevail, as his ancestors had so many times before. Everything depended on keeping the Theodosian Walls intact.

The Theodosian Walls had made Constantinople a standing affront to Islamic supremacy, 'a bone in the throat of Allah'. They confronted any would-be conqueror with three parallel layers of defences: a walled ditch, followed by a high protective outer wall, followed by an even higher inner wall, with a network of platforms, battlements and defensive towers on each level. So long as the walls could be adequately manned, the defenders could protect the city against an invasion force ten times as large. But the emperor's forces were sparse, and Mehmed had arrived at the walls with a new weapon for a new age of warfare: the bronze cannon, hauled by fifty oxen and two hundred men. It was the biggest gun in the world, and it had the power to smash gaping holes in the Theodosian Walls.

By 1453 the conquest of Constantinople seemed both impossible and inevitable.

THE WESTERN ROMAN EMPIRE expired in ignominious circumstances, but the death of Roman civilisation in the east a thousand years later has all the qualities of an epic tragedy. At least, it does to western eyes; from a Turkish point of view the conquest of Constantinople is a moment of triumph and renewal, a victory that allowed a clapped-out city to be reconsecrated to a new faith and a fresh imperial project.

The mural of Mehmed and his army that my son and I stumbled on in that dingy underpass is a work of Turkish propaganda, an invocation of that glorious day in 1453 when their ancestors broke through the walls and took the capital of the world for themselves, the moment when God confirmed their greatness as a people. It's just as well the artist chose lurid colours, because there are fantastic scenes in the story of Constantinople's last days that would be difficult to believe, had they not been separately recorded by historians, priests and a ship's doctor who lived through the city's spectacular downfall.

But the painting only tells half the story; absent are the city's defenders. Unlike Romulus Augustulus, Constantine XI did not resign his throne. Instead he drew on every reserve of courage, resilience and ingenuity he could find, within himself and his people, to make a last stand, and the defenders held out for seven weeks against their doom.

It was all in vain. Mehmed's armies eventually broke through, and Constantinople was remade as Istanbul, the capital of the Ottoman Turks and the new centre of Islamic power in the world. The Ottomans would go on to create their own distinct civilisation, inspired as much by the example of Roman grandeur as by the faith created by their Prophet. Today, Istanbul is a boomtown, the largest city in Europe, but traces of Constantinople still linger, visibly and invisibly. The local Istanbullus have become accustomed, even indifferent, to living with a ghost in their house, the disembodied spirit of Byzantium.

Once you know the story of this lost empire, you feel the ghost of Byzantium pressing against you at the crumbling land walls. You become suffused with it when you stand under the golden dome of the Hagia Sophia, and you glimpse it within the shadows of the underground cistern of Justinian. The story of how Constantinople flourished into greatness and expired in terrible violence is one of the strangest and most moving stories I know. I wanted my son to have that story too.

CHAPTER ONE

Radiant City

Constantinople, from the Nuremburg Chronicle (1493).

A Second Firmament

A THOUSAND YEARS AGO, Constantinople was the greatest and richest city in Europe. It dwarfed its rivals in size, splendour and sophistication. The city contained half a million souls, more than ten times the population of London or Paris. At a time when western Europe was ensnared in a dark age of poverty and illiteracy, the people of Constantinople enjoyed the pleasures of the metropolis: they bought exotic goods in the marketplaces of the city's great marbled squares and cheered for their teams at the Hippodrome, the world's biggest stadium. Students attended universities and law academies. There were schools for female education and hospitals with women doctors. The city's libraries conserved precious manuscripts by Greek and Latin authors, ancient works of philosophy, mathematics and literature that had been lost or destroyed elsewhere.

Constantinople was the greatest wonder of its age. It was an imperial capital, an emporium, a shrine and a fortress. Venetian merchants arriving after a long sea voyage would see the gold and copper domes of the skyline appear out of the Bosphorus fog like a hallucination. First-time visitors were stunned by the monumental scale and beauty of the city. They reacted like European peasants arriving by boat into Manhattan, not quite believing the impossible metropolis looming in front of them.

Traders came to Constantinople from all over Europe, from Asia and Africa. Russian galleys cruised down from the Black Sea, laden with fish, honey, beeswax and caviar. Amber was brought from the shores of the Baltic Sea to be exchanged for gold or silk. Spices from China and India were carried overland into the city and sold on to western Europe.

Constantinople was a holy city; its majestic churches and monasteries housed the most important sacred relics of Christendom – the crown of thorns, fragments of the True Cross, the bones of the apostles and a portrait of Christ believed to have been painted from life by St Luke himself. Pilgrims came to Constantinople by the old Roman road, down through Thrace. Passing through the Charisian Gate in the land walls, the pilgrim would push his way through the crowds on the Mese, the city's broad central avenue, passing shops, colonnaded squares paved with marble, and tenement blocks. Beggars and prostitutes would loiter in doorways while a holy fool, smeared with grime and filth, displayed the scars of his mortification to jeering children. The crowds on the Mese would part for a procession of chanting priests parading a wooden icon, followed by a train of ecstatic believers hoping to catch a glimpse of the icon weeping miraculous tears or dripping blood.

The emperor's procession among his people would bring city traffic to a standstill. Heralds with dragon banners would appear, strewing flowers on the path ahead, followed by an entourage of imperial guardsmen, clerics and ministers. The voices of a choir would then lift up and sing, 'Behold the Morning Star! In his eyes, the rays of the sun are reflected!' Finally the emperor would appear, swathed in crimson and gold silk, his feet clad in the distinctive thigh-high purple boots reserved for the occupant of the throne.

Columns of Constantinople.

THE CITY WAS ALMOST supernaturally beautiful. Visitors from western Europe could find nothing on Earth to compare it to, describing it in their letters as 'the all-golden city', 'a second firmament'.

Constantinople was created to invite such comparisons. Its emperors, bishops and architects were attempting to build nothing less than a mirror of heaven, reaching for something they called *theosis*, union with the divine, a state of ecstatic oneness with the Holy Spirit. In this way, the magnificence of their city became an expression of their moral virtue.

This longing for *theosis* reached a kind of perfection in the Hagia Sophia, the Church of Holy Wisdom, constructed with astonishing speed in fewer than six years. When completed, the Hagia Sophia became the supreme expression of Byzantine genius, blending art and technology into a seamless whole in order to flood the senses with wonder and pleasure.

Court and church ritual in Constantinople was extraordinarily complex and correct. A Russian pilgrim who witnessed an imperial coronation described the painstakingly slow procession of the uncrowned emperor to the throne:

During this time, the cantors intoned a most beautiful and astonishing chant, surpassing understanding. The imperial cortege advanced so slowly that it took three hours from the great door to the platform bearing the throne ... Ascending the platform, the Emperor put on the imperial purple and the imperial diadem and the crenated crown ... Who can describe the beauty of it all?

OUTSIDE THE HAGIA SOPHIA, under a domed shelter, stood the Milion, the golden milestone that measured the distances from Constantinople to the faraway cities claimed by the empire. All roads, it seemed, led to this New Rome, to this singular place, the heart of God's empire on Earth.

The city's glittering reputation extended in all directions for as far as it was possible for any one person to travel in a lifetime. Serbs, Bulgarians and Russians called it Tsarigrad, 'The City of the Caesars'. In medieval China it was known as Fu-Lin, a city of fantastical creatures and enormous granite walls. Viking warriors who had served as mercenaries in the emperor's Varangian Guard returned to their little villages in Iceland and Norway with tales of the distant, golden city they called Miklagard, 'The Big City'. Their stories of Constantinople became the dream architecture of the mythical realm of Asgard, the heavenly walled city where Odin, the king of the gods, dwelt. Stories of Constantinople invaded the dreams of people who would never live to see it. Its sacred rites and architecture were so heavenly, they could dazzle whole nations into the faith.

'We cannot forget that beauty'

PRINCE VLADIMIR OF KIEV was the ruler of a Slavic people who worshipped many gods. One day in 987 AD, he told his court that he and his people should no longer be pagan. But, he wondered, should they adopt Judaism, Christianity or Islam? Vladimir sent his best men to distant parts of the world to determine the one true religion of God.

Envoys were sent to the Muslims. When they returned, they told Prince Vladimir that there was no gladness among these people.

'Drinking alcohol is prohibited to them,' they told him. 'This might be too burdensome for our people.'

Vladimir had heard enough: 'Drinking is the joy of all Russia. We cannot exist without that pleasure.'

Next Vladimir called in representatives of the Jews and asked them where their homeland was.

'Jerusalem,' they replied.

'If God were truly with the Jews,' he replied, 'He wouldn't have scattered them from their homeland. Would you wish the same fate for us?' he asked. And with a wave of his hand he dismissed them.

Then Vladimir received a message from the envoys he'd sent to the Christians of Constantinople. In their letter they struggled to express how moved they were by what they'd seen in the Hagia Sophia:

We knew not whether we were in heaven, or on earth. For on earth there is no such splendour or such beauty, and we are

at a loss how to describe it to you, only this we know: that God
dwells there among humans, and that their service surpasses the
worship of all other places. For we cannot forget that beauty.

And so Vladimir was baptised into the Christian faith, and
in return he was given the Emperor's sister as a bride. Which is
how the Russian people came to be Orthodox Christians.

Another version of the story claims it was Emperor Basil II who
approached Vladimir first, asking for military aid against a rival
to the throne. Vladimir agreed, but demanded in return the hand
of Anna, Basil's sister. Vladimir's conversion therefore was simply
a necessary pre-condition for the marriage. In the first story the
Russians arrive at Christianity through the eerie beauty of the
Orthodox rite; in the other version it's a simple matter of political
expediency. But in Constantinople, the spiritual, the aesthetic and
the political were often fused together. The city was a showcase of
both Orthodox Christianity and Roman power, designed to enthral
people into the faith, and to cement their allegiance to the empire at
the same time.

WITHIN THE IMPERIAL PALACE lived the most enigmatic
figure in the city, the emperor himself, who sat at the summit of
church and state. In Constantinople, the emperor assumed the title
TOTIUS ORBIS IMPERATOR, 'Commander of the Whole World'. In
ancient times, Roman emperors had styled themselves as the first
among equals. But with the passing of the centuries, they began to
bolster their authority by swathing themselves in mystery. Court
ceremonies became more formal and elaborate. Emperors wore
make-up and donned robes embroidered with precious jewels, and
required visitors to prostrate themselves in their presence.

The Diplomat and the Singing Tree

IN 949, A VENETIAN GALLEY pulled into the Golden Horn, carrying an Italian diplomat, Liutprand of Cremona, the representative of King Berengar of Italy. Liutprand stepped ashore, presented his credentials and requested an audience with the emperor.

Liutprand was admitted to the palace through the Chalke Gate near the Hippodrome, and led through a marbled vestibule into the palace complex. Soon he was brought to the Chrysotriklinos, the 'golden reception hall', where two eunuchs hoisted him onto their shoulders and carried him into the throne room.

As he entered the glittering octagonal room, Liutprand was amazed to see a gilded bronze tree, its branches filled with mechanical singing birds, each emitting birdsong according to its species. Liutprand was carried closer to the massive throne and saw another mechanical wonder: at the base of the throne were two gilded lions with automated tails that struck the ground, and mouths that roared as they opened and closed. He looked up and there on the throne was the emperor, Constantine VII Porphyrogenitus, adorned in brocaded purple vestments, glittering with jewels. Liutprand dropped to the ground and prostrated himself three times, as required by protocol.

When Liutprand raised his head he saw Constantine's throne had somehow shot up some nine metres from the floor, raising the emperor almost as high as the palace ceiling. The emperor had also, somehow, changed his robe.

Conversation over such a great distance was awkward. After a short while a courtier indicated it was time to leave and Liutprand respectfully withdrew. He was quartered within the palace and his belongings were brought up from his ship. Liutprand was somewhat embarrassed that Berengar had given him no gifts to present to the emperor, only a letter that he knew was 'full of lies'. So he thought it best to hand over his personal gifts to the emperor as though they had come from Berengar, including nine armoured breastplates, seven embossed gilded shields, several precious cups and four child-eunuch slaves.

The emperor was well pleased with these gifts and invited Liutprand to join him at a feast in the Palace of the Nineteen Couches, adjacent to the Hippodrome, where the imperial family could eat and drink with their guests while reclining on couches in the style of the ancient Romans. Liutprand witnessed more automated wonders at the feast, as golden trays of food and wine were lowered mechanically from the ceiling to the table.

Coin of Constantine VII Porphyrogenitus.

IN ALL, THERE WERE NINETY-NINE emperors in Constantinople from the city's founding in 330 to the final siege of 1453, as well as several empresses who ruled in partnership with their husbands or governed as regents over their young sons. A very small number of empresses ruled alone, straining against every convention in a male-dominated society that would otherwise have relegated them to the women's quarters of the palace or a convent cell. In this long chain of rulers we see every human variation of what happens when an individual and great power intersect.

An emperor was much more than a political leader – he was a spiritual figurehead, God's regent on Earth. Imperial princes were taught in their lessons that Jesus came into the world during the reign of the first emperor, Augustus, and that surely this was no coincidence. Clearly it was the will of God that Roman emperors should serve as Christ's representative on Earth, in the interregnum between the crucifixion and the Second Coming.

And yet, for all that, something of the soul of the old Roman republic still remained in Constantinople. As in ancient times, emperors had to be mindful they governed on behalf of the senate and the people. An emperor who strayed too far from public opinion might end up torn to pieces in the Hippodrome.

The Flickering Lamp

HEAVENLY CITIES, doomed emperors, robotic trees, Crusaders, saints, floating nuns and the ever-looming apocalypse – it was this rich stew of stories that had brought me to Istanbul with Joe. Our common enjoyment of history was a source of quiet and deep joy to me. It wasn't hard to infect him with the history bug. Even as a small boy Joe was looking to place himself in the great long stream of events and people, needing to understand what had taken place before his entry into the world. The long, long story of the ancient Romans appealed to him as much as me.

For some reason, men and boys tend to talk more freely side by side, rather than face to face, so when Joe was little, I often took him on long walks with me. On these walks, he would pepper me with questions about the Nazis and the Industrial Revolution. By the time he was twelve we'd moved on to the Russo–Japanese War and the Cuban Missile Crisis.

Knowing the shape of these stories gave him a confidence that was hard for him to find in the classroom. Despite his evident brightness, Joe struggled in his first years of school. He was oddly reluctant to learn how to write. When required to do so in class he would often scrawl out his letters in mirror form, from right to left. He flipped letters, words and phrases around on the page, and he started to fall behind. A mild form of dyslexia was identified and overcome.

While he was alienated from the written word, Joe developed the compensatory interrogative skills that are common in dyslexic children and adults – he set about drawing down everything I knew from my reading. I was stronger on the history than the science, but I took all of Joe's questions seriously. In doing so I was trying to emulate my own dad, who had patiently absorbed my own boyish inquiries and always tried to give me his best answer.

A love of history can sometimes come across as a distraction from the more urgent business of the here and now. But without a grasp of the flow of events that have carried us to the present day, we are all a bit untethered from our place in time and space, condemned to live in an eternal present. A child's interest in history is a particularly lovely thing because it arises from some larger philosophical questions pertaining to life's deepest mysteries: how did we come to be here? History also offers us a defence against the sickly sweet temptations of nostalgia, the conviction that in times past things were simpler, people nobler and children more obedient.

Edward Gibbon, author of *History of the Decline and Fall of the Roman Empire*, joked that the discipline of history was 'little more than the register of the crimes, follies and misfortunes of mankind'. For me, history has always seemed like a trove of riches, an everlasting storehouse of stories that will never, ever be depleted. This thought has been my shield against boredom and melancholy.

Winston Churchill absorbed and wrote history to fend off his black dog, the depressive episodes that sapped his energy and robbed him of his usual *joie de vivre*. Churchill understood the value of placing yourself in the timeline of world events, noting that 'the longer you can look back, the farther you can look forward'. History offered him ballast for his restless soul, even if its insights were imprecise. In his eulogy for Neville Chamberlain to the House of Commons, he likened it to a lantern: 'History with its flickering lamp stumbles along the trail of the past, trying to reconstruct its scenes, to revive its echoes, and kindle with pale gleams the passion of former days.'

For anyone wanting to follow the trail of the Romans, the flickering lamp must travel a long way through time and space. And as we trace their path through the centuries, they evolve beyond recognition several times over.

The History of the Romans in Five Paragraphs

WE GLIMPSE THEM FIRST in their tribal origins as farmers, squatting on Palatine Hill, muttering prayers in the rain to Jupiter. There are seven legendary kings. Then the monarchy is overthrown for a republic and the lamp starts to gleam. The battle-ready Romans defeat the other tribes of Latium. Then they conquer the Etruscans to their north and the Greek colonies in the south, and the whole of the Italian peninsula is under their dominion.

As they become more powerful and prosperous they adopt the sophisticated clothes, habits and culture of the Greeks. The conquest of Sicily is the opening round of a fight to the death with Carthage, a rival power on the North African coast. In revenge, the Carthaginian general Hannibal crosses the Alps with soldiers and elephants and the Romans are almost finished. But they hang on, regroup and push back. Carthage is completely annihilated and Roman dominion expands across the Mediterranean, creating tensions over land and power that fracture the republic. Civil wars break out repeatedly but resolve nothing.

The lamp now casts a dazzling light on a generation of famous Romans: the dictator Julius Caesar, the general Pompey Magnus, the lawyer and orator Cicero, and the doomed lovers Marc Antony and Cleopatra. All of them are overshadowed by the towering figure of Octavian, who keeps the outward forms of the republic but kills its spirit, gathering up its most important offices for himself and assuming the title of 'Imperator' – commander. Octavian brings decades of civil war to an end and is awarded the title 'Augustus' or 'Revered One' by a grateful senate. Augustus is followed by a string of degenerate emperors: Tiberius, Caligula, Nero. Then the empire reaches a dizzying apogee under the rule of the Five Good Emperors, and Roman dominion extends ever further, from Yorkshire to Mesopotamia.

Then come fifty years of war and chaos. Twenty-six emperors take the throne and almost all are murdered or die in battle. We see the empire break into two, then three, pieces. The Emperor Diocletian puts it back together but in a different shape. Christianity emerges as a persecuted minority cult within the empire, first among slaves, then soldiers and senior officials. An emperor named Constantine adopts Christianity and shifts the capital east to Byzantium, which is remade as Constantinople.

The city of Rome declines, and is sacked by barbarians. Twice. The last western emperor resigns in humiliation, but the Roman name and legacy is conserved in the east. The lamplight slowly changes colour, as the Romans evolve into Greek-speaking Christians in Constantinople. The empire flourishes, and then falters, as the insurgent Muslim armies arrive at the gate. After several cycles of conquest, plague and defeat, the empire recovers its strength for another three glorious centuries, until Constantinople is wrecked by the western Crusaders. In 1453, the lamp draws deeply on the last of its fuel, for one last burst of light, and then it is extinguished forever.

HERE, SURELY, was a story big enough to fill the imagination of a history-besotted fourteen-year-old and his father. In Jewish and Aboriginal culture there are longstanding coming-of-age ceremonies to mark a child's entry into incipient adulthood. No such traditions exist for Anglo-Irish Australians, so I hatched a plan: Joe and I would go on a history road-trip from Rome to the New Rome in Istanbul, and we would conclude this father–son adventure at the site of the epic death of the eastern Roman empire by walking the full length of the legendary land walls, from the Sea of Marmara to the Golden Horn.

It has since been explained to me that the bar mitzvah is not so much for the benefit of the kid, but for the parents, to ease them into accepting that their child is no longer a helpless infant and will, in due course, be leaving the nest. This went some way to explain the zeal with which I planned this coming-of-age adventure with Joe. It would be as much for my benefit as for his.

Joe has a curious mind, an eye for the big picture, and an even temperament; I knew he'd make a good travelling companion. I selfishly wanted to enjoy a month imagining the ancient and medieval world with him before he was old enough to go out into the world on his own, without me.

This plan for a father–son escapade took some explaining to my wife Khym and my daughter Emma, who wanted to know, quite rightly, why they weren't invited. I explained that fathers and sons should have at least one adventure together on their own, and that I was fully supportive of a similar mother–daughter adventure should they care to undertake one. I thereby managed to assuage their misgivings, if not my own guilt, for getting on a plane without them.

THREE GREAT emperors dominate the story of early Byzantium: Constantine, Justinian and Heraclius. Each knew what it was like to stand at the summit of world power. All three had controversial marriages marked by murder, incest and unmistakable passion. And all of them lived long enough to suffer terrible loss. But it is the first of the three emperors who looms largest, who shifted the direction of the whole world decisively and forever.

To tell the story of Constantine and the birth of New Rome, Joe and I began in old Rome, in a courtyard designed by Michelangelo, to find the man who gave his name to the Queen of Cities.

CHAPTER TWO

Rome to Byzantium

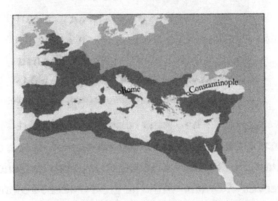

The Roman empire in 330 AD, at the founding of Constantinople.

Colossus

THE BOY LOOKS UP at the massive head propped up on a pedestal against the wall. Joe and I are standing among the dismembered bits and pieces of a colossal statue of Constantine the Great, in the courtyard of Rome's Capitoline Museum. The head, made of white marble, is two-and-a-half metres tall, big enough to crush a Volkswagen. The face is not conventionally handsome – the aquiline nose juts out crudely, as does the cleft chin – but it is noble, imperial, the expression distant and serene. Next to the head is Constantine's gigantic, muscular upper arm; on the other side, a hand with an outstretched finger pointing piously to heaven. Who is the god invoked here? The god of the Christians or Constantine himself?

Colossus of Constantine, Capitoline Museum, Rome.

In its original form, this colossus of Constantine sat on a throne and was as tall as a four-storey building, a hulking presence crafted to impress everyday Romans with the great leader's accomplishments. Colossal barely covers it: Constantine the Great is among the most truly transformative human beings who ever walked the Earth. Historians place him in the company of Jesus, the Buddha and Muhammad. We are, all of us, still living with the consequences of what this man said and did 1700 years ago.

His name means 'constant' or 'steadfast', and Constantine was certainly capable of holding to a course of action, year after year, patiently grinding down his rivals until he became the most powerful man in the world. He was the outstanding military leader of his time and, to some extent, an old-fashioned Roman general: a man of hard, relentless application to the task at hand. But once he mounted the throne, Constantine revealed himself more fully as an audacious and visionary leader.

Constantine will forever be remembered for two achievements: the foundation of Constantinople, New Rome, which endures today as Istanbul, and his promotion of Christianity from minority eastern cult to the majority religion of the Roman empire, a move that shifted the future direction of the world morally, politically and spiritually. Constantine is why the provinces of Europe and eventually the Americas would eventually form themselves into the self-described Christian nation states that endure today. For this, he was made a saint by the Church, ranked alongside the apostles of Jesus. But although he was a great man, he could not be said to be a good man.

CONSTANTINE WAS THE SON of low-born parents. His father was an army officer nicknamed Constantius Chlorus – 'Constantius the Pale' – for his light complexion. Strong, ambitious and intelligent, Constantius Chlorus gravitated towards other talented young officers and became part of a generation of hard-as-nails generals from Illyria who won their positions on merit and pulled the empire out of its third-century death spiral.

One night, in a tavern in Bithynia, Constantius Chlorus met a young barmaid named Helena. They noticed they were wearing the same silver bracelet, which inclined them to think the gods had brought them together. Helena became his consort and followed him on campaign. In 272 their son Constantine was born in the garrison town of Naissus in modern-day Serbia.

Constantius Chlorus was promoted to become the emperor's personal bodyguard, and in 282, he was appointed governor of Dalmatia. His star rose ever higher two years later when Diocletian, an old colleague from the imperial guard, became emperor.

Diocletian's accession to the throne marked the end of a protracted crisis for an empire weakened by civil war, foreign invasions and economic instability. The new emperor began a program of root-

and-branch reform, but soon came to realise the job had become too big for one man. So he decreed there would now be *two* emperors, each with the title of Augustus. Diocletian would rule over the richer, more populous eastern provinces from the city of Nicomedia in Asia Minor. The western half would be managed from Milan by his friend Maximian, a general fiercely loyal to Diocletian.

Soon afterwards, Diocletian divided the imperial tasks once again. A sub-emperor, given the title of 'Caesar', would now support each Augustus. This system would come to be known as the tetrarchy, the rule of four.

In 289 Constantius Chlorus divorced Helena to marry Maximian's daughter, Theodora, smoothing the way for his appointment as Caesar of the west. Helena and her teenage son Constantine were sent east to Diocletian's palace in Nicomedia. Constantine would not see his father again for another twelve years.

The Four Emperors of Diocletian's Tetrarchy.

CONSTANTINE LIVED WELL in Nicomedia, but in reality, he was something of a hostage, kept close at hand to ensure his father's loyalty to Diocletian. He was formally educated in literature and philosophy, and in 297 he caught his first glimpse of the realities of war, when at the age of twenty-five, he accompanied Diocletian's arrogant deputy Galerius into battle against the Persians. Constantine naturally concluded he was being groomed to join his father one day in the tetrarchy.

By the time he was thirty-two, Constantine had fathered a son with a woman named Minervina. They named him Crispus, and it seems that Constantine was a loving and protective father.

While in Nicomedia, Constantine received a first-class education in the messy realities of politics, simply by observing Diocletian and his court, who were attempting to reorganise the whole of Roman society along the lines of an orderly army camp. Diocletian had a military man's love of a straight line, a tidy barracks and a clear chain of command. He suppressed the threat of rebellion from powerful governors by reapportioning the imperial territories into smaller chunks, and by dividing military and civil authority in each province, with a *dux* ('duke') to assume military leadership, and a *vicarius* ('vicar') to oversee civil administration.

Diocletian's hapless predecessors had tried to pay for their expenses by minting more money, which had led to runaway inflation. Diocletian responded characteristically by attempting to nail down prices with a hammer, introducing price controls on every saleable commodity – bread, wine, beef, grain, cloaks, sausages and shoes.* He put tight constraints on job mobility by tying peasants to the land and making most professions hereditary. His tax policies encouraged the creation of large, self-sufficient estates. Diocletian was aiming for a restoration of classical Roman traditions but accidentally invented feudalism instead.

---

* The highest priced commodity was purple-dyed silk, set at a ceiling of 150,000 *denarii* per pound, a little higher than the price set for the purchase of a lion.

Despite his conservative instincts, Diocletian saw a need to reinvent the whole concept of imperial authority. Putting all pretence of republican virtue aside, Diocletian styled himself as emperor by divine right: he was the favourite of the gods, the human incarnation of Jupiter. He abandoned his soldier's tunic and took to wearing robes of purple silk and slippers studded with rubies. In court ceremonies the old soldier appeared before his awed subjects in make-up with a diadem on his head. All visitors who approached him were required to enter on their knees and kiss his robe.

Constantine witnessed the transfiguration of Diocletian from peasant-soldier to god-emperor. He saw how an emperor's authority could be magnified several times over by having a plausible claim to a divine mandate. Who would, after all, want to defy the gods?

The Last Persecution

IT WAS A QUESTION that came sharply into focus one day in 299, when Diocletian called for his haruspex, the pagan priest he used to divine the future from messages encoded in the entrails of sacrificed animals.* The emperor and his men stood by as the animals were slaughtered in the correct manner, and their entrails extracted and studied. But the haruspex appeared confused, and muttered that he was unable to read the divine portents. Diocletian asked him what was wrong.

'Sire,' the haruspex complained, 'I must tell you that as we began the divination, I saw the Christians of your household make the sign of the cross. This, I believe, has angered the gods into silence.'

Diocletian was deeply angered. Turning to his court, he declared that everyone in the room must at once make a sacrifice to appease

---

* A haruspex often wore a tall, conical cap for the ceremony; this is perhaps the origin of the stereotypical wizard's hat.

the gods. Anyone who declined was to be flogged. To Diocletian, what had taken place was more than insolence; it was Christian sabotage, a threat to the empire's security more dangerous than any barbarian army. From Diocletian's point of view, nothing was more important to the empire's wellbeing than the favour of the gods, whose goodwill had granted them dominion over all other peoples.

Anxious to soothe the gods' anger, the emperor decreed the next day that every soldier of the legions must also make a sacrificial offering. Christians who refused were imprisoned. Many Christians were ready to profess their loyalty, but infuriatingly, were forbidden by their religion to offer sacrifices to the emperor or to the pantheon of gods that Diocletian believed had made Rome so powerful.

Galerius, who detested Christians, urged Diocletian to go further, and the machinery of the empire geared up to purge the enemy within. Christians were stripped of their legal rights and property. Churches and holy books were destroyed. Christians who refused to renounce their religion were burnt alive. Diocletian's other reforms were put on hold as he allowed himself to be distracted into these pointless cruelties.

The last great persecution of the Christians was an atrocity in human terms and utterly counterproductive politically. The spectacle of innocent people thrown out of their homes and beaten in the streets appalled even non-Christians. Diocletian's prestige sank, while public admiration for the steadfast Christians climbed. Galerius, undaunted, persisted with the persecutions with undisguised glee, as Diocletian became depressed and withdrew from his imperial duties.

IN LATE 304, Diocletian became seriously ill and disappeared from public view. He emerged from his palace in March the following year, looking haggard and exhausted. In May he called an assembly of his generals and other senior figures to a hill outside Nicomedia, the same hill where he had been acclaimed emperor twenty years earlier.

Constantine stood impassively behind the old emperor as Diocletian declared he would do what no other emperor had done before – abdicate the throne voluntarily. Furthermore, he declared, his old friend Maximian, the western Augustus, would be retiring too. They would peacefully hand over their senior roles to their experienced deputies, Constantius Chlorus and Galerius.

This meant two new men would have to be brought into the tetrarchy to fill the vacant deputies' positions. Everyone in the crowd that day expected Constantine to be named as one of the Caesars. The court historian Lactantius describes the scene:

> *The gaze of all was upon Constantine. No one had any doubt; the soldiers who were present … were delighted with him, they wanted him, they were making their prayers for him.*
>
> *Then suddenly Diocletian proclaimed Severus and Maximinus Daia as Caesars. Everyone was thunderstruck. Constantine was standing up on the platform, and people hesitated, wondering whether his name had been changed. But then in full view of everybody Galerius stretched back his hand and drew Maximinus Daia out from behind him, pushing Constantine away.*

Both new Caesars were friends and allies of Galerius.

Constantine had been snubbed, as had Maximian's capable son Maxentius, who had likewise expected to be elevated. Diocletian wanted to establish the principle of succession based on merit, rather than inheritance, which suited Galerius just fine. But in this case, the two sons could make a claim based on merit *and* birthright.

Galerius, now the senior emperor, knew he'd made an enemy of Constantine, and had him watched closely. He had to assume that, sooner or later, disaffected elements in the army and bureaucracy would congregate around the snubbed prince and encourage his ambitions. Constantine for his part must have realised it was only a matter of time until he would meet some kind of tragic accident while he remained in Nicomedia.

Constantine passed each day in a state of watchful readiness, until one night when he was able to ply Galerius with wine and extract his mumbled consent to leave. As soon as Galerius fell asleep, Constantine bolted, taking off from the palace on the fastest horse in the stable, riding hard through the night from post-house to post-house, laming every horse behind him so he couldn't be followed. By the time Galerius woke up the next day, Constantine was long gone and pursuit was impossible.

CONSTANTINE JOINED HIS FATHER in Gaul. Together they crossed the Channel into Britain, travelling up to the Roman military base in York, where Constantine was introduced to his father's court. In 306 he was given troops to lead into battle against the Pictish tribes, north of Hadrian's Wall, which allowed his father's staff to observe his military skills. As winter set in, Constantius Chlorus fell gravely ill. When he died on 25 July 306, the senior staff arranged for the legions in York to acclaim Constantine as the rightful new Augustus of the west.

Constantine then wrote to Galerius, presenting his elevation as a *fait accompli*. He provocatively included a portrait of himself dressed in the purple robes of an Augustus. Who was he to say no to the legions loyal to his father's memory? Galerius was livid, but had to accept the turn of events to avoid war. Even so, he insisted on a compromise: Constantine would be promoted to the junior role of Caesar rather than replace his father as the senior Augustus. Galerius sent him the imperial robes to underline the point that it was *he* who conferred the title of 'Emperor'. Constantine was happy to accept, knowing that Galerius's acknowledgement removed any doubts about his legitimacy.

Constantine's audacious move left Maxentius, the other imperial son, seething with envy. Then, out of the blue, disgruntled members of the Praetorian Guard in Rome approached Maxentius and invited him to become emperor of Italy, if he would only promise to repeal an irksome new tax. Maxentius was only too happy to accept, but he sent his father, the retired Augustus Maximian, to smooth things over with Constantine. Constantine was offered a deal: the hand of Maximian's daughter Fausta, in return for his support. Constantine agreed, clearing the way for Maxentius to be acclaimed as emperor of the Italian peninsula, infuriating Galerius and his deputy, Severus.

Constantine's marriage to Fausta did not require him to divorce Minervina, either because they were never legally married or because she was already dead. Fausta and Constantine would have six children together, but he remained closest to Crispus, his first-born son from Minervina, and kept the boy close by his side in Gaul.

DIOCLETIAN EXPECTED the tetrarchy to endure as a permanent institution, refreshing itself every twenty years or so with new leaders. But Diocletian was the indispensable man in the tetrarchy, and the system collapsed almost as soon as he walked away. Galerius, the new senior Augustus, lacked the authority to keep his rivals in check, and the empire descended into a series of debilitating civil wars, fought between armies led by emperors and would-be emperors.

Diocletian, who had retired to a palace in Dalmatia to grow vegetables, observed the collapse of his carefully constructed new order with dismay. Galerius wrote to him, beseeching him to come out of retirement and broker a new settlement between the rivals. With a weary sigh, Diocletian did as he was asked, but the deal collapsed almost straightaway. One of his old colleagues wrote to him, begging him to return to the throne and restore peace to the empire. Diocletian wrote back, 'If you could come here and see the splendid cabbages I have grown with my own hands, then you would not ask such a thing of me.'

Meanwhile, his hand-picked successor was failing. Galerius was dying from a grotesque form of bowel cancer. The decline and death of the great persecutor was chronicled with gruesome relish by the Christian scholar Lactantius, who thought he could see divine justice at work in Galerius's nether regions: 'The stench was so foul as to pervade not only the palace, but even the whole city ... for by that time the passages from his bladder and bowels, having been devoured by the worms, became indiscriminate, and his body, with intolerable anguish, was dissolved into one mass of corruption'.

Galerius perished in agony, and an empire-wide power struggle broke out between Constantine and his rivals inside and out of the tetrarchy. The rivals fought each other for eighteen years like hungry sea creatures in a tank: the strong consuming the weak, until there were only two, and then one. It was in the course of this long struggle that Constantine underwent a dramatic spiritual experience that he believed saved him from defeat and death at the gates of Rome.

Chi-Rho

IN THE SPRING OF 312, Constantine marched his forces across the Alps into northern Italy. His quarry was now Maxentius, his brother-in-law. Their uneasy alliance had broken down. Maxentius's control of the Italian peninsula was slipping and Constantine had brought an army to take it from him.

Constantine, who was now forty, took Turin and Milan without a fight, then marched down Via Flaminia and camped outside Rome's Aurelian Walls. Maxentius had stockpiled food in the city and destroyed its bridges. It was assumed that Maxentius and his army would sit tight behind the formidable city walls and wait out the siege, leaving Constantine's forces exposed to the ravages of the coming winter.

Maxentius, however, was spooked by Constantine's apparent self-confidence. Looking for guidance, Maxentius consulted the *Sibylline Oracles*, which predicted that on 28 October an 'enemy of the Romans' would fall in battle. Maxentius naturally assumed that enemy was Constantine, and so he prepared to meet his brother-in-law's forces in open battle outside the city walls.

The night before the battle, Constantine was said to have experienced a jangling, hallucinatory dream or a vision. Unlike the *Sibylline* prophecies, the message of Constantine's vision was utterly direct and unambiguous. Constantine looked up at the sun and saw a blazing symbol of light over it. The cross-like symbol resembled an 'X' with a 'P' through the centre, like so:

And with it, Constantine saw these words written across the sky:

BY THIS SIGN YOU SHALL CONQUER

The fiery monogram was formed from two Greek letters, 'chi' and 'rho', the first two letters of the Greek word 'χριστός' or 'Christ'. The chi-rho was a well-known symbol of self-identification among Christians. Constantine awoke from his vision and asked his soldiers to paint the chi-rho on their shields, as they waited for Maxentius to emerge from the Aurelian Walls with his army.

MAXENTIUS CHOSE TO MAKE his stand at the Milvian Bridge, which had to be hastily reconstructed to get his troops across the Tiber River. He marched his army over the shaky pontoon timbers and prepared to confront Constantine's infantry.

Constantine's cavalry charged forward, pushing Maxentius's army back towards the bank of the Tiber. Maxentius called for his forces to retreat and regroup behind the city walls. Suddenly there was a confused crush of men and horses on the pontoon bridge; it collapsed and the Tiber was filled with drowning soldiers, weighed down by their heavy armour.

Maxentius's Praetorian Guard was now stranded on the other side of the river. They made a desperate last stand, but were slowly hacked to pieces by Constantine's men. Maxentius fell into the Tiber, where he drowned. His corpse was dragged out of the river and decapitated. The gates of the city were opened, and Constantine's men paraded through the streets, carrying Maxentius's head, spiked on a lance, to quell all further resistance.

Constantine had won the prize of Rome and, with it, complete control of the western empire. He entered the city the next day to cheering crowds. He was acclaimed in the senate, but surprised everyone when he firmly declined to give thanks and praise to the golden statue of Nike, the goddess of winged victory.

✳

WHILE IN ROME, I track down Danielle, a classics graduate and part-time archaeologist who spends a day with us in the ruins of the Imperial Forum. Danielle has lived in Rome for many years and has an answer for every question Joe and I can throw at her. Even better, she has access to the lower levels of the Colosseum, where gladiators, slaves and wild animals were once kept. The three of us have the dank subterranean space all to ourselves.

Joe points to a row of cylindrical grooves carved into the concrete floor.

'What were those holes for?' he asks.

'They were the slots that once held a series of pole winches,' Danielle explains, 'that were turned by slaves to operate an elevator platform.'

Colosseum basement.

'The Romans had elevators?' Joe asks incredulously.

'It was very dramatic. The animals and gladiators would be hoisted up from this basement onto the floor of the arena.'

'And then they'd die.'

'Actually,' Danielle says, 'some gladiators had it pretty good. Better than you'd think from the movies.'

She tells us that the best gladiators were prized athletes and celebrities who lived very comfortably and ate well between bouts. The popular ones seldom got killed, since their opponents were mostly captured enemy soldiers, who were meant to lose.

Cell in Colosseum.

Danielle leads us through the basement to a damp little cell that once held these soldier-slaves and the cruelty of everyday life in the Roman world is suddenly apparent to me. 'So you'd be a farmer, living somewhere on the periphery of the empire, and you'd join a rebellion, which would be easily crushed by the legions. You'd be carted to Rome in a cage, and then they'd dump you in this tiny cell here. After god knows how long, they'd give you a short sword and a wooden shield, push you onto the elevator and winch you up to the stadium floor, where you'd see sixty thousand Romans screaming for your death. Someone lops off your arm and runs a sword through you, and you bleed to death in the sawdust. Is that how it would go?'

'Something like that, yes.'

'Who was it that ended blood sport in the Colosseum?' I ask.

'It was Constantine,' she says.

CONSTANTINE WAS READY to give thanks and praise to the Christian God for his victory at the Milvian Bridge, but his personal adoption of the faith was very much a work in progress. It wasn't a complete and sudden Damascene conversion. Constantine was a political creature, and he took care to honour the pagan gods most of his subjects still revered.

His victory monuments sent mixed signals to the people of Rome. The Arch of Constantine, built to commemorate his victory, is Rome's largest triumphal arch – there's that fondness for bigness again – but for an emperor who had credited the Christian God for his victory, the Arch is remarkably free of specific Christian references. There are, however, plenty of images of pagan gods, particularly of the sun god Apollo.

The colossus of Constantine – the same statue Joe and I saw in the courtyard of the Capitoline Museum – was constructed and housed in a basilica commissioned by Maxentius that Constantine took over and transformed into a monument to himself. The marble colossus was something not seen by Romans since Nero's time; previous emperors had been content to have their likenesses represented by more-or-less life-sized statues. Constantine wanted himself re-created as a supernaturally large twelve-metre giant, seated on a marble throne; god-like, unknowable, seeing things beyond the mortal plane.* On the pedestal was an inscription that boasted of how he had saved Rome with the power of the chi-ro: *Through this sign of salvation, which is the true symbol of goodness, I rescued your city and freed it from the tyrant's yoke.*

Constantine never did let go of his attachment to the cult of the sun god, but his gratitude to the God of the Christians was sincere: it does seem he genuinely came to believe that the Christian God had promised him an unlikely victory and then delivered it. The question was, how would he transform the philosophy of a man who preached poverty, forgiveness and non-violence into an ideology of power?

THE ARCH OF CONSTANTINE is shielding our eyes from the late afternoon sun. 'Do you *really* think he had a vision?' Joe asks sceptically.

'Well, no I don't. I think his attachment to Christianity was real, but it crept up on him slowly. I suspect the story of the vision was something he came up with years later to frame his change of heart in a dramatic way, and to make it look like he was God's best friend.'

'He was just a man,' Joe replies.

'He was just a man,' I nod.

---

* By way of example, the seated figure of Abraham Lincoln within the Lincoln Memorial in Washington DC is just over five-and-a-half metres high, less than half the height of the colossus of Constantine.

BY 313 CONSTANTINE had destroyed all his rivals in the west. Licinius, an old friend of the late Galerius, had likewise fought his way to become Augustus of the eastern empire. The two men forged a pact, dividing the Roman world between them.

Constantine named his son Crispus as a junior emperor, and entrusted him with command of Gaul. Crispus led his legions into victories against the Franks and the Alemanni. His affability and competence made him a popular figure, compared to his aloof and grandiose father. In 322 Crispus was summoned to accompany the imperial family on a visit to Rome, a city that Constantine had never very much liked. As the imperial family paraded through the streets of the ancient capital, the loudest, most enthusiastic cheers from the crowd were not for Constantine, but for Crispus.

IT'S DIFFICULT to imagine Constantine, a man given to commissioning gigantic statues of himself, settling for a half-share of the empire. And so, despite the vast distances between their courts in Trier and Nicomedia, Constantine and Licinius began to niggle at each other. Distrust festered into on-again, off-again civil war, and then into an all-out fight to the death.

In 324, Constantine marched his army into Thrace to confront Licinius under the standard of the Christian *labarum*, a military banner crowned by the chi-rho. Licinius retreated with his forces to the minor Greek city of Byzantium. Constantine camped with his army outside the city's fortifications and waited for the arrival of his fleet, commanded now by Crispus. Perhaps at this time Constantine studied Byzantium's impressive strategic position. Perhaps the stunning natural beauty of its location on the Bosphorus Strait also beguiled him.

Crispus's fleet arrived a week later and smashed its way through Licinius's paltry assortment of ships. Crispus's decisive leadership was warmly praised on all sides; statues of the junior emperor were erected across the empire and his face was minted on imperial coins. Although Constantine had three younger sons from Fausta, Crispus was now the obvious heir apparent. Bishop Eusebius of Caesarea sycophantically compared their relationship to that of 'God the universal king, and the Son of God, the saviour of all men'.

Licinius fled the city and crossed the Bosphorus, but was caught at Chrysopolis. Constantine was at first inclined to be merciful, then thought better of it and discreetly had Licinius murdered.

The long era of civil war was over. All Constantine's rivals were dead and the empire was at peace. He was now sole ruler of all the Roman lands, touching Scotland at one end and Mesopotamia on the other.

One emperor, one empire, under a Christian God.

Of the Same Substance

CONSTANTINE SET UP his court temporarily in Diocletian's old capital of Nicomedia in Asia Minor. Having consolidated one-man rule, he now brought his immense authority to the difficult but necessary task of bringing the disparate factions of Christianity together under a single system of belief. But the faithful were in furious disagreement. The external pressure of persecution had concealed their divisions, but when Constantine invited them to the commanding heights of Roman power, underlying tensions broke out on the maddeningly complex issue of the nature of Christ.

The God of the Old Testament was singular and indivisible. What then did it mean for Christians to recognise Jesus as the 'son' of God? Was he descended from, or equal to, God the Father? The early church came up with an elegant paradox: the concept of the Holy Trinity, the idea that there is one God in three aspects: God

43

the Father, God the Son and the Holy Spirit, each one co-equal to the other two. But Christians couldn't agree on what Jesus was made from. Was he different from God the Father, or was he simply another aspect of the same God-like substance?

Arius, a tall, thin priest from Alexandria, argued controversially that since Jesus was the son of God, he must therefore be subordinate to God, the father. Arius and his followers could not accept the concept of the Holy Trinity, because Jesus was, by definition, a *created* being, a man, quite unlike the God the Father, who is eternal and uncreated.

To Constantine, this all looked like theological hair-splitting. The emperor expressed his exasperation in a letter to the Bishop of Alexandria:

> *I had proposed to lead back to a single form the ideas which all people conceive of the Deity; for I feel strongly that if I could induce men to unite on that subject, the conduct of public affairs would be considerably eased. But alas … The cause seems to be quite trifling and unworthy of such fierce contests … these are silly actions worthy of inexperienced children, and not of priests and reasonable men.*

Constantine took steps to resolve the dispute, and forge an outcome that would suit him. He announced a conference of every leading figure in the Christian church and let it be known that attendance was mandatory. And so, in the late spring of 325, more than three hundred bishops from across the empire travelled by land and sea to the town of Nicaea in Asia Minor.

IT SEEMS EXTRAORDINARY today that a Roman emperor should devote so much time and energy to fine points of religious doctrine, but Constantine's interest wasn't driven by theology as much as it was by a need to find a political solution to a problem he'd inherited from Diocletian. The cult of the God-Emperor was finished; not even Diocletian could be bothered keeping up the pretence that he was the incarnation of Jupiter. It invited ridicule when emperors retired to grow cabbages.

The death of the cult of the semi-divine emperor had left the empire without the fuel to drive it forward. It was a similar predicament faced by the Chinese Communist Party after Mao: having lost its faith in communism, the cadres had to cast about for a new governing ideology to justify their monopoly of political power settling on an appeal to crude nationalism and the pleasures of consumerism.

If Christianity was to form a new moral basis for the Roman empire, then Constantine would need to find a formula that would make his religion work as a governing ideology – a set of values and ideas that could persuasively explain why he, Constantine, deserved to rule, that would give his empire energy, cohesiveness and direction.

A Christian ruler couldn't be a god, but he could present himself as a ruler *chosen* by God, as Christ's regent on Earth, the favourite of heaven. Constantine and the emperors who followed him would place themselves in this exalted position, at the nexus of heaven and Earth, as a vessel that collects divine energy as it trickles down from heaven, and disperses it into the mortal world.

There was a divine symmetry at work. The emperor rules in Constantinople, attended by his advisors, bishops and generals, just as Jesus reigns in heaven, surrounded by angels and saints. This is why Roman mosaics of Jesus would come to portray him not as a broken pauper on a cross, but as a triumphant king on a throne. It was self-evidently the natural order of things. And to question the emperor's authority would be to question the moral order of the universe.

ON 20 MAY 325, CONSTANTINE opened the first ecumenical council in the history of the church.* The Council was charged with examining Arius's ideas before drafting a basic statement of belief that would be binding for all churches across the empire. Constantine presided but did not direct proceedings, letting the debate run its course as Arius made his case. The heretical priest was received coldly and subject to a hostile cross-examination.

When the conference ended, Constantine came down against the Arian position, putting forward a resolution declaring that the Father and Son were 'of the same substance', which was passed overwhelmingly. Arius and the two dissenters were banished, and Arianism was officially denounced as heresy.

The assembled clergy then sat down to hammer out a creed that would bind them all together. The Nicene Creed would be refined and altered over time, but the first version reads today like a careful statement of faith, blended into a combative political tract, which is exactly what it was:

We believe in one God, the Father Almighty,
Maker of all things visible and invisible;
And in one Lord Jesus Christ, the Son of God,
The only-begotten son of his Father, of the substance of the Father,
God of God, Light of Light, very God of very God,
Begotten, not made, being of one substance with the Father.

This early version of the Creed concluded with a very pointed reference to the Arians:†

---

* 'Ecumenical' meaning 'worldwide'.

† 'Arians' here refers to the followers of Arius and shouldn't be confused with the Iranian term 'Aryan', which would later be co-opted by Nazi racial ideology.

And whosoever shall say that there was a time when the Son of
  God was not,
Or that before he was begotten he was not,
Or that he was made of things that were not,
Or that he is of a different substance or essence or that he is a
  creature,
Or subject to change or conversion – all that so say, the Catholic and
Apostolic Church condemns them.

In exile, Arius contracted dysentery and died in poverty, but his expulsion failed to prevent further controversies on the nature of Christ. It was a mind-bending conundrum: every answer that was arrived at prompted more imponderable questions. How was it that God, who transcended space and time, could manifest himself in a human form? How did the human and divine elements co-exist within Jesus? Were those two natures intermingled or separate? Was he truly flesh and blood, or more like a three-dimensional spiritual hologram?

These fierce disputes over abstract and unknowable points of theology are baffling to modern eyes. Why not humbly accept the paradox and meditate on it? But for the early Christians, so much was at stake. If Jesus is fully human, then you could ask, what makes him special? But if he's fully divine, how did he die on the cross? They needed Jesus to be a manifestation of heavenly power, but also someone they could relate to as a human being, a man who endures suffering and poverty. Finding that sweet spot between the human and divine would wrack Christian thought for centuries.

Nicholas the Wonderworker

EMOTIONS HAD RUN HIGH at Nicaea. Arius's testimony to the assembly had so incensed one bishop that he had walked across the

47

conference floor and slapped the heretic in the face. The bishop's name was Nicholas of Myra, and those who knew him were shocked, for he was a kindly man, much loved by his people.

Nicholas had grown up an orphan, his parents dying in a plague epidemic when he was eight. The boy received a sizeable inheritance, but chose to give most of it away to the poor and the sick. For this and other kindnesses he was appointed Bishop of Myra in Asia Minor.

Bishop Nicholas was suspected of being the secret benefactor of many people in Myra. One man in the town despaired because he had no money to provide dowries for his three daughters. Without such dowries to attract husbands, he feared he would be forced to sell his daughters into slavery. But on three different nights a purse of gold was tossed through an open window and landed in a shoe that was drying by the fire. The man concluded the mysterious benefactor must be the bishop. Who else could be so kind?

People also told stories of miraculous deeds performed by Nicholas. It was said that during a terrible famine, three children were lured into the house of an evil butcher, who killed them and placed their remains in a barrel to cure their flesh, which he planned to sell to starving people as ham. On the day that Bishop Nicholas came into town, the butcher's crime was exposed to him in a vision. He located the barrels and resurrected the three children.

For this, and for other miraculous feats, the bishop achieved great renown as 'Nicholas the Wonderworker'. He died in 343 in Myra and was buried in his local cathedral. Nicholas was recognised as a saint by the church, his spirit credited with creating miracles long after his death. In time his reputation as a gift-giver and a protector of children blended together and it became customary to give gifts to children on his feast day of 6 December.

Different European nations came to celebrate the feast of St Nicholas in their own way. Dutch migrants to the United States transmuted the name of St Nicholas into 'Sinterklass', which became 'Santa Claus', and the gift-giving tradition shifted to Christmas Day, although gifts are still exchanged in many European countries on 6 December.

The legend of the coins in the shoe evolved into the tradition of hanging stockings by the fire on Christmas Eve. Icons of St Nicholas depict him as a thin man in the brocaded robes of a bishop, not as a large man in a red suit. Santa doesn't come from the Arctic Circle – he comes from Asia Minor.

Today Nicholas is venerated by the Orthodox church as the patron saint of children, barrel makers, sailors, merchants, the falsely accused, repentant thieves, brewers, pharmacists, archers, pawnbrokers and (mercifully) broadcasters.

The Immovable Ladder

AS CONSTANTINE was attempting to shepherd the church towards a basic statement of belief, his seventy-eight-year-old mother embarked on a mission to the Holy Land. No longer the discarded consort, Helena was now the honoured mother of the supreme Augustus. Constantine brought her out from the shadows and placed her at his side, awarding her the title of Augusta Imperatrix, and he gave her a luxurious palace in Rome.

During her time in the wilderness, Helena had become intensely Christianised. It's possible she had a hand in Constantine's decision to adopt the faith himself. Helena now became an immensely powerful and popular figure, with unlimited funds to search for holy relics. For Helena, such artefacts were more than mere souvenirs; they were holy objects, crackling with the residue of divine energy.

And so in 326, the Augusta embarked on a pilgrimage to Jerusalem, to walk in the city where Jesus once preached and died in agony. As she travelled through Palestine she showered gifts on the poor, freed slaves from their servitude in the mines, and commissioned the building of churches in significant places.

Entering the holy city of Jerusalem, Helena asked to be taken to the site of the crucifixion, identified in the scriptures as Golgotha, 'the Place of the Skull'. When she arrived she saw to her horror that a temple to Venus had been built on the site. The temple was demolished, and a team of workers began excavating the ground underneath. The traditional account records that Helena sat on a chair and supervised the digging. Soon the workmen dug their way down to a chamber carved out of the rock. When they entered this sepulchre they found three crosses. Helena concluded that these must indeed be the same crosses that Jesus and the two thieves alongside him were crucified upon.

But which was the cross of Christ? A test was called for. The Bishop of Jerusalem brought a deathly ill woman to the cavern. Timber from each of the three crosses was placed in turn upon her. At the touch of the third cross, which was stained with blood, sweat and tears, the woman instantly recovered, a sure sign that this was the True Cross of Christ.

Also found within the sepulchre, according to the legend, were the iron nails that were hammered into the hands and feet of Jesus by Roman soldiers three hundred years earlier.

Helena brought the Holy Nails and a piece of the True Cross back home with her. The rest of the cross was encased in a frame of silver and placed in the care of the Patriarch of Jerusalem. Constantine ordered that a great church be built on the site: the Church of the Holy Sepulchre, which stands there today.

*

A VISIT TO THE Church of the Holy Sepulchre in Jerusalem's Old City is an overwhelming experience. It still serves as the headquarters of the Orthodox Patriarch of Jerusalem, and is shared between no fewer than six Christian denominations, bound by intense mutual loathing.*

When I visited the church in the early 1990s, I expected some kind of hushed and hallowed cathedral, but no: at the entrance I heard a din of clashing music and voices from rival liturgies, each trying to drown out the other. It was like a rehearsal space shared between six bands. There was no single, open cavernous space, but a warren of thirty different chapels. The gloomy chambers, the clouds of incense, the clashing hymns and fervent worshippers produced a strange, electrifying atmosphere, like an unusually intense rock concert.

The six denominations share rights to the tomb itself, which is housed in a chapel known as the Aedicule. As I came out of the tomb, a very tall, bearded priest with burning black eyes confronted me.

'ONLY THE HEAD,' he boomed, glaring at me.

'I'm sorry?' I stuttered.

'ONLY THE HEAD OF JESUS IS BURIED HERE.' He gestured for me to enter a small side chapel to the main sepulchre, controlled by the Ethiopian Orthodox Church. The chapel was too small for them to lay claim to the whole body of Jesus, so instead they claimed dominion over the portion of the tomb where they believe Christ's head had once lain.

I left the Church of the Holy Sepulchre weirdly exhilarated. In the courtyard, an Australian–Israeli friend pointed to a ledge above the façade, under a window, where I could see a small ladder.

---

* Greek Orthodox, Armenian Orthodox, Roman Catholic, Egyptian Coptic, Syriac and Ethiopian Orthodox. The Protestants don't get a look-in.

The Immovable Ladder, Church of the Holy Sepulchre.

'That ladder,' he said, 'has been there for more than two hundred years.'

'Why would they leave a ladder there for that long?'

'No one can move it,' he replied.

Some time in the eighteenth century, the Ottoman authorities became weary of the infighting among the Christians in Jerusalem, so they tried to broker a peace: different portions of the church were assigned to each denomination, dividing their rights and responsibilities. It was agreed that no one priest could do anything to the church without the consent of the other five groups. Sometime later, a stonemason left the little wooden ladder on the ledge, which couldn't be moved without the express agreement of the six head priests.

'And they couldn't agree?'

'They couldn't agree. So it just had to stay there. Today they call it "The Immovable Ladder". In the 1960s, the pope was asked about it and he said the ladder could only be moved at such time in the future when the Catholic and Orthodox churches are reunited.'

'Wow.'

My friend shrugged, as if to say, 'That's life in the Holy Land.' Equally, it could have meant, 'Those crazy Christians, what are you gonna do?'

HELENA IS COMMEMORATED in the church with a chapel dedicated in her name. In the corner of the chapel is a chair, said to be the one she sat on as she supervised the digging of the Holy Sepulchre.

Helena, the former tavern girl from Bithynia, died in 327 AD the most admired woman in the Roman empire. She was made a saint, and her feast day is celebrated in Constantinople on 21 May.

He Who Walks before Me

SECURE IN HIS THRONE, with every rival dead and his official church up and running, Constantine could direct his energies towards a new project: the construction of a new imperial capital. Constantine had been born in the Balkans and educated in Asia Minor; as a young man he had led campaigns in Mesopotamia and the north of Britain. The emperor could appreciate, like no other ruler since Hadrian, the sprawl and the complexity of the empire he had won.

Rome itself was no longer a suitable capital, having lost much of its prestige and its strategic significance. Stranded halfway down the Italian peninsula, the old capital was isolated from the wealthy and cultured cities of the east, and too far from the military trouble spots on the Danube and the disputed border with Persia. Constantine had spent very little time in Rome and was free from any sentimental pangs about its historic role as the birthplace of the empire. In any case, the patrician families of Rome were too haughty and too attached to their pagan gods to be receptive to his new religion.

So Constantine looked east for his new capital. The east was richer, more populous and more cultured than the lands of the west. For a while he seriously considered the site of ancient Troy in Asia Minor, but in 323 he settled on Byzantium.

Byzantium, located on the point where Europe meets Asia at the entrance to the Black Sea, was perfect. It sat in an incomparable position, surrounded on three sides by water, and it possessed an excellent natural harbour, the Golden Horn, suitable for supply and trade.

Constantine was now in his fifties and may have sensed he was running out of time, so he put his engineers, architects and labourers to work at a cracking pace. Large tracts of the old city were demolished. Statues, relics and marble columns were plundered from Greek cities nearby. A palace complex, a bath house and a new senate building began to rise on the point of the promontory. The existing Hippodrome was improved and enlarged.

It was said that Constantine himself traced the boundaries of the first land walls with his spear. As the emperor strode ahead of his surveyors, one of them cried out, 'How much further, Sire?'

Constantine replied enigmatically, 'Until He who walks before me stops walking.'

THE EMPEROR NEEDED PEOPLE to fill his new streets, so he offered incentives for families to leave the old Rome on the Tiber for a better future in the new city in the east. The older, more established patrician families stayed put, but ambitious men and women with less impressive names made their way to the Bosphorus to try their luck.

New Rome, despite its handsome veneer, was a shoddy piece of workmanship. Construction had been rushed to fit Constantine's timelines and almost nothing of it survives today. But even if the new arrivals were tripping over gaps in the marble flagstones, they could still stroll down to Acropolis Point at the tip of the city's promontory to take in the view of the sparkling waters, inhale the sea breeze and rejoice in the panorama of the city's spectacular location.

But as Constantinople was coming together, piece by piece, the imperial family fell apart. In 326, Crispus, the oldest son and presumptive heir, was brought before a court in the town of Pola. On Constantine's orders Crispus was condemned to death and summarily executed. He was twenty-one years old. Soon afterwards, Constantine ordered the execution of his wife Fausta by suffocation in an overheated bath.

Damnatio Memoriae

BOTH EVENTS WERE unexplained, but they must have been linked.

Crispus and Fausta were close in age and had lived side by side for many years in the palace. One history of these events, written a century later, assumes that Constantine was tricked into killing his son by Fausta so that one of her sons could inherit the throne. According to this explanation, Fausta had set Crispus up by proposing an affair. As Crispus fled the palace in a state of shock, Fausta went straight to the emperor and told him Crispus had propositioned her. Deranged with anger, Constantine ordered Crispus to be executed for disloyalty. When Crispus's grandmother Helena discovered what had happened, she went to the emperor and scolded him for a fool for having been manipulated by his ambitious wife. Constantine retaliated by executing Fausta.

Another intriguing and altogether more plausible explanation for the double executions has only recently been put forward, which centres on the method of Fausta's execution. Historian David Woods noted that 'death by hot bath' was a punishment hitherto unknown to the Roman world. It was, however, sometimes recommended by ancient doctors as a means to induce a miscarriage. Perhaps Fausta and Crispus truly were lovers by mutual consent, and when she became pregnant, Constantine chose to have both of them killed. It was too dangerous for an emperor to be cuckolded by his own son.

AFTER THEIR DEATHS, Constantine declared a *damnatio memoriae* on Crispus and Fausta; their names were scrubbed from all documents and deleted from all monuments. Crispus's palace in Trier was demolished and a church was constructed in its place.

Shortly afterwards Constantine threw himself into the completion of his new capital, perhaps to distract his mind from recent events. I picture him alone, in his new palace on the Bosphorus, trembling and clutching a coin bearing the image of his dead son. It's also possible that a monstrously self-regarding creature like Constantine could put the whole incident behind him and move on.

CONSTANTINE INAUGURATED his new capital in 328 with pagan rites and Christian prayers. Byzantium was renamed 'New Rome', but from the start, people preferred to call it 'Constantinople', the city of Constantine. All religions were tolerated in the new city, but the central places of worship were set aside for the Christians. Constantine sent emissaries to gather the remains of all twelve of Christ's Apostles and inter them in a church, alongside a space reserved for his own sarcophagus. The message was clear: the emperor now meant the world to see him as the thirteenth Apostle.

In a typically pragmatic move, Constantine postponed his baptism into the faith until he was on his deathbed. Baptism at the moment of death would leave his soul pristine, cleansed of every sin, ready to ascend into heaven. It was a way of gaming the system and a common enough practice in the early years of Christianity. Perhaps the murders of Crispus and Fausta were weighing on his mind. After his baptism he refused to wear the imperial purple and his servants dressed him in a robe of purest white. Constantine the Great died in the suburbs of Nicomedia at noon on 22 May 337. He was sixty-five years old and had reigned longer than any emperor since Augustus.

The emperor's body was brought to Constantinople in a golden coffin, enveloped in purple silk. Constantinople came to a halt for the funeral of the man who had given the city its name.

CONSTANTINE RECKLESSLY bequeathed the empire to his three remaining sons from Fausta and two nephews, who were to divide the Roman lands among themselves. Constantine, of all people, must have known this could only ignite another round of murderous rivalries and fratricidal wars, which was exactly what happened. By 353 both nephews and two of the three sons were dead. The middle son, Constantius II, emerged as sole ruler of the entire Roman empire.

WHEN JOE WAS ELEVEN, he and I spent an afternoon painting a wall on the family house. To help pass the time we listened to a history podcast that traced the life of Julius Caesar. We worked in silence as the narrator took us through Caesar's ambitious early years, his abduction by pirates, the brilliant campaigns in Gaul and his rivalries with other great Romans of the age like Pompey and Cicero. We followed Caesar's march on Rome and his affair with Cleopatra, and the idyll they shared aboard her flower-strewn royal barge as it cruised down the Nile.

The sun was setting across our backyard as Caesar was being murdered on the floor of the senate. A wild-eyed senator steps forward and yanks at a corner of Caesar's tunic. Caesar, unbelieving, cries, 'Why, this is violence!' Another senator lunges with a dagger, then another and another. Caesar is stabbed twenty-three times and he dies, pulling his blood-soaked toga over his head.

As we packed up the paint tins, I wondered aloud if Julius Caesar had lived the most interesting life in the whole of human history, if he had seen and done more thrilling and unusual things than anyone else who ever lived. How would a life so rich with adventure compare to that of an *Apollo* astronaut, or Elizabeth I, or Alexander the Great?

Three years later, we are in Istanbul talking about another great Roman dictator and I wonder what Joe makes of the life of Constantine, whose oversized likeness we had studied ten days earlier in Rome. Joe turns it around in his head.

'It's too big to judge,' he says. 'There are so many good and bad things. I don't know. I can't judge.'

From the distance of seventeen centuries it is difficult to grasp Constantine's true character. His court of flatterers have scrubbed the record clean of his moments of pettiness and foolishness, although there are hints that, like Caesar, Constantine used little tricks to conceal a bald patch. Both men possessed a ruthless will to power and an unshakeable egotism that drove them to hack and slash their way to the top. And yet, once they reached the summit of

Roman power, they chose to become builders and renovators whose reforms endured for centuries after their deaths.

It's thought that Caesar drew his toga over his head in his last moments to conceal his shame at being brought down in such a sordid manner. Constantine's death is shadowed by a greater shame for the crime he tried to conceal with a *damnatio memoriae*. His deathbed baptism implies that he feared that act of damnation would rebound on him.

The Seven Sleepers

NOW THAT ALL HIS RIVALS were dead, Constantius II discovered the empire was too big for one man to govern alone, so he reluctantly appointed his twenty-three-year-old cousin Julian as his deputy, whom he mistook for an innocuous scholar. Julian, however, bore a secret hatred against Constantius, whom he blamed for the murder of his father in the wave of dynastic violence that had followed Constantine's death. Julian surprised everyone when he turned out to be a capable and resolute general. He was in the Balkans with his army, planning to march on Constantinople, when he received word that Constantius II had died of a fever, and that the soldiers were clamouring for him to accept the throne. For Julian this was proof that the gods were on his side.

Julian had spent his youth wandering the Greek world, studying with the greatest pagan thinkers and philosophers of the day. While in Athens, it seems he secretly resolved to renounce Christianity and embrace the pagan gods of the ancient world. Now Julian the Apostate, as he came to be known, no longer felt the need to conceal his true inclinations, and set about restoring the old gods to the centre of Roman life. He purged the palace staff, introduced anti-Christian laws, and increased the powers of the senate. Whether he would have succeeded in permanently reorienting the trajectory of the empire back towards its pagan, republican traditions, we cannot know, because Julian was speared in battle against the Persians in 363, and died at the age of thirty-one. Jovian, his successor, quickly re-established Christianity as the empire's preferred religion. The old gods were finished. Constantine's legacy would endure after all.

BY THE END OF THE fourth century, Constantinople's status as an imperial capital was secure. The city's skeletal frame had filled out with houses, granaries, theatres and bath houses. In 368, the emperor Valens completed the construction of an aqueduct to bring fresh water into Constantinople.* Crowds began to pack out the stands of the Hippodrome to roar their support for their chariot teams. The hundred-thousand-seat stadium became a natural forum for major public announcements and political rituals. Valens's successor Theodosius imported a magnificent pagan obelisk from the great temple of Karnak in Egypt, and placed it on the central *spina* of the Hippodrome, where it still stands today, complete with a panel on its pedestal which shows Theodosius presenting a charioteer with the laurel of victory.

Theodosius was the last emperor to rule an undivided Roman world. After his death in 395, his sons split the empire into two administrative halves, governed by an eastern emperor in Constantinople and a western emperor ruling from Milan. In time, Milan would prove to be too difficult to defend against the multiple threats to the empire, and the western emperor would relocate his court to Ravenna.

---

* The Aqueduct of Valens remains one of Istanbul's most imposing landmarks. Its arches straddle the busy traffic lanes of Ataturk Boulevard today.

A deeper change was settling into the Roman world. Christian leaders found their way into powerful roles in the empire's establishment: bishops assumed the authority and prestige that senators once enjoyed, and monks replaced philosophers as the wise elders. As Christian power grew throughout the Roman lands, the faithful came to believe that something miraculous had taken place. Somehow the faith of a carpenter's son from Galilee had changed the heart and soul of the world's mightiest empire. When the Romans took a moment to look back, they were amazed at how far they'd come, how much they'd evolved in the century after Constantine's death.

It was this joyous sense of Christian achievement that gave rise to the legend of the Seven Sleepers, which told the tale of seven young men of Ephesus during the persecutions of Decius back in 250 AD.

The seven, who were all Christians, refused to renounce the one true God and so they fled to a cave in the hills, where they fell asleep, exhausted. Their sleeping forms were discovered by the emperor's soldiers, who cruelly decided to brick up the entrance to the cave, trapping them inside. The legend records that the seven slept for 180 years, until a shepherd broke down the wall and woke them.

The seven young men rubbed the sleep from their eyes and stepped out of the cave. As they wandered down the hill towards Ephesus, they were astonished to hear church bells clanging and to see crosses on the city gates, and to hear the name of Jesus on everyone's lips.

The curious young men began to attract attention when they tried to pay for bread with coins that had not been seen for more than a century. A priest was fetched, who advised the seven that they had slept for 180 years, and that Christians were no longer persecuted and that even the emperor himself was a Christian. For the seven, it seemed like all that hatred had disappeared in the course of a single night, like a bad dream.

But even as the priest was speaking, the seven seemed to age before his eyes. Their hair became white, their bodies stooped. Then they fell down and died, and their bones disintegrated into dust.

THE TALE OF THE SEVEN SLEEPERS was retold in different forms over time. It appears in the Qur'an as the story of the 'People of the Cave', who are pious Muslims, escaping the persecution of the unbelievers, only they sleep for three hundred years. They, too, would have good reason to marvel at how their religion had prospered so greatly from such humble origins.

The legend was still well known in seventeenth-century Europe, with John Donne making passing reference to it in his most perfect love poem, *The Good Morrow*:

> *I wonder by my troth, what thou and I*
> *Did, till we lov'd? Were we not wean'd till then?*
> *But suck'd on country pleasures, childishly?*
> *Or snorted we in the seven sleepers' den?*

The Seven Sleepers were recognised as saints by the Orthodox church. Their feast day is celebrated on 22 October.

The Theodosian Walls

ON THE FLIGHT from Rome to Istanbul, Joe and I look at a map of medieval Constantinople. I trace my finger in an arc across its land boundary.

'This,' I explain, 'is something I want us to see in Istanbul, at least as much as I want to see the Hagia Sophia.'

Joe nods. He already knows about the Theodosian Walls.

CONSTANTINE HAD LAID OUT the first defensive perimeter guided by that unseen angel, but in the fifth century, the city's rapidly growing population required new land to be opened up, and a new set of walls was constructed further west, allowing room for more houses, farms and orchards. Work began in the reign of Theodosius II, for whom the walls are named, but his Praetorian prefect Anthemius deserves the credit. The first structure was a single curtain wall, five metres thick, interspersed with ninety-six high towers. Nine years later, a protective outer circuit wall was added, also fortified with battlements and towers, and a high platform running between the inner and outer layers. Then a third line of defence was added: a brick-lined ditch, protected by another low wall to keep enemy siege towers at a distance.

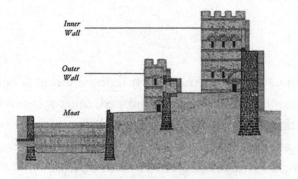

Cross-section of the Theodosian Walls.

The Theodosian Walls ran for three miles, north to south, following the undulations of the land from the Golden Horn to the Sea of Marmara, where they connected with the sea walls, enclosing the city in an impregnable seal. The result was a wonder of late antiquity, a triple-layered network of defences that formed a crippling physical and psychological barrier to any would-be conqueror. Nine fortified gates were built into the walls to allow for military and civilian traffic. The most spectacular of these was the legendary Porta Aurea, the Golden Gate, clad in marble, gold and bronze, reserved for the ceremonial passage of a triumphant emperor.

As the city accumulated more and more wealth, Constantinople became a tempting target for other powerful nations. But the presence of the Theodosian Walls made an attack on Constantinople an act of madness; it would be like attempting to devour a giant porcupine. Ambitious warlords could only watch as their armies were shot to death in a hail of arrows, while the people inside the city could simply sit tight and enjoy continuous resupply by sea. There were cisterns full of fresh water, and silos that could be stocked full of grain. And they could always catch fish from the Golden Horn.

THE THEODOSIAN WALLS are still present in Istanbul, more or less. Some sections have been demolished, other sections are slowly disintegrating, a few have been restored. But it's still possible to follow the ancient path of the walls from the Sea of Marmara to the Golden Horn. I've set aside a day for us to do this.

'I really want to stand on those battlements, Joe, and see what it was like for the poor bastards who had to charge at the walls.'

'Why? What would have happened to them?'

'First they had to get across a ditch while carrying a sword and a ladder.'

'What about the ones who did get out of the ditch?'

'Well, they would have to bolt towards the thirty-foot-high outer wall, dodging arrows and missiles. If they made it to the foot of the wall, they would have to plant a ladder and climb it, while the Romans in the guard towers above could rain rocks and boiling oil on their heads. It would be almost impossible to survive all that.'

'What about the ones who did?'

'Well, this is the cruellest part. If, somehow, a soldier managed to climb over the parapet, then the full horror of his situation would be revealed to him: he would see that he was caught in a perfect 360-degree killing zone between the towers of the outer wall and those of the much higher inner wall. In no time that guy would be pincushioned by arrow bolts from all sides.'

Nineteenth-century photo of Theodosian Walls.

The Theodosian Walls were the embodiment of every bit of tactical, strategic and engineering know-how the Romans had picked up from eight hundred years of siege warfare. Avars, Bulgars, Serbs and Seljuks would try to take the city by siege, and fail. Arab commanders who had never known defeat would fling thousands of soldiers at the walls in epic struggles that would last for years before packing up what was left of their armies and staggering home.

The walls were particularly affronting to the hordes of Hunnic and Turkic horsemen who would periodically ride out from the steppes of Central Asia into Europe, with hopes of plundering the wealth of the great city of the Caesars. They were riders accustomed to wars of movement, where a sudden inspirational dash might win the day. Instead they found themselves stuck on the outskirts of the city for months, camped in wretched conditions in front of the immovable walls. They were like the cavalrymen of World War I, obliged to abandon their horses and dig in for the slow grind of trench warfare.

The Princess and the Scourge of God

PRINCESS HONORIA was young, clever and ambitious, but for some months now she had been living in miserable seclusion within the women's quarters of the Great Palace in Constantinople. Each day she endured the withering scorn of the emperor's sisters, because Honoria was unmarried and with child.

Honoria was a very long way from her home in Ravenna. She was the older sister of Valentinian III, the boy-emperor of the battered western Roman empire. Honoria knew she was cleverer than her weak little brother; it was galling for her to see the throne handed to Valentinian in 426, but there was little she could do about it. As an imperial princess, Honoria could exercise very little power over her own life, let alone impress her will upon the empire at large. Nonetheless she was adorned with the noble title of Augusta, and upheld as a model of Roman womanhood: beautiful, chaste, saintly.

Honoria was expected to live quietly and remain a virgin until a suitable husband could be found. Bored beyond belief, she started an affair with her chamberlain, a man called Eugenius, and they conspired to overthrow her brother and rule the western empire together. The conspiracy was exposed when Honoria became pregnant. Eugenius was executed and Honoria packed off to faraway Constantinople to bear her child, away from the gossip of the emperor's court in Ravenna.

And so Honoria's days were spent wandering around a few unfriendly rooms in an unfamiliar palace: resting, eating and nursing her swelling belly, until the day came when her child was ready to be born. The fate of the child she gave birth to is not recorded.

Now that the disgraced princess was no longer a virgin, her market value as a bride had fallen considerably and her furious mother, Galla Placidia, had to abandon her hopes of marrying Honoria to a powerful prince or king. Eventually a suitable husband was found: a bland, middle-aged senator named Bassus Herculanus, who was considered a safe pair of hands.

Hemmed in on all sides, it seemed to Honoria that all the important decisions of her life had been made for her by others. Having no desire to enter into a meaningless marriage with a dull aristocrat, Honoria did an extraordinary thing: in the spring of 450 she wrote a letter, a plea for help, to the most dangerous man in the world – Attila the Hun.

THE ROMANS NAMED him 'Flagellum Dei', the 'Scourge of God'. Even today, the name 'Attila the Hun' embodies the very notion of a pitiless warlord at the head of an all-conquering horde. The Huns were to be the first of a long line of fierce nomadic peoples who would periodically charge out on horseback from the Eurasian steppe to threaten the existence of Constantinople.* Their arrival on the Hungarian plain was first registered by the Romans as a

---

* Stalin, at the end of World War II, controlled a similarly vast swathe of territory, with similar borders to Attila's empire. It's tempting to see the Great Soviet Leader – a man born in the Caucasus on the edge of the steppe – as the latest iteration in a line of spectacularly successful Central Asian warlords – Attila, Alp Arslan, Genghis Khan, Tamerlane – whose empires fall apart a generation or two after their deaths.

mysterious aftershock: in 376, imperial authorities reported a flood tide of Germanic refugees spilling into Roman territory, fleeing in panic from a horde of unknown warriors on horseback. Then the Huns crossed the Danube and all hell broke loose.

The Romans were not overly alarmed at first. They had, by now, become painfully accustomed to barbarian raids on their lands, and would usually gather their people into their walled cities, stock up on supplies, pull up the drawbridge and wait for the barbarians to lose interest or be chased away by the legions. No barbarian tribe had ever bothered to master the siege technology necessary to penetrate city walls.

The Huns were different: they used siege towers and gigantic, swinging battering rams to smash their way into Roman cities at will. At every step they introduced new tactics and technologies that made redundant the old Roman ways of waging war. Their most brilliant innovation was the composite bow – a weapon not carved from a single shaft of timber, but constructed from separate sections of wood, sinew and bone plates, which delivered much more kinetic energy to the arrow than a longbow. Hunnish warriors were highly skilled horse archers, able to adeptly manoeuvre, turn, reposition and fire. No one, it seemed, could beat them in open battle.

The Huns defeated every army they attacked and took every city they besieged. The Romans could find no answer to the Hunnish terror. Their very sight inspired primordial fear: the heads of Hunnish children were bandaged from birth, in such a way that the bones of the skull were flattened, which distorted and elongated the cranium. In the eyes of the Romans, they looked like monsters from hell.

IN 434, THE LEADERSHIP of the Hunnic tribes passed to two princes: Attila and his brother Bleda. The brothers were to rule jointly, but Attila was clearly the senior figure. A Roman ambassador described him as 'short of stature, with a broad chest and a large head; his eyes were small, his beard thin and sprinkled with grey; and he had a flat nose and tanned skin, showing evidence of his origin'.

The dominion of the Huns now extended from Central Asia to Germany, and their armies were poised on the empire's doorstep. But Attila and Bleda had no desire to conquer the Romans and burden themselves with the business of running a complex imperial bureaucracy. It was far safer and simpler to make the Romans their clients and squeeze them for gold. Every time the Romans tried to wriggle out of this extortionate relationship, Attila and Bleda would send their men across the Danube, laying waste to Roman cities and settlements until the emperor cried 'Enough!' Then, just to make sure the lesson was learnt, the Huns would double the annual indemnity.

The histories record that sometime in 445 Bleda was killed, most likely assassinated at the direction of his brother, who became sole ruler of the Hunnic tribes. Theodosius, hoping to exploit the confusion among the Huns, refused to pay the annual indemnity. Attila retaliated by launching another invasion of the Balkans. Although the Romans had had four years to dig in and strengthen their lines of defence, the Huns, once again, ran over them. A major, bloody battle was fought at the River Utus and the Roman army of Thrace was defeated and scattered. The road to Constantinople was now wide open to Attila.

Then, at this dangerous moment, an earthquake rippled across Constantinople, shaking down whole sections of the Theodosian Walls. Fifty-seven towers were brought to the ground and huge gaping spaces opened up between them. The Romans held their nerve: the emperor ordered his Praetorian prefect Constantinus to begin repairs immediately. The prefect mobilised the factions from the Hippodrome into labour battalions to repair the broken defences. Working day and night with desperate speed, the walls were restored and reinforced, the gates repaired and the towers rebuilt. A third line of defence, a trench, was excavated in front of the outer wall to stall Attila's siege engines. All of this was accomplished in an astonishingly short sixty days. The workers chiselled comments into the stonework, taking pride in their achievement.

Siege armies could only advance slowly, so the repairs were completed well before Attila and his Huns could come close to the city. Attila had no interest in throwing his precious army against the reinforced, rock-solid, triple-layered walls of Constantinople. It was never his intention to 'take' the city anyway. He didn't see Constantinople as a prize to be won; to him, the city was more like a complex machine, plugged into international trade routes that could reliably deliver wagon-trains filled with gold to him. Why would he want to pull that apart? Invading the eastern empire was Attila's way of reminding the Romans that it was in everybody's interest for them to pay the annual indemnity. So instead of putting the city to siege, Attila simply skirted around Constantinople and destroyed two nearby Roman armies.

Theodosius sent his ambassador Priscus to make peace with Attila. Priscus later recorded his observations of the 'Scourge of God' among his court:

> All the seats were ranged down either side of the room, up
> against the walls. In the middle Attila was sitting on a couch
> with a second couch behind him. Behind that a few steps led up
> to his bed, which for decorative purposes was covered in ornate
> drapes made of fine linen, like those which Greeks and Romans
> prepare for marriage ceremonies ... The eldest son was sitting

*on Attila's own couch, right on the very edge, with his eyes fixed
on the ground, in fear of his father. A lavish meal, served on
silver trenchers, was prepared for us and the other barbarians,
but Attila just had some meat on a wooden platter, for this was
one aspect of his self-discipline. For instance, gold or silver cups
were presented to the other diners, but his own goblet was made
of wood. His clothes, too, were simple, and no trouble was taken
except to have them clean.*

The Romans wearily agreed to hike up the annual indemnity to
2100 pounds of gold; they would also have to come up with the six
thousand pounds that were still in arrears.

The famous arrogance of the Romans had truly been laid low. The
rampaging Huns had placed the emperor into the role of a shopkeeper,
forced to hand over protection money to the local leg breakers.

The Most Serene Republic

ATTILA WAS BUSY making plans to hammer the western Roman
empire when he received Princess Honoria's letter, begging him
to save her from a loveless marriage. The message also contained
a jewelled ring as proof of her identity. Attila, not unreasonably,
mistook this to be a marriage proposal, which he was pleased to
accept. He fired off a message to Theodosius in Constantinople,
demanding that Valentinian surrender half of the western Roman
empire to him as a dowry for Honoria.

Exasperated, Theodosius wrote to his brother emperor in Ravenna,
explaining the situation and advising him to hand over his sister to
Attila. Valentinian flew into a rage and demanded that Honoria be
executed for treason. Their mother, Galla Placidia, intervened and
persuaded the emperor to send his sister into exile instead.

71

Valentinian replied to Attila, angrily denying that any form of marriage had been proposed. In return, Attila sent an envoy to insist that Honoria's proposal was legitimate. She had written of her own free will, and they were, to all intents and purposes, properly engaged. Attila would soon be coming to claim his wife and 'dowry'. It suited Attila to adopt the pose of a gallant suitor, flying to the rescue of an imperilled princess, when all along he had been looking for an excuse to invade the western empire. Honoria's extraordinary letter had given him the perfect pretext.

And so in 451, Attila's gigantic army surged across Gaul, taking city after city, until it reached the Atlantic coast. The Huns then turned south, but were stopped at Orleans by a coalition of Roman and barbarian armies led by the Roman general Aetius. The two armies clashed in a titanic battle on the plains of Catalaunum, east of Paris. The Romans held their position, and for the first time the Huns were pushed back. Attila lost his aura of invincibility.

Undaunted, Attila repeated his demand for Honoria's hand and his share of the western empire. He led his army into northern Italy and sacked Milan and Verona. The ancient city of Aquileia was razed to its foundations. Local inhabitants fled the fury of Attila's army by leaping into boats with whatever they could carry, and escaping to the marshy islands in the nearby lagoon. They reasoned, correctly, that the Hunnish horsemen would not bother to cross the water to chase them.

The merchants and fishermen on these muddy islands in the lagoon formed a prosperous community, untroubled by the raiding barbarians on the mainland. Trading posts, houses and wharves sprung up, and the merchants prospered. They laid foundations in the marshes by driving closely spaced timber poles into the mud until they hit bedrock, then sawing the trunks off at the top to make a flat surface. In this way they built grand houses, churches and public squares. The channels between the islands were shored up with embankments and turned into canals. And that is how the Most Serene Republic of Venice came into being, the accidental child of Attila the Hun.

ATTILA NEVER MOVED his army south of the River Po. The Italian peninsula was blighted with famine, which would have made provisioning for his army near impossible. So in 453 he withdrew back across the Danube without Honoria or his half-share of the western empire. A few months later he was dead.

There is some confusion over the cause of Attila's death, although it does seem his end was suitably bloody. Attila had taken a new wife, a beautiful young woman named Ildico. There was a great wedding feast and Attila drank himself into a stupor. Later that night he was discovered in his wedding tent, choking on blood that was flowing from his nose and mouth. Modern medical analysts suspect the blood may have come from a burst haemorrhoid in his oesophagus, a common cause of death for alcoholics.

PRINCESS HONORIA'S FATE, after being sent into exile, is unknown to us. Professor Judith Herrin has offered a tantalising explanation for her outrageous letter to Attila: it's possible that she had met him decades earlier in Constantinople when she was a child. At that time, the teenage Attila had been sent to the city as a royal hostage to ensure his uncle, King Ruga, would comply with a peace treaty. His sojourn in the Great Palace coincided with a visit from Galla Placidia, accompanied by her five-year-old daughter Honoria. Did they notice each other? Did the exotic Hunnish prince excite the young princess's imagination? Attila eventually escaped the gilded cage of Constantinople. Herrin wonders if he was fixed thereafter in Honoria's mind as a symbol of power and freedom.

AFTER ATTILA'S DEATH, the unity of the Hun tribes broke down and they receded back into the great Eurasian steppe. Constantinople shuddered with relief. But from this time, the distant badlands of the north-east would continue to haunt the Roman imagination. They were left with the nagging worry that, somewhere within those oceans of long grass, might be other hordes of implacable heathens, hell-bent on the annihilation of their God-guarded city.

Rex Italiae

AS THE EASTERN EMPIRE shored up its defences, the western empire crumbled away. Britain was abandoned. North Africa and Spain were lost to the Vandals. Gaul, which had been a Roman province for nearly five centuries, fell to the Visigoths, the Burgundians and the Franks. In its final years, what remained of the western empire became little more than an Italian client state of its eastern counterpart.

Then in 410 Rome itself was sacked by the Visigoths, an unthinkable horror for the empire's loyalists. In Constantinople three days of mourning were declared. St Jerome, writing from Bethlehem, said, 'My voice sticks in my throat ... the city which had taken the whole world is itself taken'. Christians in the city blamed the pagans for bringing the wrath of God upon the city. Pagans blamed the Christians for betraying the empire's allegiance to the old gods. Rome was sacked a second time by the Vandals in 455, and the gilt bronze tiles were torn away from the Temple of Jupiter.*

The last western emperor was fourteen-year-old Romulus Augustulus, installed in a *coup d'état* led by his father Orestes, the Magister Militum of what was left of the imperial army. The real

---

* Giving rise to the term 'vandalism'.

military power, though, was held by a barbarian chieftain named Odoacer, who, at the urging of his men, killed Orestes, entered Ravenna and occupied the palace. Odoacer felt sorry for the terrified boy-emperor and sent him into a comfortable exile on an estate in central Italy. In Constantinople, Emperor Zeno watched events with dismay, but lacked the resources to intervene.

Odoacer did not claim the title of western emperor for himself. He sent the imperial regalia to Constantinople, along with a polite letter to Zeno, telling him there was no longer any need for a separate empire in the west. Instead, Odoacer offered to rule Italy in Zeno's name. Zeno accepted the realities of the situation, probably intending to rectify the matter at a later date. He awarded Odoacer the Roman title of *patrician*, but within Italy, he was referred to as *rex*, or king. Imperial rule was upheld in principle, but in practice, it was lost.

Today we see this as a critical moment, but few people felt that way at the time. The Roman senate continued to meet, Roman magistrates were still appointed, but the western emperor had become so irrelevant that no one really noticed his absence. It was only clear in retrospect that a breach had occurred, and that the long chain of western Roman emperors that reached back to Augustus had been broken forever. A new kind of Rome would slowly grow up around the broken columns and temples of the ancient world, and people would wonder how it had ever been possible to build such colossal things.

CHAPTER THREE

The Deep State

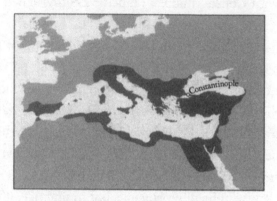

The empire in 565, at the death of Justinian.

Justin and Justinian

JOE AND I arrive in Istanbul on a cold January night. I watch the needle on the taxi speedometer waver between 160 and 180 kilometres per hour along the airport freeway, and recall reading somewhere that Istanbul is the road-fatality capital of Europe.

The driver nodded confidently when I gave him the name of our hotel, but it turns out he's never heard of the place, so he pushes his vehicle through the side streets of Sultanahmet, hammering the horn, pulling over occasionally and asking shopkeepers for directions. When he finds the hotel, he seems glad to be rid of us.

The hotel's sunken reception area is decorated with Ottoman antiques and cushions and several sleeping cats. I see an exposed slab of Roman brickwork with its characteristic red stripes. The wall once belonged to the imperial palace complex that dominated this entire district in the Byzantine era. Going up a spiral staircase, we find a quiet garden with flowers, palms and a cypress tree. A crumbling Ottoman *hamam* is attached to the back. Joe loves the place, and so do I.

It's late, so we dump our bags and go out looking for a restaurant. The fog from the Bosphorus has drifted across the city. The streets are empty and hazily lit. We round a few corners and enter a large open square and there it is, the Hagia Sophia. It is a mountain of a thing, veiled by the night fog, humped over like a giant on its haunches, preparing to stand up. The building is closed for the day and the square is empty, so we have the great church all to ourselves. Looking up, we can just see the lip of the massive dome. Joe asks me who built the Hagia Sophia.

'It was the work of thousands of labourers,' I reply. 'Probably slaves.'

'No, I mean, who designed it?'

Joe wants to be an architect. He told me this a year ago; out of the blue he announced that Frank Lloyd Wright was his hero and that he wanted to make great buildings like Wright did.

'It was designed by two engineers,' I reply, 'whose names I can't quite remember right now. In those days the architects never got the credit. All the glory went to Justinian, the emperor who made it happen. He's the guy everyone remembers.'

'Why do they remember him?'

'Well, because he built the Hagia Sophia, he reconquered Italy and North Africa, and he fell in love with the most controversial woman in the city.'

I look over at the darkened site of the Hippodrome across the square.

'Justinian also survived the bubonic plague, and murdered a tenth of the population of Constantinople in an afternoon. And he did all these things while hardly ever travelling further than a square mile from where we're standing right now.

ONE DAY, IN THE LATTER PART of the fifth century, a pig farmer named Justin left his home town of Bederiana and joined his two friends on the road heading east to the great city of Constantinople. They were young men from dirt-poor families, and they owned nothing other than the goat-hair satchels they carried on their backs, filled with hardtack for the long journey.

Justin and his friends had never seen a big city before and were amazed when they entered the metropolis, with its thronging crowds and fine buildings and statues. They were strong, fine-looking young men and soon found positions at the Great Palace with the imperial guard. In time, Justin rose to become chief of the emperor's personal bodyguard, a position of great responsibility and influence, which put him in daily communication with Emperor Anastasius himself.

Justin married a former slave girl named Lupicina, but the couple were unable to have children. So Justin invited his sister Vigilantia to send her twelve-year-old son, an ambitious boy named Petrus Sabbatius, to join him in Constantinople. Justin adopted Petrus as his own son, and gave him the cognomen Iustinianus or 'Justinian'. Conscious of his own illiteracy, Justin sponsored the boy's education in Greek and Latin culture. As he entered his twenties, Justinian was appointed to a palace regiment, where he was well placed to observe the currents of imperial politics swirling around the emperor.

Anastasius was by now an old man, and contemplating who among his three nephews should succeed him. A story was told that he arranged for three couches to be set up in his chamber, and under one of them, he hid a small piece of parchment with the word 'REGNUM' written on it. Anastasius resolved that the nephew who took the special couch should be the one to succeed him. But when the three nephews entered, two decided to share a couch and the seat with the royal message was left empty. Anastasius took this to mean that none of his nephews were fit for the throne.

That night Anastasius prayed for guidance and decided that the first man to enter his bedchamber the following morning would be his successor. When morning came, the first man at his door was Justin, the chief of his guards. Anastasius died childless in July 518 and Justin, the former pig farmer, was crowned as Justin I.

Another, less colourful, version of events suggests that Justin won the throne more straightforwardly, through his command of the palace guards and by his sizeable donations to influential senators. It's possible that Justinian, not Justin, was the hidden hand at work here.

The sixty-eight-year-old Justin lacked experience in diplomacy and was hampered by his illiteracy. A wooden stencil with the letters *legi* ('I have read it') was crafted for him, allowing him to sign off on a document by tracing the word onto the page in purple ink. Justin came to rely heavily on the advice of his clever nephew, and in this way Justinian became his uncle's regent, the de facto ruler of the Roman empire, while still in his thirties. In 521 he was awarded the old republican title of consul, which was celebrated with public games: twenty lions and thirty leopards were fought and killed in the Hippodrome. As his uncle slid into dementia, Justinian assumed more of the imperial tasks. He healed a diplomatic rift with the pope in Rome and established good relations with powerful senators.

PROCOPIUS, THE COURT HISTORIAN who is the best source for this period, records that Justinian was a plain-looking man, 'neither tall nor too short, but of a medium height, not thin, but inclined to be fat. His face was round and not ill-favoured, and showed colour, even after a two days' fast'. Justinian's growing authority in the palace was matched by his influence on the streets of Constantinople, through his connections to the powerful racing factions of the Hippodrome: the Blues and the Greens. The two factions kept horses, recruited charioteers, ran the betting action and used entertainers to amuse the crowds between events. Greens supporters tended to come from the inner city, Blues from the outer suburbs and the countryside. Over time, the Blues and the Greens evolved into powerful sporting institutions, running political and criminal enterprises on the side. Aristocratic families often paid the factions to shout political slogans at the Hippodrome, and to intimidate opponents.

Both factions had street gangs, known as partisans. The Blue partisans shocked respectable society by adopting the appearance of Huns: the front of their scalps were shaved, while their hair hung long and wild at the back. They sat among the crowds of the Hippodrome, wearing expensive, embroidered robes with tight cuffs and billowing sleeves to accentuate the muscles on their arms. Outside the track, they ran protection rackets and indulged in petty theft and street violence with impunity. Justinian, far from cracking down on the violence and disorder, openly courted the Blues' support.

Procopius, like many Roman aristocrats, secretly disdained the lower-class emperor and his ambitious nephew, who was clearly angling to succeed his failing uncle on the throne. Then, in 525, Justinian shocked the city by declaring his intention to marry the most scandalous woman in Constantinople – the former prostitute, dancer and comedian Theodora.

The Bear-keeper's Daughter

JUSTINIAN'S NEW PARAMOUR was a child of the Hippodrome, the daughter of a bear-keeper from the Green faction who died in 505. When Theodora's mother remarried, she came to the Hippodrome with her three daughters to plead with the Greens to give the bear-keeper's job to her new husband. The Greens gave her short shrift, so she turned to the Blues, who happened to be looking for a new bear-keeper, and who granted her wish. Her eight-year-old daughter Theodora never forgot this act of charity, and remained loyal to the Blue faction all her life.

On reaching puberty, Theodora was enlisted by her mother into a theatrical troupe where she became a comedian, a burlesque dancer and a prostitute. She gave birth to her first child at fourteen. Described as the most beautiful woman of her age, she became a courtesan to powerful Roman senators. After a stint in Carthage, where she shared the bed of the local governor, Theodora is said to have entered an ascetic community in the desert and experienced a religious conversion to Monophysitism, the branch of early Christianity that believed Jesus's divinity superseded his humanity. Monophysitism had been condemned as a Christian heresy, but Theodora was by nature a partisan warrior, and she lent her support to the Monophysite cause for the rest of her life, as she did to the Blues.

At twenty-one, she returned to Constantinople where she lived modestly in a small apartment. She likely met Justinian at a social event in the capital. Theodora was, by then, in her mid-twenties. Justinian was in his forties. The two fell hard for each other and began living together in the Bucoleon Palace, on the shores of the Marmara. Justinian took to calling her his 'sweetest delight' or by the literal meaning of her name, 'the gift of God'.

The couple were anxious to legitimise their union, but faced two obstacles: the first was a law from Constantine's time, prohibiting marriage between a man of senatorial rank and an actress. Justinian persuaded his uncle to alter the law, making it possible for an aristocrat to wed an actress who was 'penitent'. The second problem was the stubborn opposition of the emperor's wife, who was already embarrassed by the family's lowly origins and wanted no further controversy. When she died in 524, Justin was too senile to offer further objections and the path was open for Justinian and Theodora to be married the following year.

JUSTIN SLID DEEPER into dementia and died in 527. Justinian and Theodora were invested as emperor and empress in August that year, in a ceremony that climaxed in a triumphant procession to the Hippodrome, where they were acclaimed by the crowd. But upper-class Romans were incensed by the partnership of the upstart emperor and the whore from the Hippodrome, even if they had to smother their disdain under a veneer of deference. Well aware of their derision, Justinian and Theodora took pains to enforce imperial protocol, delighting in forcing the aristocracy to kneel at their feet and kiss the hem of their robes.

Procopius found them so insufferable he poured out his repressed bile into an extraordinary document known as the *Secret History*. While Procopius's official histories are fairly sober accounts, his pen almost seems to fly out of his hand as he records the sins and shortcomings of the imperial couple. Theodora's famous sexual exploits excited his particular interest; he describes in detail her most notorious performance piece, a burlesque parody of *Leda and the Swan*:

> *She removed her costume and stood nude in their midst, except for a girdle about the groin ... Covered thus with a ribbon, she would sink down to the stage floor and recline on her back. Slaves to whom the duty was entrusted would then scatter grains of barley from above onto her private parts, whence geese, trained for the purpose, would next pick the grains one by one with their bills and eat.*

Procopius never risked publishing his *Secret History*, which remained a secret until the manuscript was discovered mouldering away in the Vatican library in 1623. Its publication more than a thousand years after it was written titillated and scandalised Europe.

There would be other clever, powerful Byzantine women, but none quite so colourful as Theodora. Normally, an empress could only assume power when a functioning male emperor went missing. Theodora was the exception; her authority arose alongside her supremely powerful husband, who seemed happy to share the workload. Justinian lovingly acknowledged the influence of his glamorous wife in one of his decrees: 'we have taken as partner in our counsels our most pious consort given us by God'.

They were cut from very different cloth. Theodora never forgot her lower-class origins. After her death, a senior bureaucrat named John

Lydus wrote that she was 'more formidable in her understanding and sympathy towards the wronged than any other individual ever', whereas Justinian apparently never gave a moment's thought to distracting questions of social justice.

Theodora enjoyed luxury, eating well and sleeping late. Accustomed to performance, she relished the public and ceremonial aspects of her role, while Justinian lived modestly and mostly confined himself to the palace, working long hours, neglecting sleep. In modern terms, Justinian could be described as a workaholic, a perfectionist and a micro-manager. His restless mind touched almost every aspect of daily life in the capital. 'Our subjects are our constant care,' he once nobly proclaimed. And indeed Justinian often spoke of his people as creatures subject to his will, not as free Roman citizens. It's hardly surprising the senatorial class, accustomed to their ancient liberties, came to deeply resent the unsleeping autocrat in the Great Palace.

Mosaic of Justinian, Church of St Vitale, Ravenna.

Codex

IT WAS WHISPERED in the court that the source of the emperor's energy was demonic; someone claimed to have spied on Justinian in the palace late one night, and to have seen him rise from his throne, detach his head and walk about the corridors as a decapitated body. One courtier declared he'd seen the emperor's face hideously dissolve into 'a shapeless mass of flesh, without eyebrows or eyes in their proper places', before the fleshy lump recomposed itself.

The emperor's true energy source was his colossal ambition, driven by a massive ego that he never bothered to conceal. Justinian enjoyed boasting about his accomplishments, often proclaiming that no one but he could have achieved such mighty things. This bedrock of self-assurance allowed him to bring talented individuals into his inner circle and encourage them to act boldly, confident he would remain the dominant figure among them. Theodora was more suspicious of Justinian's talented lieutenants, and worked to undermine those she worried might secretly harbour ambitions to take the throne for themselves.

Justinian elevated an illiterate, low-born bureaucrat known as John the Cappadocian to act as his chief minister. John was, begrudgingly, acknowledged by Procopius as 'a man of the greatest daring, and the cleverest of all men of his time'. He streamlined the empire's bloated bureaucracy and introduced dozens of new taxes to fund Justinian's ambitious programs. The taxes and anti-corruption measures largely fell on the senatorial class, who seethed with resentment, not least because John so obviously enriched himself corruptly at their expense. The prefect began to attract powerful enemies, including Theodora, who saw him as a rival for the emperor's ear on domestic matters.

At Justinian's instigation, John set up a ten-man commission to sort through the entire corpus of Roman law. The Roman legal system was one of Rome's greatest civilisational achievements, but by the sixth century, the code had grown into a gigantic hodge-podge of conflicting and out-of-date laws that hobbled the administration of justice, which in turn undermined the authority of the state. Justinian complained there was no end to its complexity: 'We have found the entire arrangement of the law which has come down to us from the foundation of the City of Rome and the times of Romulus, to be so confused that it is extended to an infinite length and is not within the grasp of human capacity.'

Since John was illiterate, the real work of the commission was done by the lawyer Tribonian, who was guided by the elegant formulation of the ancient Roman jurist Ulpion: 'The commandments of the laws are these: live honourably, harm nobody and give everyone his due.'

The commission got to work, discarding contradictory and redundant laws, reassembling what was left into a more coherent form, and introducing new ones as needed to supersede the confusion.

Theodora instigated her own program of law reform to improve the status of Roman women. It became easier for women to own property, a husband could not take on a major debt without his wife giving her consent twice, the killing of a wife for adultery was outlawed, and rape became a crime punishable by death.

The commission delivered its draft of the *Codex of Justinian* on 8 April 529, the first comprehensive and coherent body of Roman law in the empire's history. It had been completed in just thirteen months, an astonishingly short period. Justinian crowed as he announced its publication: 'Those things which seemed to many former emperors to require correction, but which none of them ventured to carry to effect, we have decided to accomplish at the present time, with the assistance of almighty God.' Justinian presented all his reforms in this way, as the product of some unseen close collaboration between the emperor and the Almighty.

Official copies of the *Codex* were sent out to the provinces to improve the administration of justice. This was followed by the *Digest*, which collated and harmonised the work of the ancient Roman jurists into a body of fifty approved books. A guide to the elements of Roman law for students, called the *Institutes*, was produced later. All in all, the emperor's boast was correct: it was a stunning achievement.

The influence of Justinian's *Codex* lingers on, right up to the present day. Modern European civil law is founded on the work of Justinian's commission fifteen centuries ago. Justinian and Tribonian are honoured with cameo portraits, mounted on the north wall of the chamber of the US House of Representatives, alongside images of other great law-givers of world history: Moses, Hammurabi and Napoleon.

HAVING REWORKED ROMAN LAW into a new coherent whole, Justinian then set about stamping out the last flames of paganism in the empire. He introduced new laws against heretics and infidels, and against the pagan practice of homosexuality, which was to be punished with torture, mutilation and execution. The civil rights of Jews were restricted. Worship of the Egyptian god Amon was stamped out of the Libyan desert, and the cult of Isis in the Nile delta was shut down.

Almost as an afterthought, Justinian ordered the closure of the Academy of Athens, a school founded by Plato himself, terminating a thousand years of philosophical education and inquiry in a stroke.

Old Rome was an untidy warren of gimcrack tenements, temples and bath houses; it was only to be expected that polytheistic habits and practices would fester in such an unclean place. The New Rome on the Bosphorus, while not exactly grid-like, was planned, open and orderly. Old paths of spiritualism and the meandering backways of pagan belief were shut down and dismantled; the roads that brought people towards the Orthodox church were enhanced and straightened, all the better to gather the world into a single communion, with the God-appointed Justinian directing events at the centre. The Roman thought-world under Justinian became more transcendent, but also more oppressive, compared to life under the old gods.

With his domestic reforms in place, Justinian now turned his mind to the growing threat from the one foreign entity with enough might and majesty to eclipse the Roman empire: Sassanid Persia.

Dara

IN JUSTINIAN'S TIME the Persian empire of the Sassanids sprawled across modern day Iraq and Iran, parts of Afghanistan, Arabia, the Caucasus, Central Asia and Pakistan. Sassanid Persia dominated western Asia in much the same way that Rome dominated the Mediterranean world. The two empires regarded each other warily, with a mix of respect, envy and antipathy.

Sassanid Persia was ruled by a Shahanshah, or 'king of kings', named Kavadh, who lived in a staggeringly opulent palace in Ctesiphon on the banks of the Tigris River. The Shahanshah wore robes of richly coloured silk, his beard was decorated with gold, and his crown was so heavy it was suspended above his head from the ceiling. To the Persians, the Shahanshah represented an ideal of universal order and harmony, and he was depicted on coins with the sun and moon revolving around him.

Like the Romans, the Sassanids maintained pretensions of world domination. In the palace at Ctesiphon three empty chairs were placed beneath the royal throne: one for the emperor of the Romans, one for the Great Khagan of Central Asia, and one for the emperor of China, reserved for the day when these rulers came to Ctesiphon as humble vassals of the Shahanshah.

The traditional heartland of Persia was centred on the Iranian plateau, where Zoroastrianism, the state religion, was founded. But by Justinian's time the empire's cultural and financial energy had shifted west, to the cosmopolitan cities of Mesopotamia where Ctesiphon was located. The westward thrust of Sassanid Persia led to rising tensions with the Romans along the contested lands in Syria, where both sides built a string of fortresses and watched each other warily across the border.

ALONG THAT IMPERIAL faultline stood the fortified Roman garrison town of Nisibis, constructed during Diocletian's reign as a tripwire against a Persian attack.* But by Justinian's time, the Persians had pushed the border further west and Nisibis had fallen into the Shahanshah's possession.

The Romans were unsettled by the presence of a Persian garrison right on their doorstep, and so a rival stronghold was constructed at the village of Dara nearby. In Ctesiphon, the new fortress was seen as an outrageous provocation. When peace negotiations with Kavadh broke down, Justinian reinforced Dara's fortifications. In turn, the

---

* The modern-day town of Nusaybin, now located on the equally fraught border between Syria and Turkey.

Shahanshah summoned an aristocratic general named Peroz and put him at the head of a 40,000-strong army with orders to prise Dara from the infernal Romans' grip.

THE PERSIAN FORCES gathering at Nisibis included thousands of foot soldiers and horse archers, accompanied by a 5000-strong contingent of heavy cavalry known as the Immortals, a name with a pedigree reaching back to the era of Cyrus the Great. Clad in heavy, plated armour, armed with maces, swords and lances, the Immortals rode into battle astride horses draped in chainmail. They were sometimes nicknamed *clibanarii* or 'camp ovens' for the suffocating heat they endured under all that armour. Sworn to personal loyalty to the Shahanshah, the chainmailed Immortal was the Asian prototype for that most characteristic figure of the Middle Ages: the knight in armour.

Dara's defence was, for Justinian, a point of pride as much as a matter of national security. To defend it, he sent his most brilliant general, a twenty-five-year-old career soldier named Belisarius, whom he promoted to Magister Militum of the East.

The coming battle of Dara would give Belisarius his first taste of senior command. But the general's inexperience was counterbalanced by a penetrating strategic intellect and a young man's grasp of the emerging technologies that were changing the art of war. Throughout his career, Belisarius would regularly take on much larger armies and beat them, using the weight of their superior numbers against them. He possessed an uncanny ability to get inside the head of an opponent, to see the world from the enemy's point of view, and then confound their expectations. Belisarius's adversaries would go down not quite believing what was happening to them.

In 530, Belisarius rode out to the Persian front, accompanied by Procopius, who was to act as his legal secretary, and who recorded an eyewitness account of his campaigns. In Dara the general mustered his forces: twenty-five thousand in all, a mix of regular Roman foot soldiers, mercenary horse archers and armoured cataphracts, the Roman counterpart to the Persian Immortals. Lacking the resources to withstand a siege against such overwhelmingly large enemy numbers, Belisarius resolved to stand and fight in open battle outside the fortress.

PEROZ BROUGHT HIS PERSIAN forces up towards Dara, confident of victory, but reports of the Roman lines unsettled him. Belisarius had arrayed his infantry and cavalry in a wildly unconventional manner. The Romans had dug a central trenchline that zigzagged at right angles in front of their fortress, forming the shape of a set of bull's horns. Belisarius had placed his main infantry force in the rear, behind the central trench, to protect them from being trampled by the Persian cavalry. Further forward, behind the parallel trenches to the sides, were two regiments of Hunnic mercenaries armed with powerful compound bows. In the corner angles of the trenches, Belisarius placed his cataphracts, the heavy cavalry.

Peroz was taken aback. He had expected the conventional layout of infantry at the front and cavalry in the wings. Belisarius's deployment seemed to defy commonsense. Peroz spent a day in his tent with his advisors, trying to figure out what the Romans were up to.

Meanwhile the armies stood glowering at each other across the distance. Then a single horseman rode out from the Persian lines and taunted the Romans, demanding they bring forth someone to fight him in single combat. There was a buzz of chatter and a young man named Andreas came forward from the ranks. Andreas was a wrestling teacher and powerfully built, but had no combat experience. The Persian champion prepared for battle, but as he was doing so, Andreas broke into a jog, picked up a spear and hurled it into his opponent's side, knocking him to the ground. Andreas then walked over to the helpless Persian and cut his throat with a small knife. A cheer erupted across the Roman lines and from up high on the fortress battlements.

Then a second Persian horseman came forward, an older man, who pointed his horsewhip at the Romans and dared them to send forth another champion. Andreas answered the call again and was given a stallion to mount. The two horsemen charged at each other at a furious pace. As they readied their lances, the two horses crashed into each other at full speed, cracking heads, and the riders were flung into the dust. Now it was a question of who could get to his feet first. The Persian struggled up onto one knee, but Andreas was already there, standing above him, knife in hand.

FOR THE PERSIANS, it was an inauspicious prelude to hostilities. But their morale picked up the following day when ten thousand reinforcements arrived from Nisibis. The Persians now outnumbered the Romans two to one. Belisarius sent a note to Peroz, reminding him of the blessings of peace. Surely, he wrote, a diplomatic solution would be preferable to a pointless war.

'This is true,' Peroz replied, 'and I would have agreed to your suggestions, if the letter had not been written by a lying Roman.'

Belisarius wrote back that his men would fasten these letters to their banners to motivate them.

Peroz replied, 'Tomorrow I will be in Dara. Prepare my bath and my lunch for me.'

THE BATTLE BEGAN the next day at noon. The Persians advanced towards the central trench and fired off a shower of arrows; the Roman infantry formed a defensive crouch behind their shields. The Persians then launched a cavalry attack against the Roman left. As the Persians swung around the trench the Romans withdrew. Sensing a quick victory was close at hand, the Persian cavalry broke into a gallop to chase the retreating Romans, throwing up clouds of dust. In their haste, the Persians lost formation, and suddenly, Belisarius's Hunnic horse archers were upon them, tearing into their exposed flank, firing off deadly arrows at short range. The forward thrust of the Persian cavalry collapsed, like a spear knocked down in mid-flight by a sideways blow to the shaft.

Then Belisarius unleashed his masterstroke. Earlier in the day he had concealed six hundred Herulian horse archers behind a nearby hill. Now they came charging into battle and smashed into the other exposed flank of the Persian cavalry. Within twenty minutes, two thousand Persian horsemen lay dead or dying.

As one side of the Persian attack was collapsing into a morass of dust and blood, the other side was bringing its superior numbers to bear against the Roman right. Again, as the Roman infantry retreated, Peroz's Immortals charged in pursuit. Belisarius sent in his other contingent of Hunnic horse archers, which wheeled around into the rear of the Immortals, firing lethal, armour-piercing arrows at close range from their powerful compound bows. The Roman cataphracts crashed into the attack. Another five thousand Persians were cut down.

All was not yet lost for the Persians. There were still thousands of foot soldiers yet to be deployed. But most of Peroz's infantry were slave soldiers with little motivation to fight. Watching the terrible slaughter across the trench, many of them broke and ran, with the Roman cavalry in pursuit.

It was a devastating, incomprehensible loss for Peroz. At sunset, the remnant of his army collected its dead and staggered back behind Persian lines. Peroz would have to take his bath that night in Nisibis instead.

THE BATTLE OF DARA was a triumph for Belisarius, and a vindication of Justinian's faith in his abilities, a sure sign that God was smiling on his endeavours. The emperor had more plans for his gifted general, but first his services would be needed in Constantinople, where simmering discontent with Justinian was about to boil over.

The Deep State

JOE AND I HAVE COME TO ISTANBUL at a time of civil unrest. Events within the city and around Turkey are breaking into international news bulletins. I'm keeping an eye out for any signs of protest, but the historic centre of the city is a tightly controlled tourist zone, isolated from the working heartland of modern-day Istanbul. Everything here in Sultanahmet seems calm.

At the end of our third day, Joe and I find that everyone in the hotel café is talking about the day's protests in Taksim Square against government plans to restrict access to Twitter and Facebook. Police evicted the protestors from the square with water cannons and tear gas.

The protests had begun six months earlier, when local citizens organised a sit-in protest against a proposed commercial redevelopment of Gezi Park from a public space to a shopping centre. The protests escalated into mass demonstrations across the nation as a broader expression of discontent against the authoritarian Prime Minister Recep Tayyip Erdoğan. Environmental groups led the initial protests, but they were soon joined by a much broader coalition of 'the young and the old, the secular and the religious, the soccer hooligans and the blind, anarchists, communists, nationalists, Kurds, gays, feminists, and students'. Police clashed with the protestors in Gezi Park, pounding them with water cannons and tear gas. Prime Minister Erdoğan dismissed the protestors as looters, losers and extremists.

Pro- and anti-Erdoğan forces have split the country. Erdoğan's popular base is largely drawn from conservative Muslims, particularly in regional areas, who are unsettled by the rapid changes to Turkey's economy and society. His financial support comes from construction companies and property developers who are driving the frantic redevelopment of Istanbul's skyline. In this way he profits by the economic boom and the conservative backlash against it. Erdoğan's opposition, which is mostly urban and secular, accuses him of corruption, which he adamantly denies.

Another, much older, tension is being played out around these protests. Many Turkish politicians and journalists talk about something called the Deep State, a clandestine network that operates within Turkey's most powerful national institutions – the military, intelligence organisations, the parliament, the judiciary, the bureaucracy, organised crime and the media. The interests of the Deep State are said at times to be anti-democratic, anti-Islamist, anti-Kurdish and anti-worker. No group can agree on how to categorise the interests of the Deep State, which indicates that it operates not as a single conspiracy, but as a loose coalition of interests that sometimes collude with each other for mutual benefit.

The term 'Deep State' (*derin devlet*) grew out of an infamous incident in 1996, when a black Mercedes Benz crashed into a truck backing out of a service station in north-west Turkey. Three of the four occupants of the car were killed. They were an unlikely bunch: the three dead included the former deputy chief of the Istanbul police, a hitman from the ultra-right paramilitary group the Grey Wolves, and his girlfriend. The hitman was carrying a passport with the name 'Mehmet Özbay', the same pseudonym used by the assassin who shot Pope John Paul II in 1981. The fourth occupant, the survivor of the crash, was the leader of a powerful Kurdish clan and a member of the Turkish parliament.

As the story broke and the identities of the four became known, a major public scandal erupted across the Turkish media. Why on earth, Turks asked themselves, were those four sharing a ride together? The crash exposed connections between politicians, security forces and the heroin trade. An inquiry set up to investigate the incident came to nothing. This was proof, it was said, of the power of the Deep State to smother any kind of scrutiny of its workings.

Then in 2008, a police raid exposed an apparent plot by an ultra-nationalist group known as Ergenekon (the name comes from an old Central Asian fable of a she-wolf who rescues the Turkish nation). Journalists in the Turkish press claimed the gang had ties to the military and security forces, and that it was plotting a false flag operation to assassinate several secular intellectuals, including Nobel laureate Orhan Pahmuk. They were planning to exploit the resulting chaos to bring down the government.

Prime Minister Erdoğan praised the police action, and linked the Ergenekon conspiracy to the Deep State. Erdoğan stated bluntly on Turkish television, 'I don't agree with those who say the Deep State does not exist. It does exist. It always has – and it did not start with the Republic; it dates back to Ottoman times. It's simply a tradition. It must be minimised, and if possible even annihilated.' Some journalists have accused the government of using the Ergenekon case to crack down on dissent.

THE ROOTS OF THE DEEP STATE lie within the Turkish military. Atatürk, the founder of modern Turkey, empowered the military to uphold the new secular order and to covertly suppress Islamist political figures. During the Cold War, the United States set up a secret 'stay-behind' resistance group within the military's Special Warfare Department to lead a counter-insurgency in case of a Communist takeover. In the following decades, this unit formed the core of the Deep State, taking it upon itself to keep the nation safe by suppressing and assassinating Communists, Islamists, Christian missionaries, journalists and dissidents. But the Special Warfare Department lost its rationale at the end of the Cold War, and some of its leaders drifted into ultra-nationalist groups such as the Grey Wolves.

Erdoğan's Justice and Development Party (AKP) now presents the single greatest threat to Deep State power since the establishment of the Turkish republic. The AKP wants to change Atatürk's secular constitution to reflect the growing influence of pious Muslims in rural and coastal Anatolia.

Another complicating factor is the movement for Kurdish independence, which Erdoğan sees as a threat to Turkey's territorial integrity. And there's also the lingering question of whether Turkey will ever join the European Union. Since taking power, Erdoğan has changed his position on the EU, from strong support to outright hostility. He hints that the EU hasn't already admitted Turkey because it can't bear the thought of opening its borders to nearly seventy-five million Muslims. Erdoğan, it seems, has come to see the EU as Christendom in modern clothing.

KEEPING TRACK of the connections between the players in the Deep State conspiracy theories requires a detective's pinboard, photos, thumbtacks and plenty of string. When contemplating the complexity of this tangled web of self-interested conspirators, the word 'byzantine' unconsciously comes to mind. Historians of Byzantium resent the term 'byzantine' when it's used to denote something absurdly bureaucratic and arcane, seeing it as a slur arising from centuries of western prejudice.

Still, on this day, with reports of government forces cracking down on protestors on the city streets, we hear a distant echo of the ghost empire, of a massacre perpetrated here by Justinian nearly fifteen hundred years ago.

Nika

IT ALL BEGAN WITH a failed execution. On 10 January 532, Eudaemon, the prefect of Constantinople, passed a death sentence on seven violent criminals, partisans from the Blue and Green factions. On the appointed day, however, the scaffold collapsed and two men, a Blue and a Green, fell to the ground, still alive. They were picked up by a group of sympathetic monks who rowed them across the Golden Horn to the Church of St Laurentius, where the condemned men were given asylum.

The leaders of the rival factions met and agreed to a temporary alliance. They demanded the emperor let their men go free – surely the miracle at the scaffold was a sign that God required clemency in this case. Justinian refused to budge and posted guards at the doors of St Laurentius to prevent the men from escaping.

Three days later, when Justinian took his seat in the imperial box at the Hippodrome, he was heckled and abused from the stands. The mood in the stadium darkened, and at the end of the day's events, both factions united in a steady chant of *Ni-ka! Ni-ka! Ni-ka!* – 'victory' or, more ominously, 'conquest'.

That night an angry mob formed outside the city prison. They overpowered the guards and opened the cells, freeing every inmate. Revelling in its success, the mob moved on to the city's central square, the Augustaeum, where they set fire to the Chalke Gate at the entrance to the Great Palace. The flames leapt up and caught the wind, and the inferno spread across the Square, engulfing the Senate House, the Church of Holy Wisdom and another church behind it, the Hagia Irene. The ancient classical statues that adorned the Baths of Zeuxippos were smashed and destroyed.

Justinian refused to be panicked and ordered the next day's races to proceed as scheduled, hoping the excitement would distract the crowd. Instead the factions rioted and set alight the northern end of the Hippodrome. The faction leaders ratcheted up their demands, insisting the emperor sack his three unpopular officials: John the Cappadocian, Tribonian the quaestor and Eudaemon the prefect. Justinian buckled to their demands, but his concession failed to quell the rioting. Justinian concluded the real instigators of the uprising were his enemies in the senate, who were paying the factions to continue the chaos.

Justinian lost all control and for three days the city was given over to the mob, which burnt and ransacked its way along the Mese to the Forum of Constantine. The Great Palace complex was partially destroyed. The palace guards, the Excubitors and the Scholarians, refused to help. Justinian and Theodora were now in great danger.

The next day, the emperor fronted the crowd at the Hippodrome and offered a general amnesty for the three days of mayhem. He swore on a copy of the Gospels that he would keep his word, but was greeted with jeers. Meanwhile, in the Forum of Constantine, a crowd raised up an aristocrat named Hypatius – nephew of the late emperor Anastasius – and crowned him with a golden chain.

Under siege in his own palace, a badly rattled Justinian lost his nerve. He said he thought the best course of action would be to leave the city. Each one of his ministers agreed.

AND THEN THEODORA SPOKE UP, in a speech that rings down through the ages. Looking at the court, the empress said that although it was against convention for a woman to speak in a man's council, the situation was serious enough to break with the formalities. Turning to her husband, she appealed to him to stay and fight – and die, if need be:

> *For one who has reigned, it is intolerable to be a fugitive. May I never be deprived of this purple robe. And may I never see the day when those who meet me do not call me 'Empress'.*

Theodora now gestured towards the balcony:

> *If you wish to save yourself, my lord, there is no difficulty. We are rich; there is the sea, and here are the boats. Yet reflect for a moment whether, once you have escaped to a place of safety, you would not gladly exchange such safety for death.*
>
> *As for me, I agree with the ancient saying that the royal purple is a good burial shroud.*

It was Theodora's greatest performance. Her speech shamed her husband and shifted the mood of the room towards a counterstrike against the factions. Theodora and Justinian would prevail or die together.

Mosaic of Theodora, Church of St Vitale, Ravenna.

Meanwhile, just across the square in the Hippodrome, a rumour coursed through the stands that the emperor had already fled the city. Hypatius, who had thus far been a fearful conscript to the top job, now confidently took the imperial seat at the Hippodrome, and accepted the raucous acclamation of the crowd.

JUSTINIAN PLANNED to defeat his enemies through the oldest of Roman strategies – divide and conquer. The emperor wasn't able to rely on the loyalties of the palace guard, who were hanging back, waiting to see how things turned out. So Justinian turned to the military man who remained squarely in his corner: Belisarius. The general had just returned to Constantinople from the Persian front to accept the role of army commander-in-chief. Belisarius was joined by another loyal commander, Mundus, who commanded a force of fifteen hundred battle-hardened Thracian and Herulian mercenaries, men with no connections to either of the Hippodrome's factions.

As he prepared to strike, Justinian sent a palace eunuch named Narses into the Hippodrome with pouches of gold to bribe the leaders of the Blues. Narses met them in the stands and reminded them of Justinian's longstanding partiality to their faction. Then he pointed across the stadium to the imperial box, and asked if they were likely to prosper under the reign of Hypatius, a well-known ally of the Greens.

For a moment, there was some confusion as the Blues considered moving their supporters out of the Hippodrome. Meanwhile, Belisarius was leading his men across the rubble of the Augustaeum to the south-eastern entrance of the stadium. They gathered in the shadows of the gate, largely unnoticed amid the tumult and revelry in the stands.

On his signal, Belisarius's men unsheathed their swords and charged into the crowd. At the same time, another contingent of soldiers, led by Mundus, entered through a gate on the opposite side, and fifty thousand rioters were pressed in a tight space between two battalions of hacking and slashing mercenaries. Thousands were trampled underfoot in the panic, as people frantically pushed their way from one side to the other to avoid the carnage. Hypatius looked down from the imperial box, as screams of terror melded with the groans of the wounded and dying. Blood gathered in muddy pools on the dirt floor of the Hippodrome, and ran out through the colonnades into the marble square outside.

Procopius estimated the dead at thirty thousand; other contemporary writers placed the figure as high as fifty thousand. Overall, the slaughter amounted to something like a tenth of the population of the biggest city in the world.

Hypatius was arrested and brought to the palace. Justinian hesitated before pronouncing sentence on a man he'd known for most of his life, well aware that Hypatius had never really been a conspirator and had been carried along by the real plotters. As the emperor pondered his decision, Theodora intervened, reminding him that if he spared Hypatius, another conspiracy would inevitably form around him. Justinian reluctantly agreed and Hypatius was beheaded, his body tossed into the Sea of Marmara. The senators who had supported the riots were exiled and their property confiscated. Feeling under no obligation to honour his earlier commitment made under duress, Justinian reinstated John of Cappadocia as his chief minister. The power of the Blues and Greens was sharply curtailed. Justinian and Theodora had re-established their authority, atop a mountain of corpses.

Inner Radiance

CONSTANTINOPLE was quiet at last, with the peace of the exhausted battlefield. Justinian surveyed the ruins of his blackened and blood-streaked Augustaeum and, typically, saw a great opportunity. A grand redesign of the city square would go some way to healing the horror of the atrocity in the Hippodrome. A reassertion of imperial majesty would encourage his people to see him as a builder, not a tyrant.

To the south-east of the Augustaeum, Justinian ordered the construction of a new, smaller senate building inside the palace grounds, befitting its diminished status. The main entrance to the palace, the Chalke Gate, would be restored and lavishly clad in marble and mosaics. On the southern end, he ordered the rebuilding of the Baths of Zeuxippus. But his grandest ambitions were reserved for the area north of the square, on the burnt-out ruins of the second Hagia Sophia. (The first church of that name had been destroyed by rioters more than a century earlier.)

Six weeks after the massacre, workers began clearing the rubble and digging the foundations for a third Hagia Sophia, which would dwarf its predecessors in every respect. Justinian's instructions to his architects, Anthemius of Tralles and Isidore of Miletus, were simple: design the greatest building in the world and do it quickly. Absolutely no expense was spared in the creation of a church of surpassing magnificence. Construction materials were shipped into Constantinople from all over the empire: green marble from Thessaly, black stone from the Bosphorus, and porphyry of imperial purple from Egypt. Ten thousand labourers were conscripted to complete the job as quickly as possible.

Anthemius and Isidore's design was ingenious: they conceived the new Hagia Sophia as a mountain of interlocking domes, dominated by a gigantic central dome that would hover like the canopy of heaven over a vast, open interior space. Once constructed, this central dome was greeted with gasps of amazement: Anthemius and Isidore had taken the principle of the load-bearing arch and rotated it 180 degrees to create the biggest dome in the world, a feat no architect would equal for a thousand years.

Work on the Hagia Sophia was completed in five years and ten months, a dramatically short period that was taken to be a miracle in itself.* Justinian came to inspect his new church before its inauguration in 537. As he stood under the breathtaking dome, he boasted, 'Solomon, I have outdone you.'

---

* The construction of Notre Dame, by comparison, required more than a century.

THE CITIZENS OF CONSTANTINOPLE gazed in wonderment at the scale of the new Hagia Sophia. They marvelled at the intricacies of its craftwork and the harmony of its proportions. 'It exults in an indescribable beauty,' sighed Procopius. The interior was lovely beyond belief: the interplay of golden light as it streamed through the upper windows onto the green, purple and white marble reminded him of a meadow blooming with flowers.

The creation of the Hagia Sophia was a kind of victory, a triumph of the celestial over the mundane, the truest act of *theosis*. It was the point in the city where the thick curtain separating heaven and earth became gossamer thin. Justinian's great church brought an unalloyed joy to the people of the city and made them surer of the glories of the afterlife. The magnanimity of the Hagia Sophia inspired a similar generosity of spirit in those within it. Procopius saw how the church lifted the spirits of those who entered it, how, 'when present in the church men rejoice in what they see, and when they leave it, they take proud delight in conversing about it'.

But the work had been undertaken in haste, and there was no getting round the fact that there were visible flaws in the building, which had to be fixed over time. In 558 an earthquake caused the central dome to collapse. The replacement was designed by Isidore's nephew, who made the dome higher and rounder, and thus more stable. He fixed the rim of the dome to four pendentives, triangular dome segments that caught the weight of the dome and distributed the load effectively from the centre to the four corner pillars.

The Hagia Sophia and the Hippodrome, adjacent to each other, became the great complementary theatres of Constantinople, where the emperor and his people could act out different aspects of themselves. The pleasures of this life were played out in one, the joys of the afterlife were contemplated in the other.

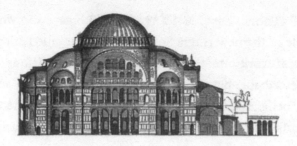

Plan of the Hagia Sophia.

A Vast Harmony

THE HAGIA SOPHIA served as a Christian house of worship
for nine centuries, then as a mosque for another five. Today it's a
museum, and Joe and I are lined up at the ticket gate. As we wait in
the queue, we overhear two elderly Texan ladies arguing behind us.
They're not enjoying their stay.

    'Let it go, Pearl.'

    'Well, Ah thought he was *rude*.'

    'Ah said, let it go.'

We purchase two tickets stamped with *Ayasofya Müzesi*, and
turn to face the entrance of the great church. We pass into the inner
narthex through a grand rectangular portal once reserved for the
ingress of the emperor. Legend has it that the heavy timber doors
were crafted from timbers salvaged from the wreck of Noah's Ark.

Then we're inside the cavernous nave of the church. Joe breaks
into a broad smile. Like all great buildings, the Hagia Sophia seems
at one moment to be completely indifferent to your tiny existence,
and in another, to be like a great big present made just for you.

An English author named Robert Hichens came to visit the great church a century ago. He arrived in a foul mood, frazzled by the noise and dirt of Istanbul. Once inside the church, his irritability fell away and he suddenly found himself 'in the midst of a vast harmony, so wonderful, so penetrating, so calm, that I was conscious at once of a perfect satisfaction'. As he gazed upwards, he felt, he said, 'both possessed and released'. This, I find, is no exaggeration. As Joe and I step under the great golden dome, an electric tingle rises from the middle of my spine to the top of my head. I have a sudden certainty that I am in the most beautiful building that has ever been made.

The threadbare grandeur of the Hagia Sophia inspires awe and affection at the same time. So many of its tessellated gold tiles have been lost or stolen; only a few of its mosaics are visible. The marbled floors are uneven, worn down over the centuries by the countless footsteps of worshippers, pilgrims and sightseers. For all that, it is a thrilling, heavenly space.

The 'Splendid Door' carved with Indian motifs, brought to the Hagia Sophia from an ancient temple in Tarsus, Asia Minor.

Standing under the great dome, I have the impression that it is somehow, impossibly, holding up the whole building. Light streams through the upper windows and is reflected and refracted on the mosaic tiles of gold and glass, suffusing the interior with a warm golden glow. To the Romans, it seemed the glow was miraculous, 'not illuminated from outside by the sun, rather that the radiance was created from within itself'. The Muslim conquerors of the city could only agree; today the dome is inscribed with Arabic script: *Allah is the light of the heavens and the earth.*

Seraphim

THE GLITTERING MOSAICS of the Hagia Sophia seem, at first, curiously flat and jaunty, lacking coherent lines of perspective. Then you notice they do indeed have a *kind* of perspective, only it's weirdly inverted. Buildings and figures are shaped not to recede into the distance, but to enlarge. The pedestal under the Virgin's throne and other box-like objects are wedge-shaped. The vanishing points don't lie somewhere on the horizon within the image, but outside it, within the eye of the viewer. When looking at these pictures, it helps if you imagine a conical field of vision, where the tip of the cone touches your eyeball and widens as the image deepens. The overall effect, like everything else in the church, is quite magical and otherworldly.

JUST BELOW THE RIM OF THE DOME, I see four huge, feathered creatures looming over us. Pairs of heavy blue wings, projecting up, down and sideways, surround their disembodied faces. A guide tells me they're archangels, but they look like no angels I've ever seen before. They remind me of monsters from Greek mythology.

The creatures in the four mosaics represent the seraphim, the highest in the hierarchy of angels and the protectors of the throne of heaven. In Hebrew, the name *seraphim* translates as 'the burning ones'. Their strange likenesses are drawn from the Book of Isaiah, where they appear to Isaiah in a terrifying vision.

Seraph from Hagia Sophia.

The prophet sees the six-winged creatures flying around the throne of God, shrieking *Holy! Holy! Holy!*, and is overcome with trembling fear and a sense of his own worthlessness. Then one of the seraphim swoops down to show him 'a burning coal in his hand, which he had picked up with tongs from the altar. He touched my mouth with it and said, "Behold, this has touched your lips; and your guilt is taken away and your sin is forgiven".'

THE IMAGES OF THE SERAPHIM in Justinian's great church are altogether more startling than the handsome golden-haired angels we've become accustomed to. Angels, we're discovering on this trip, are not quite what we think they are.

In Rome, at the beginning of our journey, I had pointed to what I thought was an angel on the Arch of Septimius Severus, a monument that dates back well before Christianisation.

Our guide Danielle smiled. 'That's no angel,' she said. 'It's Nike, the goddess of winged victory. You'll notice she has the tunic of a Persian soldier impaled on her spear. Angels don't normally do that sort of thing.'

When I asked why Nike happened to look so much like an angel, Danielle explained that when the empire was Christianised, it became fashionable for wealthy Romans to sponsor art that would depict them in the company of angels. 'The artists and sculptors would ask, "What do angels look like?" and they would say "Well, you know, they're beautiful, with wings and billowing robes." The artists already had templates for Nike so they just went ahead and used those.'

THE IMAGE OF NIKE, concealed in the form of an angel, flourished in the post-Roman world, even as her name declined into obscurity. Then, in 1971, a classically educated salesman for a sports shoe company in Oregon had a dream of the goddess of winged victory. He came to work the next day and suggested the company change its name from Blue Ribbon Sports to Nike. The new brand was attached to a 'swoosh' logo and today her name sits at the masthead of a global enterprise with questionable labour practices, just as she once did for the Roman empire two thousand years ago.

Belisarius and the Vandals

AS THE MIRACULOUS FORM of the Hagia Sophia rose up to dominate the city skyline, Justinian received word that Kavadh was dead and had been succeeded by his son Khusrau. Justinian sent emissaries to Ctesiphon where they found the new Shahanshah amenable to some kind of settlement, and so a 'Treaty of Eternal Peace' was concluded between the Roman empire and Sassanid Persia. The two emperors agreed to recognise each other as equals, and pledged themselves to mutual assistance against raiding tribes of barbarians. The treaty left Khusrau free to deal with his internal problems, and gave Justinian a free hand to pursue his most cherished territorial ambition: the recovery of the lost lands of the west.

The Romans had been thrown out of North Africa by the Vandals, who had conquered Carthage in 439 and made it the seat of their new kingdom. Early in his reign, Justinian had begun a friendly correspondence with the Vandal king, Hilderic, who had Roman blood on his mother's side and had accepted Orthodox Christianity. The emperor was coaxing Hilderic towards a voluntary re-entry into the empire, but in 531, Hilderic was overthrown by his cousin Gelimer. Justinian sent a letter of protest to Carthage. Gelimer replied by telling Justinian to mind his own business.

Justinian's mind was now set on war. He brought Belisarius back from the eastern front and ordered him to take Carthage and bring the wayward province of North Africa back into the Roman fold. John of Cappadocia set out his objections: the campaign would involve a risky sea voyage; if the venture failed it would be a year before they found out about it; and even if they did succeed, it would be nearly impossible to hold Carthage, unless they also held Sicily.

Justinian was unmoved by John's objections, and in June 533 watched from his balcony as Belisarius's fleet of transports and warships sailed past the Bucoleon Palace on their way to North Africa. Also on deck was Belisarius's wife, Antonina.

Antonina was, like her best friend Theodora, a daughter of the Hippodrome, brought up in a family of charioteers. She was older than Belisarius, and had several children from an earlier marriage. Like Theodora, she was street-smart, politically astute and closely bound to her talented husband. Belisarius relied on her advice and she accompanied him everywhere.

Also on board the flagship was Procopius, who liked Antonina no better than Theodora. Even so, he was obliged to credit her intelligence. As the invasion fleet crossed the Adriatic, the supplies of hardtack were found to be mouldy. The water supplies were spoilt too, and the jars cracked, except for those aboard Belisarius's ship. Procopius records that Antonina had arranged for a bed of sand to be constructed below deck, and had buried the glass water bottles within it, keeping the jars unbroken and the water free of algae.

THE FLEET SAILED SOUTH-WEST and anchored in Sicily for supplies, where Belisarius received some welcome intelligence that the Vandal fleet had abandoned Carthage to quell an uprising in Sardinia. The city was, for the moment, wide open to attack. Belisarius gave the order to sail at once for the North African coast. He set his infantry and cavalry down on a beach 140 miles south of Carthage, then marched north. Gelimer could do nothing to stop the Roman advance and barely escaped in time. So quick was the victory that when Belisarius and Antonina entered Carthage, they sat down to a feast that had been prepared for Gelimer and hastily abandoned.

Gelimer sent an appeal to his brother Tzazo, who was with the Vandal fleet in Sardinia, and together they regrouped and launched a counterattack. Rather than face a siege, Belisarius led his men out of the city to confront the Vandal army. Gelimer had the greater numbers, but Belisarius's troops were better trained and more disciplined, and the Goths reeled under the ferocity of the Roman attack. Tzazo was killed in the fighting and the Vandal king fled to the mountains. When he was eventually discovered by a detachment of Roman soldiers, he appeared to have lost his mind.

BELISARIUS WROTE to inform his emperor that North Africa was once again a Roman province. Justinian was overjoyed, and awarded Belisarius a Triumph, an honour not granted by an emperor to a commander for more than five centuries. Belisarius sailed back to Constantinople and was greeted as a hero. Centuries earlier, Julius Caesar had received the adulation of the crowd from a chariot; this time Belisarius simply marched with his soldiers into the Hippodrome on foot, followed by wagons of looted treasure, as the ecstatic crowd raised cheer after cheer.

Gelimer, as an honoured prisoner, was led into the Hippodrome in chains, but given a purple cloak to identify him to the crowd as the defeated barbarian king. As he saw Justinian sitting in glory upon his high throne in the *kathisma*, Gelimer was overheard to mutter, 'Vanity, vanity, all is vanity'. He was stripped of his cloak and forced to prostrate himself before Justinian, who chose to be merciful. Gelimer was awarded lands in Galatia and permitted to live there in peace with his family.

Temple Menorah.

Among the plundered goods seen in the Hippodrome that day was the menorah, the seven-branched Jewish candelabra that had been seized from the Temple of Jerusalem in 71 AD, and brought to Rome.

The menorah had, in turn, been plundered by the Vandals during the sack of Rome in 455 and carried off to Carthage. The candelabra was recognised by Jewish rabbis who were among the cheering crowds in the Hippodrome that day. The next day the rabbis came to the Great Palace to plead for the menorah's return, warning that the same bad luck that had brought down Rome and Carthage would fall upon Constantinople if the emperor did not return the menorah to where it belonged. Justinian agreed, and had the candelabra, along with other precious objects from the Temple, sent back to Jerusalem.

ALSO SITTING AMONG the cheering crowds that day, eyeing the chests of Vandal treasure circling the Hippodrome, were the ambassadors of Khusrau. In their diplomatic communications, Justinian and Khusrau had taken to referring to each other as 'brothers'. Surely, the Persian ambassadors argued, brother emperors should share their plunder, particularly when such riches had only been made possible by the peace granted to the emperor by Khusrau. Justinian could not agree to such a division of the spoils, but he took care to send lavish gifts to the Shahanshah instead, which did nothing to satisfy Khusrau's envy.

Belisarius and the Goths

THE RECONQUEST OF NORTH AFRICA opened the way for the recovery of the Italian peninsula. Both Italy and Sicily were under the control of another Germanic tribe, the Ostrogoths – or Eastern Goths – who had settled there in large numbers forty years earlier. Belisarius sailed from Constantinople with a force of 7500 men, with instructions to begin with Sicily. Procopius records that the general took the port of Palermo by an ingenious method: he sailed his ships close to the sea walls, then sent archers up high into the rigging, from where they fired down upon the garrison troops inside and then leapt down onto the battlements. The Goth defenders panicked and surrendered the port. The rest of Sicily was taken with ease.

Belisarius now had a strategic base for an assault on the Italian mainland. He transported his army across the straits of Messina onto the toe of the Italian boot, and marched his men north towards Naples. The city's walls were fiercely defended by Jews and Arian Christians, who had no desire to live under Orthodox rule. They held out for three weeks. Belisarius had a small force and no siege towers, so he cast about for another solution. One of his men followed a disused aqueduct, and found that it led into a narrow water culvert under the battlements. Belisarius sent a single file of four hundred men to crawl into it. They emerged, swords in hand, in the centre of the city, at the same time as another regiment attacked from outside the gates. The city surrendered.

Now the great prize of Rome itself lay before Belisarius. Vitiges, the king of the Ostrogoths, announced he would not defend it, and withdrew to consolidate his forces in Ravenna. Pope Silverius sent Belisarius a wary invitation to come north, and in December the imperial army marched into the Eternal City through the Porta Asinaria. 'So it was,' wrote Procopius with a sigh of satisfaction, 'that Rome once again, after a period of sixty years, became subject to the Romans.'

Theodora wanted to replace Pope Silverius with a more compliant figure, and she sent strongly worded instructions to Belisarius to strip him of his papal office. But it was the empress's friend Antonina who did the sacking.

Silverius was brought into the mausoleum of the Pincian Palace in Rome, where he saw Antonina reclining on a couch, with Belisarius sitting awkwardly at her feet.

'Tell us, Lord Pope Silverius,' she complained imperiously, 'what we have done to you and to the Romans that you should wish to betray us into the hands of the Goths?' As she spoke, a soldier stripped away Silverius's papal vestments. He was taken away, put into a common monk's robe and exiled to a craggy island in the Tyrrhenian Sea where he died of starvation.

BELISARIUS HAD NO TIME to enjoy his victory. He had only five thousand men, and he expected Vitiges to return in force before long. Preparations were set in train for a long siege. The Aurelian Walls were repaired and strengthened, but Belisarius's numbers were so thin, he had to order the closure of several gates. Early in the new year, Vitiges arrived at the walls with fifty thousand Gothic troops, ten times Belisarius's numbers. Citizens begged the general to surrender. Instead he appealed to Constantinople for troops and supplies; Justinian duly sent another sixteen hundred men to Italy.

It wasn't nearly enough. Justinian, it seems, couldn't let go of the notion that he could reconquer the west on the cheap, relying on Belisarius to keep pulling off unlikely victories. Vitiges surrounded the city, cutting off supply. Belisarius had no choice but to sit tight and wait for a change in fortune, or for Justinian to properly reinforce his small band of defenders.

Vitiges then ordered the destruction of Rome's aqueducts. After centuries of continuous use, the city's great fountains and baths dried up, and the mills used to grind flour came to a standstill. Belisarius responded to the flour shortage ingeniously, by mounting transportable mills onto the River Tiber, and so bread production could continue for the moment, but the destruction of the aqueducts would hobble Rome's growth for another thousand years.

Vitiges tried another approach. He sent four tall siege towers trundling towards the ramparts, dragged by teams of oxen. When Belisarius was alerted to the danger, he ran up to the battlements and fired two arrow bolts, felling two Gothic soldiers on the towers. He handed the bow to one of his men and told them to do the same thing to the oxen. The attack was stalled and the siege towers had to be abandoned in the field.

Still Vitiges kept feeling for cracks in the city's defences. A contingent of Goths attempted to climb the walls alongside the Mausoleum of Hadrian. Belisarius ordered his soldiers to rip out the ancient marble statues from the roof of the tomb and hurl them onto the invaders' heads as they climbed up their ladders. The attack was thwarted, but the glory of Rome, which Belisarius had fought so hard to redeem for the empire, was slowly being dismantled.

Belisarius was forced into further improvisations, as the mood soured within the city and the hardships deepened. There were food shortages and rumours of cannibalism. At last, in November, five thousand imperial cavalry and infantry arrived from the east. Vitiges asked for a truce.

During the negotiations, Belisarius sent two thousand horsemen, led by a headstrong lieutenant named John, on a raiding mission into Tuscany. John was under strict instructions not to stray too far north and get himself stranded in enemy territory. John ignored this command and led his men as far as Rimini, just thirty-five miles south of the Gothic capital of Ravenna.

When word of this reached Vitiges, he broke off truce negotiations and lashed out with a final series of attacks on the walls of Rome. The last assault was at the legendary Milvian Bridge, where Belisarius hammered the half-starved, disease-ridden Goths into a retreat. The siege, which had lasted a year and nine days, was over, but the prize of Rome was wrecked.

Vitiges marched his demoralised men north, back towards Ravenna. Belisarius saw that John and his horsemen were about to be enveloped by the enemy, and sent a message to John, ordering him to withdraw at once.

Narses

IT WAS AT THIS MOMENT that things started to get away from Belisarius. John flatly refused to obey. Belisarius was furious. Vitiges, as expected, arrived at the walls of Rimini with a far larger force than John's meagre detachment. Belisarius was pondering whether to send troops to rescue John, or simply leave him to die with his men as the price for his bad behaviour, when ten thousand imperial troops landed on the north Italian coast.

The new force was led by Narses the eunuch, one of Justinian's most trusted advisors, last seen bribing the Blues in the Hippodrome. Narses was a shrewd political operator, gifted at palace intrigue, but with no military experience. He was close to Theodora, and it might have been her idea to send a reliable operator to keep an eye on the glamorous and popular general. Narses presented Belisarius with new, carefully worded orders from Justinian: 'It is our wish that Belisarius alone shall lead the whole army as he sees fit, and he should be obeyed, as far as it is in the interest of our State.' The second part of that sentence gave Narses a loophole big enough to drive a war elephant through. Reading between the lines, Belisarius could only infer that while he would continue to direct all military decisions, Narses was now empowered to veto him in the name of state policy.

With all this in the back of his mind, Belisarius held a war council to discuss the predicament of John and his two thousand troops pinned down in Rimini. Belisarius stated bluntly that it was his belief they should leave John and his men to face the consequences of their insubordination, that it was just too risky to send a relief force so deep into Gothic territory. One by one, his officers nodded in agreement. Then Narses, who was a friend to John, spoke up. He argued that if Rimini fell to the Goths, and John and his men were captured, the empire would lose a commander, an army and a city. The enemy still had the greater numbers across Italy. If the Goths re-took Rimini, he said, it would raise their morale and put the whole Italian campaign in danger.

'As for John,' the eunuch said, turning to Belisarius, 'if he has treated your orders with contempt, it will be within your power to deal with him as you like, once the city is relieved. But you should make sure that in punishing him for any mistakes he has made through ignorance, that you don't punish the emperor and his subjects as well.'

It was an awkward moment. Belisarius backed down, and agreed they would relieve Rimini.

Belisarius buried his resentment and launched a brilliant attack on the Gothic camps outside Rimini from land and sea. Duped into thinking they were surrounded, Vitiges's men trudged back to Ravenna. Belisarius's tactics had won the day, but even Procopius had to concede that Narses had been right to insist on the rescue in the first place. Belisarius entered the city and found John looking thin and pale. The rebellious captain did not apologise for his conduct, and pointedly offered his thanks for his rescue only to Narses.

BELISARIUS AND NARSES were now rival commanders competing for the loyalties of the imperial armies. The competition at first served the empire well, as the two separate forces conquered town after town across the north of the Italian peninsula. But then the split between the rival commands widened, and the city of Milan fell into the abyss.

Milan was the largest and richest city in northern Italy. Belisarius's men had taken it from the Goths in 539 and maintained a small garrison there. Vitiges thought it might be vulnerable and appealed to the King of the Franks for aid, offering him a share of the spoils if he could send an army to help retake Milan. The commander of the beleaguered garrison inside the city smuggled out a plea for help. Belisarius at once sent an order to the nearest commander to relieve the garrison. But the commander in question happened to be John, who sniffed that he would only proceed with Narses's authorisation.

Exasperated, Belisarius wrote to Narses, who agreed to give the order, but it was too late. The Franks had made the garrison an offer: if they surrendered, they would be allowed to leave the city unharmed. To the citizens, they promised nothing. The men of the imperial garrison, who had been reduced to eating dogs and rats, accepted the offer and staggered out the city gates, leaving the city wide open to the Frankish army. Every man in the city was slaughtered. Every woman and child was either butchered or taken into slavery, and the city was burnt to the ground.

If Milan had been lost to the Romans, it had been lost to the Goths as well. A brutal famine set in across the war-ravaged countryside. A desperate Vitiges now reached out over the heads of the Romans to Ctesiphon. He bribed two Ligurian priests to carry a letter to the Persians. The letter advised Khusrau that if he were thinking of making a move against the Romans, now would be an excellent time, while the bulk of Justinian's forces were pinned down in Italy. Envious of Justinian's recent successes, Khusrau accepted the message, and planned accordingly.

The Crown of the West

BELISARIUS FIRED OFF an angry letter to Constantinople, holding Narses responsible for the debacle in Milan. Justinian agreed and recalled Narses from his command. Belisarius now had a free hand to conduct the war as he saw fit.

By late 540, Belisarius had knocked out the remaining Gothic strongholds one by one, and his men were at the walls of Ravenna. Vitiges lost hope and agreed to enter into surrender negotiations. Belisarius was on the verge of total victory when two senators arrived from Constantinople with orders from Justinian. The Persians, they said, were making preparations for war, and he was needed at once in the east. Belisarius was instructed to make peace quickly, on terms favourable to the Goths, leaving them with half their treasure and all territories north of the River Po.

Belisarius was floored by the letter. He must have thought Justinian was trying to make him insane with frustration. Why surrender so much now, when he was close to bringing the whole of Italy back into the fold? Vitiges, on the other hand, thought it all sounded too good to be true. He said he would only put his name to the deal if Belisarius, whom he respected, did so as well. But Belisarius flatly refused. He told the senators he would not sign the agreement without an explicit order from Justinian.

For a few days no one knew what to do. Then Vitiges came to Belisarius privately and put an extraordinary offer to him: how would the general like to be the emperor of a revived western Roman empire, with the army of the Goths at his disposal?

Belisarius thought for a moment, and said that he would.

BELISARIUS MADE ARRANGEMENTS with his own men, and then sent private assurances to Vitiges that he would indeed accept the crown of the west, and would do no harm to the Goths once he had entered the city. The gates of Ravenna were flung open, and Belisarius marched in peacefully with his army, bringing with them much-needed grain supplies. Procopius observed the entry of the Roman army into Ravenna, and wondered how it was that such a small imperial force could have subdued a much larger barbarian force. He concluded that God's hand was at work here, as it was with all things.

Belisarius took possession of the palace and the Gothic treasury, but keeping to his agreement with Vitiges, he left private fortunes intact. No houses were looted, the people of Ravenna were left unharmed, and Vitiges was treated as an honoured prisoner.

After five brutal years, Italy had been won back for the Roman empire, but at a catastrophic cost to its inhabitants: the cities of the ancient heartland were wrecked, its fields and crops destroyed. War and famine had left the landscape strewn with bones.

IT WAS SOME TIME before Vitiges realised he'd been duped. Belisarius had no intention of betraying Justinian and setting himself up as emperor of the west. Instead Belisarius returned to Constantinople with Vitiges, the treasure of the Goths and the glad news that the whole of Italy had been reincorporated into the Roman empire. What further proof of his loyalty could he offer Justinian than his refusal of the crown of Italy?

Belisarius was now even more wildly popular in the capital. People camped outside his house and followed him around the city, hoping to catch a glimpse of his famous figure. He was, Procopius records, 'tall and remarkably handsome', but without a touch of arrogance in his dealings with the common people.

This time, however, there was no triumph in the Hippodrome and the general received a frosty welcome from his emperor, who was furious with him for disregarding his orders to return immediately to the Persian front. In truth, Vitiges and the Goths were just a sideshow; the only power in the world that could truly threaten the existence of Justinian's empire was Persia. And even if Belisarius had proved his loyalty by renouncing the title of 'emperor' of the west, it was certainly unwelcome news – to both Justinian and Theodora – that Belisarius had been considered worthy of it in the first place. Only seven years had passed since a howling mob had set up Hypatius as a rival emperor in the Hippodrome. Hypatius had also once been a friend to Justinian.

And what exactly had Belisarius, for all his labours, 'won' for the empire anyway? Italy was a starving wasteland, Rome a ruined city, Milan burnt to the ground, and his duplicity with the Goths guaranteed they would pick up their swords again before too long. Meanwhile in the east, the Persians were ready to make their move.

IN 540 KHUSRAU'S ARMIES attacked Roman outposts in Mesopotamia and Syria. The Eternal Peace had lasted nine years. The Persians bypassed Dara this time, and swung south to take Sura, and then Aleppo, which was burnt to the ground when it refused to pay a ransom.

By June, Khusrau was at the walls of Antioch, the empire's rich but thinly defended third city. The terrified Roman garrison was allowed to leave unmolested, but the citizens of Antioch bravely resolved to take up the city's defence. The Persians prevailed through the weight of numbers, and Khusrau extracted a terrible revenge for their defiance: Antioch was sacked and burnt, and the survivors were taken into slavery. Khusrau, well pleased with his victory, walked down to the shores of the Mediterranean, took a swim, then turned back for home with wagons of gold and slaves trailing behind him.

He built a new town near Ctesiphon to house his new Antiochian slaves, and gave it the ridiculous name of 'Weh Antiok Khusrau', or 'Khusrau's Town That Is Better Than Antioch'.

Justinian was offered a humiliating new treaty: a down payment of five thousand pounds of gold, with an additional five hundred payable to the Persians every year to follow. The emperor had no choice but to accept. Even so, the next year Khusrau was tempted to break his treaty agreement again, attacking the Black Sea town of Lazica.

Justinian retaliated by sending Belisarius into Mesopotamia, where he defeated a Persian army near Nisibis, but he was unable to take the city and was recalled back home.

The great general seemed distracted. According to Procopius, his lassitude was brought on by the discovery that his wife Antonina had been conducting a secret love affair with their adopted son.

ANTONINA HAD BECOME Theodora's closest friend and co-conspirator. The two women had already engineered the dismissal of John of Cappadocia, whom they considered a mutual enemy. When Belisarius discovered his wife and their adopted son Theodosius had become lovers, he suspected the empress had had a hand in the matter. The on-again, off-again liaison sickened and depressed Belisarius, but Antonina connived with Theodora to force him to tolerate the affair. It seems likely that Theodora intended to undermine Belisarius's prestige by making a cuckold out of him.

Procopius records sympathetically that Belisarius was so broken-hearted by his humiliation, 'he failed even to remember the time when he was a man; sweating, dizzy and trembling, he counted himself lost; devoured by slavish fears and mortal worry, he was completely emasculated'. The treacherous Theodosius, however, died soon after of dysentery and Belisarius's spirits slowly recovered.

In 542 Justinian sent Belisarius back to the east to launch a counterattack against the Persians. The general swiftly took the Persian fort of Sisaurana, and sent out his Arab allies, the Ghassanids, to harass Persian settlements along the Tigris River. But the conflict ended indecisively when a strange sickness broke out in both camps, causing them to retreat in confusion.

Pestis

During those times there was a plague that came close to wiping out the whole of mankind. Now for all the calamities that fall upon us from the heavens it might be possible for some bold man to venture a theory regarding their causes ... But about this calamity there is no way to find any justification, to give a rational account, or even to cope with it mentally, except by referring it to God.

Procopius, The Wars of Justinian, 2.22.1

AS THE GLORIOUS decade of the 530s came to a close, three ominous portents were observed within Justinian's realm. Procopius records that in 536 the sky dimmed for the better part of a year, during which, he wrote, 'the sun gave forth its light without brightness, like the moon'.* A year later a comet shaped like a swordfish appeared in the skies for forty days and nights. At sea, there were troubling reports of ghostly bronze ships, seen gliding swiftly across the waters of the eastern Mediterranean, piloted by headless men in black, clutching staffs of burning bronze.

The first report of a deadly plague came in 541 from Pelusium, an Egyptian town near Suez. The outbreak travelled from village to

---

* The likely culprit was an eruption, half a world away, from Krakatoa, which would have thrown up vast amounts of dust and debris into the atmosphere.

village along the Nile and in September it reached the great port of Alexandria, the empire's second city.

Sailors and dockworkers were the first to feel the sickness, starting with flu-like symptoms: a headache, weariness, fever and vomiting. Hideous, bulbous swellings would appear on the upper thighs and around the genital area, as well as in the armpits and around the neck, accompanied by terrible, agonising pain. Often the fingertips and toes would blacken from gangrene. Sometimes the swelllings would erupt in an explosion of pus. Some sufferers would sink into a coma and die. Others would experience convulsions and madness. Many died vomiting blood, the result of internal haemorrhaging.

THE PATHOGEN RESPONSIBLE for this misery was *Yersinia pestis*, a rod-shaped bacterium that went about its deadly work under several layers of concealment, as a parasite within a parasite within a pest. The lethal microbe is ingested into the gut of a flea from an infected animal. The flea then attaches itself to the fur of a black rat, bites down into the rat's flesh and begins to draw up blood. But the bacterium blocks the entry of blood into the flea's gut, and the blood is regurgitated back into the wound, along with the bacteria, and the rat is infected. Starved for food, the flea becomes frantic with hunger and bites into any mammal it can find nearby, including humans. And in the Roman world, rats were always found near humans, feeding on their grain and refuse.

Once it enters the human bloodstream, *Y. pestis* is carried to the body's lymphatic system, causing painful swellings or buboes (hence 'bubonic plague'). Sometimes the bacteria would lodge in the lungs instead, forcing the victim to cough and project a spray of minute, bloody droplets onto others.

Flea infected with Yersinia pestis.

Carried within the hold of ships, the infected, rat-borne fleas were ferried across the Mediterranean. Merchant ships that sailed out to sea with apparently healthy crews were ravaged by the plague, leaving unmanned, corpse-laden vessels bobbing around the Mediterranean. Ships that made it to foreign ports unwittingly let loose their infected cargo into the grain stores along the wharves, and from there into the greater city. In this way the pathogen moved across the eastern Mediterranean. There would be a brief distant warning of its impending arrival, then the disaster would engulf the port, the city and the towns beyond.

THE PESTILENCE ARRIVED in Constantinople in 542. Within ten days the city was utterly transformed. There was a terrifying absence of moral logic to the plague. It struck down rich and poor, virtuous and wicked alike. Procopius records the death rate in the city leapt to five thousand a day, and then to ten – probably a wild guess, but it says something of the staggering scale of the epidemic. Hospitals were quickly overwhelmed. Doctors were helpless to explain the plague's origins, let alone how to treat it.

Family members struggled desperately to care for the sick. Inevitably, they too fell ill and died: 'houses large and small, beautiful and desirable … suddenly became tombs for their inhabitants, and … not one of them escaped who might remove their corpses out from within the house'.

The sudden onset of the plague created eerie and ghastly scenes. John of Ephesus reports of 'bridal chambers where the brides were adorned (in finery), but all of a sudden, there were just lifeless and fearsome corpses'. Workplaces fell silent: 'It might happen that a person was sitting at work on his craft,' wrote John of Ephesus, 'holding his tools in his hands and working, and he would totter to the side and his soul would escape ... The entire city then came to a standstill as if it had perished'. Outside the city, entire villages perished together, leaving fields unharvested and cattle to wander across the countryside.

At first, families were able to bury their dead, but as the mortality rate soared, every tomb was filled. The prefect of the city ordered workers to tear the roofs off the towers of the fortress of Galata, on the far side of the Golden Horn, and had the dead dumped inside. That too was quickly filled to capacity, generating a rank stench that caught the breeze and pervaded the city. Then there were not enough people left to dig burial pits and so the bodies were left to rot in the streets.

The daily round of death and infection elicited acts of great tenderness, even from hardened criminals. The Blues and Greens suspended their hostilities to help each other bury their dead. Before venturing outside, people took care to attach an identifying tag to their wrists, in case they fell down in the street. Food production came to a halt, and so the pestilence was followed by famine.

An epidemic caused by a pathogen as lethal to humans as *Y. pestis* usually runs its course quickly if it kills the host too rapidly for that person to circulate and transmit the disease. The really successful pathogens behave like the common cold, leaving their hosts well enough to go out and sneeze in crowded places. But the true target of *Y. pestis* was not a human, but a rat. The human megadeaths were just collateral damage; if anything, the corpses helped things along by providing more food for the rats. But the rats and other animals were also suffering from the plague. With such an indiscriminate killer, who could possibly understand the meaning of it all?

AFTER MONTHS OF RAGING HELL, the rat and human population of Constantinople crashed so hard that the progress of the disease halted. By August 542 the plague was mostly spent, but not vanquished. Constantinople would suffer recurrences of the plague in 558, 573 and 599. Those who survived were often marked for life with an ugly scar, a shuffling gait or a thickened tongue.

The population of Constantinople in early 542 was estimated at half a million people. Within the space of four months, it seems the city lost between 50,000 and 200,000 people, almost half of its citizens, to plague and starvation.

THE PLAGUE OF JUSTINIAN, as it came to be known, fell so quickly and violently it could only be interpreted as a punishment from God upon the whole world. John of Ephesus saw the epidemic as a mighty winepress of God's wrath, trampling people like fine grapes. The traumatised survivors sat in their silent, empty houses, homes once filled with busy people and noisy children, wondering if their sins had in some way contributed to this terrible tribulation.

Today we know the plague was the work of an invisibly small germ going about its business with no thought of the welfare of its host in mind, but the Romans of Constantinople could always see an extra element of causation in any event, good or bad. If the science of microbiology had been known to them, their likely response would have been, 'But who placed the germ in the flea? Whose hand guided the rat?'

Today we have more science at hand to explain why things happened as they did, but we are not inherently wiser nor any less superstitious. They were just as we are – bewildered people living through tumultuous times, trying to make sense of the world with limited information.

AT THE HEIGHT of the epidemic, Justinian too fell gravely ill and took to his bed, leaving Theodora in charge. The imperial couple had produced no children, so Theodora set her mind to work on who would succeed her husband if he failed to recover. As she was contemplating her next move, news of the emperor's illness reached Belisarius and the senior army command in the east. By now, wary of Theodora's intrigues, they agreed they would not recognise any new emperor chosen in Constantinople without their consent.

When she heard of this agreement, Theodora pushed back hard; she recalled Belisarius to Constantinople, and stripped him of his wealth and his personal guard, leaving the command of the eastern front in disarray. Khusrau, however, could do little to take advantage of the chaos, as the plague was also coursing through the Persian lands, creating similar scenes of devastation in Ctesiphon and other Persian cities.

Justinian recovered to rise from his sickbed and assess the damage to his capital and empire. His dream of a restoration of Roman supremacy was in tatters. The death of so many soldiers and taxpayers had devastated his armies and shrivelled imperial revenue. Despite the setbacks, he returned to his desk and authorised emergency austerity measures: road maintenance and postal services were cut, and he was obliged to turn a blind eye to the sale of governorships. The sudden absence of manpower sent wages soaring, a problem

Justinian typically tried to solve through an edict, which failed to have any effect. He was forced to suspend soldiers' pay, a dangerous move that led his army in Italy to extort money from the locals, who were already being squeezed hard by the emperor's predatory tax collectors. Landowners who couldn't pay were compelled to sell themselves into slavery. Justinian's 'Romans' were becoming deeply hated among the people they had come to save from 'barbarian' rule.

A new, revolutionary Gothic leader named Totila harnessed the discontent in Italy and rallied a new army to his cause. Totila called for the liberation of slaves, the redistribution of land and an end to imperial taxes. Before long, large numbers of imperial troops were defecting to his side. By the end of the plague year of 542, Totila was in control of Naples and most of the Italian countryside. Justinian's hapless commanders in Italy drafted a letter informing the emperor that the situation was hopeless and that Italy would have to be abandoned.

But cash-strapped and undermanned as he was, Justinian simply could not cut his losses and accept a contraction of the borders he had fought so hard to extend. And so the emperor turned unabashedly, once again, to his miracle worker, Belisarius. The general was sent to Ravenna, with a tiny force of unpaid, unhappy troops. He doggedly tried to break Totila's siege on Rome, but a discontented soldier inside the city opened the gates and the Goths rushed in. The population of the once-teeming imperial city had, by now, plummeted to fewer than a thousand souls. The remaining inhabitants were sent away unharmed while the walls, the palaces and the arsenals were pulled apart. 'For a few weeks,' wrote one historian, 'Rome was a deserted city, given up to the wolf and the owl.'

Again, Belisarius was being asked to do too much with too little by his wary emperor. He sent Antonina to Constantinople to petition Justinian, hoping that her friendship with Theodora might be of use.

But by the time Antonina arrived in the capital, Theodora was dead. Her death from cancer left Justinian in an agony of grief. As her funeral procession passed through the streets of Constantinople, Justinian reached out and attempted to fasten a necklace to her lifeless body, and then broke down in sobs. In his final years, he would often return to her mausoleum, the one he eventually planned to share with her, to light a candle to her memory. He refused to take another wife, not even to provide an heir to the throne, and would remain a widower for the rest of his days.

The year before her death, two dazzling mosaic panels were unveiled in the Church of St Vitale in Ravenna that capture the essence of Justinian and Theodora's partnership at the height of their power. The mosaics, which are still there today, are complementary, portraying Justinian and his entourage on one side of the altar, and Theodora with hers on the other. Justinian carries a basket of bread for the Eucharist; Theodora holds the wine. Together, they form a dazzling commemoration of the Roman empire's greatest power couple.

The Dear Leader

THE EMPEROR SURFACED from his grief and returned to work, the only consolation left to him. He heard Antonina's plea and recalled Belisarius from Italy, awarding him an honourable retirement. Without Theodora to fuel his paranoia, Justinian greeted Belisarius like an old friend on his return to Constantinople, and erected a gilded statue of him in the Augustaeum.

The emperor accepted the dire assessment of the situation in Italy and dispatched a much larger force under the command of

Narses, now in his seventies. Narses moved with great speed and crushed the Gothic army at the battle of Taginae in central Italy. Totila was mortally wounded and died in the nearby village of Caprae. The final battle took place later that year in the shadow of Vesuvius (near the long forgotten town of Pompeii), and the Goths were finished in Italy. The remaining Gothic forces agreed to head north outside the Roman frontiers, taking whatever they could carry with them.

The war was over. Justinian had won.

THEN, INCREDIBLY, Justinian recovered southern Spain for the empire as well. The Visigoths had ruled the province of Hispania for more than a century, but a civil war in 551 between rival chieftains led to a call for imperial help. Justinian dispatched a small detachment of two thousand men under the command of another octogenarian general named Liberius. Through force of arms and skilled diplomacy, Liberius brought Mediterranean Spain and the Balearic Islands back into the orbit of the Roman empire.

In 558 the plague returned to Constantinople. This outbreak was less acute but lasted longer. People wondered why, this time, it seemed to carry off so many children. We know now it was because the young lacked the immunity to *Yersinia pestis* that was hard won by the survivors of its first outbreak.

IN HIS FINAL YEARS, Justinian seemed to lose interest in fighting for imperial territory, preferring to use diplomacy and gold to pay off hostile neighbours. In 559, the Kotrigur Huns crossed the Danube and invaded Thrace, riding alarmingly close to Constantinople. It was an embarrassment for the emperor who had boasted of being master of all lands from Spain to Mesopotamia to find an enemy in his front yard, and Justinian was roused into action. To lead the counterattack, Justinian called one last time on the loyal Belisarius.

The general was no longer a young man, but had lost none of his tactical cunning. He brought together a tiny force of veterans, volunteers and guardsmen and set up camp near the Kotrigurs. That night he ordered the lighting of many fires to give the impression of a much larger force. The following day, as the Kotrigurs approached, he told his inexperienced volunteers to bang loudly on their shields, which baffled the enemy. As the horsemen charged towards the exposed foot soldiers, Belisarius's veterans emerged from the woods behind them, armed with spears and arrows. Surprised by the attack on their rear, and spooked by the banging infantry in front of them, the Kotrigurs turned and retreated to their base near Arcadiopolis. It was yet another stunning victory for Belisarius against a much larger force.

At this point, the old imperial jealousy started twitching. Justinian stepped in to personally assume command from Belisarius, but only to bribe the Kotrigurs to withdraw across the Danube. For this dubious achievement, Justinian awarded himself a Triumph. On the way, the procession detoured to the Church of the Holy Apostles so he could light a candle at Theodora's tomb.

JUSTINIAN HAD ONE FINAL indignity in store for Belisarius. In 562 the general was accused of conspiring with others in a plot against the emperor. Again, he was stripped of his wealth and honours until he was found innocent of all charges eight months later and allowed to return to his retirement. Belisarius died in March that year, at the age of sixty. A legend would arise, centuries later, that Justinian had had his eyes put out and sent him to Rome, where he lived out his final days as a blind beggar near the Pincus Gate. The legend is entirely untrue, but it lent extra poignancy to the story of the most gifted military leader of his age, who had been treated so shabbily by an ungrateful emperor.

JUSTINIAN DIED a few months later on 14 November at eighty-two. He had ruled the Roman empire for thirty-eight years, longer than anyone other than Augustus and Theodosius II. As with other long-reigning autocrats such as Louis XIV and Stalin, his death was welcomed in some quarters with relief, but with widespread anxiety in the larger population. The dead emperor's body was laid out on a golden bier, and covered in fragrant honey and oil. After lying in state it was carried in a torch-lit procession from the Great Palace to the Church of the Holy Apostles, passing through streets filled with a hundred thousand weeping citizens. He was wrapped in a silken shroud embroidered with scenes from his greatest triumphs, then laid in a porphyry sarcophagus next to Theodora. Hardly anyone could remember a time when he hadn't been emperor. How on earth were they going to survive without him?

AFTER A WEEK IN TURKEY, Joe and I still can't get our mobile phones working, so we go into a Turkcell outlet to get new SIM cards. Joe scans the back wall of the shop and spots yet another framed portrait of Mustafa Kemal Atatürk, hero of Gallipoli and the founder of the modern Turkish republic. We've seen his picture in restaurants, in ticket offices and on banknotes. In the Turkcell office, he looks like an old-fashioned movie star, nattily turned out in a tailored three-piece suit with a floppy white handkerchief.

Joe looks at the picture and then looks back at me like he's about to ask something, but I widen my eyes and gesture for him to wait until we're outside the shop. The cult of Atatürk is said to be the longest running cult of the personality in modern times. Travel advisories warn never to speak ill of him while in Turkey. There is a law that makes it a criminal offence to insult his memory, punishable by three years in prison.

Back on the street, I'm checking my Twitter feed for news of anti-government protests, and Joe asks, 'So, why are there pictures of Atatürk everywhere in Istanbul?'

'I think it's because they still love him and what he did for the country. Most of them do, anyway.'

'It's a bit like Kim Jong-Il, isn't it? Is he like the Dear Leader of Turkey?'

Joe is fascinated with North Korea. He's amused and intrigued by the far-out weirdness of totalitarianism. At home he's borrowed some of my books on totalitarian art and propaganda. I was drawn to those images when I was his age too. I always thought there was something particularly awful about being force-marched by a Dear Leader or a Great Helmsman towards some hellish utopia that lies just over the horizon.

'It's not really like that with Atatürk,' I say, looking around to see if I'm being overheard. 'He was quite a progressive leader. He introduced democracy, women's rights, that kind of thing. And most of the memorials and statues were put up after his death. They want to remember his greatness. It's not such a big deal.'

'But it seems like everyone has to put his picture up, whether they want to or not,' Joe retorts, smiling at my wariness. 'And why are you whispering, Dad, if it's not such a big deal?'

TO HIS DEFENDERS, Justinian's greatness was self-evident: all they had to do was point to a map of the empire, showing a reincorporated North Africa, Italy and Spain. And it did seem, for a while, that the losses of the previous century had been an aberration and that Rome's ancient supremacy, the normal state of affairs, had been restored.

But it was all an illusion. Justinian's passing marked the end of the Roman superpower, and their dominion would never again stretch so far. In the centuries to follow, the empire would slide into a dark age. In time it would recover and become a great power once more, but it would never resume its place as the incomparable giant of Europe and the Middle East.

Justinian's successors were saddled with debt and imperial obligations they could not fulfil. Imperial overstretch and the depredations of the plague led to a thinned-out military and poor lines of communication. Discontent towards the distant, unresponsive capital festered in the far-flung provinces, followed by counter-productive attempts to reassert imperial authority. Just three years after Justinian's death, much of northern Italy was lost to another Germanic tribe, the Lombards. The Roman toehold on Spain was lost to the Visigoths within fifty years. North Africa would fall in the Muslim conquests of the seventh century.

Justinian was the last Roman emperor to speak Latin. His successors would speak and write in the same Greek language as their subjects. As use of Latin declined, another link to the ancient past was severed.

Justinian's most impressive accomplishments survived the collapse of his military adventures and remain with us today: the codification of Roman law and the creation of the Hagia Sophia. But there was yet another, less obvious, accomplishment that would in the long run cement Constantinople's place as the economic powerhouse of the eastern Mediterranean and sustain its empire for centuries to come.

Serica

IN 552, TWO NESTORIAN MONKS arrived at the Chalke Gate in Constantinople and requested an audience with Justinian. The monks presented the emperor with a remarkable story. The previous year, they explained, they had travelled from India to China, where they had witnessed with their own eyes the secret of manufacturing silk.* Justinian was intrigued: the method of producing the luxurious fabric had been, for centuries, a maddening and costly mystery to the Romans.

The arrival of slippery, smooth Chinese silk in the empire some six hundred years earlier had created a sensation in the Roman world, particularly among upper-class women, who adored its comfort, its rarity and its shimmering beauty. Conservative Roman men denounced the foreign fabric as immoral. Seneca thought a woman clad in silk was a shameful spectacle; the flowing fabric made her every curve visible to the public. She might as well, he concluded, be walking around naked.

No one in the empire could explain how this luxurious fabric was manufactured, and so it had to be transported all the way from China, passing through the hands of many middlemen, including the Persians, who all took their cut. By the time it arrived in Rome, it fetched a higher price than gold. Pliny the Elder complained of the vast sums of money flowing out of the empire's borders so that a Roman lady might be able to 'shimmer' in public. Pliny estimated

---

* China was known as 'Serica' by the Romans, taking the name from *seres*, the Latin word for 'silk'.

that the importation of silk drained more than 100 million *sestertii* a year from the Roman economy, more than a tenth of the annual budget.

Silk was just as popular in Justinian's time, worn by court ladies and the Orthodox clergy, but the ongoing wars with the Sassanid Persians had disrupted trade and sent the price soaring. Justinian attempted to establish new silk routes that skirted around Persia, but without much success. The profits from the silk trade continued to flow out of the empire and into the hands of the Sassanids, which was why Justinian was so eager to hear what the Nestorian monks had to say.

The monks explained what they had learnt in China: silk thread was gleaned from a particular worm that ate only the leaves from a certain bush. They now proposed to make a return journey to China and smuggle out some of these precious worms, as well as saplings of the mulberry bush they fed from. The emperor gave the monks' proposition his blessing. A deal was struck for an unknown amount of gold, and the monks set out on a mission of industrial espionage that took them around the northern edge of the Persian empire, across the Caspian Sea and through Central Asia, skirting along the edge of the Gobi Desert before dropping down to the silk factories of Xi'an.

The Chinese had mastered the production of silk thousands of years before the birth of Christ, and they did it this way: masses of newly hatched silkworms (*Bombyx mori*) are allowed to gorge on freshly cut mulberry leaves in warm, dry conditions. They feed until they have enough energy to produce their cocoon, which they spin around themselves from a gelatinous internal fluid that hardens on contact with air. The puffy white cocoons are left to settle for a week. Then they are steamed to kill the pupa inside, before it can hatch as a moth. The lifeless cocoons are then placed in hot water to unravel into a single, long strand. Five or six of these vanishingly thin filaments are woven together to form a single thread.

Bombyx mori.

Having arrived in China, the monks procured some silkworm eggs or larvae, and smuggled them out by concealing them inside a hollow walking stick. Somehow, the monks were also able to transport small mulberry shrubs in earthenware pots on the 6500-kilometre journey. At the end of their two-year round trip, the monks returned to Constantinople, giving Justinian the silkworms and the shrubbery he needed to set up a native silk industry.

MANY HISTORIANS now regard this story as a fable, but in the later years of his reign, Justinian did establish silk production within the empire's borders, near modern-day Beirut. True to his autocratic style, he made the industry a state monopoly, creating an ongoing revenue stream for the imperial treasury, and choking off the eastward flow of Roman gold to the Persians.

A little noticed consequence of the home-grown silk industry was that Justinian and his successors were suddenly much less interested in a proxy war they'd been running in the Arabian peninsula against the Persians. The Romans had a longstanding alliance with a group of Christianised Arabs known as the Ghassanids, who often warred against another Arab group called the Lakhmids, who were allies of the Persians. At stake for the two imperial powers was control of a new silk route that would reach Constantinople via the Red Sea, bypassing the Persian tax collectors.

Now that Romans could grow their own silk, Roman and Persian influence among the Arabs started to wane and they lost interest in the goings-on within the Arabian lands. This lapse would leave both great powers completely unprepared for the hammer blow in the next century that would cleave one empire in half, and destroy the other completely.

The Sunken Palace

IN THE YEAR 1544, a French scholar named Pierre Gilles arrived in Istanbul, the capital of the Ottoman empire. He came to stay for three years. Gilles was a natural scientist with a fondness for fish and marine life in general, but he also had some expertise in topography, the business of mapping the features of the surface of the Earth. These two separate disciplines would come together and lead him to make a strange discovery.

Nearly a century had passed since the conquest of Constantinople, but many of the Roman buildings were still in place, and although most of the great statues had been toppled, their broken remains were lying in the streets and squares. Gilles set about sketching and measuring these monuments. Drawing from life was forbidden to Muslims, and so his sketches attracted a small crowd of curious onlookers who marvelled at his ability to bring the scene to the page.

As the Frenchman fell into rudimentary conversation, he heard a story of a house in a street near the Hagia Sophia (now renamed the Aya Sofya) where the householder was somehow able to drop a bucket into the dark space below his floorboards and haul up a pail full of fresh water. Occasionally, it was said, this man would find a fish swimming about. Gilles was intrigued and decided to investigate.

The Frenchman took himself to the door of the house. Gilles explained himself as best he could, and the master of the house agreed to take him downstairs to his basement, where there was an opening in the floorboards. Peering into the inky blackness, he heard the slap and trickle of water, echoing through some kind of cool, cavernous space. The householder fetched a torch and the two men lowered themselves through the hole into a small skiff bobbing on the water's surface. On the floor of the boat was a barbed spear. The master of the house passed Gilles the torch and he began to row across the mysterious body of water.

Through the torch-lit gloom, Gilles began to make out the trunks of gigantic stone columns, evenly spaced, rising dramatically out of the water to support the vaulted roof above their heads. At the base of some of the columns were stones shaped into ghastly, grimacing heads. The space was like a flooded underground temple, but this was no Christian house of worship: Gilles realised they were inside a vast underground water cistern, built in Roman times and long since forgotten. Gilles's host paddled the skiff towards a point directly below the opening of a well where a single beam of light descended onto the water. A fish came up for air and was speared for the man's dinner.

Justinian had commissioned the cistern in the sixth century to ensure an adequate water supply for his palace complex. Fresh water was scarce on the peninsula of Constantinople, so it had to be delivered by a chain of aqueducts that led all the way back to a reservoir near the Black Sea.

The cistern had the capacity to store up to 100 million litres of water for the Great Palace. The rows of pillars – 336 in total – were scavenged, on orders from Justinian, from nearby pagan temples. When the imperial residence shifted to the Blachernae Palace at the other end of the city, the cistern was closed and forgotten.

Gilles returned to the surface and advised the authorities of his discovery, but the Ottoman rulers were indifferent. For centuries afterwards it was used as a dumping area.

Medusa head from Basilica Cistern.

TODAY THE CISTERN, known as Yeribati, 'the Sunken Palace', is one of Istanbul's major tourist attractions. Evocative lighting and music intensify the drama of the space. Sean Connery filmed a scene here as 007 in *From Russia with Love.*

In a corner of the cistern, at the base of two columns, Joe and I see two stone blocks bearing the face of Medusa, the snake-haired Gorgon of Greek mythology. One of the head-blocks is placed on its side, the other is upside-down. The reason for this strange placement isn't clear; perhaps it was intended to rob the pagan stones of their demonic power, or maybe the stones were just rotated to fit the columns they support. Still, the sight of the Gorgon's head, with her half-submerged, baleful gaze, is troubling. She looks like a demon suffering the torments of hell. If the Hagia Sophia is the heaven of this ghost empire, Justinian's cistern is its abandoned underworld.

CHAPTER FOUR

Persian Nightmares

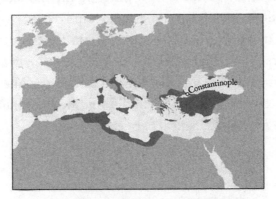

The empire in 610, at the accession of Heraclius.

Salep and Kaymak

THE BLUE MOSQUE confronts the Hagia Sophia across the expanse of Sultanahmet Park like an ambitious younger sibling.* Justinian's great church set an example that no sultan or architect could ignore, and so, despite a gap in age of eleven centuries, the Blue Mosque bears a strong resemblance to its older sister across the way.

Joe and I enter the mosque through the door reserved for non-Muslims. We remove our shoes and pad comfortably across the carpeted space. This is the first time I've been inside a mosque since I was a schoolkid and I'm surprised by the effect that shoelessness

---

* 'The Blue Mosque' is a colloquial name inspired by its shimmering blue tiles; its official title is the Sultanahmet Mosque.

has on me. In a church, I'm accustomed to feeling footsore and uncomfortable sitting on those hard wooden pews, but here, the open sprawl of carpet feels comfortable and generous, like the living room of someone's home. And some home it is: almost every part of the mosque is decorated with intricate tile mosaics of cerulean blue, like the inside of a gigantic aquarium. There are no images of God, Muhammad or Muslim saints: Islam forbids the creation of such images. The visual allusions to Allah are purely abstract; tiles form swirling lines of Qur'anic text and complex geometric patterns, displaying the Islamic tradition of finding the sublime within calligraphy and mathematical perfection.

Outside the mosque, Joe is intrigued by a cart selling something called *salep*. I order two cups and we are presented with a creamy hot drink. I hand a paper cup to Joe, who takes a long, slow sip. He closes his eyes and smiles, like he's just found something he was looking for.

'Right,' he says emphatically, 'we're having *salep* every day while we're here.'

Salep is a gooey mixture of milk, rice flour, sugar and rosewater, but the crucial ingredient is derived from the tubers of wild orchids, which are washed, boiled, dried and ground. The milky concoction is poured into a cup and garnished with cinnamon or crushed pistachios. Turkish people claim that *salep* is a medicinal drink, effective against all kinds of complaints including bronchitis and heart disease, but Joe and I are happy to drink it for the sweet contentment it brings on a cold morning.

That night we tell Yasin, the desk clerk at the hotel, how much we love *salep*.

'*Salep* is no big deal,' he says. 'The really great thing to have in Istanbul is *kaymak*.'

Yasin scrawls a name on a post-it note: Pando Kaymak.

'The best *kaymak* is here,' he says quietly.

The next day Joe and I walk down to Eminonu to catch a ferry to the crowded inner-city suburb of Beşiktaş (pronounced like 'Beshiktash') on the European shore of the Bosphorus.* Beşiktaş is a gentrified shopping precinct with kebab shops, mobile-phone outlets and burger joints. Joe and I find our way to the cobalt-blue shopfront. This modest café is an institution in Istanbul, like Pellegrini's in Melbourne or Veselka in New York City; rundown but spick and span, informal but charismatic. The clientele is a mix of old-timers and young Turkish hipsters.

Joe and I take a seat at a marble-top table as an ancient man shuffles past, tentatively carrying a plate of eggs. This is the proprietor Pando, a man in his nineties with close-cropped hair and white whiskers. Pando and his wife Döne are some of the few remaining Greek

---

* Beşiktaş was once the site of the waterfront pleasure palace of Michael III (r. 842–67), the playboy emperor. Michael is said to have enjoyed parading through the streets with a group of friends dressed as bishops, in a parody of an Orthodox procession. The role of Patriarch was played by a man known as Theophilos the Pig, who was said to have a talent for blowing out candles by breaking wind on them.

Christians in Istanbul. Clustered on the walls are framed photos of Pando's proud ancestors: moustachioed men with burgundy fezzes perched on their heads.

Pando Kaymak.

Pando's café and cream shop was founded in 1895; he was born and raised in this cramped two-storey building. As a boy in the 1920s, he met Atatürk, the founder of modern Turkey, who came by and shook his hand.

The café serves a delicious breakfast of fried eggs and sausages, washed down with tea or Turkish coffee. But people mostly come here for the *kaymak*, which I discover is a kind of clotted cream formed from buffalo milk. It's a traditional Turkish food, originating from Central Asia.

Döne comes to our table. She wears an apron over her black cardigan and her grey hair is pulled back into a bun. She bows her head with a degree of old-world formality and smiles at us, ready to take our order.

I have no Turkish so I grin apologetically, point at the items on the menu and say querulously, '*Kaymak*? Turkish coffee?'

Döne smiles. '*Avec du sucre?*' she enquires.

A little taken aback, I reply, 'Ah yes, I mean, *oui.*'

She's speaking beautiful French to me, this lovely Greek grandmother in Istanbul.

'*Vous êtes Americain?*' she enquires politely.

'*Non, madame,*' I stutter, summoning my schoolboy French. '*Nous venons de l'Australie.*'

'*Ah! Mon mari a un cousin à Melbourne.*'

'*Je suis né à Melbourne.*'

She jots down our order, '*Alors, deux plats de kaymak, et cafe turc avec du sucre.*'

'*Merci, madame.*'

She smiles and withdraws. Joe is agog.

'We've been here all this time,' he gasps, 'and you speak fluent Turkish?'

I arch an eyebrow enigmatically. It's hard to impress a teenage son.

THE *KAYMAK* ARRIVES in creamy white dollops on metal platters, with a basket of fresh bread and a pot of honey. After watching what everyone else is doing, I slather some *kaymak* onto a chunk of bread, drizzle a spoonful of honey across it and take a bite. The spongy bread pushes the *kaymak* onto the roof of my mouth. The creaminess is very light and delicate, not oily at all, dissolving instantly into a milky sweetness. Then the taste of the honey comes in from the sides – syrupy, aromatic, not too sweet, with a clean finish. The difference between this and regular honey is like the difference between Champagne and Fanta. To eat this every day for breakfast would probably kill me in five years, but it might be worth it.

Kaymak.

Kaymak is made like this: fresh buffalo milk is slowly simmered for hours until a thick layer of rich cream forms on the surface. The *kaymak* is left to cool and then rolled into delicate cylinders. It has a shelf life of barely a day. Pando used to get his milk from a herd of buffalo his family kept in a pasture outside the city. Eventually it became impossible to maintain the herd, and now he buys it in.

Pando and Döne are among the last of their kind. A hundred years ago there were as many as 130,000 Byzantine Greeks living in the city. Today there are just three thousand. The pre-World War I Ottoman empire was comfortably multi-ethnic, but the modern nation state of Turkey has witnessed the steady departure of the Greeks into other lands.

The year 1953 marked the quincentenary of the Ottoman conquest of the city, and the Turkish government of the time thought it best to commemorate things in a low-key manner. But two years later, the same government, struggling for public support, chose to inflame nationalistic and religious fervour against minorities. Rioting broke out in the city; Greek and Armenian shops and homes were vandalised. A mob burst into Pando's shop and shattered one of his marble counters.

After the riots, many younger Greeks and Armenians concluded there was no future for them in Turkey. More Greek Christians left Istanbul after 1955 than in the fifty years after the conquest of 1453. Pando and Döne chose to stay, but kept their fractured counter in place, as a mark of shame against the rioters, and as a reminder to themselves that a mob might one day reappear on their doorstep.

On the day of our visit, Pando's café was busy, prosperous and evidently much loved. Its future seemed secure, as long as Pando was still living, at least.

Six months after we left, Pando received an eviction notice. His landlord had plans to renovate the two-storey building and convert it into a *bufe*, a fast-food outlet. Several Turkish journalists and lawyers took up the cause to keep the cream shop alive. There were passionate articles in the local press, and a Twitter-hashtag campaign briefly flared into life. Nothing, it seems, could be done. Pando Kaymak closed its blue doors for the last time in August 2014, and another tiny fragment of Byzantium died with it.

King of Kings

JUSTINIAN'S EXHAUSTED, overstretched empire was passed into the care of his nephew Justin II, who tried to get on top of the empire's financial troubles by cutting back on the round of indemnities Justinian had been handing out every year to well-armed neighbours. Justin cancelled the annual payments to the Avars, nomadic warriors from Pannonia, who in turn put pressure on the Lombards, who invaded northern Italy, wiping out most of the territorial gains achieved through decades of war and sacrifice by Belisarius and Narses. The Lombards put down roots in the area and married into Italian families, strengthening their hold on the territory.* At the same time the Visigoths began to push the Romans out of their newly reconquered lands in Spain. The empire created by Justinian was so complex and fragile, it seems only Justinian could run it.

Justin accepted the losses in the west because he thought he saw opportunities in the east. He cancelled the annual indemnity to Khusrau and sent his armies to attack Persia. The ageing Shahanshah retaliated by overrunning the Roman lands in Syria and taking the fortress of Dara, which Belisarius had defended so brilliantly forty-three years earlier. Justin was so troubled by these defeats, he seems to have suffered a breakdown, and he had to be restrained from jumping out the window of the Great Palace. As his mind further unravelled, his attendants found they could only calm him by dragging him around the imperial apartments in a little wagon.

Justin's wife, Empress Sophia, stepped in to pick up the reins of government. Sophia, who had already been supervising the finances of the empire, paid off the Persians with an extortionate amount of gold in return for a year's peace. In the meantime she recalled a capable general named Tiberius to Constantinople to act as co-regent.

When Justin died in 578, Tiberius became sole Augustus of the Roman empire. The war with the Persians resumed, and Tiberius was forced to agree to another round of protection payments to the marauding Avars to keep them on the far side of the Danube.

Tiberius ruled for eight difficult years and passed the throne to another competent general named Maurice, to whom he delivered his last words: 'Make your reign my finest epitaph.'

---

* The Lombards gave their name to the region known today as Lombardy. The word derives from the Latin *longobardus* or 'long-beard'.

MAURICE PROVED to be a capable administrator who brought some stability to the empire and, for a while, even extended its borders. When the great Khusrau I died in 579, Maurice deftly exploited the crisis of succession in the Persian court. Khusrau's grandson, Khusrau II, was forced to flee Ctesiphon and seek asylum with the Romans. The Persian prince offered to give up Dara, Persian Armenia and the frontier outposts of Mesopotamia if Maurice would help install him as Shahanshah. Khusrau, supported by a Roman expeditionary force, returned to Persia and won back his throne. He kept his bargain with Maurice and surrendered the fortresses. Peace was won, the eastern border was secured, and Constantinople was no longer on the hook for the crippling annual payment to the Persians.

Maurice could now happily shift his attention and resources to his European borders to settle the problem of the Avars. But he was undone by his own parsimony: he cut the rations of the soldiers on the Danube and cancelled their winter leave, which left his men facing the prospect of spending several frozen months on the front, shivering in their tents. When Maurice economised further by cutting their pay, the army on the Danube mutinied and raised a centurion named Phocas onto their shields. Phocas and his rebels abandoned their posts and marched towards Constantinople.

Alerted to the danger, Maurice begged the Blues and the Greens to defend the capital against the mutineers, but food shortages had left the population sullen and restive. A riot broke out in the capital, and Maurice and his family escaped in a boat to Chalcedon.

Phocas entered the city in 602, flinging handfuls of gold to the cheering crowds in the streets. He assumed the throne and sent his soldiers to track down his predecessor. Maurice was captured and forced to watch as his children were beheaded. Then it was his turn.

The headless bodies were thrown into the sea. A large crowd came down to watch the corpses bobbing around on the water.

HISTORIAN EDWARD GIBBON thought Phocas's appearance spoke of his degenerate character, writing of 'his diminutive and deformed person, the closeness of his shaggy eyebrows, his red hair, his beardless chin, and his cheek disfigured and discoloured by a formidable scar'. Phocas was aware his authority was tenuous. He could hardly claim, as Constantine and Justinian did, to be the favoured son of heaven when everyone knew he was a crude opportunist who had murdered his predecessor. Phocas tried to crush disquiet among the people and the aristocracy with a reign of terror, punishing his enemies, real or otherwise, through slow torture and execution.

The turmoil in Constantinople encouraged ambitious warlords and kings on the empire's fringes to prod its borders. The Avars began to eat away at the rich imperial lands in Thrace, sending raiding parties right up to the Theodosian Walls. Phocas, distracted by internal dissent, agreed to pay more gold to the Avar leaders to make them go away.

Khusrau II.

But a far greater danger was brewing in Persia. Khusrau's deal had been with Maurice, the emperor who had come to his aid and rescued his throne. The Shahanshah simply refused to recognise the man responsible for his murder, and when Phocas sent an ambassador to make formal contact, Khusrau had the man arrested. The interminable war between the Romans and the Persians was about to move into a dangerous new phase, and its ultimate beneficiary would be a power that no one in either empire saw coming.

KHUSRAU II, KING OF KINGS of the Sassanid Persians, was in his early twenties when he was raised to the throne by his two uncles, who had led the palace coup that blinded and killed his father Hormazd.

Khusrau grew his beard into ringlets and wore gowns of heavy embroidered silk. Visitors to his palace in Ctesiphon entered through the Great Arch of Khusrau, the biggest unsupported arch in the world,* passing into an immense ceremonial hall with a 90-metre carpet made of silk, embroidered with gold and pearls. The basement of the palace contained a vast inner sanctum that was said to house a harem of three thousand concubines. The Shahanshah also kept a summer palace in the cooler highlands of the Persian plateau maintained with hunting grounds and a private zoo of exotic animals.

Khusrau's enjoyment of his kingly pleasures was tempered by the shakiness of his position in Ctesiphon. The Zoroastrian priesthood resented his toleration of Christianity – his queen and his finance minister were both Christians – and there was broad discontent among the people over the deal he had struck with a Roman emperor to win back his throne. Maurice's murder offered Khusrau a chance to shore up his failing authority. When a foreigner showed up in Ctesiphon claiming to be Maurice's only surviving son, Khusrau declared war on Phocas, in the name of this spurious pretender.

---

* Today the Great Arch is the only visible remnant of the palace, located near the Iraqi town of Salman Pak.

Khusrau's armies crossed the Euphrates and overran the Roman outposts in Mesopotamia with astonishing ease. Encouraged by his easy victories, the Shahanshah ordered his forces to keep marching west.

A year later the Persians took the fortified city of Edessa. Then, in a series of cascading defeats for the Romans, Khusrau's soldiers crossed the Taurus Mountains and swept into Anatolia. The Persians now picked up a deadly momentum that carried them right across Asia Minor to Chalcedon. Suddenly, shockingly, Khusrau was at the doorstep of Constantinople itself. Persian campfires across the strait were visible from the windows of the Great Palace.

A tremor of fear coursed through the streets of Constantinople. Phocas, for all the terror he could inflict upon his own people, was evidently powerless to stop Khusrau's outrageous incursions into their lands. The Romans believed that God made winners of the righteous, and Phocas, clearly, was cast as a loser. Phocas heard the rumblings of dissent and cracked down hard, lashing out at his enemies in the city. To deflect blame, Phocas launched a persecution of Jews across the empire. The Jews of Antioch retaliated with a massacre of the local Christians. Within Constantinople, Greens partisans rioted and burnt down several buildings.

News of the chaos in Constantinople travelled across the Mediterranean to North Africa, where the Roman governor commanded a sizeable army and a fleet of ships. In the summer of 610, the governor sent his fleet to Constantinople, led by his thirty-five-year-old son, Heraclius.

HERACLIUS WAS HANDSOME and charismatic, described as 'robust, with a broad chest, beautiful blue eyes, golden hair, fair complexion and wide, thick beard'. As his armada set out across the Mediterranean, he rallied his men by strapping an icon of the Virgin to the prow of his flagship. The fleet reached the shores of the Bosphorus in early October. Impressed and no doubt relieved by the sight of all the ships in the harbour, Phocas's allies deserted him and Heraclius entered Constantinople without a struggle.

Phocas was arrested, stripped of his imperial robes, and brought before Heraclius, who quipped, 'So this is how you governed your empire?'

Phocas snarled, 'Will you govern it any better?'

Heraclius pushed him away with his foot.

Phocas was taken away to be executed; his skinned body and severed head were paraded through the streets of Constantinople. Heraclius was acclaimed by the senate and crowned in the Chapel of St Stephen within the Great Palace.

Heraclius had to find a good answer to Phocas's provocative question, and find it quickly. The presence of Khusrau's army across the Bosphorus was alarming, but the Persians, as yet, had no ships and they had no means to penetrate the immense Theodosian Walls. But Heraclius lacked the tools to drive the Persians back: the army was demoralised and depleted, the war had choked off trade, and the imperial treasury was empty. Phocas's grisly death was symptomatic of the poisonous apocalyptic atmosphere in the city; many thought they could see the hand of God at work, guiding events towards a great climax in the history of the world, the End of Days foretold in the Book of Revelation.

Heraclius had to somehow turn it all around. His challenge was twofold: to bring his badly rattled people together behind his leadership, and gather up what remained of his army to stall Khusrau's momentum. A victory was desperately needed, a triumph he could present to his people as a sign of God's favour.

Heraclius tried to get on the front foot: he sent an army to intercept the Persians near Antioch, but it suffered a crushing defeat at the hands of Khusrau's brilliant general, Shahrbaraz. In 613 Shahrbaraz took Damascus, completing the Persian conquest of Syria. Khusrau gloried in these victories, which had carried his men far deeper into Roman territory than he had dared hope.

THEN HERACLIUS SUFFERED an even worse blow: his popular wife Eudoxia suffered an epileptic seizure and died, leaving him without a companion and consort. Her death deepened the pall of gloom on the capital.

Soon afterwards, Heraclius scandalised Constantinople by announcing his intention to marry his young niece, Martina. According to church law, their union was taboo, an act of incest. Sergius the Patriarch tried to talk Heraclius out of it, but the emperor stubbornly insisted. Sergius reluctantly performed the marriage rite, crowning Martina as Augusta. The partnership appears to have made Heraclius very happy; he couldn't bear to be separated from Martina and brought her on campaign with him. But his subjects were displeased. Martina was widely blamed for having beguiled their emperor into an unholy union, and the Augusta became a reviled figure, the most hated woman in the city.

AND STILL KHUSRAU'S ARMIES kept tearing off pieces of Heraclius's empire with impunity. In 614, Shahrbaraz arrived at the gates of Jerusalem, where the Christians of the city surrendered to him. Shahrbaraz installed a Persian garrison and placed Jewish leaders in control of the city. But after the general left, the local Christians rose up and slaughtered the Persian garrison, massacred the Jews, and then closed the gates.

Shahrbaraz turned back and recaptured the city in a bloody siege. Shahrbaraz's revenge was brutal. For three days the Christians of Jerusalem were put to the sword or carried off into slavery. The Persians set fire to the Church of the Holy Sepulchre and carried off the True Cross of Christ, the most precious relic in Christendom, as a trophy of war. It was an attack designed to inflict the most terrible psychic agony on the Romans. The war had gone beyond a struggle for territory; the Romans and Persians were now bound by intractable hatreds.

When news of the horror in Jerusalem reached Constantinople, the Roman aristocracy lost its nerve. The senate leaders pressed Heraclius to sue for peace on any terms. Ambassadors were sent to Khusrau with an extraordinary message. In his letter, Heraclius hailed Khusrau the 'supreme emperor', he acknowledged the Persian empire as superior to that of the Romans, and he signed off with an act of obeisance, describing himself as Khusrau's 'obedient son, one who is eager to perform the services of your serenity in all things'. In six hundred years no reigning Roman emperor had ever written such an abject letter to a foreign king.

Khusrau read the letter and had the ambassadors arrested. There would be no peace – Khusrau was not looking to dominate the Roman empire, but to exterminate it. Revelling in his seemingly limitless power, the Shahanshah responded to Heraclius with all the bombast of a Marvel Comics supervillain:

> Khusrau, greatest of Gods, and master of the whole Earth, to
> Heraclius his vile and insensate slave. Why do you still refuse to
> submit to our rule, and call yourself a king? ... I will pardon your
> faults if you submit to me ... Do not deceive yourself with vain hope
> in that Christ, who was not able to save himself from the Jews, who

killed him by nailing him to a cross. Even if you take refuge in the
depths of the sea, I will stretch out my hand and take you.

THE SHAHANSHAH WAS GIDDY at the turnaround in his fortunes. No longer a weak, embattled figure, he was now tightening his grip around the throat of the Roman empire. From here he could see the endgame: complete control of the remaining eastern Roman lands, followed by the conquest of Constantinople itself.

Ohrmazd and Ahriman

AS THE ROMANS BECAME more singularly Christian in the fifth and sixth centuries, so too did the Persian court shift into a more militant phase of Zoroastrianism, a religion named for Zoroaster, its founding prophet.

Zoroaster taught his followers that the universe was divided into two primal forces: Ohrmazd, the God of Light, Truth and Wisdom, and Ahriman, the God of the Lie.* These two principles, he said, were in constant conflict, and every human being, no matter how lowly their status, had a part to play in the struggle of Ohrmazd to renew the world through fire. The role of the Shahanshah, like that of the Roman emperor, was to act as the divinely appointed protector of the state religion.

Even so, Khusrau remained close to certain Christians in his inner circle, particularly his third and most influential wife, Shirin. He tolerated the presence of Nestorian Christians in his empire and donated money to their shrines. But as the war with the Romans intensified, religious attitudes hardened on both sides.

---

* Ohrmazd, also known as 'Ahura Mazda', inspired the name of the Japanese car manufacturer.

The ideals of radical Zoroastrianism – renewal of the world through purifying fire – melded well with military conquest. Priests would follow the army into the newly won Roman territories, set up Zoroastrian fire temples and aggressively proselytise among the conquered peoples. The holy men of both empires were waging a war for the soul of humanity, to be redeemed either by the body and blood of Christ, or by the sacred fires of Ohrmazd.

The Roman position continued to deteriorate. In 618, Shahrbaraz's armies stormed into Egypt. After a year-long siege, the crucial seaport of Alexandria fell to the Persians. Egypt, the empire's granary, was lost. The next year the plague broke out yet again in Constantinople, further reducing its manpower and revenue. There seemed to be no end to God's displeasure with the Romans.

FOR TEN YEARS, hemmed in on every side, Heraclius had nothing to offer his people but sacrifice, defeat and more sacrifice. He repaired the imperial finances by halving official salaries and soldiers' pay: a dangerous move for any emperor. It's a testament to his remarkable political skills that he was able to persuade his soldiers to swallow their disgruntlement, but elements of the aristocracy defended their privileges and obstructed his reforms. Exasperated beyond belief by their mulishness, Heraclius threatened to abandon Constantinople for Carthage, where he said he could marshal the empire's forces and take the fight to the Persians from there. His subjects couldn't bear the thought of being abandoned by their emperor and all remaining opposition to his emergency measures cracked. A contrite delegation of senators led by Sergius the Patriarch begged him to stay. Heraclius said he would, but only if they were prepared to accept the hardships he required of them, and they meekly assented. The church even agreed to hand over precious gold ornaments and silver plate to refill the imperial treasury. With his enemies outfoxed and his authority enhanced, Heraclius entered the Hagia Sophia and swore an oath, in the presence of the Patriarch, that he would never abandon Constantinople. The fate of the emperor, the city and the church were now intertwined.

Heraclius tried to invoke a mood of Churchillian defiance among his people through a steady drumbeat of propaganda stories of Persian atrocities in Jerusalem. Lurid tales of the destruction of churches and the desecration of icons were circulated in the city. Hatred was also directed at the Jews who, it was said, had opened the gates of the holy city to the invaders and eagerly participated in the mass slaughter of Christians.

In 622, Heraclius personally led a successful counterattack against the Persians in north-west Anatolia, but maddeningly, he couldn't press his victory. The sudden arrival of the Avars at the Theodosian Walls forced the emperor to drop everything and rush back to the defence of Constantinople.

Heraclius paid off the marauding Avars from his dwindling reserves of gold. Now he could focus his remaining forces on the Persians. He had just one army left: every other Roman army had been destroyed, enslaved or dispersed. Heraclius retrained this last body of men as a guerrilla force, and galvanised their broken morale with Christian zeal.

In the spring of 624, Heraclius was ready to take the fight to the Persians. On 25 March he farewelled his twelve-year-old son and left Constantinople with his men. He would not return to the capital for another four years.

The Tower of Darkness

HERACLIUS MARCHED his army northwards from Trebizond into the mountains of Armenia. He could not hope to defeat Khusrau's forces in open battle, so he simply bypassed them, leading his men through Armenia's hard, bony mountain ranges. In the summer they entered the Caucasus, then turned south into the Persian heartlands, laying waste to several cities, taking Khusrau's thin defences completely by surprise.

Now, deep inside the Persian lands, the emperor made plans to destroy the Shahanshah's prestige and take revenge for the theft of the True Cross with an act of sacrilege. He sent a detachment of his men to attack the temple of the Fire of the Stallion.

The Persian Zoroastrians revered three sacred flames that were housed within three great fire temples: the Fire of the Stallion, the Fire of the Farr (the holy spirit), and the Fire of Mihr-is-Great, which was housed in the east. The Zoroastrians had come to believe that these three sacred flames had been lit by Ohrmazd himself at the creation of the world, to bring light and order to the universe. A special order of turbaned temple priests was charged with the awesome responsibility of keeping the fires burning. The threat of extinguishment was nothing less than a threat to the integrity of the cosmos.

The temple of the Fire of the Stallion was perched on the summit of a hill in Media, next to a cool mountain lake replenished by underground mineral springs. Every newly crowned shah was expected to make a pilgrimage on foot from Ctesiphon to this temple. Khusrau II had come there to pray for victory against the Romans, and he had lavished royal gifts on the shrine.

The hilltop temple was ringed with two protective walls and thirty-eight towers. Perhaps the hill was poorly defended that day because Heraclius's men seemed to have little difficulty storming it. The Romans entered the ornate temple complex and killed the horrified priests. The soldiers followed the long corridor into the fire sanctuary, a dramatic domed room girded by a stucco frieze around its walls. In the centre of the room was a three-stepped pedestal leading up to the sacred fire-altar itself. Heraclius's men gleefully smashed down the altar and stamped out the fire. A final, thin trail of smoke ascended from the ashes up to the dome and dispersed into nothingness.

Now it was Persia's turn to recoil in horror and revulsion, to suffer the trauma of a spiritually disordered universe.

HERACLIUS'S FORCES RANGED around the lands north of Ctesiphon, striking suddenly, plundering the smaller settlements, and then disappearing. Khusrau sent three armies to locate and destroy them, but Heraclius outmanoeuvred and defeated each of them in turn.

Heraclius was wintering by Lake Van when he heard worrying news: the Persians in Asia Minor had joined forces with the Avars and were converging on Constantinople from east and west. Shahrbaraz was confronting the city from the Asian shores of the Bosphorus, while the Avars had hauled their new siege engines up to the Theodosian Walls. This put Heraclius in a terrible bind, as Khusrau surely knew it would. He stood to lose his capital, but if he were to leave and march his army way back to Constantinople, he would lose the initiative – all his recent gains would have to be surrendered and there would be no hope of recovering the True Cross.

So Heraclius took a deadly gamble. He would stay where he was, and send only a small force, led by his brother Theodore, to harass the invaders. He would leave the Queen of Cities to fend for herself. He chose to place his trust in the hands of God, the Theodosian Walls and the defiant spirit of the people of Constantinople.

DESPITE THEIR VASTLY superior numbers, nothing seemed to go right for the besieging armies. The Avar catapults failed to dent the reinforced land walls. The city's most precious icon, a portrait of the Virgin, was paraded on the battlements. It was said that the Khagan of the Avars realised his siege was futile when he witnessed a Christian miracle: the ghostly figure of the Mother of God floating above the walls.

At the same time, the Roman navy easily destroyed the rickety Persian transports on the Bosphorus, leaving Shahrbaraz's troops stranded on the other side. Although the Avars and the Persians had brought massive armies to Constantinople, the siege petered out after a couple of weeks and both the Khagan and Shahrbaraz withdrew.

Heraclius, immensely relieved and heartened by these signs of God's favour, offered to make peace with Khusrau, but the shah of shahs, incredulous at his sudden reversal of fortune, stubbornly refused. The Romans swept down from the mountains onto the plains of Mesopotamia; Heraclius intended to ruthlessly illustrate to the Persians the powerlessness of their heaven-cursed leader.

On 12 December 627, the Romans crushed a Persian army outside Nineveh. Shamed by the defeat, the local Persian commander killed himself. Khusrau ordered the commander's body be packed in salt and brought to him, whereupon he ordered the corpse stripped and flailed until it was a bloody, shapeless mess. It was whispered around the palace that the Shahanshah was not altogether sane.

MEANWHILE, HERACLIUS'S MEN, hungry and exhausted, invaded Khusrau's summer palace and raided his royal zoo. The exotic animals were killed, roasted and fed to the Roman troops. They were mocking Khusrau's impotence.

Heraclius then marched his men down the banks of the Tigris to raid the outlying suburbs of Ctesiphon, creating terror and anguish within the city. Now it was the Persian capital's turn to tremble at the sight of enemy fires outside the walls.

And with that, the Persians decided they'd had enough.

A delegation representing Khusrau's ministers came to the Roman camp in secret. Heraclius was informed that moves were afoot within the palace to depose Khusrau, and to reach an understanding with the Romans. Two days later, Shahrbaraz sent two of his sons to arrest Khusrau, who was suffering from terrible dysentery. Khusrau was locked into a chamber known as the Tower of Darkness for five days with no food. Instead his guards brought in a heap of gold, silver and precious stones, saying: 'Do enjoy these things which you have loved insanely and amassed'. On the sixth day, the guards returned and slowly shot the befouled and half-starved Khusrau to death with arrows.

News of Khusrau's demise was sent back to Constantinople with ringing words: 'Fallen is the arrogant Khusrau, the enemy of God! He is fallen and cast down to the depths of the Earth, and his memory is utterly exterminated!'

KHUSRAU WAS REPLACED by his son Kavadh-Shiroe, who immediately opened peace negotiations with the Romans. The war was over. In the space of eighteen years, Heraclius had engineered the most stunning comeback in Roman history. The emperor, glad of heart but weary in spirit, left his representatives to conclude a treaty with the Persians, and began the long journey home alongside his wife Martina.

Six months later Kavadh-Shiroe too was dead, killed by the plague, and his infant son Ardashir took his place on the throne. Heraclius's ambassadors concluded a peace deal with Shahrbaraz, who agreed to restore to the Romans all their former territories in Syria, Palestine and Egypt. The Romans demanded the return of the True Cross, located in the palace at Ctesiphon. It was handed over to them.

And with that, it seems, the Persian leadership simply disintegrated. The child Ardashir was murdered by Shahrbaraz, who replaced him on the throne. Then Shahrbaraz, too, was murdered in a palace coup.

WHEN HERACLIUS AND MARTINA caught sight at last of their palace in Heira, on the Asian shore of the Bosphorus, they saw thousands of grateful citizens gathered at the palace gate with olive branches and lit candles. Heraclius was deeply moved, but said he would not re-enter Constantinople until he could bring the True Cross with him. The holy relic duly arrived in Heira in September as preparations were underway for a triumphal homecoming.

On the morning of 14 September 628, a massive crowd gathered at the Golden Gate for the procession. First to pass through the gold-plated doors was the True Cross, accompanied by victorious soldiers. Next to emerge were four Persian elephants, the first ever to be seen in the city.

Then, with a shout of joy, the crowds caught sight of their emperor, who had aged visibly since they had last seen him. Heraclius was cheered along the Mese, all the way to the Hagia Sophia, where a thanksgiving mass was held. Patriarch Sergius grasped the True Cross and lifted it up towards the great dome. It was a golden moment, a perfect triumph.

Chatrang

AS THE GRAND strategic games of Heraclius and Shahrbaraz rolled back and forth across Mesopotamia and Asia Minor, thousands of smaller strategic struggles played out on the tables of west Asia.

The game of chess is thought to have originated in northern India, between the third and fifth centuries. The Indians named it *chaturanga*, which means 'four divisions', a reference to the pieces that represented infantry, cavalry, elephants and chariots. The game's popularity carried it into Sassanid Persia, where its name was Persianised into *chatrang*.

Chatrang was played on a chequerboard of eight by eight squares. Each player had sixteen pieces: a *shah* (king), a *vizir* (prime minister), two *pil* (elephants), two *asp* (horses), two *rukh* (charioteers) and eight *piyadeh* (foot soldiers). Players would call *shah* when the opposing king was threatened, and *shah mat* – 'The king is finished' – when it could no longer escape the enemy.

The conquering Arabs, fond of mathematics and games of strategy, took up the game eagerly. They called it *shatranj*. Pilgrims and traders brought *shatranj* to western Europe, where it evolved into modern-day chess. In Europe the powerful *vizir* became a queen, the elephants evolved into bishops, the horses became knights, and the charioteers retained the title of 'rook', but took the shape of castle turrets. The eight little *piyadeh* became pawns.

Chess seems to have taken off quickly in Constantinople, even though killjoys in the Orthodox Church condemned it as a form of gambling. Princess Anna Comnena mentions it in passing in the pages of the *Alexiad*, describing it as a 'game invented by the Assyrians and thence brought to us'. She writes that chess was a comfort to her father, the emperor, who would occasionally play it in the early morning to dissipate the worries that had beset him through the night.

ON MY EIGHTH BIRTHDAY, my favourite uncle gave me a handsome illustrated book titled *Chess for Children*. Inside, the origin of chess was told as a fable:

There was once a great Shah of Persia, a ruler who loved games so much he appointed a learned man to his court, to act as his official Vizier of Games. The Shah asked the man to invent a game of strategy so that he might hone his skills as a military leader. The Vizier went away and came back to him with the game we all know as chess.

The Shah was delighted with chess. He admired the way it could produce such complexity from simplicity. He adored the struggle and the drama embedded in each turn of the game. After playing it for many days he summoned the Vizier to him.

'Chess is the greatest diversion anywhere on earth!' cried the Shah. 'I am very pleased and you may name your reward.'

The Games Vizier thought for a moment. Then he said, 'Sire, my wish is a simple one and can be reckoned according to the squares on the chessboard.'

'How so?' inquired the Shah.

'For the first square I should like a single grain of rice. For the second square I would like two grains of rice. For the third square, double it again to four grains, eight for the next, and so on.'

The Shah admitted to being bewildered. 'This would be a modest reward indeed for such fine and clever work, but I will grant you this wish.'

The Shah's treasurer withdrew to his chambers to calculate the exact amount of rice owed to the Vizier of Games. The treasurer returned to the throne room, his face full of amazement.

'Sire,' he reported, 'it seems Your Majesty now owes his Vizier of Games more than 18 billion billion grains of rice.'*

---

* 18,446,744,073,709,551,615 grains to be exact. Such an amount would form a heap of grains bigger than Mount Everest.

This was more rice than could be grown in Persia in a million years. The Shah could not fulfil his rash promise to his Vizier, and so, even though it grieved him, he had no choice but to chop off the man's head.

The fable is told to illustrate the power of exponential sequences. It's fun to imagine the shah's treasurer following the tally of grains across each square of the board: 1, 2, 4, 8, 16, 32, 64, 128 gets you to the end of the first row without too much fuss. On the second row the numbers begin their steep ascent: 256, 512, 1024, 2048, 4096, 8192, 16,384, 32,768 ... By now the Shahanshah is into a serious commitment of rice and we still have six more rows to go. *Shah mat!*

The Message from the Prophet

THE TRUE CROSS, recovered from Persian captivity, had one more journey to make. On 21 March 630, Heraclius entered the holy city of Jerusalem, not as a conquering emperor, but as a humble pilgrim, barefoot and stripped of his imperial regalia. In his hands he carried the holy relic down the Via Dolorosa to the Church of the Holy Sepulchre, where it was handed over in a moving, candlelit ceremony.

Heraclius then unleashed a campaign of forced baptism of the Jews in the city, in retaliation for their real or imagined treachery, which only deepened their longstanding resentment of Roman rule.

ACCORDING TO MUSLIM TRADITION, when Heraclius entered Jerusalem, he was brought a letter, written by an obscure Arab desert leader:

> In the name of Allah, the Beneficent, the Merciful. This letter
> is from Muhammad, the slave of Allah and his Apostle, to
> Heraclius, the ruler of the Romans. Peace be upon him who
> follows the right path. Furthermore, I invite you to Islam and
> if you become a Muslim you will be safe, and Allah will double
> your reward, and if you reject this invitation of Islam you will be
> committing a sin by misguiding your subjects.

Heraclius, it was said, had no idea as to the identity of the author of this audacious message; nonetheless the Muslim accounts say he treated the demand respectfully and expressed some curiosity about this 'Muhammad, slave of Allah'. According to Islamic tradition, Muhammad sent similar letters to Khusrau, to the Negus of Ethiopia, the governor of Syria and the rulers of Egypt and Bahrain. The likelihood that such a letter was ever written or conveyed to Heraclius is a matter of some debate between secular and Islamic historians, but it is beyond dispute that the followers of Muhammad were soon to make their presence known to Heraclius.

Yarmouk

A GRATEFUL SENATE awarded Heraclius the title of 'Scipio', ranking him with the legendary commander who defeated Hannibal. His place in the pantheon of the greatest Roman generals seemed secure.

A German historian once argued that if Hitler had died in 1938, historians would remember him as Germany's most successful statesman. Something like that is surely true for Heraclius. Had he suddenly dropped dead after returning the True Cross to Jerusalem, Heraclius would have been accorded a place alongside Augustus and Constantine. Instead he is remembered as the emperor who lived too long.

On the surface it seemed Heraclius had restored the *status quo ante bellum*, but everything had changed. Twenty years of ruinous warfare followed by plague had left the empire a burnt husk of its former self. Roman lands were littered with blackened churches and fortresses, ravaged croplands and empty villages.

The emperor sent his bureaucrats to Palestine, Syria and Egypt to pick up where they had left off, but things just weren't the same; the Romans had been absent for so long, and they had been kicked out so ignominiously. It was like the British returning to Singapore after the Japanese occupation; all the pomp and circumstance in the world could not disguise the fact that everyone had seen the mighty empire take a beating. Still, Heraclius's authority among his people was immense, and he spent the next seven years travelling from province to province, patiently rebuilding Roman administration in Damascus, Edessa and Antioch. But the ineffable prestige of the Romans, once so useful in subduing lesser peoples, had been punctured.

THE FIRST SIGNS of the coming cataclysm were felt as distant tremors on the desert frontiers, as flickers on the empire's nerve endings.

In 629, just a year after the cessation of hostilities, a Roman garrison in Palestine was attacked by a group of Arab raiders. The Romans drove them off and the raiders retreated into the desert. Rumours filtered into the empire of turmoil among the Arab tribes, and of movement along the borders. The Romans had once called these desert Arabs 'Saracens', but these new Arab insurgents preferred to call themselves *muhajirun* or 'emigrants'.

There were more raids, this time on small towns and settlements. The raiders would hit hard, plunder and disappear before the imperial troops could regroup and counterattack. The Roman military position in Syria and Palestine was starting to fall apart.

The Arabs were well known to the Romans as soldiers and traders. Both the Romans and the Persians had employed Arab mercenaries to fight proxy wars on the desert borders. Over time these tribes had come to rely on Roman gold, but now the war was over and money was tight, so Heraclius cancelled the annual tribute. The Arab border tribes angrily ended their alliance with the Romans. Intelligence from the Arabian peninsula was completely cut off, which left Heraclius completely unprepared for the coming storm.

IN 634, HERACLIUS WAS IN ANTIOCH when he received a report that a massive army of *muhajirun* had poured into Syria. The Roman army sent to drive them out was utterly destroyed. A year later, the Arabs took Damascus.

It was a shocking yet preposterous turn of events. The Romans were accustomed to seeing the desert dwellers as a lesser people – sometimes an ally, sometimes a nuisance – who would pick over the scraps left behind by the great powers. How had they become so organised, so lethal? Procopius had written a century earlier: 'Saracens are by nature unable to storm a wall, but are the cleverest of all men at plundering.' Now, somehow, they *had* learnt to storm a wall – and to take the city behind it.

Heraclius received an anxious letter from Yazdegerd III, the latest (and, as it would turn out, the last) Sassanid shah of Persia. Yazdegerd was similarly bewildered by a sudden flood of Saracens across *his* borders. The two powers agreed to assault the Arabs simultaneously: Heraclius would prepare to attack in Palestine while the Persians would mount a counterattack in Iraq. But just as Heraclius was gathering his armies, the Arabs cannily proposed peace negotiations with the Persians, and Yazdegerd's government, exhausted and broke, were only too happy to come to the table.

Heraclius, no doubt sick at heart at the prospect of having to win back Syria all over again, assembled a massive allied imperial force at Antioch of fifty thousand Romans, Christian Arabs, Slavs, Franks, Georgians and Armenians. The *muhajirun* fell back to a position near the river Hieromyax, known by the Arabs as Yarmouk, south of the Sea of Galilee. On 15 August 636, the armies confronted each other on a dusty plain, edged by a deep ravine known as Wadi-ur-Ruqqad.

THE ROMAN FORCES WERE LED by an experienced Armenian general named Vahan. His frontline infantry soldiers were armed with spears and swords; behind them were lines of missile troops carrying javelins and composite bows. Supporting the infantry was Vahan's heavy cavalry, his cataphracts, draped in scale armour.

The Arab leader, Khalid ibn al-Walid, was the most gifted Arab general of his time, having already won four quick victories against the Persians in lower Mesopotamia. Khalid had brought an army to Yarmouk that was half the size of the Roman forces, but his soldiers were masters of desert warfare, accustomed to navigating their way from waterhole to oasis, riding on camels and horses.

The first day of battle began with skirmishing and duelling. On the second day, Vahan launched an impressive frontal attack, which forced Khalid's right flank to retreat. The battered Arab infantrymen staggered back into their camp, but their wives jeered and threw rocks at them until they were shamed back into battle. The day ended with heavy casualties but inconclusively.

On the third day, Vahan again tore into the Arab right flank, but on the fourth, Khalid's army launched a fierce counterattack. Still, the Roman cataphracts had wounded and blinded so many of Khalid's soldiers, it became known as the 'Day of Lost Eyes'. On the fifth day, there was no battle, but Khalid moved his troops to cut off every possible escape route for the Romans.

At the dawn of the sixth day, Khalid unleashed a full attack on the Roman left flank. The Roman positions suddenly collapsed under the pressure. Then the Arab forces wheeled around and moved in for the kill. The remaining Romans were encircled. Some soldiers fell into the ravines of the wadi. Others escaped and ran for their lives, but most were slaughtered; the Arabs were taking no prisoners that day. Khalid and his mobile guard chased the escaping Romans all the way to Damascus where they were caught and killed.

IN ANTIOCH, HERACLIUS was brought the news of his army's destruction at Yarmouk. Now unable to defend the city, he was forced to retreat with his remaining forces over the Taurus Mountains into Asia Minor. After decades of bitter sacrifice, the Roman province of Syria was lost to him again. It seems Heraclius also resigned himself to the loss of Palestine, because he took the precaution of transporting the True Cross from Jerusalem to Constantinople for safekeeping.

It was just as well. The next year the Arab high command sent its forces to conquer Jerusalem, putting the city to siege for four months, until the Roman authorities surrendered in April 637. The city watched the disposition of its new Arab rulers closely. Were they Christians, pagans or something else? Jewish hopes in the city soared when Caliph Umar ordered the rubble to be cleared from the Temple Mount, the site of the legendary Temple of Solomon, which the Christians had been using as a garbage dump. Jewish leaders were heartened when the new Arab rulers of Jerusalem referred to them respectfully as *ahl-al-kitab*, People of the Book.

Three years later, Egypt fell to the disciplined fury of the *muhajirun*, opening the way for the Arab conquest of North Africa. Conquest was followed by consolidation, as the Arabs picked up the Roman habits of administration in their newly won lands.

In the space of thirty years, the Romans had lost two-thirds of their empire, won it back, then lost it all over again. In the east, the Arab gains were even more spectacular as huge swathes of Sassanid Persia fell to the unstoppable Arabs: the conquest of Iraq was completed in 638, followed by the whole of Iran. Yazdegerd III, the last Shah of the Sassanids, fled to his easternmost city of Merv, where he was murdered in the street. He was thirty-four years old. Yazdegerd's children died in exile in China. And just like that, the empire of the Sassanid Persians was gone forever.

THIS THIRD DRASTIC change in the fortunes of his empire left Heraclius a broken man, and he retreated to his palace in Heira. His people were inclined to blame his misfortunes on his incestuous marriage to Martina. To his critics, it seemed their marriage was cursed: of their ten children, three had died in childhood, one had a paralysed neck and another was a deaf-mute.

Heraclius was now sixty years old. The full crown of blond hair had fallen away, his body was stooped and he was afflicted with oedema, a build-up of fluid in the legs, which caused him terrible pain. It was said that at this time, Heraclius was also beset by hydrophobia, an anxious fear of water, which kept him stranded outside Constantinople, afraid to cross the Bosphorus. His officers ordered the construction of a pontoon bridge of boats, which allowed the emperor to cross the water to the capital.

His oedema worsened, confining him to bed. When death came for him in January 641, Heraclius must have welcomed it.

George of Pisidia, the court poet who had accompanied Heraclius on his brilliant campaign through Persia, wrote some sombre lines during Heraclius's final years:

Suddenly fades the splendour that surrounds
And all the unstable vanity of human glory
Stretches out and again constricts ...
The whole course of life
And the soft lump of everything human
Passes like a ball inflated with air.

A Terrible Foreboding

ISLAMIC HISTORIES RECORD that on the dawn of the first day of the Battle of Yarmouk, as the two sides stood glaring at each other across no-man's land, a Christian unit commander named George rode forward from the Roman lines towards the Arabs, shouting that he wanted to change sides and was ready to become a Muslim. George was welcomed into the ranks by Khalid and renamed 'Jirjah'. It's recorded that Jirjah was killed on the first day of battle.

Reports of the religious views of the Arabs were certainly mystifying to the Romans. The Arabs accorded respect to Christians and Jews, but required them to pay a *jizya*, a special tax levied only on non-believers. There were Christians in the conquered lands prepared to convert to the new religion simply to avoid the tax.

It's difficult to fathom the intensity of the spiritual terror suffered by medieval people after a defeat at the hands of an army sworn to a different faith. In the bitter aftermath there would be no shortage of holy men in the streets crying out that the cataclysm was God's punishment for some perceived wickedness or heresy among them.

A further defeat could unleash a far more dangerous thought: could it be that the 'infidel' is right, that we have been wrong all along? Do I choose a martyr's death or do I choose, like Jirjah, to gallop over to the winning side? For God must surely be with the winners. Such uncertainty could induce crippling anxiety, for what was at stake was not just your life in the here and now, but the everlasting fate of your immortal soul.

For all their imperial confidence, the ancient Romans never could entirely shake a melancholic sense of the transience of their glory. A premonition of a faraway doom lingered in the mind of a Roman general one night in 146 BC as he watched his men put the city of Carthage to the torch. The annihilation of Carthage, Rome's most hated enemy, should have been a jubilant moment; instead he wept and muttered to a Greek companion, 'I have a terrible foreboding that one day the same doom will be pronounced on my country'.

In 146 BC, that reckoning was a long way off. The Roman empire was just beginning its steep ascent towards domination of the entire Mediterranean. In the following centuries, the Roman world would periodically lurch into cycles of crisis, recovery and then reinvention at the hands of Augustus, Diocletian and Constantine. It was easy to assume the empire had a fixed place in the scheme of things.

But at the time of Heraclius's death in 641, the Romans of Constantinople were acutely conscious of a fall from grace, a demotion from superpower status to being just one among many powers in the Mediterranean. Decades of warfare and plague had left the Romans grief stricken and highly strung, an emotional state exacerbated by one of the most powerful aspects of Christian belief: an expectation that the return of Christ was imminent. Every churchgoer in Constantinople who recited the creed knew of the promise that Christ would 'come again in glory to judge the living and the dead', a moment when the dead would be resurrected, the wicked condemned and the whole world redeemed. Heraclius had been all too successful at equating the fortunes of the empire with God's plan for the world. What did it mean when the Arabs, of all people, driven by a mystifying faith, had conquered so many of their lands?

CHAPTER FIVE

Children of Ishmael

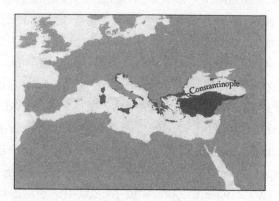

The empire in 718, at the second Arab siege of Constantinople.

Prayer is Better than Sleep

JOE AND I have fallen into a routine whereby we retire after dinner at an early hour and get up at daybreak when the first call to prayer floats out of the minarets of the Blue Mosque: *Come and flourish, God is great, Prayer is better than sleep.*

Joe is not so sure about that last part. He finds the call to prayer grating, but I don't mind it at all. After a while it mixes into the general hubbub of the city and I barely notice it. Istanbul is, as Constantinople once was, the largest city in Europe and the benefits of pausing for a moment of peace and reflection several times in the course of a busy day are suddenly obvious to me. But at Joe's age, I think I would have hated it too.

I am trying on this trip to open Joe's mind to the glory and emotional intensity of sacred art and architecture. Khym and I have

180

not brought our kids up as Christians and they've never shown an interest in any kind of religion. Joe has almost no acquaintance with Bible stories, so the Byzantine mosaics of Istanbul are as incomprehensible to him as a column of hieroglyphics. His exposure to religion thus far has also been an entirely negative experience. Evangelical Christians are active in our suburb and he's had arguments with kids his own age who insist the world is only six thousand years old, that Darwin was wrong and that humans coexisted with dinosaurs.

'Don't be too hard on them,' I tell him. 'They're just trying to be loyal to their parents and to the creed they've been raised on.'

'But they're so *annoying*. They say I'll go to hell if I don't agree with them.'

'Is there any part of you that believes that?'

Joe screws up his face, 'Of course not. I don't believe in God at all.'

Blue Mosque, interior.

Some years ago I interviewed biologist and well-known atheist Richard Dawkins. I mentioned in passing something I'd been taught in first-year philosophy: that we can apprehend knowledge through either reason or faith. Dawkins didn't like the faith part of that equation, and replied in his distinctive staccato, 'Well, *I* don't see how *any* responsible academic could *ever* utter such a *foolish* proposition ...'

Dawkins takes a very dim view of religious fundamentalists who present creation myths to children as scientific fact. It troubles me too; teaching kids to believe six impossible things before breakfast will probably, in the long run, be counterproductive, or convince them they can assert whatever 'facts' they like, so long as they do it confidently and self-righteously. I want Joe to be open to religious art and philosophy, but I want him to hate bullshit as well.

To prepare for the Dawkins interview I watched a British documentary he had written and presented called *The God Delusion*, where he travelled to America and the Holy Land to investigate the baleful effects of religious superstition and bigotry. Dawkins finished the program in Jerusalem, where he stood in front of the Dome of the Rock deploring the intractable hatreds inspired by the city's three great religions.

But, I thought that as he spoke, he seemed oblivious to the glittering golden beauty of the great mosque behind him. To him, the Church of the Holy Sepulchre was just a rabbit warren of fanatics and charlatans. Beauty, he says, can be found in science, in the elegance of a twist of DNA, in the song of a blackbird or in the complex symmetry of a flower. Well, yes, but I wondered if there wasn't a degree of philistinism among some of the new atheists too, if their aversion to the sacred has left them indifferent to its beauty.

Dawkins, naturally enough, sees religious fundamentalism as an attack on the values of the Enlightenment: reason, scepticism and a stubborn sticking to the facts, no matter how unwelcome they might be. Edward Gibbon, the eighteenth-century historian whose work did so much to give Byzantium a bad name, was also very much a man of the Enlightenment, who cared not at all for the Greek-speaking Romans of Constantinople.

'Superstition riveted their chains,' he sighed. To him their history was 'a tedious and uniform tale of weakness and misery'. Voltaire was similarly disgusted by the God-haunted Byzantines, denouncing their thousand-year civilisation as 'a disgrace to the human mind'. As a result of this chorus of enlightened disapproval, the word 'byzantine' is embedded in the language as a slur, a cliché used to describe anything pointlessly complex and bureaucratic. There are still a great many people today who know the meaning of the word 'byzantine' but almost nothing of Byzantium.

In the twentieth century a new generation of western historians looked afresh at Byzantine history and concluded that these gentlemen of the Enlightenment had thrown a very large baby out with the bathwater. The critics had failed to answer the obvious question: if the Romans of Constantinople were so effete, so paralysed by superstition, how did their civilisation endure for so long? How did they inspire so many with their vision of heaven on Earth? Was it all just a silly hoax, bolstered with conjuror's tricks?

I can't help but love and admire Byzantium's readiness to turn its back on the self and fix its gaze directly into the face of Creation. There is something in me that is drawn to the numinous, the sacred. I feel its gravitic force drawing me towards it like an invisible planet. It's sometimes led me to the gate of a church, but never made me want to stay. Several times in foreign countries I've slipped into the back of a cathedral to witness a mass so that I might absorb the beauty of the liturgy in a language I can't understand. If I could, I'm certain it would irritate me no end. I'd rather be an observer than a participant: I don't want to be required to recite creeds I don't believe in.

My father, Alan, was never comfortable in a church. On those occasions when he was obliged to be present for weddings, for funerals and on Christmas Eve, he would distract himself by observing the antics of children in the congregation who were as bored as he was, impishly goading them to misbehave. Mum would stifle a laugh and whisper, *Stop it, Alan*.

Alan had a terrible childhood. His mother, my grandmother, died of tuberculosis when he was three, and his father, a veteran of the Great War, neglected him. Dad was given a cursory education at a Christian Brothers Catholic school where the Brothers tried to beat godliness and obedience into him.

My mother, Pamela, had a much happier exposure to Christianity. She was raised an Anglican in a small country town, and had fond memories of church and the seasonal rhythm it brought to community life.

Pamela and Alan on their wedding day.

They were married in 1959, when Catholic–Protestant unions were still, in some places, frowned upon. Pamela said she was happy to convert to Catholicism, but Alan wasn't interested, so they were married in an Anglican church in Adelaide. Sectarianism was dying in Australia anyway, and they were by no means an odd couple –

they looked like they were made for each other. In their wedding photos they're movie-star good-looking: Dad resembles a young John Barrymore, Mum is as luminous as Grace Kelly.

The Hollywood wedding photos belie their very modest circumstances. My sister and I were brought up in the outer suburbs of Melbourne and Sydney, and educated in suburban state schools where religious instruction was kept at arm's length. Pamela wanted us to be familiar with the Bible stories and hymns of her childhood, so she took us to the local Anglican church. When I entered high school, church attendance petered out as my Sunday mornings were given over to sleeping in and watching TV, but at fifteen I joined a local Anglican youth group, not because I was particularly spiritually curious, but because I wanted to meet girls.

Youth group meetings involved some kind of social activity on a Sunday afternoon followed by Evensong. The local minister's approach was low-key rather than evangelical. Some of my friends were Christianised by their years in youth group, but I wasn't, which disappointed them. Temperamentally I'm a doubter rather than a believer. And I wasn't able to reconcile the God of love and forgiveness in the New Testament with the angry, mercurial creator of the Old Testament.

The stories of Genesis are, for me, still so beguiling and strange. The book begins by taking us into the mind of God as He creates the heavens and the Earth. It's a creation myth that can be read today like a poetic interpretation of Big Bang theory: there is a lump of primordial matter, a ripple of energy and then a sudden burst of light, followed by the creation of the Earth and all life upon it.

Yahweh, the God of the Hebrews, is as awesome and as harsh as the Land of Canaan. In *Genesis* he walks with Abraham and wrestles with Jacob. In Exodus he appears as a pillar of fire and as a disembodied voice within a burning bush. He drowns the population of the world because humanity has become irredeemably corrupt, but he spares Noah and his family. Yahweh evades all human understanding; His reasoning is too large for us to grasp.

Christianity appears in Palestine like a viral mutation of Judaism. Jesus comes to Jerusalem as the messiah, the anointed one of the Hebrew prophecies. He redefines the relationship between God and his human creations, and countermands the ancient laws given to Moses with new commandments of love and kindness. After his crucifixion, the Christians are a small Jewish sect until Paul of Tarsus brings Jesus's new monotheism to the wider Roman world. Christianity gives hope and dignity to slaves and the poor, who in turn begin to convert their masters. There is a new moral perspective. The humble sermons of a carpenter's son eventually conquer the Roman empire.

Six hundred years after the death of Christ, an Arab desert merchant named Muhammad delivers a third and final refinement of the religion revealed many times before by Abraham, Moses and Jesus (who is named as a prophet, not as the son of God). There would be, he said, no further refinements. Muhammad leaves no room for doubt. The word this time, transcribed into the Holy Qur'an, is not mediated and diluted by mortal men; the Qur'an is presented to the world as nothing less than pure, unadulterated language from the mind of God.

The Prophet

THE ORIGINS OF ISLAM are shrouded in uncertainty, at least for non-believers. The earliest written accounts of the life of Muhammad are based on oral traditions, transcribed by pious Muslims centuries after the Prophet's death. The traditional Muslim version of events currently exists in a state of tension with modern historical inquiry, based on non-Muslim accounts from the time.

ACCORDING TO ISLAMIC TRADITION, Muhammad was born in Mecca in 570. His mother died when he was still a child, and he was raised by his grandfather and his uncle, Abu Talib.

Muhammad belonged to a tribe known as the Quraysh, which worshipped Allah, the supreme God, but also a collection of lesser goddesses, who were believed to be the daughters of Allah. As a young man, Muhammad accompanied the trading caravans that passed between Mecca and Syria, and he was introduced on his travels to Jewish and Christian teachings. At 25 he married a wealthy widow named Khadija.

While the traders of the Quraysh enjoyed their worldly pleasures, Muhammad was drawn to a simpler, ascetic life, and he would sometimes retreat into a tiny cave in Mount Jabal al-Nour, to pray and meditate.

One night, while in his cave, Muhammad's mind was flooded with a single dramatic command: *Recite!*

In a terror, he ran outside the cave, where it is recorded that he was confronted by an angel so immense that he covered every part of the sky and spoke with a voice like thunder: *Recite in the name of your Lord who created man from clots of blood! O Muhammad, you are the prophet of God and I am Jibrīl.**

And from Muhammad's lips poured divinely inspired words. More recitations would follow over the next twenty-three years, which were memorised by Muhammad's followers and written down on parchment, stones and palm leaves and carved into the shoulder bone of a camel.

The revelations were physically painful to Muhammad. 'Never once did I receive a revelation,' he said, 'without thinking that my soul had been torn away from me.'

---

* The Arab name for Gabriel.

AT FIRST, MUHAMMAD only spoke of these revelations to his family, then to a few friends. After three years, he began to preach to members of his tribe, the Quraysh. Muhammad's message to his people was as simple and as stark as the desert lands it came from: your old gods have failed. There is only one God, Allah, and everyone must submit to his will, for the day of judgement and resurrection could come at any moment: 'When the sky is rent asunder; when the stars scatter and the oceans roll together; when the graves are hurled about; each soul shall know what it has done and what it has failed to do'.

Muhammad demanded justice, humility and charity from his followers. His was a call to a properly ordered moral life, and his words were warmly received among those of the Quraysh who were troubled by the greed and arrogance of the newly wealthy merchant class. His followers were expected to give over a portion of their income to the destitute, to abstain from food within daylight hours during the month of Ramadan and to acquaint themselves with the hardships of poor and hungry people.

Muhammad's radical message began to win him powerful enemies among the wealthy leaders of the Quraysh. In 622 Muhammad escaped Mecca, foiling a murder plot against him. He and his followers migrated to Yathrib (later named Medina) where he was welcomed by his many supporters in that city. Those who accompanied the Prophet to Medina were called *muhajirun*, 'emigrants'.

In 624 a Quraysh army clashed with a much smaller force of Muhammad's *muhajirun* at Badr. The Muslims were victorious, with Muhammad crediting the victory to a host of invisible angels. A truce was signed, and in 629 the Prophet was permitted to enter Mecca unharmed. He came directly to the black, cubic shrine of

Mecca known as the Kaaba, and demanded that it be cleansed of its pagan idols and reconsecrated to the one God, Allah.

The dignity and breadth of Muhammad's vision dissolved ancient rivalries and united the tribes of Arabia under his leadership. The Prophet preached that all willing servants of God form a single community, an *umma*, and prepare themselves to engage in a struggle, a *jihad*, to serve the purposes of God on Earth. Unlike Jesus, Muhammad never claimed divinity for himself: he was a prophet, not a messiah. Where Christians agonised over the intricacies of the Holy Trinity, Muhammad offered a jewel-like clarity: 'There is no God but God'.

MUHAMMAD DIED OF A FEVER IN 632, but there were many followers willing to pick up his banner. Leadership passed to the Prophet's good friend Abu Bakr, who became the first caliph.* Abu Bakr launched successful invasions of the exhausted, plague-raddled Roman and Persian empires. Umar the second caliph completed the Arab conquest of Iran and Iraq to the north-east, along with Syria, Palestine and Egypt to the north-west. The cascading victories of the armies of Allah carried the Arabs far beyond anything their tribal ancestors could have known or imagined, and left them with a sense that something extraordinary had happened. An anonymous Muslim pamphleteer from the tenth century would later write:

We set out, barefoot and naked, lacking in every kind of
equipment, utterly powerless, deprived in every sort of armament
and devoid of all the necessary provisions, to fight the peoples
with the most widely extended empires, the peoples that were

---

* Taken from the Arabic *khalīfah*, meaning 'successor'.

most manifestly mighty, possessing the most numerous troops ...
namely the Persians and the Romans. We went to meet them
with small abilities and weak forces, and God made us triumph
and gave us possession of their territories.

For the *muhajirun*, it was living proof of the correctness of the
Qur'an's message that a society living in harmony with God's laws
would flourish and prevail over the enemies of God.

Hagar and Ishmael

THE EMERGENCE OF the Arab juggernaut tormented the
Christians of Constantinople. The Romans of the ancient world
had regarded the Arabs with a mix of contempt and uneasiness that
characterised their attitudes to all the barbarian tribes lurking on the
empire's borders. The Arabs were known to be fierce and resourceful,
but feuding between the tribes had always prevented them from
constituting a real threat. Now they were united, apparently
unstoppable, and moving inexorably towards Constantinople.

In Jerusalem there was hope among both the Christians and the
Jews that their new Arab rulers were people of the same faith. The
Romans in the city noted that they called themselves 'believers' – but
in what? Who were these people in the eyes of God?

One clue can be found in a letter from this time that records a
meeting between the patriarch of Antioch and the new emir of Syria.
The document notes that the Arab leader quizzed the patriarch on
the laws and beliefs of the Christians and the Jews, but the emir's
people are referred to not as Muslims or followers of Muhammad,
but as *Mhaggráyé* or 'Hagarenes'.

Another clue can be gleaned from the words of an arrogant Arab
demand, issued to Heraclius, that claimed the province of Palestine

as their birthright: 'God gave that country as the inherited property of Abraham and of his sons after him. We are the sons of Abraham. It is too much that you hold our country. Leave in peace, and we shall demand from you what you have seized, plus interest.'

The Prophet Muhammad was described as 'a man of the sons of Ishmael'. And in that name, the Romans could find an answer of sorts why the blessing of heaven had fallen so manifestly upon the Arabs. The explanation lay within the first book of the bible, the Book of Genesis.

ABRAM WAS A FAVOURITE of Yahweh, the God of the Hebrews. The meaning of his name was 'exalted father', but Abram despaired because he was 85 years old and had not been blessed with children.

One night, Yahweh appeared to him in a dream. Yahweh led Abram outside his mudbrick house into the cool evening air and showed him all the stars shimmering in the night sky. Then Yahweh said to him, 'Count the stars, if you can. For that is how numerous your offspring shall be.'

Yahweh invited Abram to make a blood sacrifice. Abram slaughtered a calf, a goat, a ram, a dove and a pigeon in turn, and suddenly he was plunged into a terrifying darkness.

The voice of Yahweh again came into his mind. Yahweh told Abram that his descendants would have to suffer four hundred years of slavery, but they would one day inherit all the lands stretching from the Wadi of Egypt to the Euphrates River.

Abram awoke from the dream and turned to his wife Sarai.

'Yahweh has promised me I shall have as many offspring as there are stars in the sky,' he said, his face full of wonder.

But Sarai was seventy-five years old. She clutched at the loose skin on her face and at her breast.

'Look at me, Abram,' she said. 'Everyone can see I am now too old to bear children.'

Then Sarai called for Hagar, her Egyptian handmaiden.

'Go, sleep with my slave,' she said to Abram, bitterly. 'Perhaps I can build a family through her.'

So Abram took Hagar as his concubine. Soon she became pregnant. Sarai watched Hagar and her swelling belly with a jealous eye. Sarai believed her slave had become proud, and this made Hagar hateful to her eye. Sarai confronted Hagar and accused her of nursing a secret contempt. Hagar began to fear for her life and fled into the desert.

After some time Hagar stopped to rest at a lonely spring, where an angel found her.

'Hagar,' the angel asked, 'where have you come from, and where are you going?'

'I'm running away from my mistress, Sarai,' she replied.

'Go back to your mistress and submit to her. Do as I say and you will have more offspring, so many you will not be able to count them all.'

The angel then told Hagar she would give birth to a son. 'His name will be Ishmael' (which means 'God has listened').

And then the angel offered Hagar a warning. 'Ishmael will be a wild donkey of a man; his hand will be against everyone and everyone's hand against him. He will live in hostility towards all his brothers.'

Hagar did as the angel told her to. She returned to the house and in time she gave birth to a son. Abram named him Ishmael.

Ten years passed. Abram was now ninety-nine years old.

Yahweh came to him in a dream once more. 'No longer

will you be called Abram; from this day your name will be Abraham' (which means 'Father of a Multitude').

Yahweh repeated his promise, that Abraham would be the father of many nations.

'In return,' Yahweh said, 'you and all your descendants must keep a new covenant with me: a covenant of the flesh.

'Every male among you must be circumcised. Every one of them: you, your sons, your slaves. This will be proof that you have kept your covenant with me.'

Then Yahweh told Abraham that his wife Sarai would have a new name too. 'From this time she must be called Sarah, and she will now bear a son by you. I will bless her so that she will be the mother of nations; kings will come from her.'

Abraham bowed with his head to the ground and began to laugh.

'How can a son be born to a man who is a hundred years old?' he asked. 'And, I might add, how will Sarah, who is ninety, even bear such a child? And what of my son Ishmael? Why can't he live under your blessing?'

Yahweh's presence shone in Abraham's mind like the blazing sun. 'Listen to me,' he said. 'I tell you that Sarah will have a son and you will call him Isaac. I will establish this everlasting covenant through him, and his descendants.'

Abraham listened and said nothing.

Yahweh said, 'As for Ishmael, I have heard you, and yes, I will bless him too. I will make him the father of twelve princes and make him into a great nation. But my covenant will be with the descendants of Isaac.'

And when Yahweh finished speaking he floated up into the sky.

THAT SAME DAY, Abraham, along with his son Ishmael and every other male in the house, was circumcised with a knife, just as Yahweh had instructed.

A year later, Sarah gave birth to their much longed-for son, Isaac.

Abraham was, by now, a hundred years old.

Isaac grew out of infancy and a feast was held to celebrate his weaning. At the feast, Sarah saw that Ishmael was making fun of her little Isaac and she became enraged.

'Abraham,' she whispered, 'get rid of that slave girl and her son. That Ishmael will never share in the inheritance with my son Isaac.'

Abraham was torn, because Ishmael was his son as much as Isaac.

But then Yahweh came to him and told him, 'Listen to Sarah and do as she asks. Do not worry. I will protect Ishmael and make a nation from him too, because he is your son.'

At dawn the next morning, Abraham gave Hagar some bread and a skin of water. He placed Ishmael on her shoulder and sent them away.

Hagar and Ishmael wandered into the desert of Beersheba, and Abraham never saw them again.

IT WAS NO STRETCH AT ALL for Christian scholars to recognise the conquering Arabs as the long-lost descendants of Hagar and Ishmael, having come out of the wilderness to seek their birthright. And that portrayal of Ishmael as a 'wild donkey of a man' with his 'hand set against everyone' ... well, did that not perfectly describe this strange horde of believers, clutching scimitars atop their camels?

Then a more disturbing thought: if the desert warriors were indeed the children of Ishmael, then the Arabs could, like the Jews, claim an ancient bloodline descending from Abraham, something that Roman Christians could not do.

The Fallen Colossus

AFTER THE DEATH OF HERACLIUS, Constantinople was thrown into turmoil. His funeral was followed by a complicated power struggle between the emperor's unpopular widow Martina and the branch of the family related to Heraclius's first wife. A few months later, Martina and her son Heraclonus were exiled to Rhodes, and Constans, the eleven-year-old grandson of Heraclius, became sole emperor. The Roman empire was by now greatly diminished, covering not much more than lower Thrace, Asia Minor, Armenia, North Africa and isolated fragments of Italy. Constans II ruled for twenty-seven years in the shadow of the ever-growing caliphate.

Meanwhile, the Arabs set up effective governments in the former Roman provinces of Syria, Palestine and Egypt. The caliphate now had control of major port cities on the eastern Mediterranean coast, but the Roman navy continued to dominate the shipping lanes.

The new governor of Syria was an aggressive general named Mu'awiya, who saw at once the need for the Arabs to have a Mediterranean fleet of their own. Mu'awiya approached Caliph Uthman for permission to embark on a major shipbuilding program. Uthman agreed and Mu'awiya set up dockyards along the Syrian coast.

After just two years, Mu'awiya had built an impressive fleet of ships, manned by Christian sailors and Arab marines. In 649 he launched a naval attack on Cyprus and won a quick victory. The following year he set his sights on the island of Rhodes, an important Roman trading post between Constantinople and Alexandria.

RHODES HAD BECOME FAMOUS in the ancient world for its glorious Colossus, a thirty-two-metre-tall bronze statue of the Greek sun god Helios.* The statue was constructed to celebrate the victory of Rhodes over the king of Cyprus, and completed in 280 BC. The sight of the massive statue by the entrance of the harbour was by all accounts astonishing, and it was hailed in ancient times as one of the Seven Wonders of the World.

The Colossus stood upright for just fifty-six years, until it was toppled by an earthquake in 226 BC. The superstitious Greeks never tried to re-erect it, accepting its downfall as the will of the gods. The fallen colossus became a popular destination for sightseers in the ancient world. Pliny the Elder wrote that 'even lying on the ground it is a marvel. Few people can make their arms meet round the thumb of the figure, and the fingers are larger than most statues'.

Rhodes was easily captured by Mu'awiya's navy in 653. The colossus was either an abomination or an irrelevance to Mu'awiya, and so the bronze ruins were dismantled and sold for scrap to a Jewish merchant from Edessa. Nine hundred camels were needed to carry it away. The bronze was taken to Syria and melted down into coins. It was a moment of decay, and renewal: the Colossus of Rhodes, a wonder of the ancient world, atomised into thousands of particles and dispersed into the medieval world.

TWO YEARS LATER, the new Arab navy won a smashing victory over a much larger Roman fleet in a clash that became known as the Battle of the Masts. Emperor Constans was present at the battle and lucky to escape with his life. He fled to Sicily for his own safety.

---

* Roughly the same size as the Statue of Liberty.

Five hundred of his *dromons* were sunk, along with Roman naval domination of the eastern Mediterranean.

Mu'awiya became caliph in 661 and he shifted the Arab capital to Damascus. Seven years later, Constans was killed in Syracuse by his bath attendant, who struck him over the head with a soap-dish. The Romans believed it was God's punishment for having abandoned Constantinople.

Colossus of Rhodes.

Garum

ONE OF THE MANY blessings conferred on Constantinople, even in its darkest years, was the ready supply of fish in the waters of the Golden Horn. The ancient custom of catching and grilling fish on the wharves of the harbour continues to this day. And so at lunchtime, Joe and I catch the tram down to Eminonu on the Golden Horn to grab a fish sandwich from one of the famous fish-sandwich boats of

Istanbul. Bobbing in the tide, next to the Galata Bridge, we see a row
of gaudy timber galleons. On deck, the men are cooking fish fillets on
sizzling hot plates, making conversation, and shouting instructions
to each other.

We order from the dockside counter. The woman calls out the order
over her shoulder; behind her, on the boat, a kitchen worker stuffs a
grilled fish into half a baguette, along with salad, onion and lemon
juice. He wraps it in paper and tosses it across the water to the counter.

Joe and I pull up a couple of stools and sit down to eat, alongside
dozens of Istanbullus on their lunch break. The sandwich is very
cheap at just five Turkish *lira* apiece, but it's surprisingly bland, and
the fish is so bony it's almost inedible. We decide to discard our
half-eaten sandwiches and fill up on a couple of big Turkish pretzels
instead. Later I discover the fish is not, in fact, freshly caught from
the polluted waters of the Bosphorus, which is probably just as well,
but imported Norwegian mackerel.

The plentiful supply of fish in a protected harbour helped
Constantinople withstand long sieges that would have broken other
cities. Aside from fish, the people of Constantinople ate a mostly
vegetarian diet of carrots, leeks, mushrooms, onions and spinach.

Olives, cheese and eggs played a large part in the diet of lower-
class people, while wealthier citizens enjoyed expensive meats such
as pork, lamb and poultry, as well as oranges, lemons, pomegranates
and apples. Caviar was so plentiful and cheap it could be enjoyed
by anyone. Spiced wines were popular; Liutprand of Cremona
complained in his letters of the 'resinated wine' served at the
emperor's table, which sounds a lot like retsina, the white wine
flavoured with pine resin served in Greek restaurants today.

Liutprand also sarcastically recorded in his journal that the
emperor had sent him a 'wonderful gift', a roasted baby goat 'proudly

stuffed with garlic, leeks and onions and smothered in garum'. It was the *garum* that bothered him the most: a pungent fish sauce that the Romans sprinkled on nearly every dish to enliven otherwise bland food. Western visitors often reviled *garum*'s fishy aroma, but ambassadors to the imperial court had little choice but to eat it up with a grin.

This is how *garum* was made: fish blood and intestines were salted, smashed up and placed in a vat to ferment in the sun. After several months a clear liquid, the *garum*, would rise to the top. A closely woven basket filter was lowered into the vessel to strain the *garum*, and to leave the remaining 'feculence' behind. The product was probably similar to the fish sauce that gives Vietnamese food its delicious pungency.

Byzantine fishermen from an illuminated manuscript, the Madrid Skylitzes.

THE ARAB CONQUESTS changed the way the Romans ate and drank. The loss of Egypt cut off the grain supply that had once fed their empire. It was replaced in Constantinople by a yeasty northern wheat grain that rose into a loaf when baked. The loss of Syria forced people in Constantinople to do without olive oil for some time, so food was increasingly boiled, not fried. Houses had to be lit with candles instead of oil lamps.

In ancient times, wealthy Romans had dined while reclining on couches; food was served by slaves and eaten with the fingers. From the seventh century, the Romans began to sit at tables. The end of the spoon was sharpened into a spear to pick up food. In time, a second prong was added and the fork became commonplace at the table, alongside the knife.

Personal hygiene changed too. Luxurious Roman bath houses had been the pleasure palaces of everyday people in the ancient world, but in the seventh century, Christian suspicion of the flesh led the church to frown upon public bathing and the use of Constantinople's Baths of Zeuxippus fell away. In time the complex was given over to military use, then one part of the bath house was converted to a prison, the other to a silk factory. The easy sensuality of the ancient world dimmed and then winked out altogether.

THE LOSS OF LAND, income and people made the seventh century a dark age for the eastern Roman empire. The society became poorer and more militarised, and the influence of the cultured senatorial class began to recede and disappear. Fewer histories were written, and culture became the preserve of a relatively small group of people within the clergy.

Under repeated assaults, the empire withdrew behind its high walls. The old Roman swagger retreated into a fearful defensiveness. The empire would one day recover, reconquer and enjoy a glorious efflorescence, but in seventh-century Constantinople, such a future was barely conceivable, as people went about their lives to a dismal drumbeat of war, plague and violence.

Slit-Nose

IN 669, A FEAST WAS HELD in Constantinople to celebrate the birth of a son and heir to the Emperor Constantine IV and his consort Anastasia. The little prince had a fine pedigree: he was the great-great-grandson of Heraclius and his parents named him Justinian, in the hope that he might some day match the achievements of the first Justinian, conqueror, lawgiver and builder of the Hagia Sophia.

Young Justinian received a classical education, in the expectation he would become a just and wise ruler. The boy was twelve when his father nominated him as his co-emperor. Two uncles were also raised to deputy-emperor status, which presented Justinian's father with a dilemma: how could he ensure that these men would not overthrow his son after his death?

The solution he hit upon was to have their noses slit. Emperors were required to be free of all visible imperfections; nose-slitting made both men too ugly, too disfigured to entertain any hope of stealing the throne from the boy. The mutilation was cruel, but considered essential for the stability of the empire.

Constantine IV died four years later and his son was crowned Justinian II at just sixteen years old. Despite his youth, the new Justinian acted like he had no time to lose. First he sent an army to drive the Arabs out of Armenia. The Caliph Abd al-Malik, distracted by internal divisions, was forced to come to terms. A jubilant Justinian II then sent his soldiers north into Thrace where they defeated the Bulgars of Macedonia and took back the city of Thessalonica. Justinian II entered the city in triumph.

Success emboldened Justinian II to move some pieces around the imperial chessboard; he uprooted the Slavs of Thrace and the Christians of Cyprus and ordered their populations to be shifted to a town in Anatolia he renamed Justinianopolis. Five years after the forced deportation, Justinian II drew on this population of sullen, dislocated Slavs to create a new 30,000-strong army. Now he was ready to attack the Arabs once again

His first strike against the Arabs was successful. Then it all fell apart. The new Slavic army had no love for the Roman cause or for the young emperor who had uprooted their families so ruthlessly, so the Arabs had no difficulty bribing them to swap sides. Two-thirds of Justinian II's troops slipped across enemy lines and turned on the Roman army. The Roman forces broke apart and Justinian II was forced to flee across the Sea of Marmara back to Constantinople.

Stung badly by his first major defeat, he lashed out, ordering the wives and children of the defecting Slavs be put to death. The Slavs who had stayed loyal were punished anyway for the treachery of their countrymen. The senior general of the campaign, Leontius, was summoned to Constantinople, given a dressing down by the emperor and thrown into prison.

Still seething, Justinian II launched a crackdown on a range of religious practices that he deemed unorthodox. He convened a new ecumenical council to create new church law, but Pope Sergius in Rome was angered by the council's new rules and refused to accept them. Justinian II sent soldiers to Rome to place the pope under arrest, but the pope's men refused to let the arresting officers come anywhere near him. Justinian II had given an order that he could not enforce, a dangerous moment for any ruler. It was also a sign of the empire's waning influence in Italy.

Public opinion within Constantinople soured on the young emperor. His ambitious building program had obliged him to raise taxes and prosecute evaders, which deepened resentment among the wealthy and the poor alike. He tried to mollify the aristocracy by freeing the scapegoat Leontius from his prison cell, and soon enough a group of dissident senators gathered in secret at the general's house. Everyone agreed they were sick to death of the bumptious young emperor. He had to go.

The conspirators enlisted the backing of the Blues faction from the Hippodrome. Even Callinicus, the Patriarch of Constantinople, agreed to turn a blind eye.

On the agreed night, a group of senators and military leaders met at Leontius's house and acclaimed him as emperor. Leontius then led his followers to the Praetorium, the Constantinople jail, where they freed all of Justinian's political prisoners. Agents of the rebellion took to the streets, shouting, *Christians! Come to the Hagia Sophia!* Sleepy citizens were roused from their beds, anxious to see what was going on. A crowd gathered at the great church and began shouting abusive slogans directed at the emperor. Leontius arrived at the Hagia Sophia accompanied by the Patriarch Callinicus, who gave the uprising his blessing. Someone in the crowd spat an old Roman curse at the emperor: *Let the bones of Justinian be dug up!* The rebellious mood turned murderous.

At dawn the crowd surged over to the Hippodrome. A delegation of soldiers was sent to seize the emperor. Justinian was dragged out of the palace and across the Augustaeum and flung onto the floor of the Hippodrome. Leontius, now in the imperial box, looked down on him. The howling mob, revelling in the thrill of revolution, wanted blood. Leontius chose restraint: Justinian was still the legitimate ruler in the eyes of the world, and cutting his throat would set a dangerous precedent. But some form of permanent disqualification was required to keep Justinian from the throne.

The solution was obvious. Justinian was held still, a knife was produced and, like his uncles before him, his nose was sliced away. Then his tongue was slit in two.

Bloodied, disfigured and traumatised, the dethroned emperor was sent into exile. He was dumped into a boat, and taken out onto the Black Sea, towards the city of Cherson on the southern tip of the Crimean peninsula.* He was, by now, twenty-six years old.

IN CHERSON, Justinian nursed his wounds and brooded on his ordeal, in no way prepared to accept that his disfigurement had made him unfit to rule. In his mind he was still the rightful emperor, the descendant of the great Heraclius, chosen by God.

Cherson was a small provincial city, and the presence of a dethroned emperor generated excitement among the locals. Despite his wounds, Justinian was still a figure of glamour and public curiosity, and as the tale of his cruel treatment spread, he became the object of considerable sympathy. A growing band of supporters met at his house, where he openly plotted his return to power. The local authorities, loyal to Leontius, pondered whether to send him back to Constantinople or to simply have him killed. As they deliberated, Justinian was tipped off and slipped out of town. He and his supporters headed north-east, into the Caucasus, to a place where he hoped and expected to find sanctuary: the land of the Khazars.

The Khazars of Khazaria

THE KHAZARS OF KHAZARIA are surely among the most intriguing peoples of the Middle Ages. Like the Huns and Avars, they were originally semi-nomadic horsemen from the steppes of Central Asia who settled along the western stretch of the Silk Road, roughly in the area of modern-day Ukraine. Sitting on the crossroads of Byzantium, Arabia and China, the Khazars traded silk, sable, wax,

---

* The site of modern-day Sevastopol.

silverware, spices and honey. They herded sheep and cattle, and sold fish from the Volga River.

In time, the Khazarian empire incorporated people from different races and religious traditions, welcoming Christians, Jews, Muslims and worshippers of the Mongol sky-god Tengri. Sometime in the ninth century, the Khazar nobility decided to convert to Judaism, which is astonishing, because unlike Muslims and Christians, Jews have rarely sought to convert other peoples. The Khazar legend of the conversion tells of Bulan, the Khagan of the Khazars, who summoned sages from the three great faiths to come to him and debate which was the best religion. The three sages argued for two days, and on the third day, the Khagan turned to the Christian priest.

'What do you think, priest?' he asked. 'Which of the *other* two religions do you prefer?'

'My lord,' he replied, 'the religion of the Israelites is better than that of the Muslims.'

Then the Khagan of the Khazars turned to the Muslim imam and asked, 'Which do *you* prefer, the religion of the Jews or the Christians?'

'The religion of the Israelites is preferable,' he replied.

'Well,' said the Khagan, 'you have both admitted with your own mouths that the religion of the Jews is better. Therefore I choose the religion of Israel.'

THE KHAZARS SPOKE a Turkic language, but after their conversion, their court documents were written in Hebrew. They cheekily issued coins with the legend 'Moses is the messenger of God', in imitation of the inscriptions on Muslim coins claiming that role for Muhammad. Although their Judaism set them apart from the great powers, it did, for a while, help them maintain a degree of independence from the Christian Romans and the Muslim caliphate. Both powers could tolerate a Jewish presence on their borders more readily than the religion of their rival.

Situated on the crossroads of different cultures and different faiths, Khazaria was rich, pragmatic and tolerant, a natural haven for the desperate and persecuted, and an obvious refuge for the deposed Justinian, who hungered for vengeance.

JUSTINIAN THE SLIT-NOSE and his band of followers arrived at the Khazar city of Doros, where they were warmly welcomed by Khagan Busir. The Khagan was happy to grant Justinian asylum, figuring it would be no bad thing to have a Roman emperor in his debt should Justinian ever return to power. The Khagan offered to bind them closer together by offering Justinian his sister's hand in marriage, which was accepted. We can only wonder what misgivings the Khazar bride might have had on her wedding day as she stood next to her new husband, a mutilated Roman emperor preoccupied with black revenge. Nonetheless, it does seem that a genuine affection grew between them. Justinian gave his bride a new Roman name, the highest he could bestow: Theodora, after the wife of the first Justinian. The newlyweds were given a home by the Sea of Azov, where Justinian settled down and waited to see how many soldiers the Khagan was prepared to grant him.

MEANWHILE IN CONSTANTINOPLE, the usurper Leontius crashed and burned. As Leontius struggled to hold his unhappy people together, Caliph Abd al-Malik sent an expedition to seize Carthage in North Africa. Leontius dispatched the imperial fleet to retake the city, but Arab reinforcements overwhelmed them, and the defeated fleet slunk back to Constantinople. North Africa was slipping out of the grasp of the Roman empire forever.

On the voyage home, the worried Romans wondered aloud how much blame Leontius would heap on them when they arrived in Constantinople. Then it occurred to someone that the loss would be much easier to explain to the emperor if the emperor were one of them. A vice-admiral named Apsimar was put forward as their leader. When the fleet disembarked, Apsimar's men bribed the guards at the Blachernae Gate to let them in. The rebels stormed the palace and Leontius was deposed. Now it was Leontius's turn to suffer disfigurement; his nose and tongue were slit, and he was banished to a monastery in the city.

The rebel leader Apsimar sat himself down on a very unsteady throne. He could claim no birthright and no real moral justification for seizing it. He was further troubled by the news from Cherson, that Justinian had escaped the city and was now the guest of the Khazars, and most likely plotting his return.

Apsimar wrote to the Khazars, offering fantastic bribes and gifts in return for Justinian's head. The Khagan, swayed by the prospect of gold today rather than a vague promise of gold tomorrow, sent a detachment of guards to Justinian's house for his 'protection'. Two men, Papatzys and Balgitzis, who were known to Justinian, were given orders to assassinate him.

But Theodora had been tipped off. Pregnant with their first child, her loyalties were now with her husband. Justinian made the first move: he invited Papatzys over, and when they were alone, Justinian strangled him with a cord. Then he sent for Balgitzis and strangled him too.

Justinian hastily farewelled Theodora and sent her back to her brother's house. A fishing boat was found. Justinian and a few followers climbed aboard and sailed out once again onto the Black Sea. The little boat pulled ashore near Cherson, where he was still a wanted man. Justinian kept out of sight while two of his men slipped into town to fetch supplies, and to organise a bigger, more robust ship.

The next day, Justinian and his band of supporters pushed out their new boat onto the Black Sea. After several hours the sky darkened and the seas began to churn. As the boat rolled and pitched on the stormy waves, the men on board began to fear for their lives. Justinian's manservant reached out to him, and begged him to make a deal with God.

'Promise Him you will be lenient with your enemies,' the manservant shouted, 'if God in his mercy will spare our lives through this storm.'

Justinian glowered, rose to his feet and shook his fist at the blackened sky.

'If I should spare a single one of them,' he bellowed, 'then may God drown me here!'

THE STORM PASSED and the sailors piloted the ship into the mouth of the Danube, into the lands of the Bulgars. Justinian sent a message to Tervel, the Bulgar Khan, and a deal was struck: a promise of gold, land and a Caesar's crown in return for fifteen thousand horsemen. After ten years of thwarted plans and near-escapes, Justinian the Slit-Nose had his army.

Golden Nose

IN THE SPRING OF 705, Justinian rode towards Constantinople at the head of fifteen thousand Bulgar horsemen. Intelligence of their impending arrival reached Apsimar, who sent an army to hold them off, but Justinian's forces had taken a different path through Thrace, slipped past Apsimar's men, and arrived at the foot of the Theodosian Walls unharmed. The Bulgars had brought no siege engines; Justinian had assured them that, as their rightful ruler, he was sure to be welcomed by his people, and that the gates would be flung open for him. But when Justinian arrived at the gate and appealed to the loyalty of the guards on the wall, they showered him with abuse and taunted him.

As Justinian suffered their insults helplessly, the Khan's men began to suspect they'd been sent on a fool's errand. They were dangerously exposed at the walls: when Apsimar's army returned, they could be outflanked, attacked from front and rear.

Running out of time and desperate to find a way in, Justinian led a band of soldiers on a night-time expedition to the north-west corner of the outer wall, where the fortifications bulged out to wrap themselves around the Blachernae Palace. The former emperor was familiar with the workings of the palace, and uncovered a narrow water conduit. Wasting no time, Justinian dived into the pipe, followed by his men. They crawled through the filthy tunnel and emerged inside the city unopposed. Apsimar, unsure of the loyalty of his troops, bolted from the palace.

It was a bloodless *coup d'état*. After an absence of ten years, the mutilated prince was once again the master of Constantinople.

JUSTINIAN SENT HIS GUARDS to track down Leontius and Apsimar. The usurpers were arrested and dragged through the streets in chains. The crowd were encouraged to jeer and throw shit and rubbish at the two men as they were hauled onto the floor of the Hippodrome. As they looked up they saw a strange spectacle: there in the imperial box was the gleaming visage of Justinian II, wearing a solid gold prosthetic nose.*

At Justinian's command, Leontius and Apsimar were brought into the imperial box and made to kneel before him. The emperor placed a foot on the neck of each man, then sat back to enjoy the races. When the day's events were over, Leontius and Apsimar were taken away and beheaded. Army officers loyal to Apsimar were arrested and executed, their bodies hung on a wall. The Patriarch Callinicus, who had joined the rebellion against Justinian all those years ago, was blinded and banished to a monastery in Rome.

Tervel the Bulgar Khan was welcomed into the city and rewarded, as Justinian had promised, with gold and land, and honoured with the title of Caesar, making Tervel the first foreigner ever to receive the ancient title.

Now it was time to reunite his family. He sent warships across the Black Sea to Khazaria to fetch his wife Theodora and their infant son Tiberius. Khagan Busir was only too happy to hand them over. The loyal Theodora was awarded the title of Augusta, and little Tiberius was crowned as co-emperor.

THE SECOND REIGN OF JUSTINIAN II was as restless and as unhappy as the first. He reinstated a reign of terror against his enemies, real and perceived. Paul the Deacon records that the emperor would order an execution almost as often as he would use his hand to wipe his runny butchered nose.

Regretting his decision to honour the deal with Tervel, Justinian sent an army to take back his lands, but his forces were routed.

---

* How a prosthetic nose might be mounted on the face isn't clear, and some historians have cast doubt on whether Justinian ever did wear a golden nose. It may have been part of a golden mask; such things were often worn by high-born leprosy sufferers.

The new Arab caliph invaded Anatolia and tore away more Roman territory for himself. Then a revolt broke out in Cherson. Justinian sent an expedition to suppress the rebellion, but at Cherson, his army decided to join the rebellion instead, denouncing Justinian and acclaiming their general Bardanes as their emperor. Justinian, on his way to Armenia, turned around and raced to get back to Constantinople before Bardanes could take his throne from him, but he was too late. Bardanes and his men entered the palace and began a purge of Justinian's supporters.

Theodora saw what was coming. She took the hand of little Tiberius and fled to the Church of St Mary in a desperate bid for sanctuary. Two of Bardanes's henchmen entered the church, where they found the terrified boy clinging with one arm to a leg of the altar table, and clutching a fragment of the True Cross in the other hand. Protective amulets had been strung around his neck. Theodora begged for mercy. One of the henchmen, Strouthos, seized the boy, took the True Cross from his hand and placed it on the altar table. He removed the amulets and placed them around his own neck. The boy was murdered in the doorway of the church. There is no record of what happened to Theodora.

Justinian was intercepted outside Chalcedon and arrested. All of his men deserted him. His son was dead. A rebel bodyguard named Helias, whose family had been killed on Justinian's orders, pushed through the crowd of soldiers and sliced off the emperor's head with a dagger. The dynasty of the great Heraclius was terminated at the point of a sword.

THE TALE OF JUSTINIAN THE SLIT-NOSE comes to us mostly through the *Chronicle of Theophanes*, an historical work compiled a century after Justinian's death, from other sources that are now lost. The tale of the disfigured emperor hellbent on bloody vengeance has the qualities of a Greek tragedy and a 1970s horror movie. Theophanes had his own axes to grind, and there is no way to know how much of Justinian's story is his own invention.

I'm struck, as I tell Joe this story, by the undertow of hatred and violence in Constantinople at this time. Death demands more death, and a moral threshold is crossed. This is one of those moments in history when psychopathic leaders gain the upper hand, and the normal human sanctions against killing disappear: the Jacobin terror of revolutionary France, Indonesia's year of living dangerously, the *Kristallnacht* of the Nazis, the Rwandan massacres. In such moments, death becomes as commonplace as eating and drinking. Passionless political killing mutates into casual murder for pleasure, and something unravels as the sight of helpless people invokes not pity, but its opposite, a kind of smiling contempt. The killing picks up momentum and corpses pile up until death has had its fill and can consume no more.

The modern mind might shrink from metaphysical representations of evil, but in the medieval world, the real culprit behind the chaos was easily identified. *Netherlandish Proverbs*, a sixteenth-century work by Pieter Bruegel, is a sprawling portrait of a Flemish village swirling with anarchy. Within this topsy-turvy world Bruegel illustrates 112 separate proverbs of stupidity and wickedness: a man fills in a well after his calf has drowned in it, another man tries to shear a pig, two naked arses shit from a broken privy into the stream below, the blind are leading the blind, and a fool in a cap bangs his head against a brick wall. And in the centre of it all, seated on a wooden throne, is the author of this spiralling madness, the Devil himself: a fat woodland creature with buckshot eyes and two dead branches sprouting from his head.

Detail: Netherlandish Proverbs, Pieter Bruegel.

Gog and Magog

THE YEARS OF ARAB conquest were, for the Romans, an anxious time. Many Christians in their former provinces willingly converted to Islam, if only to avoid the *jizya*, the tax levied by the caliphate on non-Muslims. Those who stayed loyal to the faith looked for reassurance, or at least an explanation for why so much misfortune had been brought upon the Christian empire of the Romans.

The hour was late. It was surely only a matter of time before the Arabs would focus their attention on Constantinople; the Queen of Cities was too great a prize to be ignored. The stakes were so very high because the fate of the city was linked to the fate of the universe itself. If Constantinople, the Christ-guarded city, was to be overrun by the Ishmaelites, then its destruction must inevitably trigger the apocalypse.

To make sense of the horribly disordered world they now found themselves in, Roman scholars turned to the prophecies embedded in the scriptures, to Revelation, the hallucinatory endnote of the Bible. The author of Revelation, John of Patmos, prophesied that in the final convulsion of the apocalypse, there would be a war between Satan and the Heavenly City:

> *When the thousand years are over, Satan will be released from his prison and will go out to deceive the nations in the four corners of the Earth – Gog and Magog – and to gather them for battle. In number they are like the sand on the seashore.*
>
> *And they came up on the broad plain of the earth and surrounded the camp of the saints and the beloved city, and fire came down from heaven and devoured them.*

The eyes of priests and scholars lit upon the mysterious names Gog and Magog. Who were these numberless hordes dwelling in the far reaches of the earth?

They found a clue in the legend of the greatest general of the ancient world: Alexander the Great. Alexander had perished some three hundred years before the birth of Christ, but the tales of his conquests were told and retold, written and rewritten. A collection of stories of his exploits known as the *Alexander Romance* became wildly popular in the early Middle Ages, particularly in Constantinople. In these tales, Alexander enjoys fabulous adventures: he meets centaurs and sirens, travels to a city with twelve towers of gold and emerald, encounters an island with a fleshy surface that turns out to be a whale, which plunges into the depths, nearly drowning him.

The hero of the *Alexander Romance* bears only fleeting resemblance to the historical Alexander; he was presented to Christian readers not as a pagan, but as a kind of harbinger of Christianity, a pious follower of the One True God. And it was here that Christians thought they could see the hand of God at work centuries before the feet of Jesus walked the Earth.

ALEXANDER OF MACEDONIA, young, brilliant and handsome, set out one day to fight the Belsyrians, who had refused to submit to his rule. Alexander's men, clad in golden breastplates, were victorious and they pursued the fleeing Belsyrians for fifty days into the wilds of the north-east, all the way to the borders of the Unseen World.

Eventually Alexander and his men chased the Belsyrians to a pair of dark mountains, known as 'the Breasts of the North'. The people of this place were of a foul and unclean nature; some with a single horn growing out of their heads, others with the feet of an elephant or the head of a wolf. The wretched creatures ate 'dogs, flies, snakes, aborted foetuses, dead bodies and unformed human embryos' and the names of their nations were Gog and Magog.

Alexander understood at once that these creatures posed a mortal threat to the civilised world. He studied the pass between the two mountains, and realised that if he could somehow close it up, all the hordes of the Unseen World would be trapped behind it. He fell to his knees and asked almighty God to bring the two mountains together. With that, the mountains groaned and shuffled and the gap was closed.

The young conqueror then ordered his men to construct gigantic gates of bronze to stop up the narrow space that remained between the two mountains. Alexander, well pleased with his work, went on his way. And the people of Gog and Magog remain trapped in that dark place to this day, seething at the bronze gates, waiting ... waiting ...

Detail of mosaic of Alexander the Great.

THE NAME-CHECKING of Gog and Magog in the *Alexander Romance* was further proof to the Romans, if any was needed, of the soundness of the scriptures, and of Revelation. But still, the holy book left them puzzled as to what role they would play on the Day of Judgement. The waters of the Apocalypse had been muddied somewhat by the ideas of the early Christians. Revelation had been written at a time when the empire was still pagan, and emperors were persecutors. Many early Christians had taken the most lurid figure in John's vision, the Great Whore of Babylon, as a symbol of the Roman empire in all its wickedness and cruelty. But now that the Romans had been redeemed in the blood of Christ, the old correlation between the empire and the Great Whore could no longer be accepted. A different role had to be found for the empire, and for the emperor, in the final crisis before the Second Coming.

THEN, AT THE CLOSE of the seventh century, a powerful new vision of the apocalypse surfaced in Constantinople. The vision was attributed (falsely, as it turned out) to a fourth-century father of the church, Methodius of Olympus.

The *Apocalypse of Pseudo-Methodius* put Revelation entirely to one side and drew on other isolated strands of scripture to find a much more favourable and central role for the Roman empire in the final war between heaven and hell. Although the author's vision was somewhat bleak, ultimately he offered reassurance that the victories of the Ishmaelites were all part of the plan, and that Christendom would ultimately be redeemed by the return of Christ in triumph.

The *Apocalypse* speaks of a time when the Ishmaelites will overrun the lands of the Persians and the Romans. From the vantage point of the late seventh century, these prophecies had uncannily already come to pass. In the next phase, the book predicts the walls of Constantinople will be breached: 'Woe to you, city of Byzantium, because Ishmael overtakes you. For every horse of Ishmael will pass through, and the first among them will pitch his tent before you and will break down the Gate of the Wooden Circus.'

But the invasion of Constantinople will mark a turning point. God will galvanise the emperor and the Romans into action. They will retake the lands stolen from them by the Muslims, and extract a terrible vengeance. The emperor's anger will burn up the conquered lands until they are barren and quiet once again.

For a brief interregnum there will be joy and peace for the Christians. But then, the *Apocalypse* prophesies, Satan will open up the gates of the north, and the unclean nations of Gog and Magog will stream out across the face of the Earth like locusts.

Then, when all seems lost, a mighty angel will descend from heaven and annihilate the hordes of hell in a single moment. With Gog and Magog dead, the last emperor of the Romans will perform one last solemn duty:

> The king of the Romans will go up to Golgotha, where the timber of the Cross was fixed at the place in which Christ our lord endured death. And the king of the Romans will take his crown and place it on the Cross and spread out his hands to heaven and deliver the kingdom of the Christians to God.'

At this moment the emperor's diadem will ascend into heaven and the last emperor, having completed his duties, will drop dead at the foot of the cross, and the Earth will be given over to the temporary rule of the Antichrist.

FOR THE BELEAGUERED ROMANS, the *Apocalypse* gave a shape and meaning to events that would otherwise seem symptomatic of a disordered universe. Its fierce imagery was imprinted on the Byzantine imagination, and its prophecies remembered when the empire entered its death throes at the end of the Middle Ages.

But as the Christian calendar clocked over into the eighth century, the Romans continued to lose more lands to the caliphate. The armies of Allah expanded eastward into Central Asia and westward across North Africa, all the way to the Pillars of Hercules in modern-day Morocco. Still restless for conquest, they sent their transports across the straits of Gibraltar into Spain.*

---

* 'Gibraltar' is derived from the original Arabic name *Jabal Ṭāriq*: 'Mountain of Tariq', after Tariq ibn-Ziyad, the Umayyad general who spearheaded the Muslim invasion into Spain.

The sudden eruption of Arab power constitutes one of the biggest power shifts in the history of the world, all of it achieved less than a century from the death of Muhammad. By 712, an Arab trader could conceivably set out from the banks of the Indus River and ride west continuously through Arab-controlled lands all the way to the surf of the Atlantic coast.

The despised desert nomads were no longer embattled upstarts. Winning an empire had made them supremely self-confident, and they now sought to crown their glory with the Queen of Cities, which their Caliph planned to remake as his new capital.

MEANWHILE, Constantinople had fallen into a cycle of almost continuous upheaval. Bardanes, who had taken the throne from Justinian II, was a man of limited ambitions. He took his elevation to the purple to mean that he was done with the tiresome struggle for power, and he now had licence to pursue his twin passions: getting into complex theological disputes with church leaders, and gorging himself on whatever pleasures he could purchase with imperial gold.

Just nineteen months into his reign, after enjoying a long morning banquet with his friends, Bardanes settled into an afternoon nap. A group of soldiers entered his chamber, dragged him into the Hippodrome and gouged his eyes out. This was, like the slitting of the nose, a disfigurement that stopped short of regicide, but still effectively disqualified him from any hope of a return to power

Anastasius II, a competent bureaucrat, stepped up to the vacant throne. The new emperor got to work, fixing the mess left to him by his predecessor. The strategic outlook had further deteriorated. Imperial spies in the east brought alarming news to Constantinople: the Arabs were building ships in their Mediterranean ports and moving troops towards the border. All the evidence pointed to a major assault on Constantinople by land and sea.

The Dream of al-Qustantiniyah

THE CALIPH OF THE ARAB EMPIRE was a popular and admired leader, famous for his appetite and oratory skills. His name was Sulayman bin Abd al-Malik, and in that promising summer of 715 his mind was filled with the singular object of his longing: al-Qustantiniyah, the city of Constantinople. The caliph's poetic imagination had been inflamed by an Islamic prophecy, which foretold that the capital of the Romans would one day fall to a great Muslim leader with the name of a prophet. Sulayman (Solomon) believed he might be that man. Sulayman now made a dramatic prophecy of his own, vowing, 'I shall not cease from the struggle with Constantinople; I will either force my way in, or I will bring down the whole Arab dominion'.

Sulayman was too ill to lead the expedition himself, so he entrusted the leadership of his armies to his brother, Maslama, providing him with a military force of overwhelming strength: a hundred thousand men and eighteen hundred ships, equipped for an assault by land and sea.

As word spread of Maslama's campaign, thousands of volunteers from all over the Muslim world rushed to join up, inspired by the call to *jihad* and enticed by the fabulous riches that were said to be within the Queen of Cities. Rich men donated weapons, horses, camels and donkeys, in the expectation they would be repaid many times over.

AS SULAYMAN MOVED HIS FORCES into a state of readiness his designs on Constantinople became clear to everyone in the eastern Mediterranean. It dawned on the Romans that a critical moment in the history of the world was almost upon them. Like the Arabs, they saw themselves as central actors in a great cosmic-historical drama, but the script was being handed to them a page at a time, and now the plot seemed to be directing them towards some terrible climax, an apocalypse. The full might of the Saracens was gathered and pointed at their precious city, the beating heart of Christ's kingdom on Earth. Surely, they reasoned, God would not abandon his chosen people in this critical hour? Fervent prayers were directed to the Blessed Virgin, begging her to intercede on their behalf.

Emperor Anastasius went about preparing the city for the coming siege. Catapults were hauled up onto the ramparts of the Theodosian Walls, the sea walls were repaired and strengthened, the city's granaries were filled to the brim and an edict was issued, stating that every family should store enough food to sustain itself for three years. Anyone unable to do so was advised to get out now. Meanwhile Anastasius tried to stall for time by attempting to negotiate a diplomatic settlement.

But as Anastasius diligently prepared for the frontal assault, he was brought down by a stab in the back. The same feckless troops who had installed him two years previously now objected to his strict measures and deposed him, sending him to a monastery. The army cast about for a compliant figure to replace Anastasius, and found one in a meek tax collector named Theodosius, who was terrified by their proposal and fled into the forest to hide. He was duly tracked down and urged at the point of a sword to accept the crown. Then, in March 717, Theodosius too was deposed by a skilful young general, who would come to be known as Leo the Isaurian.

Konon the Fox

LEO THE ISAURIAN was not born with the name Leo, and neither did he come from Isauria. His name was Konon and he was from a peasant family in the Syrian border town of Germanicaea, near the Taurus Mountains.* His village had been absorbed into the Arab caliphate before he was born, and so Konon grew up familiar with Arab customs and he spoke the language fluently.

Konon joined the army, where his talents were spotted by Justinian II, who appointed him as military commander of Anatolia. He was headquartered at the frontline fortress of Amorium in Asia Minor, which was where the legend of his fox-like cunning began to emerge.

The Arab generals in Anatolia were hoping to soften enemy resistance by exploiting rivalries and jealousies among the Roman leaders. The Arabs knew that Konon was being spoken of as a future emperor, and so, when they approached the fortress of Amorium, their soldiers fanned out along the walls, and mischievously began to chant 'Long live the Emperor Konon! Long live the Emperor Konon!'

The Arab commander then sent a message to Konon inside the fortress: 'We know that the empire will soon devolve upon you. Let us talk peace together.'

Konon replied, 'If you truly desire peace, then why do you blockade my fortress?'

The general promised to pull back his men if Konon agreed to talk.

The details in the historical accounts are confusing, but it seems the Arabs offered Konon a deal: if he agreed to become a vassal of

---

* Now known as the Turkish city of Maraş, famous for its production of *salep* and Turkish ice-cream.

the caliph, they would pay him secretly and help to install him in Constantinople as the 'King' of the Romans. This, they explained, would be a good outcome for everyone: Konon would get his throne, and Constantinople would be won for the caliphate without bloodshed. Konon, with his easy familiarity with Arab ways, would make a perfect puppet king.

What followed next isn't clear. In some histories it's surmised that Konon told the general that yes, of course he would agree to the deal, but his people would never accept him as emperor if they suspected he was the caliph's agent, so it was in everyone's best interests for the Arab armies to withdraw from Amorium.

The general agreed. Having confused the Arab commander for the moment, Konon escaped from Amorium with his men, and marched on Constantinople, which was in a state of anarchy. At the Theodosian Walls, Konon gave assurances to the hapless Emperor Theodosius that if he abdicated, he and his family would be well treated. Theodosius was only too happy to comply and he retired to a monastery. Konon, having won the support of the senate and the Patriarch, entered the city through the Golden Gate and was crowned Emperor Leo III in the Hagia Sophia. Later he would be nicknamed Leo the Isaurian.

LEO HAD COME TO THE THRONE, like Heraclius, in a moment of mortal peril. His forces were weak and his people demoralised. Constantinople had boiled over with revolutionary violence seven times in the past twenty-two years. While the Romans were preoccupied with internal divisions, the Bulgars had chipped away at their lands in the Balkans, and the Arabs had torn away at their heartland in Asia Minor. And now the armies of Allah were less than six months away from the capital of Christendom itself.

The Burning Ships

THE SENSE of impending doom in the city only deepened as Maslama and his hundred-thousand-strong army marched across Asia Minor to the shores of the Hellespont to meet their transport ships, which ferried them over to the European side of the strait. On 15 August, Maslama arrived on the outskirts of Constantinople, and positioned his men in fortified camps along the entire length of the Theodosian Walls.

Maslama's confidence may have been bolstered by an expectation that the emperor was secretly on his side. Maslama had no need to sacrifice his magnificent army with an assault on the walls; all he had to do was wait for Leo to persuade his people that resistance was useless, and that it was in everyone's best interests to open the gates and avoid a bloodbath. Maslama assumed, not unreasonably, that Leo would rather be the puppet king of an intact city than a dead ruler in a smoking ruin. Leo, in his letters to Maslama, hinted that surrender would be the only humane solution, but still the city's gates remained closed and barred.

The tone of their correspondence became increasingly tense as Leo stalled for time. With each day, Maslama's hopes of a bloodless victory faded into bitter disappointment.

In the meantime Leo struck a deal with Tervel, the Bulgarian khagan, who had concluded he was better off with the weaker Romans as neighbours than the dangerously strong Arab caliphate. Late one night Tervel sent a group of Bulgar raiders on a surprise attack into the Arab camps. Dozens of soldiers, including some men belonging to Maslama's personal guard, were cut down. Several days later, a party of Arab soldiers went foraging for food in a nearby forest and ran into another group of Bulgarians, and were killed to a man.

Maslama was put on notice that it was now too dangerous to

send his men to forage for supplies in the Thracian countryside. Reluctantly, he was forced to accept he'd been duped by Leo, who clearly had no intention to surrender. The only strategy left to Maslama was to bring in his navy to blockade the city, choke off its food supply and force the Christians to come to terms.

ON 3 SEPTEMBER, the Caliph's 1800 war galleys were sighted on the Sea of Marmara. Men and women watching on the walls could only gawp in wonder and terror as the vast armada swept into the Bosphorus. But as the rearguard of the Arab fleet passed Acropolis Point, the wind fell away, and twenty heavy transport galleys, ferrying two thousand marines, dropped out of formation, and were dragged by the current towards the sea walls.

Leo seized the moment and gave the order to attack. A squadron of *dromons* – Roman war galleys – charged out of the Golden Horn and bore down on the straggling Arab transports. The Arab marines on deck fired a volley of defensive arrows, but the Roman ships still pushed forwards, closing the distance.

Then, with a roar and a blast of thick black smoke, a jet of liquid fire spewed from the prows of the Roman galleys. The Arab transports were suddenly engulfed with a flaming, sticky fluid that set the sails and decks ablaze. Arab marines and sailors were burnt alive or compelled to leap into the fast-moving currents of the Bosphorus.

The prows of the Roman ships spewed more of this liquid fire onto the water, but somehow the flames were not extinguished, and the hellish substance continued to burn on the water's surface, igniting more of the slow-moving Arab ships. The rest of the fleet could only look on as their transports were incinerated, the roar of the flames mixed with groaning timbers and the screams of dying men. The charred hulks broke apart and disintegrated.

*Image of Greek Fire, from an illuminated manuscript, the Madrid
Skylitzes. The caption above the dromon reads: 'the fleet of
the Romans setting ablaze the fleet of the enemies'.*

THE EXACT FORMULA for this flaming liquid, which became
known to the world as Greek fire, is unknown. It was the Romans'
most closely held state secret and the recipe died with the empire.
Most likely it was some combination of pine resin, crude petroleum,
quicklime, sulphur and potassium nitrate, mixed up to form a
thick, black liquid. The incendiary fluid was carried aboard Roman
warships in a heated cauldron to make it less viscous. Once the
ship came within range of the enemy, the liquid was siphoned up
bronze pipes to a nozzle fitted to the prow, where it was ignited, and
then spewed out, like a flamethrower. It's not hard to imagine how
its use could have backfired horribly, but careful engineering and
meticulous seamanship brought the full power of Greek fire to bear
on the empire's enemies at the critical moment. And it was no less
effective as an instrument of propaganda: what better way to destroy
an infidel navy than by sending it to a flaming hell?

Typically, the Christian Romans credited the invention of Greek
fire not to their own human ingenuity but to divine favour. They
preferred to think of themselves as righteous and pious, rather than

clever and resourceful. And if they *were* clever and resourceful, that was surely a sign of God's favour too.

The destruction of the Arab transports was a stunning victory, witnessed by many on the city walls, and an unmistakable sign that the Blessed Virgin had come to the aid of her people at last. The larger part of the Arab fleet was still intact, but the spectacle had shocked and demoralised Maslama's men. Their ships withdrew to safer positions upstream, and a disappointed Maslama resumed his post at the Theodosian Walls.

THE WARMER MONTHS faded into autumn and the news came to Constantinople that Caliph Sulayman had dropped dead in Ramla at the age of forty-three.* This, too, was seen by the Romans as an encouraging sign from God. Then a brutal winter descended on Constantinople, the coldest anyone could remember.

Maslama's men suffered badly as they shivered in their flimsy tents outside the walls. Disease ran through the camps, and the Arab soldiers were forced to eat their camels, horses and donkeys. The winter snow came early and lay on the ground for three months. As the ground became hard and frozen, the invaders found they could no longer bury their dead, and had to throw their corpses into the Marmara.

Arab sources record that it was at this time that Leo reopened negotiations with Maslama. Leo was still being coy, holding out hope that he might yet surrender the city to end the siege.

According to these sources, Leo's correspondence with Maslama went something like this: 'If I am to surrender my city to you, I must persuade my people that all further resistance is futile.'

'How can I help you to persuade your people of this?'

---

* Sulayman's tomb in the Syrian town of Dabiq was demolished in 2014 by ISIS fighters.

'If you were to burn your remaining grain supplies, it would signal to my people that you are preparing for an all-out attack … that you are so completely confident of success, you can afford to destroy your supplies.'

The Arab histories record, implausibly, that Maslama did indeed burn his grain supplies.* Leo did not open the gates, and left Maslama and his starving men still stranded outside the walls.

Byzantine accounts say nothing of this episode and the story sounds preposterous, but historians have struggled to understand why the Arabs would fabricate such a tale, given that it paints their leadership in such a poor light. Perhaps the point of the Arab account was to shift the blame for the debacle entirely onto Maslama, or perhaps it's simply one of those fables of medieval trickery that the Arabs enjoyed so much, a tale intended to illustrate a larger truth about Leo's cunning and treachery.

UMAR, THE NEW CALIPH, shocked by the reports he was receiving, sent a new armada of nearly eight hundred ships, stocked with food supplies and weaponry, for the beleaguered Maslama. The Arab ships entered the Bosphorus, but the crews were made up almost entirely of Christian Egyptian galley slaves, and when they caught sight of Constantinople they defected en masse to the Romans, rowing over to the sea walls with their supplies, shouting 'Long live the Emperor!'

The Egyptian Christians were only too eager to tell Leo everything they knew of the positions of the Arab fleet. Leo sent out another squadron of *dromons* to destroy it with Greek fire. The cargo of the relief ships was plundered and brought into the city. Maslama had

---

* In another version, Leo persuades Maslama to hand over his grain supplies to *him*.

been counting on those supplies to get his army through the coming months. Instead, his own relief ships had resupplied the city, while his army continued to starve.

The caliph sent another reserve army to meet up with Maslama. But the Romans were tipped off. The emperor despatched a platoon of soldiers and officers, who slipped across the Bosphorus, and ambushed the relief army on the road to Nicomedia.

Maslama was agonising over whether he should break off the siege when Tervel's Bulgarian horsemen descended once again on his exhausted, sick and hungry troops. In what must have been a pitiful, bloody sight, an estimated 22,000 men were slaughtered.

And with that, Caliph Umar ordered an end to the siege and a complete withdrawal of all the Arab land and sea forces. But more tribulations were in store for what was left of the caliph's navy: as the fleet set out on its return voyage, it was hit by a storm on the Sea of Marmara. Dozens of ships were lost, but the fleet pressed on. Another storm struck them off the coast of Rhodes and more ships were destroyed.

There was still a final blow to come: as the remainder of the caliph's ships passed warily through the Aegean Sea, the volcanic island of Thera erupted, sending a shower of sizzling ashes onto the decks and sails of the fleet. Of the 2600 ships that had left the Arab coastal ports to conquer Constantinople, only five returned.

'HOW CAN THAT story possibly be true?'

Joe is shaking his head. We're on the ferry to Kadıköy, on the Asian side of the Bosphorus, not far from where Maslama's defeated army crossed back into Asia Minor. In Roman times, Kadıköy was the city of Chalcedon.

'Well, it's something that happened thirteen centuries ago. There are two Roman accounts of the siege, but they were written a century later. The Arab histories were compiled long after the event too, but all the accounts pretty much agree on the basic details: the Umayyad Arabs came in great numbers by land and by sea, and they put the city to siege for thirteen months, but Leo outfoxed the invaders, who were also let down by a horrible streak of bad luck. Both sides also thought that God had intervened decisively; what else could explain the horrible ordeal the Arabs went through?'

'I dunno. It's just bad luck.'

'They didn't believe in bad luck. The Arabs saw it as punishment for their own arrogance and pride, a sin the Prophet had warned against many times.'

THE DEPARTURE of the Arab forces was greeted with wild joy and gratitude on the streets of Constantinople. The end of the siege coincided with the feast of the Assumption of the Blessed Virgin Mary, and the Roman victory was ascribed to her divine intervention.

All the Christian lands to the west of Constantinople owed the city a great debt. The shield of Constantinople had absorbed the hammer blows of Islamic power and kept them safe from the caliph's conquering armies. In some parallel universe, there is a moment when Leo opens the gates of Constantinople, and the caliphate incorporates all of Europe into the House of Islam. But, as it happened, the shield of Constantinople enabled a feeble and fragmented Christian Europe to survive, stabilise and eventually thrive.

Arab self-confidence was momentarily chastened, and the focus and enthusiasm of the caliphate shifted to the richer, more dynamic societies of the east, where its interaction with Indian and Persian cultures would inspire a golden age of Arab science and literature.

Europe, cut off from the cultural riches of the east, became a lonely backwater.

CHAPTER SIX

Uncreated Light

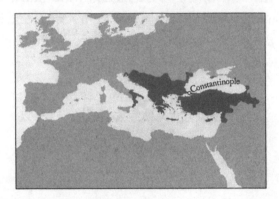

The empire in 1025, at its greatest extent in the medieval era.

Bucoleon

OUR HOTEL IS IN A RENOVATED nineteenth-century building in an older district between the Hagia Sophia and the Sea of Marmara. The streets are narrow and cramped, lined with three- and four-storey buildings, tourist shops and restaurants with laminated menus in English and German. There is a railway line a few blocks away, with houses and apartments pushed up together on both sides of the tracks. A thousand years ago, this was the emperor's polo field.

This whole area is built on the site of what was once the Great Palace: the empire's administrative nerve centre, a complex of pavilions and terraces that ran from the Augustaeum down to the sea walls. This was the home of Constantine, Justinian and Heraclius.

On most days, hundreds of staff members and courtiers would scuttle between the colonnaded pavilions. The Magnaura Palace served as the meeting place for the senate. The imperial family entertained their guests at the lavish Banquet Hall of the Nineteen Couches, where they dined like the ancient Romans. Emperors held court in the Chrysotriklinos, the marble-panelled octagonal throne room. The four hundred men of the palace guards were housed in two sets of barracks, while the imperial family slept in the perfumed halls of the Palace of Daphne.

The polo field, the Tzykanisterion, occupied an open, grassy space between the hall of the palace guards and the sea walls. Polo, like chess, was a game imported from Persia and adapted to local rules. Two teams competed on horseback to lob a leather ball into the opposing team's goal, using sticks with little nets on the end. Byzantine polo was played hard and fast: Alexius I Comnene was badly injured in one bout, Alexander III died on the field from a heart attack.

TODAY, IN THIS RESIDENTIAL DISTRICT, nearly every visible sign of the Great Palace has been obliterated, aside from one lonely ruin, which Joe and I are trying to find. We cross the railway bridge and thread our way through some narrow lanes down to Kennedy Caddesi, the waterside motorway that follows the contours of the old sea walls. We walk for a block to a small park and look up. High up on a wall, we see an unremarkable set of three marble-framed doorways, set in a crumbling wall of Roman bricks. In Justinian's time, these porticos opened out onto the marbled balcony of the Bucoleon Palace. On summer nights, he and Theodora would have passed through these doors to admire the moonlit view of the Sea of Marmara. But today these three frames are all that's left of the

Bucoleon Palace; the other ruins were demolished in the nineteenth century to make way for the railway line.

As we gaze at the porticos, I try to conjure up the lost grandeur of what was once the most beautiful palace in Europe, but it's not really working and I feel a bit silly and defeated. I can see Joe's wondering why we've spent half an hour hiking through the back streets of Istanbul just to look at some vine-entangled frames beside a roaring motorway.

Later that day we stop to stare at what appears to be the façade of a ruined Byzantine building, a three-storied set of brick arches. Was this also part of the imperial palace? A local guy stands next to me, sipping coffee, also staring at the ruin.

'It's amazing, isn't it?' he says.

'Yes. It must have been a great building. Maybe a palace?' I reply.

'A great palace. Yes, a great palace. But ...' he lowers his voice conspiratorially, 'there is a more important palace nearby.' He gestures at the shop behind us. 'It is my carpet warehouse.'

He grins at me good-naturedly and we both burst out laughing.

THE GREAT PALACE didn't die of Turkish neglect, but fell into disuse long before the Ottomans arrived. In its later centuries, the empire's rulers preferred to live in the Blachernae Palace at the other end of the city. As the empire declined, there was barely enough gold to pay for the city's defence, let alone for the upkeep of the Great Palace. When Sultan Mehmed II inspected his newly conquered city in 1453, he found the Great Palace in such an appalling state, he had most of it demolished.

In the twentieth century, an archaeological excavation uncovered stunning Roman floor mosaics from the palace near the Blue Mosque, which are on display at Istanbul's Mosaic Museum. The mosaics are dated to Justinian's reign and contain dramatic scenes of conflict between natural and mythological creatures: a gryphon devouring a lizard, a lion fighting an elephant. Elsewhere a man milks a goat and a mare suckles its foal. Further archaeological discoveries have been made in the area, but so much of the Great Palace still lies undisturbed, like a ghostly mausoleum, under blocks of apartments, the railway line and the Blue Mosque.

The Broken Icon

VISITORS TO THE GREAT PALACE COMPLEX would enter through the Chalke Gate, a grand marble vestibule with heavy bronze doors, located in the south-east corner of the Augustaeum. Above the entrance to the Chalke Gate stood an icon of Christ the Pantocrator, the universal ruler.

Reconstruction of the Chalke Gate (Antoine Helbert).

One evening in 726, a team of soldiers appeared at the gate, and to the shock of the passersby in the square, they set to work pulling down the icon. A riot broke out and two of the soldiers were lynched. Word spread through Constantinople about the incident: what was the emperor thinking, removing a much-loved, holy object from his palace gate?

Emperor Leo III had deftly led his people to a great victory against the might of the Arab empire in the 717 siege, but for all his success, Leo's authority was clothed in only the thinnest fabric of legitimacy. He was still a usurper, and the Arabs were still strong.

Leo tried to curry divine favour by issuing a new set of laws outlawing abortion and prescribing the death penalty for homosexuality. But even this was shown to have little effect when, two months later, the volcanic island of Thera blew its top, shrouding the whole region under a plume of ash and smoke. Leo concluded it was time to crack down on the worship of icons.

THE VENERATION OF ICONS linked the empire to its pagan past; ancient Greeks and Romans had enjoyed portraying the gods in their art and sculpture. It was only natural that the manufacture of sacred likenesses should have been carried over into the Christian era. Nike was transmuted into an angel, Zeus into God the father. Jesus, with his nimbus of golden light, resembled Sol Invictus, the god of the unconquered sun.

In the homes of Constantinople, the household icon of a saint would be spoken of with great respect and affection, like an honoured member of the family. These golden representations of wide-eyed saints and martyrs seemed to stare searchingly into the soul of the devotee. Women, in particular, treasured the direct access to the divine that icons brought into their daily lives, a relationship unmediated by priests, monks and bishops. Icons brought the stories of the Bible to the illiterate, delivering the full emotional power of the scriptures in a single moment.

Icons appears to have been wholly uncontroversial until the rise of Islam forced a rethink. Muslims accused the Christians of pagan idolatry, of backsliding against the second commandment delivered to Moses, 'You shall not make for yourself a graven image, or any likeness of anything that is in heaven above, or that is in the earth beneath, or that is in the water under the earth; you shall not bow down to them or serve them'.

The ancient commandment could hardly have been clearer. And yet, in the eyes of Muslims and Jews, icon worship was proof the Romans had slipped back into their bad old habits of bowing down to stone and wooden idols. In 721, Yazid II banned Christian icons throughout the caliphate, a decree that may have shamed the Romans: were the Arab infidels forcing the Christians to do something they should have done anyway? Iconophiles or 'icon lovers' were quick to point out the difference between icon veneration – the paying of respect – and full-blown adoration or idolatry. But the eruption of Thera prompted the emperor to draw the line. In 726, Leo decreed that the crucifix, the image of Christ crucified, should be replaced everywhere by the simple cross. Furthermore, public icons in the city were to be destroyed or covered in whitewash.

The attack on holy images, which was later dubbed 'iconoclasm', the breaking of icons, provoked an immediate and hostile reaction from the population. Theodore, the abbot of the monastery of Stoudios, was so incensed and distressed, he upbraided Leo to his face: 'Your responsibility Emperor,' he warned, 'is with affairs of state and military matters. Give your mind to these, and leave the Church to its pastors and teachers.'

Fortunately for Leo, the introduction of the new icon policy was followed by several years of Roman military success in the struggle against the Arabs, which allowed him to claim divine approval for the ban. But in 740, an earthquake shook Constantinople, an event predictably interpreted by iconophiles as a sign of God's anger at the destruction of holy images. This constant taking of God's emotional temperature, agonisingly reassessed after every military campaign or natural disaster, was exhausting and dispiriting. Iconoclasm was a self-inflicted wound on the empire that would be reopened again and again.

LEO III DIED OF OEDEMA in June 741 and the throne passed on to his eldest son, crowned Constantine V. The new emperor made it known he would keep hammering away at the iconoclastic nail. Military success against the caliphate emboldened him to take matters a step further. In 753 Constantine V decreed that the veneration of icons would henceforth be regarded as a heresy, and he launched a persecution of the iconophiles: monasteries were destroyed, dissident monks and nuns were forced to renounce their vows and marry each other in mock ceremonies in the Hippodrome. Those who refused to renounce icons were tortured and blinded.

In 766 Constantine rooted out a conspiracy against him by iconophile sympathisers within the palace. Everyone associated with the plot was beheaded, blinded or flogged. After that, he encountered no more conspiracies, but he had created deep divisions within the empire, and alienated church leaders outside the empire's frontiers. In 775 Constantine was struck down with a fever while leading a campaign against the Bulgars. He died on the way back to Constantinople.

CONSTANTINE V HAD BEEN a competent, if somewhat cruel, ruler, but the man's name and reputation suffered greatly at the hands of Theophanes the Confessor, the chief historian of this period and an ardent iconophile. Other Constantines would have phrases like 'the Great' or 'Born in the Purple' chiselled after their names; Constantine V, however, is remembered as Constantine Copronymus – 'Constantine the Shit-Named', after iconophiles spread a spiteful rumour that the emperor had disgraced himself as a baby by defecating in the baptismal font at his christening.

NOW THE THRONE PASSED to Constantine's eldest son, Leo IV. The new Leo was of a milder temperament than his father, and quietly attempted to heal divisions in the capital while maintaining official opposition to icons. In 780, Leo was shocked to discover two icons hidden among the belongings of his wife, the Empress Irene, which had been smuggled into the palace by members of his own staff. Leo was furious that his wife and his servants had conspired to keep secrets from him, and had his chamberlain flogged. The imperial couple became estranged, and Leo refused to share the marriage bed with Irene.

Then in September, Irene emerged from the palace with shocking news: Leo was dead. The emperor, she said, had been behaving strangely. He had demanded a jewelled crown be brought to him, but when he placed it on his head, the precious stones caused boils to break out all over his scalp. The infection was followed by a fever, then death.

This unlikely story has led historians to assume Leo's demise was engineered by Irene, acting in concert with senior palace officials with iconophile sympathies. But no one saw fit to question the story, and so Irene's nine-year-old son, Constantine VI, became emperor, with his mother the empress-regent. But Irene never saw herself as a stopgap ruler. She was twenty-five years old, and just getting started.

Basilissa and Basileus

IRENE WAS BORN into a prominent family in Athens. It's likely she was selected as a suitable wife for Leo in a bride-show, a ceremony where beautiful, refined young women were paraded for inspection before the imperial family. Her future father-in-law arranged for Irene to enter Constantinople in style on All Saints' Day 769: she crossed the Bosphorus in a Roman galley, surrounded by imperial warships festooned with silk streamers. Cheering crowds greeted her procession through the city. She was crowned Irene Augusta and married to Leo in a church within the palace grounds.

Irene lived in the shadow of power as empress-consort for twelve years before her husband's death opened the way for her to become the most powerful empress in the long history of the Roman empire, more powerful even than Theodora, who shared her imperium with Justinian.

SEEING THAT CONTROL of the empire had passed to a woman and a child, ambitious men thought they could sense weakness at the top. A conspiracy formed, almost immediately, to replace Irene and her son with one of Leo's half-brothers, Nicephorus. Irene disposed of the plot cleverly and bloodlessly by forcing Nicephorus and his four brothers to be tonsured and ordained as monks, which immediately disqualified them from the throne. Irene 'honoured' their entry into the priesthood with a splendid ceremony in the Hagia Sophia, where the unhappy brothers were compelled to perform the rite of communion for her, letting everyone in the Great Church know who was the dominant figure in the room.

Realising that male generals would be affronted to receive orders from a woman, Irene appointed eunuchs to key positions in the court and the army, men who would not blanch at feminine leadership. The foremost of these eunuchs was Stauracius, who became her chief minister.

Irene dextrously exploited her iconophile sympathies to win over key figures in the aristocracy and the church who would otherwise abhor the presence of a woman on the throne. But iconoclasts still controlled the army and some sections of the bureaucracy, and seethed at her leadership.

The empress took steps to bring the clergy to her side. She appointed a sympathetic new Patriarch and then convened an ecumenical council in 786 to rescind the policy of iconoclasm. The council met in the Church of the Holy Apostles while Irene looked on from the gallery with her young son Constantine. But soldiers from the *tagmata*, the imperial troops of the capital who were faithful to the ideals of the previous emperor, raucously interrupted their deliberations, and the council had to be dissolved.

Irene would not be thwarted. She relocated the rebellious troops to Asia Minor on the pretext of preparing for an imminent battle against the Arabs, which failed to eventuate. Once they were there, she ordered the regiment to be split up and dispersed through the various provinces. She replaced the *tagmata* in the capital with loyal troops from Thrace and Bithynia. The following year she summoned a new council outside the capital in Nicaea, attended by around three hundred and fifty bishops and a hundred monks. Proceedings went smoothly and the prohibition of icons was officially lifted.

MEANWHILE, IRENE'S SON Constantine VI was growing older, and would soon need a wife. A union was arranged between her son and a daughter of the Frankish king Charlemagne, but relations with the Franks soured and the engagement was broken off.

Still, a suitable consort had to be found, and so in 780, the empress organised a bride-show for Constantine. Thirteen eligible young women came to the capital to be paraded in front of the young emperor, but it was Irene and Stauracius who selected the bride, Maria of Amnia, the granddaughter of a saint. The two were married, but Constantine, increasingly resentful of his domineering mother, neglected his wife after she gave birth to a daughter.

AS CONSTANTINE ENTERED his late teens, he yearned to set his mother aside and assume sole occupancy of the throne. Irene and Stauracius had no intention of surrendering power, and relations between mother and son deteriorated. Constantine's attempts to assume a greater role in the palace were repeatedly thwarted by Stauracius. In his naivety, Constantine simply couldn't imagine the chief minister was acting on orders from his own mother, so he concluded that Irene had become the puppet of the wily eunuch.

Constantine conspired with a group of friends to overthrow Stauracius, but the plot was easily exposed. When Irene was told, she summoned her son to the throne room, slapped him across the face, and confined him to quarters. His co-conspirators were arrested, flogged and exiled.

A somewhat rattled Irene insisted the army swear to uphold her name above that of her son's. For once, she badly miscalculated: half the army mutinied and demanded the captive Constantine be brought safely over to them, whereupon they installed him as sole ruler of the Roman empire. Irene was allowed to retain her title of empress, but was confined to her palace overlooking the Sea of Marmara.

Constantine VI, a nineteen-year-old of no executive experience, soon found himself sorely in need of his mother's advice, which Irene was only too happy to give. But after several military debacles, Constantine's support within the army began to dwindle. He repudiated his wife Maria and married another woman, which was seen by church leaders as an adulterous relationship. Sentiment was now drifting back to Irene, who was remembered as a competent administrator.

In October 796, Constantine was staying at the hot springs of Prusa in Asia Minor, accompanied by Irene, when he received news that his new wife Theodote had given birth to a son. Constantine rushed back to Constantinople to be at her side, leaving his mother to conspire with the *tagmata* commanders in his absence.

In May the next year, Constantine was leaving the Hippodrome when a group of soldiers fell on his personal guard and tried to arrest him. He fled across the Bosphorus, but was captured and brought back to the Great Palace. On his mother's orders, he was dragged by soldiers into the purple marble chamber where Irene had given birth to him, and a soldier gouged his eyes out. Constantine VI died several days later of his wounds. He was twenty-six years old. Theophanes records that after his death, an eerie darkness fell upon Constantinople for seventeen days, which was attributed to the horror of heaven.

Gold solidus of Empress Irene with globe and sceptre.

It's unclear whether the cruel circumstances of Constantine's death were widely known among the people of Constantinople, and with Irene firmly back in charge, it was probably unwise to ask too many questions anyway.

Irene's sole occupancy of the throne created a major legal problem: all of her edicts thus far had been issued in the name of her son. With Constantine dead, it wasn't at all clear that a woman would have the legal authority to issue laws in her own name. Irene circumvented the problem by signing laws under the name of *basileus* – 'Emperor' – instead of *basilissa*, 'Empress'. The army was a problem too; she didn't dare issue orders to her restive generals in case they were not obeyed. Still, Irene was popular among the people and in the monasteries, and was able to shrewdly navigate the political currents of Constantinople as she always had.

In Easter 799, Irene paraded through the streets of Constantinople in a golden chariot, drawn by four white horses, with her four chief commanders holding the bridles. It was a dizzying moment for the woman who had risen to the commanding heights of a thoroughly patriarchal empire.

The following month she fell ill, and Stauracius's rival, another eunuch named Aetius, came to her bedside to warn her of her chief minister's disloyalty. Stauracius was made to apologise, but he too fell ill, and then died. Irene had just recovered from her illness when shocking news from Rome threw all her plans into disarray.

Karolus Magnus

ON CHRISTMAS DAY 800, Charlemagne, the King of the Franks, strode into the shrine of St Peter in Rome without his royal insignia to participate in mass as a humble Christian. But as he knelt at the altar for communion, Pope Leo III placed a golden crown upon his head, and proclaimed him Karolus Magnus, emperor of the Romans. The congregation cheered and hailed Charlemagne as their Augustus, as the pope prostrated himself at the new emperor's feet.

From Constantinople's point of view, the coronation of a barbarian king in Rome as 'Emperor' was an outrageous intrusion on their imperial prerogatives – only Constantinople had the right to name an Augustus. But there was little they could do about it. The eastern Roman empire was no longer the empire of Justinian, having lost too much territory and manpower. Sooner or later someone in the west was going to call Constantinople's bluff on its imperial pretensions. It was unfortunate for Irene, but no coincidence, that it happened during her reign. Pope Leo justified his audacious move by claiming that since everyone knew a woman was ineligible to be emperor, Charlemagne was merely filling a vacancy.

The coronation had more to do with Pope Leo's need for Frankish protection than Charlemagne's vanity. Charlemagne was now the ruler of a sprawling empire that covered modern-day France, western Germany, Austria and northern Italy, the largest political unit to emerge in western Europe since the death of the western Roman empire. Although nowhere near as culturally sophisticated, Charlemagne's kingdom was, embarrassingly, twice as large as Irene's empire.

Looking for allies, Charlemagne had put out feelers towards the court of Caliph Harun al-Rashid, who had responded warmly and sent Charlemagne an elephant as a gift. Then Charlemagne thought better of an Arab alliance, and in 802, sent envoys to Constantinople with a proposal of marriage for Irene, a union that would unite the eastern and western empires under one crown.

Irene was intrigued and inclined to accept, but her counsellors were horrified by the idea of being ruled by a coarse barbarian. On 31 October, while Irene was recovering from a minor illness, a cabal of senior bureaucrats and military officers acted pre-emptively against the alliance by seizing control of the Great Palace and deposing Irene. She was replaced on the throne by a bureaucrat named Nicephorus. Irene accepted her overthrow gracefully and was sent into exile to the island of Principo in the Sea of Marmara. A year later she was dead. Irene had ruled alone or alongside her son for twenty-two years. There would be other influential empresses in the years to come, but none so powerful as Irene of Athens, the only woman to claim the title of 'Emperor'.

IRENE'S REIGN MARKED the beginning of a turnaround in the empire's fortunes. After centuries of dispiriting defeats, plagues and natural disasters, the Romans were at last to get some breathing space that would allow them to slowly recover. An era of rebirth and expansion was about to begin. Constantinople's economy steadily improved as more people were drawn to the city, and districts that had lain dormant since the plague were rebuilt and repopulated. The apocalyptic gloom lifted for a while, and Constantinople recovered its old confidence.

The Arab expansion was checked and the frontiers expanded. The Thracian farmlands, the island of Cyprus and the city of Antioch were restored, for a while, to imperial control, and the empire settled into a shape that roughly resembled a double-headed eagle, a motif that would later be adopted as the empire's emblem. There was a European wing, encompassing Thrace, Greece, Sicily and parts of the Balkans, and an Asian wing covering the Anatolian peninsula and Cyprus.

The highwater mark would be reached under the reign of Basil II, 'The Bulgar Slayer'. Basil earned his grim nickname by blinding fourteen thousand Bulgarian prisoners of war, leaving a single one-eyed man in each cohort to lead the rest of his mutilated men back to their ruler. It was said the Khagan was so distressed, he suffered a stroke and died two days later. The Bulgars were completely defeated and their lands brought back into the Roman orbit. Other border peoples were simply absorbed into the multi-ethnic, multilingual empire.

The city's newfound wealth ignited a revival of culture and education. Manuscripts of literature, mathematics and philosophy from ancient Greece were salvaged and taught in schools and academies. Encyclopaedic tomes were compiled on history, medicine and zoology.

Such was the gravitational power exerted by Constantinople at this time that the Slavs and eastern Europeans were brought into the orbit of the Orthodox church. Visitors who were subject to the full force and majesty of the liturgy in the Hagia Sophia were left in no doubt as to the chosen religion of the One True God. The envoys of Prince Vladimir of Kievan Rus' were lost for words to describe it: 'only this we know: that God dwells there among humans, and that their service surpasses the worship of all other places. For we cannot forget that beauty'.

Ison and Melody

ON A SUNDAY MORNING, while in Rome, Joe and I went out looking for pastries and coffee. Church bells were clanging musically throughout the neighbourhood, summoning people to Mass. In the Piazza della Madonna dei Monti we heard choral music emanating from two open doors. The plaque beside the door identified the church as the Chiesa dei Santi Sergio e Bacco, a

Ukrainian Catholic house of worship that practises the Byzantine rite. I was hoping we could sneak into a back pew, but the church was already overcrowded, and we couldn't even get through the door. The scent of sandalwood floated over our heads as we lingered in the doorway, absorbing the deep resonance of the male voices raised in holy song.

A BYZANTINE CHANT has two parts, the ison and the melody. The ison is the underlying heavy drone, the sustained choral note that anchors the chant. The ison doesn't move, and so exists outside of time. It represents nothing less than the uncreated light of God, eternal and sublime.

The ison sustains the melody, which moves up and down through time. This represents the unified voice of the church. The chants travel through scales that are distinctly different from the familiar major and minor scales used in western music, shifting unexpectedly through semitones that sound beautifully strange. The ison and the melody combine to form harmonies that shimmer and ring in your head. It feels exciting and soothing at the same time. On some occasions listening to this music I've felt tears pricking at my eyes and wondered where on earth they had sprung from.

Joe stood next to me, patiently waiting for me to get my fill. I can hardly expect a fourteen-year-old kid to enjoy Byzantine choral music as much as I do. I knew he was bored, but I loved that he didn't whine about it, that he doesn't mind daydreaming while his father loiters outside a church doorway. There's a gentleness in Joe that is revealed in these moments, and a quiet underlying strength that is present even here, despite the absence of breakfast.

Most places were closed for the Sabbath, but near the square we found a café run by godless hipsters and decorated with Italian kitsch from the 1960s. While we waited for our pastries, I thought about the previous evening, when we'd walked past a hole-in-the-wall whiskey joint and I'd suddenly wished I could borrow Joe's older self for a night so we could sit at the bar, sample six different kinds of scotch and tell funny stories. And it occurred to me that Joe, as that young man, will be far more plugged into contemporary culture than me, and able to introduce me to new things bubbling up into the culture. At some point we'll switch roles, and Joe will become the cultural guide. I only hope he'll let me tag along.

I told him there'll come a time when our relationship will change. 'I will no longer be the dad who makes decisions for both of us. I'll stop bossing you around and we'll be more like equals. Like brothers.'

Joe shrugged. That day seemed a long way off to him.

Byzantine sheet music.

I try to envisage the moment when Khym and I are required to resign our parental authority over Joe. I imagine a dignified ceremony, something like the British handover of Hong Kong to the Chinese. There'll be a solemn lowering of the parental ensign and the raising of a shiny new banner of self-determination, and he'll look at his parents, now aged and shrunken, festooned with medals from campaigns that no one remembers, and try to remember how it was that we had once loomed so large in his eyes.

Melusine

A WAITER IN A PRISTINE white jacket brings us a plate of grilled *kofte* with long green pickled chillies, along with a dome of pilaf rice. On the side is a spicy chilli sauce. Joe and I have been eating here most nights. The room is too brightly lit, but the food is cheap and good. The aroma of the grilled meat, mixed with parsley, mint and lemon juice, awakens our caveman carnivore instincts, like a sausage sizzle at a hardware store. The sour, vinegary chillies complement the lamb *kofte* perfectly.

Over dinner I offer to tell Joe a fairytale.

'I'm a bit old for that now, Dad,' he sighs.

'You're never too old for a real fairytale. I'm talking about old folktales that are much darker than that Disney stuff you got fed as a little kid.'

Joe groans.

'Do you know the original version of *Little Red Riding Hood*? The wolf comes to the grandmother's house, kills her and eats her. He puts on her nightdress and gets into the bed. Then, when Little Red Riding Hood comes to the house, the wolf, in disguise, offers the girl a plate of blood and meat. So she cannibalises her grandmother without realising it.'

'That wasn't in the version I heard.'

'Exactly. Then the wolf orders Little Red Riding Hood to remove her clothes and throw them into the fire. She does as she's told. And then ... he swallows her whole.'

'What happens then?'

'Nothing. That's the end of the story.'

'Hmmm ...'

'So let me try the story of Melusine on you. It's a folktale from France, but the woman it was based on really did exist. She was born in Constantinople, just around the corner from here.'

RAYMOND DE LA FORÊT was born into a noble family in France that had fallen on hard times. The Count of Poitou took pity on Raymond's penniless father, so he adopted the boy and raised him as his son in his castle at Poitiers. In time Raymond grew up to be a handsome and charming youth.

One day the Count invited Raymond to join him on a hunt for a wild boar. As they travelled deeper and deeper into the dark forest, they realised they had become separated from their servants. The boar had escaped and they were lost. The forest grew dark and so Raymond and the Count set up camp and lit a fire.

The two men were warming themselves against the blaze when they heard a rustle in the undergrowth. Suddenly the wild boar leapt out and pounced on the Count. Raymond seized his sword and swung wildly at the beast, but his blade struck his master instead, hacking into his side. Raymond swung again and this time the boar fell dead at his feet. As he wiped the blood from the sword, Raymond saw that he had accidentally killed his master, a good and kind man who had loved him like a son. Raymond mounted his horse and rode off in a daze.

Time passed strangely that night. In time, the dark forest opened up and Raymond entered a glade, illuminated by the silvery moonlight, where a pebbly stream ran from a bubbling fountain. Next to the fountain were three young women in iridescent white dresses. They were indescribably beautiful.

One of the young women rose to her feet and gently advanced towards him.

'Why are you so frightened?' she asked.

Raymond broke out in tears and he told her how he had unintentionally killed his master and protector. The young woman listened, and when he finished she said, 'I think I have a solution. Remount your horse,' she suggested. 'Return to Poitiers. Act as though you have no knowledge of what has taken place. Then when the body of the Count is discovered, it will be assumed that he died while slaying the boar.'

Raymond thought this was a very good idea and agreed to act on her advice. As they fell into conversation, Raymond was overwhelmed by the young woman's beauty and charm. At dawn he realised he was in love with her, and made her promise to be his.

She said, 'I will do as you say. But in return I ask of you two things. Firstly I require you to obtain a grant of land for me around this fountain, but only so much as can be covered by the hide of a stag. Upon that space I will build a great palace.'

'And what is the second thing you require of me?'

'I will marry you ...' and here she paused to look at Raymond very earnestly, 'but every Saturday, you must agree to leave me in complete seclusion. You must never intrude upon me on that day. For my name is Melusine and I am a water-faerie of great wealth and power.'

Raymond agreed and returned to the castle. He obtained the grant of land around the fountain from his stepbrother Bertram. Raymond then cut the stag hide into tiny threads and succeeded in covering a much greater parcel of land than Bertram had expected.

Now that the land was hers, Melusine erected a magnificent castle upon it. And in that castle she was wed to Raymond in a ceremony that everyone agreed was the greatest and most beautiful they had ever seen. At the moment they were wed, Melusine's lovely eyes filled with tears of joy. Again she implored Raymond never to intrude upon her privacy on a Saturday.

'Please do not ignore my warning, Raymond,' she said softly, 'for if you do, we will be separated forever.'

Raymond swore to uphold her wishes.

Melusine extended and improved the castle, making it the most beautiful in the whole of France. She called it Lusinia, after her own name (eventually it would become known as the Château de Lusignan and its ruins are still there today). Melusine and Raymond lived very happily together for six days of the week, and every Saturday she would withdraw into her apartments. Raymond took care to keep his promise and leave her to her privacy.

In time, Melusine bore several children. The first was a son called Urian, who was born with a large mouth and long ears. One of his eyes was red, the other green. The second son, Cedes, had a scarlet face. The third, Gyot, was handsome, except that

one eye was positioned higher than the other on his face. The
fourth, Anthony, was covered in hair and had long claws on his
fingers. The fifth son had only one eye. The sixth was known as
Geoffrey-with-the-Tooth for the boar's tusk that protruded from
his jaw. More and more sons were born, but all were in some
way disfigured.

'Geoffrey-with-the-Tooth?' Joe smiles. 'That's what they called him?'
'That's what they called him.'
'It's like a name that's supposed to be scary, but doesn't quite get
there.'
'It probably sounds more fearsome in French.'

TIME PASSED, and Raymond's father came to live with them
in their castle, while his brothers were furnished with money
and servants.

One Saturday, Raymond's brother took him aside and told
him that Melusine's weekly absences were the subject of idle
gossip in town.

'Brother,' he said, 'you should look into it. If only to set your
mind at ease.'

Raymond pondered on this, and as he did so, he wondered
if Melusine was keeping company with another man. He burst
into his wife's private apartments and checked each room, but
all were empty. Only one locked door remained: the entry into
her bathroom.

Raymond could hear Melusine singing from within. Slowly, he lowered himself to peer through the keyhole. As he spied on her naked form, he saw that from below the waist, Melusine took the form of a double-tailed fish.

Raymond recoiled from the keyhole, shocked, but not in any way dismayed by what he had seen. He knew he loved her just as much as he always had, but he was ashamed of his rashness. He had broken his covenant with her and realised he must now lose her.

As the days passed, Melusine showed no awareness that her true nature had been observed by her husband. Then one evening, as they dined at the castle with Raymond's old father, they received news that their son Geoffrey-with-the-Tooth had attacked a local monastery, burning it to the ground, with a hundred monks trapped inside.

Raymond wailed in horror at the terrible news. As Melusine rushed to comfort him, he pushed her away, shouting, 'Get away from me, you foul serpent! You contaminator of my honourable race!'

Melusine fainted with shock. Raymond, full of sorrow and regret, held her slumped form. As she awoke, she held Raymond's face in her hands.

'I leave you with two little ones in their cradles,' she said softly. 'Look after them tenderly, for they must now lose their mother.'

Raymond nodded wordlessly.

Then, with a shriek of grief, Melusine leapt from the window. As she did so, she left a foot impression on the stone floor. Raymond ran to the window ledge and saw that his wife had transformed herself into a fifteen-foot-long winged serpent.

Melusine the dragon circled the castle three times, howling, and then flew off into the night sky.

Raymond's happiness was forever destroyed.

But Melusine had not completely abandoned her children. On many nights, the nurses caught sight of a shimmering figure hovering near the cradles of the two babies, an apparition with twin fish tails, speckled from the waist down with blue-and-white scales. The apparition took the babes into her arms and suckled them until dawn.

THE LEGEND OF MELUSINE was written in 1387 by Jean d'Arras. The tale grew up around the legend of a Byzantine princess known as Melissena of Constantinople.

This real-life Melissena was the fruit of a particularly exotic family tree, born sometime in the middle of the ninth century as the granddaughter of the Emperor Michael I Rangabe, who was descended from the Khazars. Michael's wife, the Empress Procopia, was part-Khazar too, but she could trace her ancestry all the way back to the Han emperors of China. So the twin streams of Byzantine and Chinese royal blood flowed through Melissena's veins.

Melissena was considered a very desirable potential bride until her family's political fortunes collapsed. Her father was castrated by his enemies, and the poor girl was sent away to a convent. When Melissena came of age she was married off to a Viking warrior called Inger, a humble soldier in the Varangian Guard.

Inger was well pleased with his bride, and brought her with him to the court of the King of the Franks, where he boasted of her double royal lineage. Word of the exotic princess from Constantinople spread through France, and Melissena became an object of fascination in the courts of western Europe. Her exquisite manners and cultural education set her apart from the crude westerners, and made her seem other-worldly.

After she died, the story of Melissena evolved into the folktale of Melusine. The double fish tail of the water-faerie symbolises the twin streams of Melissena's royal blood.

THE WAITER BRINGS ANOTHER plastic basket of bread to the table. On the wall, old framed photos of fez-hatted Turkish men look down upon us as we finish our meal.

Joe turns his head to the side and looks off to the middle distance, like he always does when he's turning something over in his mind. After a moment he says, 'I like how, at the start, you think Raymond is going to be the hero of the story, because he's this good guy who comes from a poor family.'

'Yeah, but he isn't the hero at all. Raymond's a blunderer. He accidentally kills this man who's been like a father to him. He's upset, but when Melusine tells him how he can wriggle out of it, he's happy. Then Melusine creates this wonderful, happy life for him. And all he had to do was to leave her alone on a Saturday.'

'It's one of those stories you think is going one way, and then it goes somewhere else.'

'All the best folktales do that. They wander off the path, even though the iron law of these stories is that you should never, *ever* stray from the path.'

THE IMAGE OF MELUSINE was popularised in the Middle Ages, and several towns placed her distinctive likeness on their crests: a naked maiden with a crown and long tresses of hair, floating above the waves, holding her twin fish tails.

Today Melusine can be seen everywhere, emblazoned on coffee cups all over the world, as the corporate logo of the US coffee chain Starbucks. Melusine, once an emblem of unearthly feminine power, has become the face of understrength, oversweetened American coffee.

Melusine.

Born in the Purple

CONSTANTINE,
IN CHRIST THE ETERNAL EMPEROR OF THE ROMANS,
TO HIS OWN SON ROMANUS
THE EMPEROR CROWNED OF GOD AND BORN IN THE PURPLE

SO BEGINS *De Administrando Imperio* – 'On the Governance of the Empire' – perhaps the most detailed manual of government created by an overbearing father for his son. The author is Emperor Constantine VII, known to history as Constantine Porphyrogenitus, 'the Purple-Born'. Constantine is writing for a readership of one: his teenage son and co-emperor, Romanus II. He wants his son to sit up straight and pay attention: 'A wise son makes a father glad, and an affectionate father takes delight in a prudent son ... Listen to me, my son, and you shall be counted prudent among the wise and wise among the prudent'.

The book was given to Romanus not long after he turned fourteen, Joe's age now. It's written as a kind of emperor's manual, a useful compendium of advice that Romanus could consult after his dad was gone.

Constantine VII was a popular ruler. He was a scholar, a painter and a patron of the arts. It was he who charmed Liutprand of Cremona at the Great Palace, seated on his mechanical throne, beside a gilded tree of automated singing birds.

De Administrando Imperio brings together the strands of Constantine's scholarship and his administrative experience. First, he advises Romanus to stay on good terms with the Pechenegs, since, like all tribes from the north, they are implanted with 'a ravening greed of money, never satiated, and so they demand everything and hanker after everything'. It's best to give the Pechenegs what they want in gold and gifts, otherwise they'll go raiding in the Crimea and take the gold anyway. Far better to buy their alliance, then turn them around and point them at the Turks and the Slavs.

If foreigners demand to be given the imperial robes or crown jewels, he advises his son to tell them they were given to Constantine the Great by an angel, and that the curse of Constantine would fall upon anyone misusing them.

Constantine does a poor job of explaining the Muslims and how they came to be. He mistakenly claims that the Muslims pray to the star of the pagan goddess Aphrodite – they cry out '*Alla wa Koubar*', which means, he says, 'God and Aphrodite'. Islam was clearly a poorly understood phenomenon among the Romans at this time.

On it goes. Constantine VII's stated concern is for the welfare of the empire, but the candour and gentleness of his voice speaks of a fatherly love, and a worry that his son might be swamped by his imperial responsibilities. Romanus would choose to heed his father's advice at times, and at other times to completely ignore it.

CONSTANTINE PORPHYROGENITUS died in the autumn of 959, and the succession passed smoothly to Romanus. The new emperor was, at first, widely regarded as a lightweight, for his love of pleasure and for his insistence on marrying a low-born wife, an inn-keeper's daughter named Anastaso, who was given the more respectable name of Theophano, which means 'divine manifestation'.

Fortunately for Romanus, his father had placed capable generals on the empire's frontiers and the young emperor was quick to capitalise on their talents. But after just three years on the throne, Romanus was killed in a hunting accident. Suspicion fell on the dead emperor's widow, but Theophano had nothing to gain from her husband's untimely death and everything to lose. Shunned by the court as a vulgar upstart and encircled by scheming bureaucrats, she reached out for protection to the empire's most brilliant general, Nicephorus Phocas.

The Pale Death of the Saracens

NICEPHORUS WAS THE MASTERMIND behind a string of stunning victories for the empire: he had driven the Muslims from Crete, and taken Aleppo in Syria by storm; here the Arab defenders were cut to pieces, earning him the grim nickname 'Pale Death of the Saracens'. Nicephorus was said to possess great physical strength, able to thrust a spear so forcefully it could skewer an enemy soldier right through his armour. For all that, he was not a particularly appealing man: he was short and mole-like in appearance and humourless in temperament. Nonetheless his victories had made him the most popular man in the empire. When Nicephorus received Theophano's plea for help, he rode to the capital at once and received a hero's welcome.

Theophano was described as the most beautiful woman in Constantinople. Nicephorus was the empire's greatest military hero, but he was twice her age and physically ugly. Despite their differences, it seems the stony general fell hard for Theophano, and he swore allegiance to her and to her two sons. Nicephorus would remain devoted to her until the end, even though it cut across the grain of who he was.

Nicephorus's first wife, Stephano, had died years earlier while he was away on campaign. Overcome with grief and guilt, Nicephorus had taken a vow of chastity. Then, when his only son was killed in a horse-riding accident, he stopped eating meat. His asceticism was such that he habitually wore a long black hairshirt to bed each night to show repentance for his sins. Nicephorus often spoke of his desire to eventually retire from army life and enter a monastery to end his days in prayer and contemplation. Marriage to Theophano would require him to surrender these earnest ambitions. And yet he did it anyway. The union was arranged by his talented nephew and chief lieutenant John Tzimisces.

Nicephorus's prestige in Constantinople was such that he easily prevailed over Theophano's enemies at court and sent them into exile. Nicephorus was crowned Emperor Nicephorus II on 16 August 963 and he married Theophano in the Hagia Sophia the next day. But once on the throne, Nicephorus fell out with John Tzimisces and other former allies. The emperor's brutal honesty and impatience with niceties made him a poor politician and an even worse diplomat.

The Return of Liutprand

IN THE SUMMER OF 968, Liutprand of Cremona stood on the deck of a Venetian galley as it cruised into the Sea of Marmara. Liutprand must have felt a pinch of excitement. Twenty years had passed since his first voyage to Constantinople, when he had come on behalf of King Berengar of Italy.

Much had changed in the interim. The affable Constantine VII was dead, and Liutprand was now serving King Otto I of Germany, who had made him a bishop, and entrusted him with a delicate diplomatic mission: to arrange a union between the Holy Roman Empire and Constantinople through a royal marriage.

Relations between the German king and Constantinople had been badly strained by Otto's military conquests in Italy, in lands that the eastern capital of the Romans still claimed for itself. But Liutprand had advised Otto that peace with Constantinople would ultimately prove more profitable than conflict. To that end, he had been sent to arrange a union between Otto's son and a Byzantine princess. The marriage would seal a treaty of peace between the two empires.

Much depended on the attitude of the emperor. Liutprand was no doubt aware that Nicephorus was a blunt warrior from a famous military clan. Still, he hoped his diplomatic skills and evident goodwill could smooth over the tensions with Nicephorus. But when Liutprand presented himself at the Chalke Gate, he was told to wait until a court official could be found to welcome him. Hours passed and a light afternoon shower turned into heavy rain, drenching Liutprand. Still no one came to admit him.

At five o'clock, a very damp Liutprand was finally admitted into the grounds of the Great Palace and he was taken to his lodgings, a draughty and barren stone house. The house was without water, and the wine that was left for him was flavoured with pitch and pine resin, which was disgusting to his taste.

For two days Liutprand was left to stew in this manner. On the third day he was led into a conference with Leo, the emperor's brother and chief advisor, and the two men bickered over the question of titles. Liutprand insisted that in their discussions, Otto, his master, must be referred to as a fellow emperor (*basileus*). Leo said this would not be possible, and that Otto would have to settle for being called a king (*rex*). Liutprand objected strenuously. Leo accused him of trying to stir up trouble.

The next day, Liutprand was led into the octagonal throne room for an audience with the emperor. Here, for the first time, he caught sight of the Pale Death of the Saracens. Liutprand recorded his impressions of the emperor's appearance:

> He is a monstrosity of a man, a dwarf, fat-headed and with tiny mole's eyes. A short, broad, thick beard disfigures him, half going grey and disgraced by a neck scarcely an inch long, which is pig-like by reason of the big close bristles on his beard. In colour he is like an Ethiopian and, as the poet says, 'you would not like to meet him in the dark'.

Nicephorus, for his part, gave Liutprand a severe dressing down.

'It was our duty and our desire,' he began icily, 'to give you a courteous and magnificent reception. But that has been rendered impossible by the impious behaviour of your master.' The emperor then unleashed a tirade against Otto for attacking his allies in Italy, and concluded by accusing Liutprand of being a spy. The two men debated fruitlessly for an hour, until the emperor called a halt to their argument.

'It is past seven o'clock,' he said wearily, 'and there is a church procession which I must attend.'

Liutprand joined the emperor's entourage as it proceeded in a stately manner from the palace to the Hagia Sophia. Both sides of the road were lined with men carrying shields and spears. Liutprand was directed to sit on a platform near the choral singers. The adulation of the emperor was, to him, a ridiculous spectacle.

> As Nicephorus, like some crawling monster, walked along, the singers began to cry out in adulation: 'Behold the morning star approaches: the day star rises: in his eyes the sun's rays are reflected: Nicephorus our prince, the pale death of the Saracens!'

After the service, Liutprand was invited to dine with the emperor, but he was given a place of low status at the table and served food that was prepared with olive oil and *garum*. As Liutprand choked his way through his meal, the emperor taunted him from the far end of the table, mocking the strength of Otto's armies.

Provoked beyond endurance, and ignoring further attempts to silence him, Liutprand rose to his feet.

'When we are angry,' he cried, 'we can find nothing more insulting to say than "You Roman!" For us, in the word "Roman" is comprehended every form of lowness, timidity, avarice, luxury, falsehood and vice.'

The exchange had a chilling effect on the dinner. Nicephorus ordered Liutprand's table be removed and for him to be escorted back to his lodgings. Too much had been said in anger. An imperial marriage was off the agenda.

Liutprand was held for another four miserable months in his 'hated abode' before being allowed to depart. He bade Constantinople a bitter farewell, 'that once most rich and flourishing, now half-starved, perjured, lying, wily, greedy, rapacious, avaricious, vainglorious city'. As he left, customs officials confiscated the five lengths of purple silk he had bought in the city to adorn his church. He was given no compensation.

LIUTPRAND had caught Nicephorus at a bad time. The emperor's reign, which had started out so promisingly, was teetering badly. Tax increases had been levied to fund his war plans, and a grain shortage had inflated bread prices, which led to protests in the streets. While making his procession through the city, two women had thrown bricks at him from a rooftop. The women had been arrested and executed, which only deepened public anger. On another procession, Nicephorus had been assaulted by an angry mob, who lobbed rocks and insults at him, while his personal guard protected him with their shields.

Beset by rumours of plots and uprisings, the emperor turned the Bucoleon Palace into a citadel, fortified with battlements. But his most dangerous enemy lay within the palace complex.

LIKE EVERYONE else in the city, Empress Theophano had grown weary of her unpleasant, older husband, and so she formed a secret alliance with John Tzimisces, his former lieutenant. Tzimisces could hardly have been more different from his taciturn uncle: he was a charming and good-looking young officer, with dark blond hair and blue eyes, who had served Nicephorus well on the battlefront. But for some reason the emperor had become displeased with his nephew, and had banished him to Anatolia.

Theophano persuaded Nicephorus that he had treated his nephew unjustly. Nicephorus relented and lifted the banishment, so long as Tzimisces agreed to stay in his family home in Chalcedon, just across the Bosphorus. Perhaps Nicephorus suspected something was up between his wife and his former lieutenant. Tzimisces was soon making secret nightly excursions by boat across the strait to a corner of the palace where Theophano waited under cover of darkness. The lovers hatched a plot against Nicephorus. Whether Theophano or Tzimisces was the chief instigator is not known.

THE NIGHT OF 10 DECEMBER was bitterly cold and windy; snow was blowing about the palace grounds. Nicephorus entered his bed-chamber, read for a while, then donned his long hairshirt, lay down on a bearskin on the floor and fell asleep. At around eleven, Tzimisces crossed the choppy waters of the strait in a rowboat with three associates. A rope was dropped from Theophano's window and the assassins climbed up into the palace. A eunuch led them to Nicephorus's bed-chamber. They drew their swords and silently entered the room.

The four men were momentarily taken aback to find the bed unoccupied, but then the snoring figure of Nicephorus was discovered on the floor. After a few hard kicks the emperor woke up and stared at his assassins. The first sword blow landed across the brow of his head. The accomplices dragged the semi-conscious emperor to John Tzimisces, who now sat on the imperial bed.

'Tell me,' he shouted, 'was it not me who made you emperor? Why then did you send me into exile? I am a man of nobler birth than you. Who will save you now?'

Tzimisces then tore out clumps of Nicephorus's hair and beard. The other assassins hit him with their sword handles until one of them thrust his curved blade into the emperor's back and ran it through him. Nicephorus's head was cut off and the rest of his body thrown out the window.

John Tzimisces's men ran out into the snow-covered streets of the city, shouting 'Hail John! Augustus of the Romans!'

The Varangians, the emperor's Viking bodyguard, heard the tumult, picked up their axes and rushed to the gates of the Bucoleon. As they tried to force open the iron gates, they looked up and saw one of the assassins holding the emperor's severed head from the palace window. All the Varangians could do now was shrug: they were too late.

John Tzimisces strode into the golden octagonal throne room, sat down, pulled on the emperor's purple boots and immediately got to work.

IF THEOPHANO WAS a co-conspirator in her husband's assassination, it availed her nothing. She was now a roadblock to her lover's ambitions. John Tzimisces came to the Hagia Sophia to receive the imperial diadem, but the Patriarch objected, refusing to lay the crown upon the head of an assassin with bloodstained hands. In reply, Tzimisces said it was not he, but his accomplices, who had delivered the deathblows to Nicephorus. And in any case, they were only acting on the orders of the empress, who instigated the whole thing. The Patriarch insisted that Tzimisces atone for his sins by publicly denouncing his accomplices and by tearing up certain decrees that had been laid down against the church by Nicephorus. Tzimisces readily agreed to all this and was crowned on Christmas Day 969.

For her treachery, Theophano was sent into a miserable exile on the island of Proti in the Sea of Marmara. At some point she escaped and slipped back into the city, where she came to the Hagia Sophia and demanded asylum. Basil, the court chamberlain, was sent to persuade her to return to exile. In her fury, she lashed out, punching Basil hard in the head, leaving the marks of her knuckles on his temple. Theophano had to be dragged from the Hagia Sophia and sent away into a final exile in the distant province of Armenia.

Nicephorus's headless body lay in the courtyard all day in the snow. Then his remains were collected and carted to the Church of the Holy Apostles, where they were laid in a coffin. His tomb was inscribed with the words: *You conquered all but a woman.*

The Golden Fork

DESPITE THE BLOODY MEANS by which he had ascended to the throne, John Tzimisces became a popular and effective ruler. He strengthened his legitimacy by marrying Theodora, a born-to-the-purple princess.

Shortly afterwards, John Tzimisces sent a message to Rome, asking Otto to revisit the idea of an imperial marriage between the eastern Roman empire and the Holy Roman empire of the west. His letter was warmly received, and so Tzimisces sent a young bride named Theophanu to Germany, to be married to Otto's son, the seventeen-year old Otto II.*

Theophanu arrived in Rome in 972, accompanied by a large entourage of servants and heavy treasure chests laden with extravagant gifts. She was just thirteen, barely a teenager, entering a strange land to marry someone she had never met and whose language she couldn't speak, but the dignity of her bearing and her elegant clothes deeply impressed the Germans and Italians of Otto's court.

Then there was some confusion when the Germans realised the bejewelled girl before them was an impostor. Theophanu was not

---

* Not to be confused with the exiled former Empress Theophano.

the purple-born princess that Otto had been expecting, but John Tzimisces's niece. Some of Otto's advisors recommended he call off the marriage and send her back to Constantinople, but Otto thought better of it; he was pleased with Theophanu and the wedding went ahead as planned.

THEOPHANU AND HER SHORT, red-headed husband Prince Otto the Younger were married by the pope in St Peter's Basilica on 14 April 972. They arrived at the wedding banquet and were seated together in the place of honour. A plate of food was laid in front of her and then Theophanu did something completely unexpected: she produced a little doubled-pronged golden implement, and used it to scoop up her food and bring it to her mouth.

The raucous wedding banqueters were shocked. No one in Otto's court had ever contemplated such a thing. In Constantinople, use of the table fork had been commonplace for centuries, but in the west, even at a royal table, food was consumed noisily and with the hands. Some of the revellers at the wedding saw at once that the use of such an implement would avoid unnecessary mess across the table and on the clothes. Others saw the fork as a symbol of effete eastern decadence. St Peter Damian of Italy would later denounce it as an ungodly implement.

Theophanu's daily bath was also controversial, a practice that made her appear pristine and ethereal, compared to the pungent westerners in Otto's court. This, too, was seen in some quarters as conceited and unchristian. But that was just the isolated grumbling of a few malcontents. By and large, Theophanu's Byzantine glamour simply dazzled the coarse Germans. Frankish celebrations became more refined, and probably much less fun.

A YEAR AFTER THE WEDDING, the old emperor Otto the Great died and Theophanu's husband was crowned Otto II, holy Roman emperor of the west. Theophanu became empress and co-ruler. Otto was happy to leave much of the business of government to her, and with each passing year her influence grew, eclipsing that of her mother-in-law, Adelheid. She and her husband appear to have genuinely been fond of each other, and had five children.

After eleven years of marriage, Otto died at the age of twenty-eight of a sudden illness and was buried in St Peter's Basilica. Their three-year-old son was crowned Otto III, with Theophanu ruling as empress-regent until the boy came of age. She reigned successfully until her death in 991, still only in her thirties. Theophanu was buried in Cologne in the monastery of St Pantaleon, the saint whose relics she had brought with her from Constantinople. Her sarcophagus is still there today.

Even the most chauvinistic commentators of the time had to concede that Theophanu had governed cleverly and prudently. A German chronicler concluded that although she was 'of the fragile sex, her modesty, conviction, and manner of life were outstanding, which is rare in Byzantium'.

Theophanu had, for better or worse, given upper-class Germans and Italians a taste for luxurious clothes and food. But her longest-lasting legacy is the introduction of the fork to the tables of western Europe. In the eleventh century, Italians discovered the joys of pasta, which could not be eaten with the hands without making a splattering mess. Then they realised that linguine could be consumed effortlessly if impaled and twirled around a fork.

Which is why, whenever you pick up pasta with a fork, you enact, in a very small way, a symbolic union of Rome with Constantinople, and a reunion of the eastern and western empires.

Varangians

IN THE HAGIA SOPHIA, on the parapet of the upper gallery, Joe and I see some Scandinavian runes scratched into the marble. The markings trace back to the ninth century and are only faintly visible today. They look like little stick figures. Translated, they say: *Halfdan carved these runes*. We're looking at medieval graffiti, etched a thousand years ago by a bored Viking.

For several days Joe and I refer to ourselves in the third person as 'Halfdan', as in, 'Halfdan hungry', 'Halfdan kill bear for supper' and 'Halfdan tired. Halfdan want to go back to room and watch Turkish TV now'.

Halfdan's runes in the Hagia Sophia.

Halfdan was a soldier of the Varangian Guard, the emperor's elite bodyguard, composed of Viking warriors from Scandinavia and Russia.* The Varangians, with their tall frames, reddish-blond hair and beards, were a novelty on the streets of Constantinople. In the imperial army they stood out like bears in the company of wolves. Strolling along the Mese, they formed an impressive sight in their blue tunics and scarlet cloaks, their double-bladed axes slung over their shoulders.

The Varangians were entrusted with the personal security of the emperor, and required to swear an oath of loyalty to him. All too

---

*   'Varangian' was the Greek name for Viking.

often they would, like poor Halfdan, be required to silently stand guard and keep watch as the emperor participated in stultifyingly elaborate ceremonies. In battle they would be held back until the critical moment, when they would charge forward, axes swinging left and right, scattering the emperor's enemies. Off-duty, the Varangians were free to get as drunk as they liked. They became notorious in Constantinople for their Viking revelries. People called them 'the emperor's winebags', although not, presumably, to their faces.

Varangians had served in the palace since 874, when a treaty between Byzantium and Kievan Rus' required the northerners to send a contingent of warriors for the imperial army. The excellent pay attracted more ambitious warriors from Norway, Sweden, Iceland, Russia and England. Emperors quickly saw the benefit of having these tall Vikings in their service – as foreigners they were removed from dynastic palace politics, and were ultimately more trustworthy than local soldiers. Varangians were indulged by the emperor and even allowed to plunder his belongings after his death.

The Vikings who joined the Varangian Guard came to Constantinople in search of adventure, fame and treasure. As foreigners in a strange land, they formed a close brotherhood and kept something of their ancestral Viking code of honour. In 1034, a contingent of Varangians was wintering in Thrace when one of their number attempted to rape a local woman. In desperation, she snatched his dagger and stabbed him through the heart. When the Varangians learnt of the circumstances of his death, they came to the Thracian woman to honour her and give her all of their disgraced comrade's possessions. Then they threw away his body without burial.

A VARANGIAN, if he survived his tour of duty, could look forward to returning to his faraway village in Scandinavia with a sack of gold, a silken cloak and a set of impressive battle scars. Great value, too, was set upon the stories they brought back with them from the fabulous metropolis they called Miklagard, the big city.

The most famous of the Varangians ever to come to Constantinople was Harald Hardrada, whose adventurous nature carried him across the world and whose name resounds in the sagas of Iceland.

EVEN AT FIFTEEN, Harald was hungry for glory. When his older brother Olaf called for allies to help him win back the throne of Norway, Harald rallied six hundred men to the cause. The battle was lost and Olaf was killed. Harald escaped with some of his men to a farmhouse, where he nursed his wounds through the winter.

In the summer Harald and his friends resolved to leave Norway and seek their fortune in the wider world. They rode through the back roads over the mountains towards Sweden.

'Who knows,' Harald sang to himself as he rode on his horse, 'my name may yet become renowned far and wide.'

Harald met up with more fugitives from King Olaf's army. They found longboats and sailed across the Baltic Sea, into the lands of Kievan Rus'. Harald was warmly welcomed in Novgorod by Grand Prince Yaroslav, who made him a captain in his army.

After seven years of fighting for Yaroslav, Harald and his men agreed it was time to venture south and try their luck in Miklagard, the great city of the Romans. They sailed their longboats southward, along the Dneiper to the Black Sea and then into the Bosphorus. And in 1034, Harald Sigurdsson, who had never in his life set foot in any settlement larger than a village, found himself in the glittering metropolis of Constantinople.

Harald and his Vikings were welcomed into the ranks of the Varangians, and they pledged their loyalty to the imperial family. For their first mission Harald and his men were sent into the Mediterranean to hunt down a band of Arab pirates. They sank the pirates' ships and laid waste to their coastal bases, killing everyone they found. The emperor was well pleased, and Harald was made commander of the Varangian Guard.

Harald's Varangians were then sent to fight the Arabs in Asia Minor. It was said that at this time, Harald travelled all the way to the Holy Land, where he walked the streets of Jerusalem, and bathed in the River Jordan.

The Roman emperor sent Harald and his men on missions across the Mediterranean. They were given orders to take a town in Sicily with high fortifications. Harald noticed the sparrows flying out from the castle each day to fetch food for their young. He ordered his bird-catchers to capture the sparrows and fix a small chip of wood, doused in sulphur, to their backs, and set fire to them. The frantic birds flew back at once to their nests in the roof beams of the castle and ignited the whole building. The people inside the town surrendered.

HARALD WAS SOON WEALTHY beyond all his expectations. He longed to return home and use his riches to take the throne of Norway, but he had fallen out of favour with the emperor and was thrown into prison, either for theft or of murder, it's not clear. Perhaps his real crime was seducing Maria, the empress's niece, which excited the jealousy of the empress, who had her own designs on Harald.

Harald and his friends were rescued one night by some allies, who hauled them out of their prison tower with a rope. They had to escape Constantinople at once, but first Harald went to claim his revenge against the ungrateful emperor who had thrown him in prison. He led a contingent of Vikings into the imperial bedchamber, where they seized the screaming emperor and gouged out his eyes.

Harald and his men left the palace in great haste. On their way to the harbour they stopped by Maria's house and abducted her. They brought her down to the Golden Horn, where they stole two galleys. As they pulled out, they saw the heavy protective chain stretched across the mouth of the harbour. Harald ordered his oarsmen to row towards the chain as hard as they could; the other passengers were sent to the stern of the boat with their luggage. Both galleys charged forward at full speed and pitched up onto the iron chain. Then he ordered his men to run forward to the bow. Harald's galley teetered on the chain, and then tipped forward into the waters on the other side. The other galley fared less well; it splintered across the middle and broke apart.

Once they had cleared the harbour, Harald ordered his boat to pull over to the shores of Galata, where he released Maria, asking her to remind the empress that this proved she had no power over him. Harald then bid farewell to Constantinople forever. He had departed Miklagard on bad terms, but he would retain his admiration and affection for the great city for the rest of his life.

BACK IN NOVGOROD, Harald asked to marry the king's daughter. Yaroslav consented to the union, and handed over the treasure that Harald had been sending to Novgorod for safekeeping.

Harald returned to Norway with a Russian princess on his arm, chests full of treasure and a string of tales of his adventures in Miklagard. His wealth and reputation helped him win the throne of Norway.

HARALD BECAME A BLUNT, uncompromising monarch. His subjects nicknamed him Harald Hardrada, 'the Hard Ruler'. He died in 1066 at the Battle of Stamford Bridge in Yorkshire, while attempting to conquer England.

Harald's death was foreseen before the battle, by one of his Viking warriors in a dream. The man said he saw the enemy's bannered army, led by a huge, ghastly witch-wife riding a wolf. The witch-wife was feeding one bloody Viking carcass after another into the wolf's mouth, all the while singing:

> *Skade's eagle eyes**
> *The king's ill luck espies:*
> *Though glancing shields*
> *Hide the green fields,*
> *The king's ill luck she spies.*
> *To bode the doom of this great king,*
> *The flesh of bleeding men I fling*
> *To hairy jaw and hungry maw!*
> *To hairy jaw and hungry maw!*

Harald knew the witch-wife was his death coming for him. He was cut down in the heat of battle and struck in the throat by an arrow while in the grip of a berserker fury, with both hands clutched around his sword.

---

* Skade or Skaði, the Norse goddess of winter.

THE VIKINGS who returned to Scandinavia from Miklagard were greatly celebrated. But many never came back. Today there are thirty or so tall runestones scattered around Sweden that commemorate the Vikings who left their villages to make their name and fortune in Grikkland – 'the land of the Greeks' – and never returned. The runestones are carved with ribbons of text, the inscriptions direct and unemotive, but implying a world of feeling for the lost sons and husbands who joined the Varangian Guard.

> *Folkmarr had this stone raised in memory of Folkbjörn, his son.*
> *He also met his end among the Greeks.*
> *May God help his spirit and soul.*

> *Ástríðr had these stones raised in memory of Eysteinn, her*
> *husbandman, who attacked Jerusalem and met his end in Greece.*

> *These landmarks are made in memory of Inga's sons.*
> *She came to inherit from them, but these brothers – Gerðarr*
> *and his brothers – came to inherit from her.*
> *They died in Greece.*

Manzikert

AT THE DEATH of Basil II in 1025, the Roman empire was once again the largest and strongest in Europe. But in the decades that followed, it was undermined by paralysis and intrigue, its economy weakened by inflation and a debased coinage.

Constantine X, among the most blinkered and incompetent of emperors, undercut the empire's defences at a time when a new Turkish tribe, the Seljuks, were pressing at the border. Regiments of the *tagmata* were replaced by units of foreign mercenaries operating under contract. The regular troops were cashiered and the frontier fortresses fell into decay. Nearly all the remaining imperial lands in Italy were lost to the Normans. On his deathbed, the wretched Constantine forced his wife Eudocia to vow never to remarry, to ensure succession would pass to his sons.

Eudocia was installed as empress-regent but, overwhelmed by the poisonous intrigues of her dead husband's family, decided to revoke her vow and marry an aristocratic general named Romanus Diogenes.

ROMANUS DIOGENES was said to be an exceptionally handsome man, with a strong frame and bright, pale eyes. When Eudocia called for him, he was actually languishing in prison for his part in a rebellion against the late emperor. When Romanus was brought before Eudocia, she wept. It's not known whether her tears were brought on by profound relief or by a premonition of disaster. The Patriarch was persuaded to destroy Eudocia's handwritten oath to her dead husband, and to give his blessing to the union. Romanus IV was crowned on 1 January 1068.

The new emperor turned his full attention to the long neglected army, and to the growing power of the Seljuk Turks, who were raiding imperial strongholds in Syria and Cappadocia. On paper, the empire's forces were far superior to those of the Turks. Romanus intended to hit them hard. In the summer of 1071, he led a gigantic, multi-ethnic force of soldiers and mercenaries through Asia Minor to confront the Turks and their sultan head on.

ALP ARSLAN, the sultan of the Seljuk Turks, was, like Romanus, a fine physical specimen. Arab historians record that he was immensely tall and exhibited great physical strength. It was said that his moustache was so long, he had to knot it behind his head while riding into battle to keep it from flying into his eyes. Arslan's court included mathematicians, philosophers and poets. The Persian scholar Omar Khayyam served in Arslan's court as an astronomer, but his name would forever be associated with his sublime poetry:

Awake! for Morning in the Bowl of Night
Has flung the Stone that puts the Stars to Flight:
And Lo! the Hunter of the East has caught
The Sultan's Turret in a Noose of Light.

Despite the raids on Cappadocia, the sultan wasn't really interested in taking on the might of the Roman empire. The Seljuks were newly converted to Sunni Islam and intent on waging holy war against the Shi'ite Fatamids of Egypt. While besieging the Fatamid stronghold of Aleppo, Arslan was brought news that the Romans were marching en masse towards them. He broke off the siege and turned back into Asia Minor to confront Romanus.

The two armies set up camp, a mile and half apart, near the fortress of Manzikert, north of Lake Van. That night, Seljuk skirmishers launched repeated assaults on the Roman camp, creating confusion and panic. When dawn broke the next morning, the Roman forces were appalled to discover their Uz mercenaries had defected to the Seljuks.

Arslan, still uncertain of his prospects for victory, proposed a peace treaty, which Romanus rejected out of hand. Romanus was commanding a 100,000-strong force of infantry, heavy cataphracts and artillery, including a wall-shattering mangonel, capable of hurling a stone weighing half a ton. The Seljuk forces were far smaller. As he prepared to go into battle, the sultan donned a white tunic resembling an Islamic funeral shroud, indicating his readiness to die a martyr's death in the field. He made his officers swear an oath of allegiance to his son, if he should fall.

The Seljuks formed a broad arc in front of the imperial forces. As the Roman infantry slowly advanced from the centre, the Seljuk centre withdrew, firing volleys of arrows as they retreated, and a loop began to form around the Romans. Seljuk horsemen launched hit-and-run attacks on the Roman flanks. As dusk fell, the frustrated emperor ordered his men to withdraw. Seizing the moment, Arslan launched an all-out attack, and the Roman line was thrown into confusion. The officer in charge of the rearguard, a treacherous rival named Andronicus Ducas, deliberately misinterpreted the signal to withdraw, telling his men that the emperor was dead and the battle was lost. Ducas fled from the battle and his men followed.

In the last minutes of daylight, the Roman centre was overwhelmed. The emperor, surrounded by his personal guard, tried to rally his troops until his horse was cut down from under him. He surrendered only when his sword hand was wounded. All night, Romanus lay on the ground, among the wounded and dying.

The following morning, Romanus was picked up and brought to Arslan's tent in chains. The sultan refused to believe the bedraggled man before him was the Roman emperor, until several other prisoners confirmed his identity. The sultan then rose from his throne and ordered Romanus to kiss the ground before him. As Romanus prostrated himself and placed his lips on the ground, the sultan placed his foot on the emperor's neck.

It was an act of symbolic humiliation, but once it was over, Arslan quickly helped Romanus to his feet, embraced him and said philosophically, 'That's life'. For the next week, the emperor stayed in the Seljuk camp as an honoured guest, going on long walks with the sultan, and eating at his table.

Alp Arslan places his foot on the neck of Emperor Romanus IV.

One night, Arslan asked Romanus, 'What would you do if I was brought before *you* as a prisoner?'

'Well,' replied the emperor, 'I would probably torture and kill you, then parade you through the streets of Constantinople.'

'I have a worse punishment in store for you,' replied the sultan. 'I'm going to forgive you and set you free.'

Romanus was happy to agree to a treaty. In exchange for his freedom, the Seljuks would receive 1.5 million gold pieces, and one of the emperor's daughters would be given as a bride to Arslan's son. The sultan now told Romanus he should return to Constantinople as quickly as possible, while he still had a throne. Romanus wrote a report to the senate, then left the Seljuk camp for the capital, picking up the scattered remnants of his defeated army along the way.

IN CONSTANTINOPLE, the court was in an uproar. John Ducas, brother of the treacherous Andronicus, exploited the confusion to declare the throne vacant, and Eudocia's young son Michael VII was proclaimed sole emperor. Eudocia was arrested and sent to a convent. The treaty with Arslan was repudiated.

John and Andronicus Ducas sent an army to intercept Romanus's forces, and the ex-emperor was defeated. He agreed to resign the throne and retire to a monastery in return for a promise that no harm come to him. John Ducas reneged on the agreement, and sent soldiers to blind him on 29 June 1072.

John Scylitzes, a contemporary historian, records the last days of Romanus Diogenes, where he was 'Carried forth on a cheap beast of burden like a decaying corpse, his eyes gouged out and his face and head alive with worms, he lived on for a few days in pain with a foul stench all about him until he gave up the ghost.'

The terrible thing about what was to follow was that it was all so unnecessary. If Romanus had been allowed to resume his throne and honour his treaty with Arslan, the Seljuks would have returned to stalking their real quarry: the Fatamid Egyptians.

But it was not to be. The repudiation of the treaty with Arslan was followed by a flood of Turkish tribesmen into Anatolia from the north-east. The degraded Roman defences were powerless to stop them.

Two years later, Michael VII chose to officially recognise the Seljuk hold on Anatolia in return for Turkish support against a Norman mercenary who had set up an independent state in central Anatolia. In this manner the Turks were granted control of Asia Minor, the empire's heartland and the source of most of its food supply and manpower. Arslan's successor Sulayman titled himself the 'Sultan of Rum'.

The Seljuks had taken the Roman name for themselves.

CHAPTER SEVEN

The Starlit Golden Bough

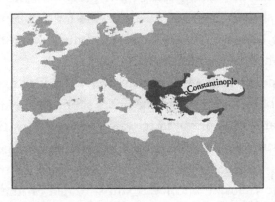

The empire at the summoning of the First Crusade by Pope Urban II, 1095.

Don't Move – I'll Be Back

THE SITE OF THE HIPPODROME is now a park in central Istanbul; the park maintains the outline of the historic racetrack. Its long central spine is still there, along with its original crop of ancient Egyptian and Greek columns.

Joe and I walk past a scowling man holding out flyers for a tourist cruise line. We see him here every day, half-heartedly chanting the same one-word phrase to sightseers, 'Bosphoruscruz? Bosphoruscruz?'

An old man with a shoeshine box is sitting on one of the Hippodrome benches. My boots are dusty, but as a visitor, I feel uncomfortable asking a local to clean them for me. Then he says to me, 'My God! Your boots are terrible! A disgrace! It's an embarrassment for you.'

Joe laughs and pushes me towards him. Two minutes later my boots are gleaming. I pay the guy and he looks at me like I'm now fit to mingle in human society.

We catch one of Istanbul's sleek new trams down to Eminonu on the Golden Horn. Walking along the crowded waterfront we see the tall, pencil-shaped Tower of Galata on the far side of the harbour, built by the Genoese in the fourteenth century, when the area was granted to them as a trading colony.

We decide to catch another tram over the bridge to take a look. The tram glides to a halt and the doors slide open. No one on the crowded platform is prepared to wait, they just push their way on board. I gesture to Joe to hang back for a moment to politely allow the disembarking passengers to come out. I board the tram, but the doors are now closing and Joe is still stranded on the platform. I reach through the crush of commuters to jam my arm between the closing doors, and Joe cries out 'Dad?' from the platform.

The tram starts to move. The system is automated and it doesn't care that my arm is wedged in the door. This is why the passengers were pushing so hard to get in on time. I look directly at Joe and shout 'DON'T MOVE. I'LL BE BACK.' I yank my arm inside, the tram speeds along and my son disappears from sight.

Inside the carriage I'm breathing heavily, sick with worry. I promised Khym I would take good care of our son, and now I've abandoned him on a tram platform in Istanbul. And neither of our phones are working.

Several commuters around me see my distress and reassure me, in English, 'It's okay. He'll be safe. You can get off at Karaköy and get the next tram back.'

These people are being so nice but I'm feeling shaky, and terrible scenes are playing out in my head. I've always been able to cope with mishaps in foreign countries before – theft, imminent violence. The rules: stay calm, be patient, remain polite, heighten your situational awareness and look all around you for opportunities to find a way out. I said something like that to Joe as travel advice before we left. But right now I'm badly frightened. Why am I so undone?

The difference is that it's my boy's wellbeing at stake, not mine. The tram trundles over the Galata Bridge. Being on the other side of the water makes it much worse somehow. The man next to me points to the electronic display above the doors. His eyes are kind. 'Next stop is here: Karaköy. Your boy will be okay.'

The tram comes to rest and the doors swish open again. I thank the guy and push my way out. I run through an underpass to emerge on the other side of the tracks, then sweat it out for an agonising eleven minutes for the next tram.

Oh, the poor kid. I hope he's not too scared. What if he's not there? How will I explain to the Turkish police that I accidentally left my son on a platform? What kind of a father am I?

The loss of a child is something I've never allowed myself to contemplate for longer than a few moments, for fear the thought might haunt my life and spoil the pleasure I take in my children. Now, absurdly, I feel I'm right on the edge of that fathomless ravine of pain.

The tram arrives and takes me back across the bridge to Eminonu, where Joe is waiting for me. He's fine, of course. I tell him he did the right thing by keeping calm and staying put, but I feel stupid because I'm gasping like I'm going to have a heart attack.

'Next time we catch a tram, we barge on like everyone else, okay, son?'

'Okay, Dad.'

Anna and Alexius

My life has been one long series of storms and revolutions.
– Anna Comnena

IN THE FIFTY YEARS after Basil II's death, imperial blunders cost the empire the larger part of its army, half its territory and the wealth of its treasury. The hapless Michael VII was pushed aside in 1078 in favour of another Nicephorus. Long past his prime, Nicephorus directed all his feeble energies into fighting off pretenders to his throne and handing out gold to his cronies.

Hopes were raised when an aristocratic young general, Alexius Comnenus, took power in a *coup d'état* in April 1081. He was twenty-five years old. The brilliant and wily Alexius was the most adroit politician to sit on the throne since Heraclius. He would have to improvise his way out of the disasters he'd inherited.

WE KNOW SO MUCH about Alexius because his daughter Anna chronicled the story of her father's life and times in a classic work known as the *Alexiad*. Anna Comnena is the world's first known female historian, and in the *Alexiad*, we hear her lively voice, carried across the distance of a thousand years. She's hardly an impartial observer, but her discerning eye and close proximity to events more than make up for any absence of objectivity.

The *Alexiad* was conceived as an act of devotion to a father whom she loved and admired, but the real star of the book is Anna herself. She begins by insisting we take her seriously as an historian and an intellectual:

I was not ignorant of letters, for I carried my study of Greek to the highest pitch, and was also not unpractised in rhetoric; I perused the works of Aristotle and the dialogues of Plato carefully, and enriched my mind by the 'quaternion' of learning. (I must let this out, and it is not bragging to state what nature and my zeal for learning have given me, and the gifts which God apportioned to me at birth and time has contributed.)

ANNA COMNENA WAS BORN in the purple birth chamber of the Great Palace in December 1083. The infant Anna was adored by her father and given a crown, in the expectation she would be enthroned one day as *basilissa*. The birth of a little brother thwarted those hopes.

With her parents' support, she received an excellent education in history, mathematics, astronomy and philosophy. At fourteen, she married Nicephorus Bryennius the Younger, a capable officer who shared her love of intellectual pursuits. Anna was put in charge of a large hospital and orphanage in Constantinople, where she taught medicine. As her father entered his final illness, Anna plotted for the succession to pass to her husband, and thus to her, but her plans were knocked over by her younger brother John, who visited Alexius on his death bed and stole the emperor's ring. John flashed the glittering bauble to the court, claiming it as proof that *he* was the desired successor.

Anna felt cheated of her inheritance, and contrived to have her brother assassinated at Alexius's funeral, but the conspiracy was exposed and she was forced to retire from court life. After her husband died, Anna was sent to live in a convent, where she put her restless mind to work by writing the *Alexiad*.

Anna never became empress, but the *Alexiad* ensured her fame would eclipse her father's. Through her eyes we see how Alexius

Comnenus managed, with a mix of diplomacy and cunning, to keep the empire afloat, and how he accidentally lit the fuse that ignited a holy war.

Alexius Comnenus.

EMPEROR ALEXIUS'S first challenge in 1081 was to respond to the Norman attack on Greece, led by the formidable Robert Guiscard. The Roman forces suffered several painful defeats, but Alexius deployed diplomacy and intrigue to pull the rug from under Guiscard: he persuaded Henry IV of Germany to attack the Norman lands in Italy, and simultaneously bribed some discontented Norman barons in the south to revolt. Guiscard, on the cusp of victory in Greece, found his Italian stronghold collapsing behind him, and was forced to go home to sort out the mess. It took Guiscard two years to push back the Germans and quell the revolt. He returned to Greece, ready to pick up where he'd left off, but an outbreak of the plague swept through the Norman camp, and carried him off with it.

Leadership of the demoralised and plague-ravaged Norman army in Greece now passed to Guiscard's son, Bohemond. The young prince was no match for the shrewd Alexius, who harassed the Normans with hit-and-run attacks. At the same time, Alexius offered Bohemond's lieutenants large bribes to defect. Eventually, Bohemond threw up his hands and signed a peace treaty, handing back the imperial territories in Greece.

ALEXIUS'S NEXT CHALLENGE was located closer to home, in Thrace, where another steppe people known as the Pechenegs had joined forces with the Seljuks and were preparing an attack on Constantinople. The shrewd Alexius bought the support of a rival tribe, the Cumans, and in 1091 his forces linked up with their 40,000-strong army to attack the Pechenegs at the mouth of the Maritsa River. The night before battle, Alexius called his men together for evening prayer and, according to Anna Comnena, they fixed small candles to the tips of their spears, 'lighting up the heavens with the gleam of many stars'.

The Pecheneg forces were annihilated the next day, and their families, who had followed them on campaign, were massacred. Alexius won battle after battle this way, re-arranging alliances so that his over-confident enemies would find the ground beneath their feet crumbling away.

With Greece and Thrace secured for the moment, Alexius could look to reversing the empire's losses in Asia Minor and Syria. Seeing that the Seljuks were convulsed by dynastic infighting, he judged that now would be a good time to strike and he looked around for potential coalition partners. In March 1095, Alexius sent an emissary to Pope Urban II with a letter asking for western help against the Muslim occupiers of the eastern provinces. Pope

Urban's response went far, far beyond anything Alexius had imagined or indeed wanted.

The Sword and the Cross

IN THAT YEAR OF 1095, people across Europe looked to the skies and saw a meteor shower, a comet and a lunar eclipse. The aurora borealis was witnessed as far south as France. It was all very unsettling. The celestial activity portended something, but what?

Alexius's letter to Pope Urban II was the pebble that caused the landslide. It seems that Urban had been brooding on the Muslim successes in the east for some time. To him it was a sign of a disordered universe and a portent of the end times. Fired with Christian zeal, Urban travelled to Clermont in France where on 27 November he delivered one of the most incendiary speeches in the history of the world, a speech that gathered up the squabbling, discontented masses of western Europe and galvanised them into action.

Urban shocked the Council of Clermont with lurid – and entirely imaginary – stories of atrocities committed by Muslims against innocent Christians in the east. Innocent pilgrims to the Holy Land were being robbed and slaughtered, he said, by the Muslim overlords of Jerusalem. He called for nothing less than a new kind of 'armed pilgrimage', a crusade – a war of the cross – to expel the Muslims from the east, and free up the Holy Land for Christian worship. He held out a tantalising promise to his flock: those willing to take up the challenge would receive a remission of sins, and martyrs could look forward to the full reward of heaven.

The pope's speech unlocked enormous latent energies within the people of western Europe. Princes, knights and commoners alike swore an oath to take up the banner of the cross and carry it all the way to Jerusalem. As their leaders rolled out their maps, they saw they would need to pass through Constantinople on the way.

EIGHT MONTHS LATER, Emperor Alexius was advised that a strange mass of foreigners had appeared at the Theodosian Walls. These were the first of Urban's Holy Warriors to show up at the gates of Constantinople. As the emperor looked out at the assembled masses from Blachernae Palace, he saw that this was an army like no other.

This was the 'People's Crusade', led by a charismatic French monk named Peter the Hermit, who rode up to the city walls on a donkey, wrapped in a cassock of coarse cloth, bearing a heavy crucifix around his neck. Behind him was a vast, shuffling army of forty thousand beggars and peasants whose enthusiasm had been inflamed by Peter's apocalyptic rhetoric to the point of near hysteria. Whole families, including women and children, had followed Peter across Europe, creating mayhem and perpetrating mass murder against Jewish settlements along the way. By the time the People's Crusade staggered up to the walls of Constantinople they'd been driven half-mad by blood, exhaustion, starvation and disease, sustained only by the dream of the glittering prize of heaven that might await them at the end of a Saracen spear.

The sight of the starving fanatics at the gate shocked Alexius, who had been hoping for units of disciplined mercenaries, not a swarm of hollow-eyed, unarmed paupers. Peter the Hermit was brought into the palace to meet with the emperor. Alexius warned him that leading such an army into battle against the Seljuk Turks would be suicidal, but the monk was undeterred. Alexius probably didn't argue the point; he was receiving reports of robberies and rapes from the Crusader camps. Alexius and his counsellors agreed that the sooner they were gone the better.

The emperor arranged for Peter and his paupers to be transported across the Bosphorus into Asia Minor, from where they kept marching. As Alexius predicted, they were ambushed by the well-trained Seljuk Turks, and the People's Crusade was completely and utterly destroyed. But there were other, much more formidable Crusaders on the way.

The Massacre of the People's Crusade, led by Peter the Hermit. Detail from Passages d'outremer (Overseas Voyages), by Sébastien Mamerot, c.1475.

THE FOUR MAIN CRUSADER ARMIES had each taken different routes from Europe, and arrived at the walls of Constantinople over a six-month period between November 1096 and April 1097. These armies were no rabble, but disciplined, heavily armed warriors, led by powerful princes from France and Germany. Among the Crusader leaders was Bohemond the Norman prince.

This time, Alexius was ready for them. The emperor had encountered Bohemond before, and he simply did not trust the stated high Christian ideals of the Crusaders, suspecting that if he allowed them to enter the glittering streets of Constantinople in force, they would be tempted to take it for themselves and plunder its wealth. Alexius said he was happy to supply them with food, but he insisted they remain outside the city walls. Only a few unarmed Crusaders would be admitted through the gates at any one time, and they would be closely monitored.

Nothing could have prepared these hard-handed princes of western Europe for the culture shock of Constantinople. They had come from a land of damp and draughty castles, surrounded by crude peasant dwellings, to a metropolis of bright silks, marble statues and monumental architecture, and warm sea breezes spiced with the scent of *garum* and garlic. Constantinople was built to intimidate such men.

Each of the Crusader princes was brought into the palace, where he was left alone for days, until he was called into the majestic throne room. There he would be met by a sombre Alexius, who would ask him to swear an oath: that if he should conquer, he would return to Constantinople any possessions that had once belonged to the Roman empire. As soon as the prince was sworn, Alexius would smile and shower the prince with expensive gifts and entertain him at lavish banquets.

There was a moment of boorish awkwardness when Baldwin of Boulogne came to the throne room in the company of his knights. As Alexius entered, one of the knights refused to rise; instead he audaciously lounged on the emperor's throne and boasted that he had never been bested in battle. Baldwin barked at him to get off the throne.

Each of the princes wanted to be named by the emperor as supreme leader of the Crusades. Alexius played them off against each other, and hinted that he, too, might take up the cross and join the fight for the Holy Land.

Alexius kept a close eye on Bohemond in particular, whom he figured for a cynical opportunist. When asked to swear an oath, Bohemond had agreed all too readily, which aroused Alexius's suspicions. Anna, the Emperor's daughter, who had a keen eye for the male figure, studied Bohemond's physical appearance closely:

> Bohemond's appearance was, to put it briefly, unlike any other man seen in the land of the Romans (for he was a marvel for the eyes to behold, and his reputation was terrifying) ... he was so tall in stature that he towered over the tallest by nearly one cubit, narrow in the waist and loins, with broad shoulders and a deep chest and powerful arms. And in the whole build of the body he was neither too slender nor overweighted with flesh, but perfectly proportioned ...
>
> His skin all over his body was very white, and in his face the white was tempered with red. His hair was yellowish, but did not hang down to his waist like that of the other barbarians; for the man was not inordinately vain of his hair, but had it cut short to the ears ... His blue eyes indicated both a high spirit and dignity; and his nose and nostrils breathed in the air freely ... A certain charm hung about this man but was partly marred by a general air of the horrible.*

IN MAY 1097, ALEXIUS FAREWELLED the last of the crusaders with a heavy sigh of relief. He was under no illusions that they would keep their oaths to return the Roman lands to him, but he had done what he could.

---

* The *Alexiad*, 13:10.

The experienced, heavily armed Crusaders hammered the Seljuks and put their capital of Nicaea to siege. But in the night, the citizens of Nicaea surrendered not to the Crusaders, but to the Roman units accompanying them. When the Crusaders awoke to see Roman banners fluttering over the city, they felt outraged and betrayed.

They pushed on towards Antioch, once the third most important city in the empire. Despite the harsh conditions, the Crusaders took the city, but they were soon besieged by a much larger Turkish army. The westerners appealed to Constantinople for help, but Alexius figured they were doomed and did nothing. The Crusaders now considered themselves released from their oaths, and prevailed over the Turks anyway. Antioch became the possession of Bohemond, and the capital of the first of the Crusader states in the east.

ALEXIUS'S POPULARITY DECLINED in the last two decades of his life. After another successful campaign in Asia Minor, he began to suffer from gout and severe asthma, an affliction which 'accompanied the emperor like a noose, and never left off strangling him'. Anna cared for her father in his final illness, even as she conspired to succeed him, but when he died in 1118 the crown was passed to her brother John instead. Anna consoled herself by writing the *Alexiad* from her lonely convent cell, where she remained until her own death at seventy.

FOR ALEXIUS'S SUCCESSORS, it was galling to see these crude westerners make themselves at home in the Holy Land, in former provinces of the Roman empire. Despite the harsh and unfamiliar conditions, the Crusaders set up little feudal states in the fabled cities they knew from their Bibles: Jerusalem, Antioch and Edessa.

Their victories in the Holy Land had made many of them famous in their homelands, and inspired the creation of several *chansons de geste* in France, but the westerners could never feel completely at ease in their new homes in the east. The Great Seljuk Empire lay just outside their borders, and the Crusaders knew the day would come when the infidels would return in force.

Prester John

TO THE CHRISTIAN MIND, the distant north-east was the very hinterland of the world, the home of Gog and Magog, a place littered with all the broken and unclean things of God's creation. These dark lands were sometimes called the Womb of Nations, and every so often it seemed they would labour and bring forth a new horde of terrifying horse archers who would stampede all the way to the Theodosian Walls. The riders came in different guises over the centuries, as Huns, Avars, Pechenegs, Bulgars and Seljuks.

Seen from another perspective, the arrival of Turkic nomads on the empire's doorstep was a natural product of the geography of the Eurasian steppe, which ran from Mongolia all the way to modern-day Hungary. The nomads of Central Asia saw the steppe not as a wilderness, but as a long, grassy highway running across the Eurasian landmass, with two of the richest cities in the world – Beijing and Constantinople – at either end. It's hardly surprising that these horsemen, arriving at the western terminus of the highway, would be tempted by the riches of the great Roman capital nearby. Constantinople was like the pot of gold at the end of the rainbow.

And so for centuries the Romans were forced to fight them off or pay them tribute to make them go away, only to be confronted by another horde, with different customs, led by a new khan. All too often these Turkic riders would carry the banner of Islam. Was it too much to hope that the east lands might one day bring forth a hitherto unknown tribe of Christians, so they might join forces and crush the Saracens from either side?

HOPE, FEAR AND RUMOUR swirled through the Crusader states of the Holy Land as the Turks regrouped and attacked their Syrian kingdoms. When Edessa was put under siege, Constantinople offered only token support, so in 1144 the Crusaders sent an emissary to the pope to plead for help. Hugh, the bishop of Jabala, was selected to make the long, arduous journey to Italy. Arriving in Rome, Hugh met with Pope Eugenius III and did his best to explain just how dire the situation was in the Holy Land. The pope was eager for gossip, and Hugh couldn't resist passing on an exciting rumour that was circulating around the Crusader camps, of a mysterious Christian conqueror from the Far East, a stupendously wealthy Priest-King named Prester John who was said to rule the lands beyond Persia.*

The Crusaders had heard a story that this Prester John had crushed a Muslim army in a bloody battle at Ecbatana. He had apparently intended to keep marching to Jerusalem to help the Crusaders, but his army had been unable to cross the Tigris River. In any event, no such rescue ever materialised. Hugh also mentioned the intriguing story of Prester John to the German historian Otto of Freising, who published it in his *Chronicon* of 1145.

While Hugh gossiped in Rome, the Crusaders continued to struggle against the resurgent Seljuk Turks. Prester John's armies never appeared, but rumours of this fabulous Priest-King of the east never quite went away either, and tales of his wealth and majesty only got larger in the telling. It was said he was descended from the

---

* 'Prester' comes from 'Presbyter', meaning 'priest'.

three Magi who attended the birth of Christ and that he carried a sceptre made of emerald.

THEN, IN 1165, a startling letter appeared in Constantinople, addressed to Alexius's grandson, the emperor, Manuel Comnenus. It began with a hearty salutation,

> *John, priest by the almighty power of God and the might of our*
> *Lord Jesus Christ, King of Kings and Lord of Lords, to his friend*
> *Manuel, prince of Constantinople, greeting!*
> *Our Majesty has been informed that you hold our Excellency*
> *in love and that the report of our greatness has reached you.*

The author of the letter identified himself as none other than Prester John. In his extraordinary message he casually boasted of the fabulous land he ruled over, one literally 'streaming with honey and overflowing with milk':

> *Our land extends beyond India, where rests the body of the holy*
> *apostle Thomas; it reaches towards the sunrise over the wastes,*
> *and it trends toward deserted Babylon near the Tower of Babel ...*
> *Our land is the home of elephants, dromedaries, camels,*
> *crocodiles, meta-collinarum, cametennus, tensevetes, wild asses,*
> *white and red lions, white bears, white merules, crickets, griffins,*
> *tigers, lamias, hyenas, wild horses, wild oxen, and wild men –*
> *men with horns, one-eyed men, men with eyes before and behind,*
> *centaurs, fauns, satyrs, pygmies, forty-ell high giants, cyclopses,*
> *and similar women. It is the home, too, of the phoenix and of*
> *nearly all living animals.*

The letter caused a sensation in Constantinople. Minstrels put some of its phrases into song. No one was certain what kind of a creature a 'tensevete' or a 'meta-collinarum' was, but it all sounded so intriguing, and, given that so little was known of the lands in the Far East, it seemed at least possible that such things might exist.

The ancient Romans were long accustomed to bizarre tales of eastern marvels spread by returning sailors and merchants. India was known to be the home of men with dogs' heads, of headless people with faces on their chests, and of wild men without mouths who lived on the scent of flesh, fruit and flowers.

THE LETTER FROM THE great Christian kingdom of the east raised the question: who were these Christians, and how did they get there? There could only be one answer: they had to be Nestorians.

The Nestorians had left the eastern Roman empire more than six hundred years earlier. They were followers of a fifth-century Patriarch of Constantinople named Nestorius, who had become embroiled in those early arcane disputes about the nature of Christ. Nestorius had come up with his own formula: that Jesus contained both human *and* divine elements that were distinctly different, but which coexisted within his nature like separate islands in the same sea. Unfortunately for Nestorius, his ideas were deemed heretical; he was sacked from his office and sent into exile.

But even as Nestorius faded into obscurity, his two-in-one concept picked up support throughout the empire. The proponents of this formula were labelled 'Nestorians' by their opponents and expelled from the church. In time, the Nestorians tired of official persecution and drifted east, into lands almost entirely unknown to the Romans.

The seventh-century Arab conquests disrupted the usual lines of communication between Constantinople and its former provinces in the Middle East, so contact with the Nestorians petered out. But from time to time, travellers and merchants would wander into Constantinople with intriguing tales of a mysterious Christian people who were said to dwell in India and in the lands beyond Persia.

PRESTER JOHN'S LETTER was a hoax, of course, some kind of medieval prank. But the author had told the Christians of Europe just what they wanted to hear. The letter was translated into several languages and copied all over Europe. Pope Alexander III was intrigued enough to reach out to Prester John in a letter, hailing him as the 'illustrious and magnificent king of the Indies'. The pope entrusted the delivery of the letter to Philip, his court physician and closest friend. Philip sailed out from Italy on a Venetian galley and disembarked somewhere near Palestine. He was last seen heading out into the desert, looking for a kingdom 'near the Tower of Babel', and was never heard from again.

THE LEGEND OF PRESTER JOHN was a case of Chinese whispers: second-, third- or fourth-hand accounts that got grander in the telling. But there was a germ of truth inside the story. Those vague rumours the Crusaders had picked up in the Holy Land were most likely distorted accounts of the Battle of Qatwan, where a heavy defeat was inflicted on the Seljuks by the warriors of Yelü Dashi, the great Khan of the Mongols.

Yelü Dashi's victory at Qatwan had made him the master of Central Asia; his followers acclaimed him as Gur-khan, 'the Universal Khan', a title that may have been translated in Syriac to Yuhanan, which is close enough to the Latin name Johannes or John. Yelü Dashi was not a Christian, but many of his subjects were indeed followers of the lost church of Nestorius, descendants of Mongol tribesmen converted by Nestorian missionaries five hundred years earlier.

THE EXILED NESTORIANS had established churches first in Persia, and then Arabia and India. In the seventh century, Nestorian Christianity came to Tang-dynasty China, where it blended into Buddhist beliefs and practices.

Today, in the ancient Chinese capital of Xi'an there still exists a stele, a black limestone slab erected in 781, that proudly tells how Nestorian Christianity came to China. The headpiece features a cross surrounded by dragons and a lotus blossom, and is titled *Memorial of the Propagation in China of the Luminous Religion from Daqin* ('Daqin' being the ancient Chinese term for the Roman empire).

Nestorian priests in Palm Sunday procession, Gaochang, China.

A wall painting in the abandoned city of Gaochang depicts a Palm Sunday procession from the seventh century, with a Chinese priest performing holy communion, while three other priests carry palm fronds in their hands.

Nestorian Christianity thrived in China until the fourteenth century, when the Ming dynasty overthrew the Mongols and expelled all foreign influences from the Middle Kingdom. The Mongols of Central Asia converted to Islam.

POPE ALEXANDER EVENTUALLY gave up all hope of seeing his friend Philip again, or of receiving a reply to his letter to Prester John. Still, the Christian leaders held out hope of a grand alliance with the mysterious Priest-King of the east. In 1221 there were fresh rumours of another crushing Muslim defeat at the hands of a 'King David of India', said to be the son or grandson of Prester John. Again, it seems a Mongol khan had been mistaken for a Christian King: the 'King David' in question was actually Genghis Khan, who had just won a shattering victory over the Khwarezmian empire of Persia.

The Mongol conquests opened up the east to European trade once again, and Prester John's letter transformed the mysterious east of the European imagination from a wild hinterland filled with terrors to a glittering kingdom of wonders that enticed many to the Silk Road, including curious and ambitious merchants such as Niccolò and Maffeo Polo, father and uncle of Marco Polo.

But if Prester John's letter had led the Romans to believe the Far East was a land of marvels and fantastical beasts, the Chinese had long believed the same to be true of the west. A tenth-century history called the *Book of Tang* records a surprisingly accurate description of Constantinople, which the Chinese knew as the distant city of Fu-Lin:

The walls of their capital are built of granite, and are of enormous height. The city contains in all over 100,000 households. In the south it faces the great sea ... In the palaces, pillars are made of lapis lazuli, the floors of bronze, the leaves of folding doors of ivory, beams of fragrant wood …

When, during the height of summer, the inhabitants are oppressed by heat, they lead water up and make it flow over the platform, spreading it all over the roof by a secret contrivance so that one sees and knows not how it is done, but simply hears the noise of a well on the roof; suddenly you see streams of water rushing down from the four eaves like a cataract; the draught caused thereby produces a cooling wind.

The Romans and the Chinese shared surprisingly similar misconceptions of each other as they peered at one another from either end of the Eurasian landmass. The ancient Romans believed the Chinese harvested their silk by combing it from the leaves of a tree. The Chinese in turn believed the Romans procured their cotton by combing the hair of a special kind of 'water sheep'.

Creature from the Classic of Mountains and Seas.

An ancient Chinese book, the *Classic of Mountains and Seas*, contains stories and illustrations of the freakish people who were said to dwell in the distant lands to the west. The Slavs are portrayed as ogres with flaming red hair and round green teacup eyes that can project green rays of envy. The Hun-like nomads of the north-west are depicted as bizarre savages, whose children are born without bones and who sometimes grow wings. And, as in Constantinople, there are stories of torso-faced dancing savages, only it was claimed that these abominations were creatures of the west.

THE FALL OF CONSTANTINOPLE in 1453 coincided with the advent of Europe's Age of Exploration, and the slow, dawning understanding that headless, torso-faced dancing people were nowhere to be found anywhere in the world. As the last unmapped parts of the globe were charted in the nineteenth and twentieth centuries, the new literary genres of science fiction and fantasy arrived to identify places where fantastical creatures of the imagination might still be discovered. HG Wells put his monsters on Mars. Jules Verne conceived of an imaginary opening to the centre of the Earth in Iceland, which led to a subterranean world of dinosaurs and giants. In the twentieth century, it was possible to imagine that humans might encounter weird creatures on other planets, but now, as we comprehend the vast distances of interstellar space, we've had to resign that hope. An astronomer once told me he was secretly longing for NASA's Huygens probe to reveal the presence of extraterrestrial fish swimming beneath the icy crust of Titan. The probe sent back disappointing images of a brown, pebbly surface. Hard scientific truths are driving us further into fantasy.

The Romans of Constantinople had no need to push all the weird creatures of their imagination into the sky or under the ground. In their minds, all that was required was to push out in a boat, or climb onto a camel, and head towards the distant horizon.

The Floating Nun

TODAY, if we think of saints at all, we think of them as serene and forbearing creatures, but in medieval Constantinople, saints were like superheroes, gifted men and women who could fly through the sky, read minds and hurl fireballs at demons. The convents of the city, like the monasteries, produced their share of super-powered saints. The most formidable of these was Irene of Chrysobalanton.

IN 855, THEODORA, the empress-regent, announced a competition to find a bride for her son Michael, who had just turned fifteen. Ambitious families all over the empire sent young daughters to Constantinople to compete in the bride-show. Among them was a ten-year-old named Irene, who arrived at the city gates from Cappadocia with servants and baggage.

Irene was renowned for her 'moral grace and corporeal beauty' and had been clothed by her parents in a 'most rich and splendid outfit'. But she came too late: a bride had already been chosen for Michael. Although a child, Irene freely chose to enter the Convent of Chrysobalanton within the city.

Once she had taken her vows, Irene became inspired by the works of St Arsenios, a holy man who practised a motionless, yet strenuous, exercise to purify his soul: Arsenios would stand completely still throughout the night with his hands extended to the east. He would only drop this pose when he felt the morning sun shining on his face.

Irene begged the Abbess to be allowed to attempt this exercise herself, so that she might be cleansed of all human frailty and come ever closer to God. With the Abbess's consent, Irene eagerly took up the routine, standing still in her cell with her arms outstretched to heaven. She did this for whole days and nights.

Rumours of Irene's virtue began to spread through the city; it was said that she was more angel than human. Irene grew into adulthood and after some years, she was appointed Abbess with the blessing of the Patriarch of Constantinople.

THEN ONE DAY a strange thought came into her mind. It occurred to her that she should ask God for the gift of second sight, so that she might know what her sisters were up to in secret. Irene gave herself over to prayer and weeping until an angel appeared and granted her wish. The following day she called in each of the sisters to come and sit with her in a chamber at the rear of the church. Irene intimated to each that she knew of secret things they had said and done, provoking them to confess and to promise to reform their behaviour.

ONE NIGHT, WHILE UPRIGHT and motionless in her cell, Irene became aware there were demons in the room. The demons tried to break her stance but Irene was undaunted and moved not an inch. Then the most insolent of the demons began to taunt her.

'Irene is made of wood!' he sneered. 'She is carried on wooden legs!'

Irene said nothing and remained immobile.

'How long will you oppress us?' cried the demon. 'How long will you burn us?'

Then the creature stretched out his hand, grabbed a torch and set fire to Irene. Still she remained immobile.

One of the sisters was roused by the scent of smoke. She rushed into the cell and hurriedly extinguished the fire.

Irene at last lowered her arms. She slowly turned to the sister.

'Why did you do that, my child?' she asked.

Irene explained that while she was burning, she had received a vision of an angel who was about to place a wreath of flowers upon her head.

'But,' she said, 'because of your concern, he left me and went away with his wreath. I hate a gift that causes me a loss.'

IRENE RECOVERED from her burns and continued to practise her standing exercises. She fasted and consumed very little water, and began to look haggard. On one occasion she held her stance for a whole week but when it came time to lower her arms, she discovered her joints had lost their flexibility. Sisters were called to help, and as they did so, they heard her joints crack.

One night a sister peeped out of her cell window and saw Irene in the forecourt of the church, levitating three feet above the ground, praying with her hands extended towards heaven. The sister was amazed to see the cypress trees bow their crowns to Irene.

The following morning the sisters of the convent discovered silk scarves tied to the treetops.

THE HAGIOGRAPHY of St Irene is full of such stories. Once you remove the supernatural elements, it's possible to read it as the tale of an insufferable busybody peering in on her poor sisters in their private moments, perhaps through a hole in the wall. A clumsy accident that leads to her habit catching fire on a lamp wick is re-created into a heroic victory over demonic temptation.

A convent was one of the few places in Constantinople where a woman might enjoy a degree of independence and authority, but it came at the price of eternal vigilance against external threats to her sisters' celibacy. And indeed Irene was once called upon to deal with a young labourer named Nicholas who worked in the convent's vineyard. Nicholas had apparently fallen in love with one of the sisters and was tormented at night by his lustful thoughts for her.

Irene suspected the Devil's hand at work. She ordered Nicholas to be trussed up and strapped to a pillar in the church. Nicholas, wild with unholy fury, broke free of his bonds and attacked a priest, biting into his flesh. Irene stepped forward and commanded Nicolas to be still and he was instantly immobilised. Irene knelt and prayed for him. Then she stood up and commanded the demon to leave his body. Nicholas was cured. Thus purged of his wickedness, he was permitted to return to work in the vineyard. If the impure thoughts ever returned, Nicholas kept them to himself.

Gylo

IN CONSTANTINOPLE, sex, pregnancy and childbirth were bound up with magical practises that originated in the dim pagan past. Women drank concoctions made from rabbit blood, goose fat or turpentine, which they hoped would make them fertile. For contraception, a woman would sometimes wear a magical amulet containing a portion of a cat's liver.

If a couple remained childless, they prayed anxiously to the Virgin Mary, the defender of the city, to intercede on their behalf. But Mary was an impossible role model, having succeeded at motherhood without engaging in the sordid business of sexual congress. A new mother was regarded as unclean, and kept from the sacraments for forty days. In this polluted state, she was believed to be in danger of attracting demons and witches into the nursery that could take the lives of infant children. The worst of these demons was Gylo, a female demon whose 'body was darkness and her hair savage'; she had wings and the lower body of a serpent.

The legend of Gylo originates in ancient Babylon. She was said to be the vengeful ghost of a young woman who had died a virgin, and was driven to take the lives of children out of spite and envy. Gylo flew across the city at night and could slip into houses, even when the doors and windows were barred. She would slither through the house, up into the nursery, and strangle a sleeping child. Amulets and icons were placed over the beds of sleeping infants to ward her off.

Fear of Gylo was very real in Constantinople. A childless old woman who behaved in ways that her neighbours might regard as eccentric could find herself arrested and hauled into a courtroom, accused of being possessed by Gylo. If convicted, the woman could be subject to a harrowing rite of exorcism, in which every single one of the demon's twelve-and-a-half names had to be carefully recited by a priest.* If any one name was omitted, it left an opening for Gylo to hide inside that name, protected from the rite of the exorcism.

FOR NEW MOTHERS, no better role model existed than the Blessed Virgin. Icon painters lovingly portrayed her with her newborn child in ways that shine a light on various aspects of the intimate mother–son relationship. In the *Hodegetria*, 'She Who Shows the Way', we see the mother who wants us to appreciate the blameless virtue of her son: Mary looks us straight in the eye while gesturing towards the baby Jesus with one hand; 'You should be like my perfect son', she seems to say. In her guise as the Lady *Eleousa*, the Virgin of

---

* Gylo, Morrha, Byzo, Marmaro, Petasia, Pelagia, Bordona, Apleto, Chomodracaena, Anabardalaea, Psychoanaspastria, Paedopniktria and Strigla.

Tenderness, Mary gives herself over to adoration of the child; she's the besotted mother, with the infant Christ nestled against her cheek. Sometimes her face is flushed with sadness, as she seems to anticipate the crucifixion that awaits her baby boy.

Then we see her as the *Galaktotrophousa*, the Nursing Madonna who serenely breastfeeds her child.

The icons are heavily stylised, otherworldly. The Orthodox faithful use them to open a tiny crack in the world, to let the radiance of the heavenly kingdom shine through. But these images also warm the soul as very human portraits of a mortal woman and her infant. Her arms and robes form a throne for the object of her adoration.

The Eldest Son of the Eldest Son

JOE WAS OUR FIRST CHILD. Khym and I had been married for five years and we were in our mid-thirties. We decided it was time to start trying before we embarked on a long trip together through France, Spain and Morocco. We suspected something was up in Madrid. By the time we got to Marrakesh, Khym was uncharacteristically queasy around the spicy food. The day we returned home to our little flat in Sydney, she took the test and came out of the bathroom giggling, fatalistically.

I was a little apprehensive about becoming a father. I had wanted this baby and we had agreed now would be a good time. And I was happy Khym was pregnant. But a new person was about to enter our lives, whom we didn't know, who was going to be with us forever. In my mind, the child was an abstraction, like a baby-shaped silhouette with an 'X' in the middle of it.

I thought Khym was remarkably relaxed about the whole thing. As her belly swelled she became radiant. The remaining seven months of her pregnancy passed quickly.

Khym likes to prepare herself for the worst. When we decided to try for a baby, she warned it might not happen for years, if at all. Now that she was pregnant, she suggested we should be prepared in case she somehow didn't form that instant mother–child attachment. So much of our future happiness rested on those critical few seconds after the birth. We were counting on love at first sight. It sounded like witchcraft.

Halfway through her pregnancy, Khym woke up one morning and told me the baby had introduced himself to her in a dream: she had walked into the bedroom and there he was, a baby boy in a cradle, wearing a tight blue jumpsuit. He was standing up with his hands on the rail, looking up at her, bewildered. He said he wanted to know who he was. She said, 'Well, you're my son.' She picked him up and took him to a mirror where they stared into their reflections. He seemed shocked by what he was seeing. He told Khym his name was Joe, and that he was an artist.

ONE SATURDAY MORNING in late June, Khym came out of the bath and told me the contractions had started. The midwives cared for Khym with calm efficiency, like a guild of expert priestesses. Our friend Sally stayed close to Khym, whispering encouragement. Every woman in the room knew exactly what she was doing there.

No one will come right out and say it, but the presence in that room of the father-to-be is utterly superfluous. During antenatal classes, the instructor flattered the anxious dads-in-waiting, telling us we could help during labour by giving our partners a loving shoulder massage. Now, as I dutifully rubbed my wife's shoulders, I realised that no amount of massage was going to ameliorate the pain of passing a small human from your body. It was a deft act of misdirection: keep the man out of the way so the professionals can get on with the job.

I was still happy to be there. I could see that the men of my father's generation, who were discouraged from being present for the birth of their children, missed out. It's a kindness for us to be admitted into that room, to see how heroically women labour and suffer to bring life into the world. In that room we are properly reacquainted with our mammalian selves.

It was dawn the next day when Khym entered the second stage of labour, and the midwife told us the baby would be with us in an hour. I drew a deep breath and looked at the clock. As Khym began to bear down, a surge of adrenaline coursed through me. Soon, I thought, there will be a new person in the room.

An hour later that baby boy arrived. Khym was utterly spent, but triumphant. I exploded into tears, weeping in joy and relief and wonder. I was completely undone, sobbing, as I looked upon this strange thing, and I was instantly in love. I pulled myself together long enough to cut the cord. The midwife handed our newborn son to Khym, who held him to her breast and beamed, and said, 'Joe'.

THE HOSPITAL STAFF gave us an hour to be a new family together. I was in awe of Khym, who was relaxed and happy as she nursed Joe, even though she hadn't slept for the better part of three days. Late-morning sunshine streamed into the room and onto her hair. She was the *Galaktotrophousa*, the Nursing Madonna. She said she was looking forward to eating oysters and goat's cheese again.

I came home and sent out a mass email announcing the arrival of a healthy baby boy. Alone in the flat, I reviewed the events of the past three days in my mind and marvelled at my emotional outburst at the moment of birth. Where had that come from? I hadn't cried like that since I was a child. I called two friends who had recently become fathers and told them I'd just been though the most moving experience of my life.

'The feeling changes you forever,' one of them confessed quietly.

The other said, 'It gives you an entirely new idea of love.'

Until that moment, every new dad I'd met had said something glib about the change in life that was coming. They would chuckle and tell me to prepare for Phase Two: a life of no sleep, shitty nappies and not hanging out with the guys anymore. I think this banter is an act of concealment, a way of papering over the powerful and unsettling surge of love that fatherhood brings.

A few days later it was time for Khym and Joe to come home. I called a cab to pick us up at the hospital. The driver was from Pakistan and wearing traditional Muslim dress. He was grinning widely, delighted to be bringing a new family home for the first time. He drove ten kilometres per hour below the speed limit all the way through Sydney traffic. We got talking about kids. He had three under five.

'And what have you named your son?' he asked.

'His name is Joe,' Khym replied from the back seat, where she sat next to the baby capsule.

'Is that short for Joseph?'

'Yes, it is.'

'It is a Muslim name as well. Only we will call him Yusuf.'

He turned and looked me straight in the eye and said, 'Children are the best pleasure in life.'

A week later I received a warm letter from my Uncle Brian. He wrote that he was deeply moved that we had named our son Joseph. I assumed he was pleased that we hadn't called him 'Jayydyn' or 'Seven'.

OUR DAUGHTER EMMA was born three-and-a-half years later.

Her birth was more straightforward. She came into the world pain-free and beautiful, and fell asleep in the arms of her mother. *Eleousa*, the Lady of Loving Kindness.

There it was again, the same surge of love and tenderness.

Emma had penetrating, dark eyes. She was a calmer, more placid baby than Joe, which might have been because we were calmer and more confident parents. Her hair was tufty and black, and her eyes were dark and beguiling.

WHEN JOE WAS FIVE and Emma was two, Khym and I took them to a family function and I got talking with my Uncle Brian. I was very fond of him and hadn't seen him in years. Again, he told me he was touched by our choice of name for Joe. I asked him why. He raised his eyebrows and said he thought I knew about the family tradition.

'Ever since our ancestors came to Australia in the 1840s,' he explained, 'the eldest son of the eldest son had always been named Joseph.'

'But I'm the eldest son of the eldest son, and I'm a Richard.'

'Ah, yes. Your great-grandfather was a Joseph, but his son Joe died without children. Then your grandfather George took on the mantle. His eldest son was your dad, Alan. But I thought you knew all about this. I thought you'd named your boy Joe to re-establish the tradition.'

'It's the first I ever heard about it.'

He reached into his jacket and pulled out a dog-eared, hand-drawn family tree, which he unfolded on the table. He pointed to the names of our ancestors, who had migrated to Australia from England and Ireland. Then his finger traced the line down to their first two children, the first natural-born Australians in the family.

Their names were Joseph and Emma.

We looked at each other and heard the peal of a distant ship's bell resounding across 160 years. This was nothing more than a coincidence, but the symmetry of the past and present names pleased my uncle, who was a religious man, very much, and it pleased me too.

The Death of Andronicus

EMPEROR MANUEL I – the grandson of Alexius – was twenty-five when he ascended to the throne of Constantinople. He was a tall, slightly stooped young man, with a dark complexion and a pleasant smile. His coronation was greeted enthusiastically within the city, but on the empire's borders, the strategic outlook was deteriorating: the Normans had taken all of the imperial lands in Italy, and were planning an attack on Greece; the Seljuks were firmly in control of large swathes of Asia Minor.

Fortunately for Manuel, trade was booming. Constantinople was perfectly positioned as a thriving *entrepôt* between the rising powers of Venice and Genoa to the west, Fatamid Egypt to the south, and the new Crusader states in the east. With a treasury fattened with tax revenue, Manuel was able to spend lavishly on his army and navy.

Manuel inspired intense loyalty among his courtiers, but he never quite *looked* the part of emperor, not as much, at least, as his cousin Andronicus, who even his enemies had to concede was an impressive figure. Andronicus was tall, absurdly handsome, quick-witted and charming. He was physically powerful and his sexual appetite was said to be 'like a horse in heat, covering mare after mare beyond reason'. Andronicus's roguish, manly nature endeared him to Manuel and he became a great favourite at court, until he took his niece Eudoxia as his mistress. Whenever he was upbraided for forming an incestuous relationship, Andronicus laughed and quipped that he was from the same mould as the emperor – who happened to be sleeping with his own brother's daughter.

Falling out of favour in Constantinople, Andronicus was appointed to a military command in Cilicia in Asia Minor, and in 1152, he set out with Eudoxia to take up his post. One night, she entered his tent to warn him that her kinsmen were waiting outside, ready to assassinate him. Eudoxia suggested he call the maid in, switch garments with her, and sneak out in disguise. Andronicus dreaded the thought of being captured in such a demeaning manner; instead, he slashed an opening at the rear of the tent with his sword, leapt over a fence and escaped.

ANDRONICUS'S CASUAL disregard for propriety had earned him many enemies at court, who began to assail Manuel with tales of his disloyalty. The stories wore away at Manuel's affection for Andronicus, and he was recalled to Constantinople, and thrown into a prison within the Great Palace.

Andronicus started removing bricks from his cell floor, and spied an ancient underground passage. He pulled out some more bricks, making an opening wide enough to squeeze through, then put the bricks back in place as he exited. When the guards came to serve him his dinner, they were astonished to find the cell empty, with no apparent sign of entry or exit.

In retaliation, Manuel ordered that Andronicus's wife (who, needless to say, was not Eudoxia) be held captive as a hostage, placing her in the same cell that had held Andronicus. Using the same tunnel, Andronicus entered her cell, led her out and had sex with her against the prison wall. She would later give birth to a son, John. Adronicus's wife's name is not recorded, and it is not known what became of her.

Andronicus was soon caught and placed in heavy iron fetters. But he persuaded a young boy in the prison to make a wax impression of the key to his cell. The boy then took the wax to Andronicus's brother, who forged a new key and dropped it into an amphora of wine, which was brought in with Andronicus's midday meal. He slipped away again.

It was now too dangerous to remain in Constantinople, so Andronicus made his way north, towards the Danube, but was caught again by a party of Vlach warriors on the lookout for him. As they made their way back to Constantinople, Andronicus told his captors he had gastroenteritis. His disgusted captors allowed him to duck away to the side of the road to relieve himself. Taking his walking stick with him, he crouched down a little way from the camp. With his back to the guards, Andronicus draped his cloak around the stick and placed his hat on top; in the darkness, his clothing could pass as a man on his haunches. Leaving this scarecrow behind, Andronicus took off into the woods.

Heading north, he reached Galicia, ruled by yet another cousin, Yaroslav, who welcomed him with open arms. Emperor Manuel, worried that Andronicus might raise an army to usurp him, decided it was time to patch things up with his wayward cousin, and Andronicus was allowed to return to Constantinople in 1168.

ANDRONICUS LASTED for only a year before he fell out of favour again, by complaining noisily about the emperor's selection of his Hungarian son-in-law as his successor. Andronicus had given voice to grumblings of discontent in the capital. Manuel, who had married a blonde Norman princess, was increasingly seen as too close to foreigners from the west.

Infuriated, Manuel expelled Andronicus from the court, and sent him back to the front in Cilicia, probably hoping he'd die in combat. Andronicus's second stint proved even more disastrous than his first: he allowed himself to be drawn into a pointless battle against Thoros of Armenia, and his forces were badly beaten.

As he retreated from the battlefield, Andronicus looked over his shoulder and saw Thoros preparing to launch a final assault on his men. Overcome with the anguish of defeat, Andronicus turned his horse around and charged towards Thoros. As he neared the startled Armenian king, Andronicus flung his lance, which clanged into Thoros's shield and knocked him off his horse. In the confusion, Andronicus was able to turn around and race away.

WITH THAT, HE WAS DONE with campaigning. Andronicus laid down his armour and shield and rode south to the court of Raymond of Antioch where, it was recorded, he 'gave himself over to wanton pleasures, adorned himself like a fop, and paraded in the streets escorted by bodyguards bearing silver bows'. He seduced another beautiful Norman princess – Philippa, the sister of Empress Maria. On receiving the news back in Constantinople, Manuel was 'thunderstruck'. Still furious over Andronicus's idiotic attack on the Armenians, he demanded Andronicus be brought back to Constantinople in chains. In fear of his safety, Adronicus abandoned Philippa, and fled south, into the Holy Land, where he found refuge in the Crusader kingdom of Jerusalem, under the protection of King Almaric.

At fifty-six, Andronicus began the greatest love affair of his life, with Theodora Comnena, Manuel's niece and widow of King

Baldwin III of Jerusalem. Manuel sent a letter to Almaric, pointing out that Andronicus was a rebel and guilty of incest. He demanded that Almaric put out his eyes. The letter was passed to Theodora, who showed it to Andronicus. Choosing to share the burden of exile, they departed Jerusalem together.

The couple travelled east into the Muslim lands to the court of Nur ad-Din, the sultan of Damascus, where Theodora gave birth to two children. After several years, they resumed their wanderings, eventually settling in a castle on the shores of the Black Sea.

One day, while Andronicus was away from home, their castle was captured by the Duke of Trebizond. Theodora and the children were taken into custody and brought to Constantinople. Andronicus, in great distress, agreed to exchange their captivity for his, and he returned to Constantinople in early 1180.

THE TWO FORMER FRIENDS had not seen each other for years, and Manuel was shocked at his cousin's ragged appearance. Andronicus looked up at the emperor soulfully and shrugged off his cloak, dramatically revealing a heavy chain he had fastened from his neck to his ankles. Then he stretched out on the floor in front of the emperor, tearfully begging his pardon. The emperor was moved to see such a mighty man brought so low. He ordered his attendants to raise Andronicus to his feet, but Andronicus said he would not rise until someone had dragged him by his chain over the path to the throne, and then dashed him against it. It was no less than he deserved, he said. The emperor commanded that this be done and pardoned Andronicus. He was allowed to retire with Theodora on their estate on the Black Sea.

LATER THAT YEAR, Manuel's health declined and he died after a long fever. He was succeeded by his ten-year-old son Alexius II, under the guardianship of his mother, Empress Maria. Popular discontent with western influence in the court was now focused on the foreign-born empress-regent.

Manuel had recognised the growing wealth and power of the Italian city-states of Venice, Genoa and Pisa by granting them generous trade concessions in Constantinople. The presence of these rich Italians on the streets of the city was deeply resented. Their wealth had made them arrogant, and their Catholicism made them ungodly in the eyes of the Orthodox faithful.

Andronicus, hearing reports of discontent in the capital, raised a band of followers and marched on Constantinople. A contingent of soldiers was sent out to intercept him. Instead, they defected to Andronicus's side, along with the commander of the imperial navy. The gates of the city were opened, and Andronicus entered Constantinople unchallenged, to an emotional, almost hysterical, welcome.

Something ugly was unleashed on the capital that day. Long-festering resentment against wealthy westerners erupted into street violence. Thousands of Latin Catholics were murdered, women and children along with them. John, the papal legate, was killed and his severed head was tied to the tail of a dog and dragged through the city streets.

Andronicus, the beneficiary of all the violence, did nothing to stop it. Those who had smiled on the tall, handsome aristocrat or dismissed him as a charming rogue had missed the cruel streak in his character. The man who now controlled Constantinople, and the Roman empire, was a psychopath.

EMPRESS MARIA AND HER SON were arrested and brought before Andronicus. The boy emperor was still invested with supreme legal authority, and was forced to sign his mother's death warrant.

Maria was then strangled by two members of the imperial guard. When this was done, Andronicus compelled Alexius to accompany him to the Chalke Gate, and to recognise him as his co-emperor in front of a cheering crowd. Alexius was then taken away and strangled with a bow-string. His body was thrown into the Bosphorus.

Alexius had been betrothed to Agnes, daughter of King Louis of France. Andronicus now took her as his wife, disregarding the vast age difference between them: he was sixty-four and she was a child of eleven. His son John Comnenus – conceived that night outside the prison of the Great Palace – was appointed his junior emperor.

MANUEL HAD BEEN widely resented for his tolerance of corruption. Andronicus now instituted a crackdown on corruption and wasteful spending, and his punishments became crueller and more frequent. Attendants who failed to please were blinded or burnt alive in the Hippodrome. The chill of official terror descended on the capital. Unburdened by any moral constraint, Andronicus 'let down the fine and delicate plumb line of his cruelty to the very bottom of his soul'.

AS EMPEROR, ANDRONICUS was free to give rein to his gargantuan sexual appetites. Court historian Nicetas Choniates describes him setting out from the city, 'followed by his ladyloves, like a cock by barnyard hens … opening wide every passageway to flute girls and courtesans, with whom he indulged himself at all times in the pleasure of intercourse'. The emperor was said at this time to apply ointments to his genitals to improve his sexual prowess, and to eat crocodile meat, which he believed to be an aphrodisiac.

As he sank deeper into paranoia, Andronicus attempted to divine the future through hydromancy, by looking for signs of the unknown by peering into a basin of water. When the question was asked, 'Who will rule after Emperor Andronicus?' the waters indicated the first two letters of the name 'Isaac'. Andronicus's suspicions now fell upon his cousin Isaac Angelus.

The Death of Stephen Hagiochristophorites. Detail from Passages d'outremer (Overseas Voyages), by Sébastien Mamerot, c.1475.

The emperor sent his chief enforcer, a man named Stephen Hagiochristophorites, to arrest Isaac. Hagiochristophorites was widely feared and hated in the city. Accompanied by two attendants, he confronted Isaac in the courtyard of his home. Seeing he was cornered, Isaac leapt on to his horse, drew his sword and charged towards the men. Hagiochristophorites panicked and turned his mule around to make his escape. He got as far as the courtyard archway when Isaac brought his sword down onto his skull, cracking it in half. The other two attendants fled.

Isaac Angelus, exulting in his escape from death, now rode his horse to the Hagia Sophia, holding aloft his bloody sword, shouting he had just killed the hated Hagiochristophorites. Isaac dashed into the Great Church with hundreds of people streaming in behind him. He ascended to the pulpit and asked for sanctuary, and forgiveness for the crime of murder. Soon there were more than a thousand people in the church. By dawn the next morning, there were more people outside the Hagia Sophia, but no one came to attack or arrest them. Another crowd formed at the watch house and set all the prisoners free. Isaac was acclaimed as emperor by the crowd and the atmosphere in the city turned mutinous and murderous.

ANDRONICUS WAS STAYING at his country estate when he was told of the insurrection in the city. He returned to the Great Palace and ordered the guards to fire arrows at the angry crowd. The soldiers were reluctant to obey, so Andronicus picked up a bow and began firing arrows himself. Then, realising he was alone, he decided to make a run for it. He tore off his imperial insignia, covered his head with a bonnet, and climbed into a waiting boat, bringing with him his child bride and his mistress. The mob then overran the Great Palace, looting it of every scrap of treasure they could find. The palace complex would never recover.

Andronicus's little boat was intercepted in the Bosphorus. He was arrested and thrown into another boat, along with his wife and mistress, to be brought back to Constantinople. Andronicus was a veteran of many dazzling escapes, but there was no getting away this time. As he sat in the boat, bound hand and foot, he began to sing. It was a lament of self-pity for his unfortunate life. His voice swelled and cracked with emotion. Both his young wife and mistress began to sing with him, but his captors were unmoved.

Andronicus was shackled and paraded in front of the new Emperor Isaac Angelus. He was slapped across the face and kicked on the buttocks. His beard was torn and his teeth pulled out. Women stepped forward to pummel him with their fists. His right hand was cut off with an axe, and then he was thrown back into his cell.

Two days later, one of his eyes was gouged out, and then he was handed over to the mob. Andronicus was placed on a camel and paraded through the streets, 'looking like a leafless and withered old stump'. People struck him with clubs and poured shit on his head. All the cruelty he had inflicted upon the lives of his people was now revisited upon his body.

Somehow still alive, Andronicus was brought into the Hippodrome, seated on the hump of the camel, in a gruesome parody of a triumphal procession. He was pulled off the camel and suspended by his feet between two pillars. As he suffered these terrible ordeals, he turned to his tormentors and whimpered, 'Lord have mercy', and 'Why do you further bruise the broken reed?'

Two Latin soldiers with swords stepped forward and cleaved him apart. As they did so, he raised his handless right arm to his mouth, and then he died. He was sixty-seven years old, and he was the last emperor of the Comneni, the dynasty founded by Alexius I. His son John was killed by his own troops in Thrace.

TODAY, IN THE PLEASANT PARKLANDS of the Hippodrome, it's difficult to re-create in our minds the dark passions of the crowd that day, which exploded just a hundred metres from the church of Holy Wisdom.

Spiritually, the Romans of Constantinople were reaching for *theosis*, or union with the divine. The underlying principle that would generate *theosis* was something they called *taxis*, a divinely ordained sense of order that would infuse the world with light, harmony and holiness. A good and wise imperial government was expected to uphold this principle of *taxis*.

The opposite of *taxis* was *ataxia*, turbulence and randomness. *Ataxia* was supposed to belong to the lands beyond the empire's frontiers, a formless world of meaningless violence.

Andronicus's reign had inverted that proposition: what did it mean when the emperor himself was the source of so much *ataxia*? Constantinople was shaken, unsure of itself and completely unprepared for the cataclysm that was to come and wreck it beyond repair.

CHAPTER EIGHT

The Fourth Crusade

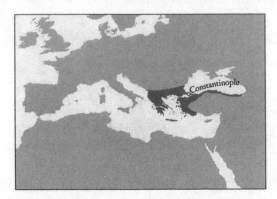

The empire in 1200, at the outset of the Fourth Crusade.

The Blind Old Duke

'There can be no doubt that the hand of God guided all of these events.'
– Geoffrey de Villehardouin

UPSTAIRS IN THE HAGIA SOPHIA, in a corner of the gallery, I spot the oddest, most unlikely thing. I call Joe over to look at it. Embedded into the stone floor is a modest tombstone, inscribed with the name 'Henricus Dandolo'.

I tell Joe that Henricus Dandolo is better remembered to the world as Enrico Dandolo, the Doge of Venice and the perpetrator-in-chief of one of the worst crimes of the late Middle Ages. Dandolo successfully connived to wreck Constantinople beyond repair and he personally led an attack on the city walls. There was no end to the mayhem he unleashed upon the world for the narrow advantage of Venice.

'And when he did all this, he was an old man of ninety, and utterly blind.'

'So why' Joe asks 'is he buried in the Hagia Sophia?'

Stone memorial to Enrico Dandolo, Hagia Sophia, Istanbul.

ENRICO DANDOLO was eighty-five when he was elected the forty-second Doge (or Duke) of the Most Serene Republic of Venice in 1192. His mind worked as well as it ever had, but his eyesight was gone. Dandolo was cagey about his blindness, and tried to conceal it with little tricks, like surreptitiously dropping a single hair into his soup and then complaining about it to anyone present.

There was a time when the young Republic of Venice had pleaded for the empire's favour and protection. That time had passed. Trade had made Venice rich and confident. Its merchant ships cruised the Mediterranean, protected by its formidable navy, the strongest in Europe. The aristocrats of Constantinople were inclined to disdain the Venetian upstarts as nouveau-riche shopkeepers and sailors. The

Venetians, in turn, saw the Byzantines as effete, impractical snobs living off the fading prestige of their once-glorious name.

Dandolo knew Constantinople well. He had travelled there decades earlier as a special envoy, charged with repairing Venetian relations with the empire. But Emperor Manuel Comnenus, irritated by Venice's growing clout, decided to withdraw the republic's trading privileges and to lock up some of its merchants. Dandolo returned to Venice humiliated. Later there would be rumours that Dandolo had been blinded during this unhappy time in Constantinople, on orders from the emperor. Another rumour had it that his eyesight was lost in a street brawl in the city. These stories were put forward to explain Dandolo's apparent hatred of Constantinople, but both were untrue; his eyesight was actually destroyed years later in Venice, by a blow to the head.

Power in the Venetian Republic was concentrated within a tightly knit upper class of merchants and property owners. The Doge was the chief executive, elected for life. Venice's leadership was drawn from a pool of shrewd and experienced men, while in Constantinople they all too often had to take potluck with a hereditary prince or a brutal general.

The Venetians were Catholics, and took spiritual guidance from the pope in Rome. In church they hoped and prayed for salvation, but in the marketplace they put aside wishful thinking in favour of hard data. The merchants of Venice were the first to properly use a new method of mapping the cash and goods flowing in and out of their businesses, a process we now call double-entry bookkeeping. It was an unsentimental exercise that burned away unrealistic hopes and grandiosity.

The financial power of Venice was reinforced by its great navy. Its ships were constructed with the most advanced maritime technology of the era and operated by the most seasoned sailors in the

Mediterranean. Venetian trading galleys were well equipped to repel attacks from pirates, and from their rivals, the merchants of Genoa.

DANDOLO HAD SERVED six years as Doge when an emissary came to his office with a report: His Holiness Pope Innocent III had issued a plea for a fresh armed struggle to liberate Jerusalem from the Muslims.

Control of the Holy Land had turned over several times since the first Crusader knights had passed through Constantinople. Jerusalem had been won, and then lost to Saladin. The Third Crusade had concluded eight years earlier, unsatisfyingly; while Acre and Jaffa had been captured, the Crusader kings had failed to retake Jerusalem, the emotional and spiritual heartland of the Crusade.

For Pope Innocent, it was simply intolerable that the banners of Muhammad should continue to flutter over the holiest city in Christendom. The thought pinched and pricked at him like a stone in his shoe. But enthusiasm for a new crusade among the kings and princes of western Europe was tepid at best. So Innocent looked to the next layer down, to the ambitious lords and younger brothers, who were eager to prove their mettle and willing to carve out new estates of their own in the Holy Land.

Richard the Lionheart had walked away from the Third Crusade telling anyone who would listen that any future attempt to take the Holy Land should consider advancing to Jerusalem via Egypt, the soft underbelly of the Saracen world. If a Fourth Crusade were to be launched, it would need a great many ships to ferry the armies of Christ across the Mediterranean. Since Venice was the leading maritime power in Europe, Pope Innocent's call to arms made it inevitable that someone would show up sooner or later to ask for Venice's help.

IN THE SPRING OF 1201 a galley entered the Venetian lagoon bearing six French knights, led by the Marshal of Champagne, Geoffrey de Villehardouin. The knights were brought ashore into the Piazza San Marco and taken to the Doge's palace. Dandolo received them warmly and inquired as to the reason for their visit. The knights confessed they were envoys of certain French noblemen. Their lords, they said, wanted an alliance with Venice, to aid them on their Crusade against the Saracen infidel.

Geoffrey de Villehardouin, French postage stamp.

The old Doge invited the six men to speak of their plan and the Crusaders got down to business. They proposed to follow Richard's recommendation to enter the Holy Land via Egypt, but they would need Venetian ships to carry their soldiers and horses. Dandolo asked how many soldiers they could rally to the cause. Villehardouin thought for a moment. He'd heard stories of a charismatic evangelist called Fulk of Neuilly, who'd recently boasted of signing up 200,000 men for the struggle.* That number was obviously fanciful, so the

---

* Fulk of Neuilly travelled around France like a modern-day televangelist, using his imposing physical presence to preach the virtue of poverty and simplicity, even as he was collecting large sums of gold for the Crusade. But Fulk was unable to bring himself to hand over the cash. James of Vitry, more in sorrow than in anger, recorded that Fulk, 'through avarice or other base motive, did not make these payments ... His wealth grew, but the fear and respect he had commanded fell away'. Fulk's reputation was badly dented by these charges of embezzlement and he died in disgrace a few years later.

knights landed on a much more conservative 33,500 men, admittedly still a huge figure. The expectation was that each one of these men would bring funds to pay for their passage.

Dandolo called a special meeting of the Great Council of Venice and a deal was struck: Venice agreed to supply transport vessels for 4500 knights and horses, nine thousand squires and twenty thousand foot soldiers, along with provisions of water, wheat, flour and wine. In return, the Crusaders would pay Venice the towering sum of 84,000 silver marks. As a show of good faith, the Venetians would throw in, at their own expense, fifty additional fully equipped galleys. In return, Venice would be entitled to receive a half share of the conquered territories.

The Great Council had given its consent, but before Dandolo could fully commit Venice to such a gigantic enterprise, he needed to win over the greater mass of the Venetian people. And so the six Crusaders were invited to attend a people's assembly at the Church of St Mark. The congregation was hushed as Villehardouin rose to his feet and delivered an electrifying appeal to the people of Venice:

> *The barons of France, most high and powerful, have sent us to you!*
> *They cry to you for mercy, that you take pity on Jerusalem,*
> *which is in bondage to the Turks, and that, for God's sake, you*
> *should help to avenge the shame of Jesus Christ ... They have*
> *come to you, because they know full well that no other people has*
> *so great a power on the seas, as you and your people. Our lords*
> *have commanded us to fall at your feet, and not to rise until you*
> *consent to take pity on the Holy Land which is beyond the seas.*

Then all six of these proud Frankish knights fell to their knees before the crowd. The sight of these good men, humbly prostrating themselves, invoked a kind of compassionate ecstasy from the crowd. The sightless Doge was himself moved to tears and the congregation cried out: *We consent! We consent!*

IT WAS ALL A RUSE – on Dandolo's part at least – because at that moment, his commissioners in Cairo were negotiating a trade contract with Egypt that stipulated Venice would not take part in any invasion of Egyptian territory. Unless he had his wires badly crossed, Dandolo, it seems, had no intention of accompanying the Crusaders into Egypt. His true destination would emerge later.

The French knights were unaware of the negotiations, and it was solemnly agreed that the Crusader armies would assemble in Venice in a year's time, on St John's Day, 1202. In the meantime, Venetian shipbuilders would put aside all other business to begin constructing the Crusaders' new fleet. Venice committed a year's worth of labour, almost all its wealth and its sea power to the cause. The Crusaders and the Venetians would proceed on this great adventure together, hand in hand, for better or worse.

The Sign of the Cross

THE NEXT SUMMER Crusader armies began to arrive in Venice in dribs and drabs, and set up camp on the Lido. The Crusade was spearheaded by a small group of wealthy noblemen from northern France and Italy. Baldwin of Flanders, one of the richest men in France, arrived early with his entourage of knights, archers and crossbowmen. Hugh of St Pol also brought knights and infantry. Louis of Blois, who had fought in the Third Crusade as a teenager, had received a thousand marks for the campaign from King John of England. Villehardouin, a veteran of earlier battles in the Holy Land, was also among the leadership group.

Baldwin, Hugh and Louis were a close-knit group of young, ambitious Frenchmen who had known each other all their lives, but they chose an outsider, Boniface of Montferrat, to lead them. Boniface was an immensely wealthy, middle-aged nobleman from northern Italy, his family connected by marriage to many of the royal houses of Europe. Boniface's father had fought in the Second Crusade and his older brother, William of the Long Sword, had married an heiress to the kingdom of Jerusalem. His court in Montferrat was famous for its chivalry and for the songs of its troubadours.

Boniface showed up in Venice in mid-August and found the camp on the Lido in a state of disarray. The call to take up the Cross had failed to rally anything like the numbers the French knights had rashly promised a year ago. The army that had showed up was less than a third of the size they were counting on to win back the Holy Land.*

The embarrassed Crusader leaders met with Doge Dandolo, who asked them how they would now pay for the new armada of ships his people had constructed in good faith. The Crusaders emptied their war chests but were still 34,000 silver marks short. Dandolo told them not one ship would leave Venice until every last one of them was paid for.

Now everyone was stuck. Calling off the Crusade was unthinkable, a terrible humiliation and a financial disaster. The pope had granted them remission of their sins for agreeing to take up the Cross. What would he say now? What would their people think?

The Crusaders pleaded with Dandolo to come up with a solution and the sly old Doge made his move: he proposed a moratorium

---

* Geoffrey de Villehardouin's account of this awkward episode is titled *First Starting of the Pilgrims for Venice, and of Some Who Went Not Hither.* For indeed, hither some of them went not.

on all Crusader debt ... for the moment. They could pay him later. In the meantime, perhaps the Crusaders could do the Republic of Venice a small service.

Further down the Adriatic coast was a city called Zara, which had been captured by the King of Hungary.* If the Crusaders were prepared to help him recover Zara for Venice ... well, he said, that might be to the benefit of both parties. Zara, he knew, was a wealthy city. The Crusaders would be entitled to half the booty. Maybe that would pay their debt to him.

The Crusader leadership agreed to the new plan, but dissent broke out in the lower ranks. A diversion to attack a Christian city, some said, was outrageous, a violation of their sacred oath to make war on the Saracens. Some of the men packed up and left Venice in disgust, vowing to make their own way to the Holy Land.

In this moment of doubt and confusion, Dandolo made a dramatic gesture. He announced that despite his age and his blindness, he would *personally* lead the Venetian fleet. Dandolo climbed into the pulpit of St Mark's to address his people: 'I am an old and feeble man who should have need of rest,' he sighed. 'But I see that no one could command and lead you like myself. If you consent, I will take the sign of the cross to guard you and direct you ... If you consent, then I shall go to live – or die – with you and the pilgrims.'

With that, the old man carefully stepped down from the pulpit and knelt before the altar. A cap with a cross was placed on his aged head. The old man had delivered a massive jolt of energy to his people: thousands of Venetian men, inspired by his valour, offered to join the Crusade. Venice's commitment had ratcheted up dramatically. The entire fleet and half the city's manpower was now dedicated to

---

* Present-day Zadar in Croatia.

the Crusade. It was to be the biggest and most expensive enterprise in all of Venetian history.

One of the Crusaders, Robert de Clari, later wrote that 'the whole army seemed intoxicated that summer night' as the Crusaders celebrated their alliance by parading through the streets of Venice with flickering candles fastened to the end of their lances.

Zara

THE VENETIAN FLEET sailed out from the lagoon in October 1202, festooned with shields and banners, led by Doge Dandolo's special vermilion galley. Dandolo was spotted standing on the deck, next to a billowing marquee of red silk, seeing things other men could not.

The fleet travelled down the Illyrian coast and pulled ashore outside the walls of Zara. They set up camp, assembled their catapults and prepared to attack. But before they could get underway, a message arrived from Rome. Pope Innocent had gotten wind of their plans to attack a Christian city, and expressly forbade the attack. All who disregarded this message, he warned, would be excommunicated. The Crusaders were dismayed, but a furious Dandolo insisted they keep their bargain to attack Zara.

'I will not in *any* degree give over being avenged on Zara!' he said. 'No! Not even for a pope!'

Now the Crusaders were in a terrible moral bind, forced to choose between dishonour and excommunication. In the end they reasoned they had better keep their contract with the Venetians, if only as a means to fulfil their greater obligation to go on to Jerusalem. The leadership agreed to keep the existence of the pope's letter a secret, lest it cause more dissent in the ranks.

Dandolo expected to conclude an agreement with the Zarans without the need for a battle. They had arrived with overwhelming numbers and the Zarans could not hope to withstand the 11,000-strong army at the gate. The Zarans came forward with an offer: they would agree to restore the city to Venetian control and surrender their possessions so long as the Crusaders agreed to spare their lives. Dandolo was ready to accept their terms when one of the dissident Crusader knights, Simon of Montfort, approached the Zarans and told them the Venetians were bluffing – there would be no attack, he said, because the Franks would never help the Venetians fight for Zara. The Zarans, thinking they had nothing to gain by surrendering, withdrew from negotiations. The Crusaders mounted an attack and quickly overcame the city.

On 24 November 1202, Zara surrendered and the city was looted. But the money they were able to plunder from the city wasn't nearly enough to pay the remainder of their debt. Now they were facing failure *and* excommunication. Angry muttering was heard within the camp. A brawl broke out between Venetians and disgruntled Crusader soldiers. A small delegation of Crusader knights hurried off to Rome to beg the pope's forgiveness, explaining the whole thing was a regrettable necessity. But Dandolo and the Venetians were unperturbed and refused to apologise; their excommunication remained in place. And they were still a long way from Jerusalem.

BY NOW, POPE INNOCENT WAS, perhaps, beginning to comprehend how little control he had over the forces he had unleashed upon the world. He accepted the repentance of the Frankish Crusaders and absolved them of their sins; the cause of the Crusade was still dear to his heart and he very much wanted them to proceed as they had promised. But there was another problem: the unrepentant Venetians were still officially in a state of excommunication, and under canon law it was now forbidden for the Crusaders to associate with such people.

Innocent asked his bishops to come up with a solution, and a loophole was found: canon law, they said, did allow for members of the flock to associate with the excommunicated, but only if the persons in question were members of the same family. Such a thing was only practical. And could it not be said that members of the same fleet, embarking on a holy mission together, were a kind of family?

Still, the Venetians would not sail until they had been paid, and the Crusaders had no way of raising the money. Hatred and resentment festered between the two parties and early one evening a riot broke out that raged for hours before the Crusader leaders could separate the combatants and shut it down. A gloomy sense of purposelessness and of moral degeneration descended on the Crusader camp. More defections were to come over the winter of 1202–3.

The Pretender

THEN A YOUNG PRINCE of Constantinople named Alexius Angelus came into the picture. Alexius was the son of Emperor Isaac II, who had overthrown Andronicus and handed him over to the mob.

Sadly, Isaac, too, had proved a disaster as emperor and had been cruelly overthrown by his older brother, who was also, confusingly, named Alexius. The usurper ordered his brother to be blinded and imprisoned. The younger Alexius (Isaac's son) had to run for his life.

Alexius Angelus found refuge with his brother-in-law, Philip of Swabia, in Germany where he brooded on the injustice that had been perpetrated by his wicked uncle. Honour demanded that Alexius the Younger seek to take back the throne of Constantinople, no matter the cost.

When Philip of Swabia realised there was a great army sitting tight in Zara with no place to go, he sent a message to the despondent

Crusaders, offering them a lifeline that would solve all their problems, ensure the success of the Crusade and make them all very rich. If they agreed to bring Alexius to Constantinople and install him on the throne as the rightful emperor of the Romans, then Alexius would reward them handsomely – very handsomely indeed. Alexius promised to hand over all the gold the Crusaders needed to pay off their debt to the Venetians. He also promised to give them another 200,000 silver marks to sweeten the deal, and to cap it off with a donation of ten thousand imperial soldiers to join the fight for the Holy Land. And just to cover off any qualms the Church might have, Alexius promised to place the whole eastern Orthodox church under the authority of the pope, ending the great schism between eastern and western Christianity.

The greedy, desperate Crusader leadership didn't need much convincing. Constantinople was the richest city in the world, known to contain unfathomable amounts of treasure. True, the Theodosian Walls were formidable, but everyone knew that young Alexius was the rightful emperor. The people of Constantinople would surely open the gates and flock to his banner. The letter had assured them of that. The Crusaders would be greeted as liberators.

SO NOW THERE WOULD have to be a second diversion. The journey to the Holy Land would have to be put on hold just a little longer. Doge Dandolo gave the new scheme his strong support, even though he must have known that Alexius could never deliver on his promises. The Crusader leaders searched their consciences, but it wasn't hard for them to construct the necessary moral scaffolding they required to sail to Constantinople. The concept of legitimacy was at the very centre of the Crusaders' feudal mindset, and the overthrow of a rightful lord by a usurper was seen as a particularly heinous crime that demanded swift retribution. But to make that work, they had to ignore or not speak of an inconvenient fact: Isaac Angelus, the blinded former emperor, was himself a usurper who had seized the throne by the sword and, as such, was no better than his brother. But all that was set aside, and the leadership agreed that attacking Constantinople would not be a sin, but a righteous deed, a just war to avenge the overthrow of the rightful emperor of the Romans.

As news of the plan to sail to Constantinople spread through the camp there were more defections. Simon of Monfort spoke for many when he chided the leadership, saying, 'I have not come here to destroy Christians.' Other doubters were bribed into sullen silence. The pope sent another angry letter completely forbidding the Crusaders to attack Constantinople, but it arrived too late. The armada had already sailed.

IN CORFU, THE FLEET picked up Alexius Angelus, who was warmly embraced by Dandolo and Boniface of Montferrat. The Crusaders spent three weeks on the island preparing their attack. Then, at this critical moment, the whole thing nearly fell apart. Discontent broke out within the ranks, with at least half the army seized by terrible doubt. Had they not vowed to God and to the pope to make war on the Saracens? Was it not sinful to attack a Christian city? The leadership begged the renegades to stay the course, telling them they would imperil the whole Crusade if they were to leave now. The doubters were slowly, reluctantly, brought back into the fold by a combination of pleading, promises, and a public vow from Alexius to fulfil the terms of the agreement.

With their final preparations complete, the armada set out from Corfu, the warm summer air filling their sails. The heavy, high-masted war galleons led the way, followed by the transport ships with the soldiers and horses, then the slave galleys and merchant ships, carrying provisions for what they thought would be a short campaign. The fleet sailed south, looped around the Peloponnese coast and entered the strait of the Dardanelles.

Venetian galley.

So Great an Enterprise

THE FLEET entered the Sea of Marmara in June 1203, and the Crusaders caught their first glimpse of Constantinople. It appeared through the summer haze like a dream. There was nothing they'd seen in their lives to compare it to. The city's population was, at half a million, more than twenty times the size of Paris. As the armada cruised past the sea walls, the sailors pointed up to the majestic colonnades of the Great Palace. As they approached Acropolis Point, the massive domed form of the Hagia Sophia swept into view.

The grandeur of Constantinople left them stupefied. Villehardouin recorded the awe among his fellow Crusaders:

> When they saw those high ramparts and the strong towers with which the city was completely encircled, and the splendid palaces and soaring churches ... they never thought that there could be

so rich and powerful a place on earth ... There was not a man so
bold that his flesh did not tremble at the sight ... for never since
the creation of the world was there so great an enterprise.

But Constantinople was more fragile than it appeared, weakened by two decades of feuds, purges and uprisings. Beset by unstable leadership, the Roman armies had suffered some painful defeats in recent years. The city was demoralised, yet complacent behind its high walls.

The invaders set up camp near Chalcedon, on the Asian side of the Bosphorus. Soon an envoy arrived with a message from the emperor. The envoy informed them that His Imperial Majesty had happened to notice the presence of thousands of men and ships in his domain, and was very keen to know their plans. If they were prepared to pass through imperial territory peacefully, as earlier Crusaders had done, the emperor was willing to give food and support.

A knight named Conon of Béthune spoke on behalf of the Crusaders. He said he didn't see how they could possibly make any such arrangements when the sitting ruler, as everyone knew, was a usurper and a tyrant. Conon was blunt: go tell your ruler that if the tyrant is prepared to surrender the throne to the rightful emperor, Alexius Angelus, and throw himself at his nephew's mercy, perhaps there will be no need for violence. And if the tyrant wasn't prepared to do this, then he shouldn't bother them with any more such messages.

THE CRUSADERS WERE READY to let everyone in the city know their true emperor was waiting outside the walls. Once the people saw Alexius, they reasoned, the populace would rise up and overthrow the usurper. A bloodless victory would be won, and they could take their gold and leave for the Holy Land at last.

The following day ten galleys rowed across the Bosphorus to parade Alexius in front of the sea walls. Alexius preened on deck in full view of the fascinated onlookers who had come to watch but they were silent and did not cheer.

Confused, the Crusaders shouted out, 'Do you not recognise your true lord and master?'

The onlookers began to laugh and heckle the westerners in the boats below. Someone threw a cabbage. The realisation must have come as a terrible shock to the Crusaders: no one knew or cared who Alexius was. There would be no popular uprising. They had come on a fool's errand to the most heavily fortified city in the world, and they had come too far to go back. The Franks and the Venetians desperately needed the money that Alexius had rashly promised them. The Crusader leaders and the Venetians agreed they would somehow have to break in through the walls and install their man on the throne by force.

The western knights, soldiers and sailors prepared for battle. Priests and bishops heard their confessions and encouraged them to make last wills. Ship after ship was boarded by knights armed with lances their horses draped in chainmail and coloured silk, alongside the battalions of archers and crossbowmen. The war drums and trumpet blasts from the camp were heard across the Bosphorus. Inside the city, people climbed onto their rooftops to get a glimpse of the strange warriors on the far side of the strait.

The Winged Lion on the Shore

THE ENTRANCE to the city's deep-water harbour, the Golden Horn, was protected by a massive chain that trailed across the water from the sea walls of Constantinople to the Tower of Galata on the other side. A party of Crusaders landed at Galata and secured the tower. Meanwhile the Venetian captains rammed their galleys up onto the chain, then rocked them over into the water on the other side, just as Harald Hardrada had done nearly two centuries earlier. The emperor's navy had suffered from years of neglect and could only put up a pitiful resistance. The Venetian ships now enjoyed the freedom of the Golden Horn.

The invaders devised an amphibious plan of attack. The Venetians agreed they would attack the sea walls from their ships while the Crusaders, more comfortable on solid ground, proposed to confront the city at the formidable land walls. Both forces would attack at different angles of the north-western corner of the city, where the land walls meet the northern sea wall as it curves around the Blachernae Palace.

To overcome the high sea walls, the Venetians constructed siege towers by fastening timber gangways onto the spars of their galleys. Bringing their vessels close to the edge of the shore, they began launching missiles from their ship-mounted catapults, and volleys of arrows from their crossbows. High up on the ramparts of the city, the defence was led by the Varangian guard, armed with double-headed axes, supported by regular archers and crossbowmen.

The Venetian galleys, coming under heavy fire, kept their distance from the shore. As the attack began to falter, the old man Dandolo rallied his men. Dressed in battle armour, standing on the prow of his vermilion ship, the Doge croaked out to his oarsmen that if they valued their lives, they must propel the ship forward towards the walls.

Dandolo's ship picked up speed and ran aground on the narrow strip of beach between the wall and the sea. Someone leapt down and planted the banner of St Mark in the muddy ground. The sight of the Doge standing on the shore alongside the winged lion of

St Mark thrilled the Venetians. Beaching their own galleys, they climbed up onto their gangways and pushed their way onto the tower defences, winning control over a section of the walls. After a few hours Dandolo was able to send word to his allies that they now held twenty-five towers.

Winged lion of St Mark, Venice.

MEANWHILE, around the corner, the Crusader army had assembled in front of the Blachernae Gate. The emperor chose this moment to ride out and make a show of force. The Crusaders tensed themselves for battle as the bronze doors of the Blachernae Gate creaked opened and the imperial army tramped out, led by the emperor himself. The Roman soldiers poured out onto the plain in such numbers that it seemed to the Crusaders 'as if the whole world were there assembled'. Geoffrey de Villehardouin estimated the emperor had forty-divisions against their six.

Both armies edged towards each other. The Crusaders offered prayers, drew their swords and prepared to die. Then on the plain outside Blachernae the imperial army came to a halt. Tense minutes went by as each army eyeballed the other, neither side moving.

And then, inexplicably, the emperor lost his nerve. He gave the order to turn around and march back inside the city. The Crusaders could hardly believe their luck.

AT DUSK, the Venetians prised open a section of the sea walls and their soldiers poured through the gap. They ran into the Blachernae quarter of the city and set fire to several wooden houses. Soon the whole street was ablaze. It was the first time any invader had penetrated the walls in nearly eight centuries.

The disgraced Emperor Alexius III, now held in contempt by his officers, frantically prepared to flee the city, taking with him ten thousand pounds of gold, a sack of jewels and his favourite daughter. In his rush to escape, he abandoned his wife and the rest of his family. As he lowered himself into his boat and sailed out into the Sea of Marmara, an orange glow lit up the night sky. The outer neighbourhoods of Constantinople were burning and the empire had no emperor.

The court officials at Blachernae sent at once for Isaac Angelus, the former emperor. Isaac was hauled out of his dungeon and brought back to his former palace. Isaac, who had once so boldly cut down Andronicus's henchman, was a pitiful sight, blinded and enfeebled by months of imprisonment. The broken, bewildered man was dressed up in imperial robes, hailed by the court as the rightful emperor and restored to his throne. It must have seemed like a strange dream.

A message was sent to the Crusader camp advising Alexius that his father had regained his throne. This put the Crusaders in yet another awkward spot. Their stated, 'honourable' objective had been met: to restore a legitimate emperor to the throne, and they had to acknowledge his legitimacy. But their real objective had been to get access to the imperial treasury. Only Alexius, not the reinstated Isaac, had agreed to help them do that.

A delegation of Crusaders, including Villehardouin, was sent to negotiate with the blind Isaac Angelus. A contingent of Vikings from the Varangian guard, equipped with battleaxes, lined both sides of the street, as the envoys made their way to the Blachernae Palace. They met with Isaac in his chambers.

'Sire,' Villehardouin began, 'you can see the service we have rendered to your son. We have kept our covenant with him. But we cannot release him until you confirm that agreement he freely entered into with us.'

Isaac asked, 'And what is this agreement?'

'To begin with, the Church of your empire shall be put in obedience to Rome. Secondly, 200,000 silver marks shall be delivered to us, along with a year's supply of food for our men. Thirdly, the empire shall contribute ten thousand men to aid our mission in the Holy Land.'

Isaac heard him out and said, 'This covenant is very onerous and I don't see how we can possibly make it happen. Nevertheless, my son and I are greatly in your debt and I will sign any document you put before me.'

Alexius entered the conquered city and was received with great joy by his trembling, traumatised father. He was made co-emperor and crowned as Alexius IV. From the Crusaders' point of view, everything had worked out fine. They could now look forward to clearing their debts to Venice and to receiving the sizeable bounty promised to them. Surely they would soon be on their way to Egypt to fight the Saracens.

THE NEW EMPEROR intended to make good on his promise of 200,000 silver marks, but his predecessor had escaped with most of the treasury's wealth. Alexius was forced to raise taxes to squeeze more wealth from the city, but it wasn't enough. He resorted to melting down the frames of valuable icons to extract their gold and silver. Even so he could only raise 100,000 marks. Half of that went to the Venetians, as they were entitled to fifty per cent of any of the spoils of conquest, so the Crusaders were still well short of paying their debt to the implacable Dandolo, who was again threatening to leave with his ships and strand them in Constantinople, unless he got what was owed to him.

As Alexius IV tried to extract even more gold out of the city, resentment festered among his people. The destruction of holy icons for payment created widespread outrage. Skirmishes broke out between Crusaders and disgruntled Roman soldiers. The city was coming to hate these crude, greedy westerners. And still the Venetians demanded their money. Alexius was being squeezed on both sides.

Dandolo requested a meeting, and so Alexius rode his horse down from Blachernae to the shore of the Golden Horn, where he met the Doge, who had been ferried across on a galley. Speaking more in sorrow than anger, Dandolo said, 'Alexius, what do you think you're doing? Don't forget that we lifted you out of your pitiable state. We made you emperor and had you crowned! Why don't you keep your promises and pay your debts to us?'

'No,' Alexius replied firmly. 'I have no intention of doing any more than I have done already.'

'You stupid boy,' said the Doge, turning back to his galley, 'we dragged you out of the shit. We'll put you back in the shit soon enough.'

Alexius returned to the palace and called for his counsellors' advice. One of them, a particularly hirsute aristocrat known as Murtzuphlus ('Bushy Brow') for the single thick eyebrow that ran across his forehead, told Alexius the westerners had gone too far. The whole city now hated the foreigners who were bleeding them dry. He told the emperor to give them no more gold. But Alexius was out of time as well as money – the next night 'Bushy Brow' entered Alexius's room and strangled him with a noose.

Murtzuphlus claimed the throne for himself. He was crowned as Alexius V, the third 'Alexius' to sit on the throne in as many months. The new emperor made it clear there would be no more gold for the hateful foreigners, and he was cutting off their food supply. Maybe now they would give up and be on their way.

THE MURDER OF YOUNG ALEXIUS shocked and outraged the Crusaders. Feeling provoked beyond endurance by the faithless Romans, the Crusaders began to plot a second attack on the walls of Constantinople. This time, there were no moral qualms; the Latin priests declared that the murder of the 'legitimate' ruler Alexius meant the Romans had forfeited all rights to their lands. The already fragile ties of religious sympathy between eastern and western churches were now severed. The schismatics inside the city walls must now be made obedient to the pope by force. One priest went so far as to denounce the Romans as 'the enemies of God'.

For all the sputtering Crusader outrage, the decision to attack was a matter of practicality as much as anything. They could neither leave safely nor stay: there was no food to forage and none coming from the city. The Crusaders were trapped, and the only way out was through Constantinople.

Reports of the Crusader activity reached Murtzuphlus within the palace, and he set to work to prepare his city for the next Crusader onslaught.

THE INVADERS CHOSE to leave the land walls alone this time and focus their efforts on the same weakened point on the north-west corner of the sea walls. The Venetians converted their ships into floating castles, fixing siege engines to the decks, and gangways to the high masts to carry their men onto the Roman ramparts.

On the morning of 9 April 1204, the Venetian galleys charged once again at the walls along the Golden Horn.

Unlike Alexius, Murtzuphlus was prepared to fight. He had personally directed the repairs of the sea walls, bolstering them with wooden towers. Platforms for catapults were hastily constructed. The Crusader ships pressed up against the sea wall, but every soldier that managed to clamber on to the ramparts was shot down by arrows and missiles. By mid-afternoon the invaders called the retreat and limped back across the water. The Romans mocked the Crusaders by baring their arses to the retreating ships. Murtzuphlus exulted in his victory.

BACK AT CAMP, several Crusader knights declared they had had their fill, arguing their defeat was a judgement from God for attacking a Christian city. They wanted to give up and leave for the Holy Land, which was – had they forgotten? – the reason they left France in the first place. But Dandolo was adamant and insisted they try again. The Venetians wearily repaired their ships. This time, however, they stabilised their siege towers by lashing the galleys together in pairs. Three days later they set out for the sea walls once last time.

The battle raged all morning. The Roman defences on the walls were holding the Crusaders at bay. The defenders were happy to fire missiles from a distance, but seemed unwilling to risk their lives in direct combat. Then a group of Crusaders, creeping along the narrow beach between the sea wall and the water, came upon a freshly bricked-up postern gate. The Crusaders began to frantically pull away at the brickwork, while the defenders directly above them rained down arrow bolts and boiling pitch upon them.

Then a fighting Crusader priest called Aleume de Clari managed to smash apart a small opening in the brickwork, leading into what appeared to be an underground armory beneath the wall. Peering through the gap into the darkness, Aleume could see the shocked faces of dozens of Roman soldiers. Without another thought, Aleume dived in through the stonework. His brother Robert grabbed at his ankles, trying to drag him back, but Aleume wriggled free and landed inside the armory. The enemy soldiers began to move towards him warily. Then Aleume produced a large knife and ran at them, and the Romans took off.

Soon the rest of the knights were inside the armory. They rushed up the stairs to confront the soldiers on the wall. At the sight of the armoured knights, the guards ran from their posts, abandoning the tower to the Crusaders.

Meanwhile, out on the harbour, a sudden gust of wind propelled two of the biggest Venetian ships right up to the edge of the sea wall. The first Venetian soldier to clamber from the mast onto a guard tower was cut to pieces by the defenders. Then a knight managed to crawl onto a rampart. The defenders hacked at him with axes and swords but, protected by his armour, the knight suffered no serious damage. He then astounded his attackers by rising to his feet and drawing his blade. Again, the defenders fled in panic. A gangway was lowered onto the wall. A party of Crusaders ran across and took the guard tower. The gate below the tower was opened and the 20,000-strong Crusader army began to stream into the city.

At the first sight of Crusaders in the streets, Murtzuphlus bolted from his fortified tent near the walls and raced across the city to the safety of the Great Palace. As more soldiers ran into the city streets, shocked and panicked residents gathered what they could and ran, pouring out of the gates into the countryside. As night fell, Murtzuphlus lost all hope. He commandeered a fishing boat and sailed into exile. Murtzuphlus would eventually be captured, returned to the city and thrown off the top of the Column of Theodosius to a messy death.

The Crusader knights, now in control of the Blachernae quarter, burnt down a row of houses to clear an avenue for defence. The conflagration ran out of control and soon the whole quarter was on fire, with Villehardouin estimating that on that night, 'more houses had been burned in the city than there are houses in any three of the greatest cities in the kingdom of France'.

The remaining residents of Constantinople woke to news that another emperor had abandoned them. Another exodus of citizens streamed through the streets towards the ancient city gates, as the Crusaders donned their armour and readied themselves to engage in hard street-by-street fighting. But as the westerners ventured tentatively along the Mese, they discovered there was no one to oppose them. A group of priests came forward to formally surrender the city, accompanied by some members of the Varangian guard who asked to change their allegiance. The cry went up among the invaders: *the city is ours!*

TWO YEARS OF BOILING frustration, greed and rage then exploded onto the terrified people of Constantinople. Under medieval custom, the invaders were entitled to three days of looting. The Crusaders rushed through the streets and into houses, seizing everything that looked valuable, and destroying whatever they couldn't carry. The Venetians, who had a better understanding of the true value of the works of art around them, carefully crated up what they found and sent it home.

A band of soldiers broke into the Hagia Sophia and began to strip the altar of its gold and precious stones. The men, giddy with the joy of conquest, got drunk on communion wine and cheered as a camp prostitute stood on the seat of the Patriarch and began to dance and sing bawdy French songs.

Some of the larger ornaments proved too unwieldy to be carried out, so mules and packhorses were brought into the church. One poor animal lost its footing on the slippery floor and fell, and had to have its throat cut; the floor of the church was splashed with blood and animal shit, the stench mingling with the scent of scattered sandalwood and rose oil.

Elsewhere in the city, unarmed men were put to the sword, women were snatched from their family homes and dragged away, nuns were raped in their convents. Icons and precious books were destroyed. Bronze statues from the ancient world were torn down and thrown into the melting pot to make copper money to pay the soldiers. Emperors' tombs were stripped of their precious metals.

As the Crusaders revelled in their revenge and their new-found wealth, terrified families cowered inside their houses, awaiting the inevitable pounding on the door.

The Venetian in the Suit of Armour

FROM THE WINDOW of a mansion near the Hagia Sophia, Nicetas Choniates observed the rampage on the streets below. Nicetas was a high government official who had served in the court of several emperors. His greatest fears that day were for his children and his pregnant wife.

To Nicetas, the Crusaders, in their long tunics embroidered with the sign of the cross, were frauds. Whatever these men said they were, they were not Christians. The worst of them, in his eyes, were the knights, the hypocrites who had raised the cross to their shoulders, who had sworn to pass through the Christian lands without bloodletting, who had vowed not to be diverted from their holy mission. These were the men who had led this savage mob to his city.

One of them would soon be at his door. Nicetas gathered together his wife and children, along with several servants and neighbours. The group slipped out and fled to the house of a friend, a Venetian wine merchant. The Venetian friend agreed to shelter them. But they were not safe. Nicetas cast his eyes about the room and saw a suit of armour. The Venetian friend agreed to put it on. Soon there were fists hammering at the door. The armoured Venetian confronted the Crusaders on his doorstep. Speaking in their language, he told them he'd already claimed the house for himself and sent the disappointed soldiers on their way.

The deception worked well enough, until soldiers began to arrive in larger numbers. Nicetas feared if they stayed they would all be taken prisoner and the women would be stolen from them. The Venetian friend came up with another ruse. He called for some rope and bound the wrists of Nicetas, his family and his neighbours, and led them through the streets, posing as their captor. Nicetas placed the women in the centre of the party, their faces smeared with mud to make them less attractive to the invaders.

The group shuffled fearfully westward through the teeming streets, towards the land walls and the Golden Gate, where they could escape the wreck of their beautiful city. As they passed by a church, Nicetas saw they were being eyed by a leering Crusader.

Suddenly, the soldier lunged into the centre of the group, pulled out a young girl and dragged her off. In the confusion, the girl's aged father slipped into a muddy hole in the road. Flailing about in the mire, the old man begged Nicetas to do something to save his daughter.

Nicetas loosened his bonds and followed the soldier. As he did so, he grabbed at another group of Crusader knights standing near the church, and begged them for help. His pleas moved a few soldiers to pity and they agreed to accompany him. They followed the girl's abductor to the door of a looted house.

Icon of St Michael, looted by the Fourth Crusade, now in the Treasury of San Marco, Venice.

Nicetas saw the soldier fling her inside, then turn and stand at his door, ready to fight his pursuers. Nicetas drew a deep breath and he beseeched the Crusaders at his side to honour their sacred oaths, 'to refrain from intercourse with married women, with maidens who have never known any man, and with nuns who are consecrated to God'.

The men stepped forward and demanded the girl be released. But her abductor was defiant. Enraged, the soldiers threatened to hang him from a stake, 'as an unjust and shameless man'. At that, the abductor backed down, and flung the girl gracelessly back into the street. Nicetas returned her to her father, who wept with relief.

Badly shaken, Nicetas's group pressed on towards the open doors of the Golden Gate. They passed through the marble arch, and across the drawbridge to the open plains outside the city. Nicetas paused and turned back, looking at the silent land walls, still intact, still impressive, yet stonily indifferent to the wrecked city behind them. To Nicetas it seemed the walls had committed a kind of betrayal. He fell to the ground in exhaustion and despair.

Nicetas Choniates eventually joined the Roman court-in-exile in Nicaea. He never returned to Constantinople.

The Ruby Apple

AFTER THREE DAYS OF LOOTING, Boniface of Montferrat called on the leadership to assemble and divide the spoils. They piled the treasure into three different churches, then the Crusaders and the Venetians gathered to pay their debts and claim their share. Villehardouin gazed at the heap of treasure in amazement, 'so great that none could tell you the end of it: gold and silver, and vessels and precious stones, and samite, and cloth of silk, and robes fair and grey, and ermine, and every choicest thing found upon the earth'.

A quarter was to go to the new emperor of Constantinople, whoever that was going to be; the rest was to be split down the middle between the Crusaders and the Venetians. At last the knights could settle their account with Doge Dandolo. The debt that had weighed upon them so heavily now seemed a trifle compared to the treasure heap in front of them.

The greatest treasure of all was the empire itself, which also was to be divided as part of the spoils of victory. But nothing in these westerners' narrow, feudal backgrounds could comprehend the complexity of the empire they had just seized, and they completely failed to appreciate its value as a buffer state, a protective seal for their own lands against the Islamic tide. One historian observed that the Crusaders fell on the empire 'as savages might fall on a watch – giving the case to one, the jewels to another, and a disjointed mechanism to a third'. The disjointed mechanism was to be handed to the new emperor.

The various imperial territories were chopped up and doled out. Dandolo now boasted, with the zeal of an accountant, that he was the ruler of three-eighths of the Roman empire. The Orthodox church of Constantinople was brought officially under the rule of the church of Rome. Meanwhile, the city's holy relics began to make their way into the churches, homes and public squares of western Europe. Seated atop their mountain of plunder in the ruined city, the Crusader knights forgot their papal vows, and their plans to take the Holy Land were quietly shelved. In the end, the Fourth Crusade was no crusade at all: they never saw Jerusalem.

The time had come to decide who the new emperor of Constantinople would be. Boniface of Montferrat expected to win, but Doge Dandolo once again managed to skew events. Voting as a bloc, the Venetians threw their support behind Baldwin of Flanders, who was seen as a more biddable creature than Boniface. And so, on 16 May 1204, Baldwin was acclaimed as the first Latin emperor of Constantinople in the Hagia Sophia. In his hands was placed a ruby the size of an apple.

The mass exodus had driven Constantinople's population down to a tenth of its former size. But the city's conquest was greeted with indifference in the west; there was no rush to colonise the imperial lands. The Franks were unable to repopulate the city, and with half the houses destroyed by fire, whole neighbourhoods were never rebuilt. The natural world began to reassert itself within the city walls. Vegetation and foliage grew in newly cleared spaces. Weeds rose up to waist height in the great forums of Theodosius and Constantine.

THE LATIN EMPIRE of Constantinople was a doomed enterprise, destined to last for just fifty-seven years. Byzantine rule would be restored in the thirteenth century, but the damage was done. In time, as more and more imperial territory fell into the hands of the Ottoman Turks, the terrible irony of the Fourth Crusade was revealed: the Crusaders had not just failed to retake Jerusalem, they had wrecked Christendom's biggest city, and destroyed a European bulwark against Islam.

The foundations were laid for centuries of Orthodox bitterness against the Catholic west.

The Four Horses

VENICE EMERGED as the true beneficiary of the Fourth Crusade. Venetian raiders helped themselves to Constantinople's plentiful array of statues from the ancient world, including the famous team of gilt-bronze horses known as the Quadriga. The statues of the Quadriga had stood majestically over the starting posts of the Hippodrome for centuries. Together the four horses formed a stunning expression of equine muscle and movement, each one twisting its neck and raising its foreleg, anticipating the charge down the track.

The Quadriga was too big a prize for the Venetians to ignore. The four statues were pulled off their mountings in the Hippodrome and dragged through the streets down to the Golden Horn, where the heads were sawn from the bodies to allow them to be properly packed and transported. The pieces were hauled onto a ship bound for Venice, and installed triumphantly above the front porch of St Mark's Basilica. The horses were given collars to conceal the place where their heads had been rebonded. The Quadriga remained atop St Mark's for five centuries, until it was taken down and brought inside to protect it from acid rain. The Quadriga you see above St Mark's today is a fibreglass replica.

The Quadriga, now in the Museum of St Mark's Basilica, Venice.

The porphyry statue of the four tetrarchs – Diocletian, Maximian, Galerius and Constantius Chlorus – embedded into a corner of the basilica is also a treasure stolen from Constantinople. The marble cladding and the columns at the doorway of the church once adorned the palaces and public places of the imperial city.

Once you know this of Venice, you can never see St Mark's in quite the same way. It looks less like a work of holy inspiration and more like a magpie's nest of plunder, a monument to a shameless act of theft.

DOGE ENRICO DANDOLO finally expired in 1205, just a year after the sack of Constantinople. At his request, he was buried in the Hagia Sophia, which the conquerors remade as a Catholic place of worship. His bones lay there undisturbed for more than two centuries until the final conquest of the city by the Ottoman Turks. The sultan's troops raided the church and Dandolo's tomb was destroyed. The modest plaque I saw that day in the eastern gallery of the great church was created by Italian stonemasons in the nineteenth century to honour his memory.

Which is why, my son, the Hagia Sophia still honours the name of the wiliest enemy the Queen of Cities ever had.

CHAPTER NINE

End of Days

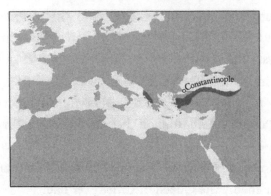

The empire in exile, 1250.

The Golden Gate

TAXIS MOVE AT an astonishing clip along Istanbul's freeways. My body is cramped with tension as I prepare to assume the brace position and I wonder how I'll be able to live with myself if Joe is injured, or worse, in a crash.

The driver is in a garrulous mood. He wants to talk about the Australian soccer team.

'I have seen your team. They are not so good.'

Joe is amused and can only agree with the driver. 'So, what's the Turkish team like?' he asks.

The driver grimaces and rotates his flattened hand to make the 'so-so' gesture. I just want him to keep both hands on the wheel.

I should ask him to slow down, but every car, it seems, is skating along at the same speed on this motorway, which borders the Sea of Marmara. Joe is now daydreaming, untroubled by the taxi velocity; he looks out the window and points to an armada of Russian oil tankers rolling through the morning haze towards the Dardanelles.

The upside of Istanbul's live-free-or-die motorways is that you tend to arrive where you want to go pretty sharpish, and so, a mere twelve minutes after we've caught our cab from Sultanahmet, we're at our destination, a little park that's more of a traffic island on the water's edge. In the middle of this patch of green is a broken slab of parapet wall, abutting a medieval tower. This marks the southernmost point of the Theodosian Walls of Constantinople. From here the walls march inland, following the contours of the landscape for 5.6 kilometres, all the way to the Golden Horn.

The Theodosian Walls at the Sea of Marmara.

Our plan on this day is to walk the entire length of these ancient stone and brick walls, to follow their path through the backstreets of Istanbul from sea to shining sea. To see and touch these walls and to take in their colossal strength is to feel the past made concrete. The colours and shapes of the ghost empire come sharply into focus here.

Turning our backs on the Marmara, Joe and I shoulder our backpacks and set off. We follow the course of the inner wall into a slum. The walls aren't really presented as a destination zone for tourists, so the area hasn't been prettied up and signposted. Istanbul has pragmatically chosen to simply ignore the Roman walls wherever possible, to build around them and, where necessary, punch a hole through them to allow traffic to pass.

We see some makeshift cabins, made from milk crates and tarpaulins, pressed up against the inner wall. The old timber houses across the street sag and lean precariously; some mangy dogs fight half-heartedly over a plastic bag. Joe has never seen a slum before and is worried we're intruding. But there are slums and there are slums and this is fine; we see no public squalor or drug use, there is no threat of violence. People go about their business.

Théophile Gautier, a French writer, came to Istanbul in 1852 and wrote of his own trek along the walls, an experience scarcely different from our own:

> We plunged boldly into a labyrinth of narrow streets and lanes of the purest Turkish character. As we advanced, the scene became more lonely; the dogs, growing more savage at each stage of our progress, glared sullenly at us and followed growling at our heels. The wooden houses, discoloured and dilapidated, with their crumbling lattices and floors out of line, looked like collapsed chicken coops.

'Look, Dad,' Joe says as he runs his hand along the wall, 'Roman brickwork.'

He's right: there are rows of granite blocks, alternating with long stripes of narrow red bricks. It's the same kind of ancient wall you might see in North Africa or Yorkshire. There's a remarkable uniformity to the Roman world; they tended to build the same things the same way wherever they went.

JOE AND I FOLLOW the line of the inner wall and pass through a stone archway into a medieval fortress: an open grassy space, ringed with towers and battlements. We pay some Turkish *lira* to an old unshaven man at the gate and enter. We have the place all to ourselves. This fortress was built by the Romans and then redesigned by the Ottomans into Yedikule (pronounced 'Yeh-di-ku-leh'): the Fortress of the Seven Towers. Today it's a derelict space.

On the far wall I notice a set of three bricked-in arches, with a few broken stones next to it. The arches are unmarked, so it takes me a moment to realise what we're looking at.

'Oh man. This is the Golden Gate of Constantinople, Joe.'

The Golden Gate at Yedikule.

This nondescript slab is all that remains of the Porta Aurea, the Golden Gate of the Caesars, the majestic, ceremonial portal into

Constantinople. Passage through this central arch was reserved for imperial coronations and triumphal entries.

A thousand years ago, the Golden Gate was clad in polished white marble, with heavy bronze doors panelled with gold sheets. A gilded dedication was inscribed in the stonework above the arch to Theodosius, the emperor who 'brought a golden age and built the gate from gold'. Heraclius entered the city here with the True Cross in 628, in a procession led by four Persian elephants.

As the frontiers receded, and the empire shrank to little more than a single embattled city, the Golden Gate had to be sealed up and converted into a citadel. Today the gate is an achingly forlorn sight. There will be no more elephants passing through this arch.

We wander around the fortress of Yedikule in silence. Joe enters one of the cylindrical stone towers and finds a mattress and a couple of empty beer cans.

Inside a tower at Yedikule.

*

The Recovery of Constantinople

BROKEN, friendless and severed from its ancient capital, the eastern
Roman empire really should have died after 1204. Constantinople's
fall seemed to echo the disastrous sack of Rome in the fifth century,
which presaged the collapse of the western empire.

But the Roman empire of the east refused to die. Although its
power had been shattered at the centre, courts-in-exile sprouted up
in Nicaea, in Epirus and in Trebizond on the Black Sea coast. The
exiles regrouped, lit their candles and waited for the hated Crusader
regime to collapse under the weight of its own incompetence.

In Constantinople, the Crusaders surveyed the city they had
won, but were at a loss to know what to do with it. Hard-handed
soldiers who had run nothing bigger in their lives than their
muddy feudal estates in northern France, they were ill-prepared
to run a foreign metropolis in crisis. The new rulers distrusted
the palace bureaucrats they'd inherited (with good reason) and
dispensed with their services, thereby depriving the government
of administrative experience and institutional memory. The
Crusaders had no understanding of shipping or commerce, so they
deferred to the Venetians in their court, who cannibalised the city's
trade revenue, starving the treasury of income. Their weak and
unhappy rule was made weaker by constant, grinding warfare with
the Bulgarians, and with the undigested segments of the empire
they had consumed.

The first Crusader emperor, Baldwin I, reigned for just one year
before he was captured and killed by the Bulgarians. Boniface of
Montferrat was killed in battle two years later. Baldwin II was the
longest serving of the colonial Latin emperors of Constantinople, but

he could do nothing to stop the city's wealth draining away like water down a plughole. In desperation, he pawned the city's most precious holy relic, the Crown of Thorns – believed to have been worn by Christ on the cross – to a Venetian merchant in exchange for 13,134 gold pieces.* Baldwin used the gold to buy himself an army, but was unable to do anything with it. As he sank further into debt to Venice, he plundered the last scraps of the city's wealth, selling the lead roof tiles from the Great Palace. Rain came in and the elegant collection of palaces by the Sea of Marmara became derelict, a ghostly shell.

The penniless Baldwin II petitioned Venice for another loan, and was forced to hand over his only son, Philip, as a guarantee for future repayment. In fewer than forty years, the Crusaders were reduced to pawning their own children for gold.

MEANWHILE, THE EMPIRE in exile in Nicaea was steadily reclaiming scraps of imperial territory in Asia Minor and Thrace. The emperor-in-waiting Michael Palaeologus was ready to take back the capital. His forces were small, but popular opinion in the city was on his side. Michael was planning for a long, hard campaign when Constantinople just fell into his lap.

Michael had sent one of his generals, Alexius Strategopulus, on a reconnaissance mission to study the condition of the city's defences. The general and his men were riding through a nearby village when they stopped to talk to a group of sympathetic local farmers. The farmers mentioned that Constantinople was, at that moment,

---

* The pawnbroker sold the Crown of Thorns to the King of France, who built a special chapel to house it. Today the relic is kept within the Cathedral of Notre Dame in Paris, where it is put on display once a month. In the summer of 2015 I came to Notre Dame on its viewing day, hoping to see it, but was defeated by a long, snaking queue of what seemed to be ten thousand tourists.

undefended: most of the Latin garrison and the Venetian fleet were away on campaign.

On the night of 24 July 1261, the general's informants slipped into the city. They crept up to a postern gate, killed the sentries on duty, and unbolted the gate. Strategopulus and his men rushed inside and seized control of the Blachernae Palace.

Baldwin II was awakened from his slumber by the sounds of fighting. He looked out the window and was astonished to see Michael's soldiers inside the palace grounds. Baldwin was defenceless. Leaving his crown and sceptre behind, he ran down to the Golden Horn on foot and escaped the city in a Venetian ship. The throne of the Caesars was vacant.

Three weeks later, Michael Palaeologus entered the city on foot through the Golden Gate, carrying himself more like a holy man than an emperor. Michael was greeted by a throng of leaping, rejoicing Romans, scarcely able to believe the happy turn of events. He was brought to the Hagia Sophia, and crowned as Michael VIII, Emperor and Autocrat of the Romans.

The Coming of the Ottomans

MICHAEL VIII was the first emperor of the Palaeologi, the final imperial dynasty. He began to pick up what remained of his empire and put it back on its feet: commissioning repairs to the Theodosian Walls, refurbishing the Hagia Sophia and sponsoring the reconstruction of a mosque that had been torched by the Crusaders.

Michael struggled to revive the flattened economy. The wharves along the Golden Horn still attracted trading ships, but the treasury could extract almost no revenue from them; Venice and Genoa were exempt from local taxes, and no decree from the emperor could force them to pay. In return for naval support, Michael ceded the neighbourhood of Galata to the Genoese, who later built a fortified tower on the north shore of the Golden Horn.

It was fortunate for Michael that the Seljuk Turks were unable to take advantage of the empire's weakness at this time. The Sultanate of Rum was completely unprepared for the arrival of the Mongols and their warlord Genghis Khan. In 1245 the Mongols swooped down on the Seljuk army near Köse Dagh, and completely shattered it. The Seljuks never recovered.

MICHAEL'S SON AND SUCCESSOR, Andronicus II, tried to repair Constantinople's budget problems by dismantling the imperial fleet of eighty ships, which left the empire even more dependent on Venice and Genoa for protection. The vulnerability of the city was painfully apparent. Lacking a sizeable army or navy, successive emperors hoped to shore up the city's defences by playing their enemies off against each other with a mixture of bribery and intrigue.

But the world was changing around them. After the destruction of the Seljuk Sultanate of Rum, Asia Minor became a lawless province, a patchwork of small fiefdoms. Bands of fanatical Muslim warriors, known as *ghazis*, wandered the countryside. Over time, they naturally gravitated to the one remaining Turkish principality, the realm of the Ottomans.

The Ottomans had come to Asia Minor from the city of Merv in Central Asia. They took their name from their founder Osman Bey, who declared independence from the Seljuks in 1299. Like the Arabs of the seventh century, the Ottomans were clear-eyed warriors in a power vacuum, fired with the power of Islam and ready to be rapidly propelled towards greatness.

The Ottomans established a small kingdom on the north-west edge of Anatolia, where they were able to observe the Romans from a short distance and study the manner in which a great civilisation carries itself. Their ranks swollen with zealous *ghazi* warriors, they put the Anatolian city of Prusa to siege for seven years, before they broke through in 1326, and remade it as Bursa, the new Ottoman capital. Capturing Bursa opened up the rest of Asia Minor: Nicaea was won in 1331, Nicomedia in 1337, remade as the Ottoman cities of Iznik and Izmit.

AS OTTOMAN POWER FLOURISHED, Constantinople shrank further in its own skin. The empire suffered further losses under the long, miserable reign of John V Palaeologus. John was just eight when he succeeded his father to the throne. A civil war then broke out between supporters of his designated regent, John Cantacuzenus, and his mother, Anna of Savoy. Anna needed gold for troops, so she pawned the imperial crown jewels to Venice for 30,000 ducats. It was a sign of the times.

In 1347, a court historian came to Constantinople to attend an imperial wedding and noted the sad state of affairs: the silverware was gone, replaced by cups made of pewter and clay, the jewels were glass and the gold was painted leather.

'To such a degree,' he wrote, 'the ancient prosperity and brilliance of the Roman empire had fallen, entirely gone out and perished.'

The empire's miseries were further compounded when the Black Death came again to Constantinople, killing a third to half of the population. The plague left people fearful and chastened. The sparse population was now far too small to fill out the capital, and the Queen of Cities devolved into a loose collection of suburbs, separated by vineyards and wheatfields.

CIVIL WAR BROKE OUT once again in the 1350s, between John V Palaeologus and his co-emperor John Cantacuzenus. John V called on the Serbs for help, whereas Cantacuzenus enlisted the support of the Ottoman army, who crossed the Dardanelles and set foot in Europe for the first time. When the walls of Gallipoli were brought to the ground by an earthquake, the Ottomans occupied the city and declared it to be the evident will of Allah that they should do so. In 1362 they seized the ancient city of Adrianople in Thrace and renamed it Edirne. Sultan Murad I made it his new European capital. Constantinople was now surrounded by the Ottomans on all sides.

IN HIS LATER YEARS, Emperor John V Palaeologus was obliged to travel to the courts of western Europe to beg for aid against the growing threat of the Ottoman Turks. It was the first time a Roman emperor had travelled abroad as a supplicant. John alienated the Hungarians by arrogantly refusing to dismount from his horse when their king walked towards him. He received nothing for his efforts. On his journey home John was detained in Venice as a debtor, a terrible humiliation for the emperor and autocrator of the Romans. In the absence of any material support from the west, John had no choice but to become a vassal of the Ottomans, required to pay tribute and provide military support to a Muslim sultan.

After John's death, the dynastic infighting among the Palaeologus family only intensified. Ottoman rulers became accustomed to receiving the envoys of emperors and would-be emperors, offering tribute in exchange for military support against a hated rival. The prestige of the imperial office declined as the Palaeologi squandered their dwindling inheritance, fighting each other for supremacy. In the eyes of the world, the Roman 'empire' slid from a thing of tragedy to an object of ridicule and, ultimately, of contempt.

The Orb and the Cross

'I, SINFUL STEPHEN of Novgorod the Great, came to Constantinople with my eight companions to venerate the holy places and to kiss the bodies of the saints' – so begins the account of Stephen, a Russian pilgrim who came to Constantinople in 1349. Stephen and his companions were bewildered by the size and complexity of the metropolis. His advice reads like a post on TripAdvisor: 'Entering Constantinople is like entering a great forest; it is impossible to get around without a good guide, and if you attempt to get around stingily or cheaply you will not be able to see or kiss a single saint.'

As Stephen and his fellow pilgrims entered the great square of the Augustaeum, they were confronted by a mighty column 'of wondrous size, height and beauty', so huge Stephen imagined it could be seen from far away at sea. Atop the column was a massive bronze statue of Emperor Justinian, nine to twelve metres high, erected in a far-off time when Roman power encompassed Italy, Egypt and the Holy Land. The statue of Justinian was crowned with a feathered headdress, his figure clad in armour astride a horse. Stephen of Novgorod noted that the right hand was stretched out 'bravely to the south, toward the Saracen land and Jerusalem', as if to hold back the Muslim tide. Justinian's left hand was grasping an orb with a cross on it, symbolising the emperor's God-given dominion over the whole world.

The orb became known in the Muslim lands as *kizilelma*, the Red Apple. For the Ottomans, the orb became a fixation, a prize that represented global domination. Eventually the idea took hold: take the city, seize the Red Apple and become the rightful rulers of the world.

Then, just as the Ottoman Turks began to encircle Constantinople, the orb dropped out of Justinian's hand and crashed onto the square below. It was a horrible portent. Several attempts were made to hoist it back up into Justinian's hand, but the Red Apple kept crashing back to the ground. And so there the Red Apple remained, on the cracked floor of the Augustaeum, the symbol of Rome's lost authority, ripe for the taking.

Drawing of statue of Justinian.

IN 1439, A SPANISH NOBLEMAN named Pedro Tafur came to visit Emperor John VIII, who he believed was distantly related to him. Pedro was warmly welcomed at Blachernae, and invited to join the imperial party on several hunting trips. In his time with the imperial family, he was able to observe their very modest living conditions. Unable to afford the upkeep of Blachernae, which had fallen into disrepair and was mostly closed off, the emperor and his family were living in a couple of cramped but well-appointed apartments in the rear of the palace.

As he wandered the city streets, Pedro was struck by the shabby state of its citizens: 'They are not well clad,' he noted, 'but sad and poor, showing the hardship of their lot.'

Pedro happened to be present to witness the great army of the 'Grand Turk' as it marched by the Theodosian Walls. It was a thrilling spectacle, but it left him unsettled:

> *I thought that they [the Ottomans] would sit down and besiege*
> *the city, but they continued their march to the Black Sea ...*
> *It was, indeed, what I desired, for we had but few men, and*
> *it would have been difficult to make much resistance. It was,*
> *therefore, a gratifying thing to see so great a host depart without*
> *peril or labour. Would to God that the people of our country were*
> *closer at hand, for there are here neither ships nor fortresses, nor*
> *is there any protection except by fighting.*

JOE AND I FOLLOW the line of the Theodosian Walls northwards. We see a cabinetmaker's workshop built into one of the postern gates. We're walking in silence now. The dilapidation of the Golden Gate has induced a melancholic feeling, an odd sense of futility.

The Greek description of *melancholia* – a weight of sadness and lethargy – sounds very much like a modern diagnosis of depression. That's not quite what I'm feeling here at the Theodosian Walls. Orhan Pamuk, in his memoir *Istanbul*, uses a Turkish word, *hüzün*, to describe a similar emotion, which pervades his childhood memories of the city. *Hüzün*, he says, is not a solitary experience, but a communal feeling that arises from living in a city crowded with the monuments and signs of a glorious past. It's a hazy sadness, a gentle conviction that one is living in a monochrome era, in a world built in a larger, more colourful age.

Today the lethargic Istanbul of Pamuk's childhood is being flattened and cleared to make way for the dynamic Turkish megalopolis of the twenty-first century. On this walk along the wall, we see blocks of slum housing being torn down. Joe and I walk into a newly cleared space and see a neat set of contemporary townhouses under construction, fitted with modern plumbing, air-conditioning and broadband. I wonder how long it will be before the new residents demand that the crumbling old wall be demolished too.

Fatih district, Istanbul.

FURTHER ALONG, near the Gate of the Rhegium, I see some ancient steps built into the brickwork. I climb up onto the parapet and haul Joe up with me. There is no protective rail, and if either of us trip, we will fall to our deaths. We plant our feet on a stable patch of brickwork and look out to the west. Below us are the ruins of the outer wall, and beyond that, a traffic flyover ramp and more makeshift housing. The modern suburbs of greater Istanbul stretch out to the horizon.

We climb into a tower and peer out the window, putting ourselves in the place of a Roman sentry, looking out at a sea of enemies on the plains beyond the walls. We climb down and walk further, to the point where the walls are bisected by a six-lane freeway. In the freeway underpass, we find the hand-painted mural of Mehmed II and his conquering army. It's the first sign of Turkish triumphalism we've seen so far. But the sultan's enemies, the Romans, are absent from the picture. This is the site of the greatest Ottoman victory, but over whom?

Joe at the Theodosian Walls near the St Romanus Gate.

The winter sun is dropping from the sky as Joe and I walk into a steep valley near the St Romanus Gate, the weakest point in the land wall defences. The outer wall has been stripped away, giving us a clear line of sight of the final stretch of the inner wall as it sweeps majestically towards the Golden Horn, interspersed with square and hexagonal towers; still upright, still vigilant, like an old soldier recalled to duty. Joe skips across a culvert that carries a thin stream of water under the wall. Was this the Lycus River? High up on a tower I see a cross etched into the brickwork, facing out to the west like a protective talisman.

Murad and Mehmed

TWO HUNDRED AND FORTY kilometres to the west of Constantinople lay the city of Edirne, the European capital of the Ottoman Turks. Edirne was flourishing under Ottoman rule; the sultan had commissioned splendid mosques, fountains, hospitals and a new palace to properly reflect their newfound wealth and power. The Ottoman Turks, once a nomadic people, were transformed by their acquisition of an empire: they became richer, more settled, better educated. Their rulers, who had once contented themselves with the title of 'Emir', now took the grander title of 'Sultan', and adopted the ceremonial trappings of a great power, to be admired and feared.

And yet, for all that, their sultan could not fail to wonder why he should dwell in the relatively modest confines of Edirne when his lands encircled another, far more famous Roman city down the road, a city ruled by an emperor of nothing in particular, who pompously styled himself as the heir of the Caesars.

Sultan Murad II had built on the success of his predecessors and the borders of his empire had grown steadily under his rule. He was astute, popular and widely admired, even by his enemies. Nonetheless, Murad found himself distracted again and again by major and minor insurrections from rebel generals or a pretender to his throne. Murad detected the hand of Constantinople in many of these irritating disruptions, and with good reason: lacking a sizeable army, the Romans were constantly trying to wrongfoot the Ottomans with subterfuge. When Murad's enemies showed up at the gates of Constantinople seeking sanctuary, the emperor was all too willing to take them in, and then send a bill to the sultan for the pretender's upkeep.

In 1421 Murad decided he'd had enough of these meddlesome Christians and led his magnificent army to the walls of Constantinople. The siege lasted three months and despite his overwhelming numerical superiority, he was forced to call a halt to the attack: the cunning Romans had sent out Murad's ambitious younger brother Mustafa to lead a rebellion in Asia Minor. Murad broke off the siege, hunted down his brother and executed him.

Despite all this bad blood, by the end of Murad's reign, the Ottomans and the Romans were at peace. Murad's chief vizier, Halil Pasha, who was secretly receiving bribes from the Romans, persuaded Murad that an all-out attack on the Christian capital risked uniting the European Christian kingdoms in a crusade against them. In the end, Murad accepted he would simply have to tolerate the presence of this city of irksome Christians in his lands.

IN 1451, MURAD FELL ILL and died in Edirne, and was succeeded by his nineteen-year-old son, Mehmed. In Europe, Mehmed was dismissed as a ridiculous teenager: rash, young and stupid. His earlier trial runs as sultan had ended in disaster, thanks to Halil's sly machinations, and on both occasions Halil had contrived for Murad to be dragged out of retirement to mend the damage.

Mehmed's accession to the Ottoman throne was welcomed with smiles of relief among the emperor's counsellors in Constantinople. But the chief advisor, George Sphrantzes, was less sanguine: "This news brings me no joy,' he said stonily. 'On the contrary, it is a cause for grief. The late Sultan was an old man and had given up on the conquest of our city. This man who has just become Sultan is young and an enemy of the Christians since childhood.'

MEHMED WAS MURAD'S third-born son, and never intended for the throne. As a boy he was an insolent student and a constant vexation to his father. No tutor could induce him to study, until Murad summoned a famous mullah with a long red beard named Ahmed Gurani. Murad presented him with a branch and gave him permission to use it.

'Your father has sent me to instruct you,' Gurani told Mehmed by way of introduction, 'but also to beat you in case you don't obey me.'

Mehmed laughed, and so the mullah gave him a terrible thrashing. Mehmed was thereafter in awe of Gurani and became a more attentive student. Gurani taught Mehmed a famous prophecy, attributed to Muhammad himself, which promised that the fabled capital of the Romans would eventually fall to the Muslims: 'Verily you shall conquer Constantinople. What a wonderful leader will he be, and what a wonderful army will that army be!'

Mehmed had no expectation of succeeding his father until his oldest brother, Prince Ahmed, died suddenly in 1437. Six years later another brother, Alaeddin Ali, was strangled in his bed, along with his infant sons. Ali was Murad's favourite, and his death filled the sultan with a terrible grief that seems to have ruined his happiness. Mehmed, at eleven, was suddenly heir to the throne.

MEHMED WAS IN MANISA, near the Aegean coast, when he was brought a sealed envelope from a special messenger. Inside was a brief note advising him of his father's death. Mehmed mounted his white stallion and cried out, 'Let those who love me follow me!' and set out for Edirne.

He was enthroned as Sultan Mehmed II on 18 February 1451. Afterwards, Mehmed called for his nobles to attend him. The treacherous Halil was nowhere to be seen.

'Why,' he asked, 'do my viziers stand aloof? Bring Halil here and tell him to take his usual place.'

Halil Pasha was found and brought forward. He dropped to his knees and kissed the sultan's hand. Mehmed confirmed him in his position as chief vizier.

Mehmed had learnt to bide his time.

SULTAN MEHMED II contained all kinds of contradictory impulses and ideas within his energetic mind. He was a dedicated jihadist who nonetheless ruled his Christian and Jewish subjects with tolerance and generosity. He was brittle and short-tempered but made long-range plans that he carried steadily to fruition. He took five wives but had several male lovers too.

A miniature portrait of Mehmed in his later years portrays him as a thoughtful man with a reddish beard, small ruby lips and a prominent aquiline nose. His expression is mild as he gently holds the stem of a tiny rose to sniff its perfume. We see in this picture one authentic aspect of Mehmed: the poet-king, a man alive to the fragile beauty of things. But in the first act of his reign we see another, equally authentic aspect: his unwavering ruthlessness.

Mehmed had an infant half-brother named Ahmed Çelebi, a son by another of Murad's wives. Mehmed called Ahmed's mother to the throne room. While she was out, an assassin entered her home and drowned little Ahmed in his bath. The distraught mother was married off to a Turkish nobleman and sent out to the provinces.

With the murder of his baby brother, Mehmed affirmed a new principle of royal fratricide, writing into Turkish law, 'whichever of my sons inherits the Sultan's throne, it behooves him to kill his brother in the interest of the world order'. Mehmed argued the execution of rival brothers was a positive good, a stabilising principle that was preferable to the turmoil that so often afflicted the Romans when it came time to choose a new emperor.

Secure on his throne, Mehmed could turn his mind once more to the question of Constantinople. Encouraged by his military advisors, the young sultan conceived himself both as an empire-builder like Alexander, and as a holy warrior of Islam who would overpower Christian civilisation with the force of *jihad*. Mehmed resolved that the ancient city of Constantinople must be his, and that the emperor must surrender it to him, or die.

Sultan Mehmed II.

The Last Emperor

AS MEHMED WENT back and forth from his bed to his desk each night, studying his model of the Theodosian Walls, his quarry lay sleeping behind those walls in the Blachernae Palace.

Emperor Constantine XI Palaeologus was forty-three years old and fated to be the very last emperor of the Romans, the final link in a chain stretching all the way back to Augustus Caesar. He was an altogether different ruler from his feckless predecessors. Constantine possessed deep reserves of courage and fortitude that would sustain him in the ordeal to come. He inspired affection and loyalty among his advisors, if not from his subjects, who bridled under the hard decisions he was forced to make on their behalf. It was his awful fate to inherit the throne just as the empire's final crisis was already engulfing it.

He was born in Constantinople in 1405 as the son of the Emperor Manuel II Palaeologus and his wife Helen Dragaš. In a coincidence that underscores the multicultural nature of their realms, both Mehmed and Constantine were born from Serbian mothers: Constantine's was a noblewoman, Mehmed's a former slave. Constantine was the eighth of ten children, and like Mehmed, he grew up without the burden of expectation that he would become emperor. His most important childhood friend was George Sphrantzes, who would become his closest advisor.

Constantine's first marriage ended after a year when his wife died in childbirth. Twelve years later, he remarried, but his second wife also died in childbirth. His older brother John, upon becoming emperor, appointed Constantine as governor of Morea in the Peloponnese, one of the last remaining imperial outposts.

One day in 1448, two envoys from Constantinople arrived with sombre news: John was dead, and they had come to invest

Constantine as the new emperor. Constantine accepted with some sadness and reluctance, and dutifully accompanied the envoys back to Constantinople.

THE NEW EMPEROR styled himself as 'Constantine XI Palaeologus, in Christ True Emperor and Autocrat of the Romans', but it was all a charade. The 'emperor' of the Romans was now a vassal of the Ottoman Turks, required to hand over an annual tribute to keep the peace. The sad truth was that Constantine had only been permitted to take the throne after Sultan Murad had given his assent.

Constantine donned the imperial robes, including the *loros*, the long narrow winding scarf, embroidered with gold and gems, and the distinct purple leather boots, but he never dared risk a full ceremonial coronation in the Hagia Sophia. The Orthodox flock was bitterly divided between those who, like the Patriarch, wanted union with the Catholic church as a matter of political necessity, and those who denounced the union as an unthinkable heresy. Constantine was advised that a full coronation would provoke public rioting, and so a shadow always lingered around his legitimacy.

Constantine could read a map as well as Mehmed, and was under no illusions about the coming storm. Like his predecessors, he sent envoys to the Christian monarchs of the west, hoping to prod their consciences into some kind of collective military action against the Muslim Turks, anything to distract Ottoman attention from Constantinople. He appealed to Rome, but support from the pope was contingent on the completion of the act of union.

Then the unionist Patriarch Gregory, tired of constant accusations of heresy, absconded to Rome where he was given papal protection. Constantine was in an awkward bind: to his own people playing down the prospect of any union, while at the same time reaffirming his commitment in his letters to the pope, all the while hoping that the sultan in Edirne wouldn't force the issue.

WHEN MEHMED SUCCEEDED his father in 1451, Constantine tried to start the relationship on a positive note, sending envoys to Edirne to congratulate the new sultan. Mehmed received them warmly and he swore by Allah, the Prophet, the angels and the archangels that the Ottoman Turks would live at peace with the city and the emperor. Constantine may have taken too much comfort in this vow, because he spoilt this friendly start with a terrible blunder.

Constantinople had given asylum to Prince Orhan, a pretender to the Ottoman throne. Mehmed's father had agreed to pay Constantinople an annual sum to provide for Orhan's upkeep and to keep him safely detained within the city. Constantine was hoping to wrangle more gold from the Turks, but he overplayed his hand. He sent ambassadors to Halil with a mischievous demand: double the allowance or Orhan will be released.

This was a game the Romans had played well for centuries: turning the power of an enemy upon itself through deception and blackmail. But the Byzantine mouse had provoked the Ottoman lion once too often. Their only ally in Mehmed's court, Halil Pasha, was put badly offside. Halil had counselled patience and tolerance of the Romans, but this new demand undermined his advice. Halil's reply to the ambassadors revealed the depth of his anger:

> *You stupid Greeks, I am sick of your devious ways. The last*
> *Sultan was a lenient and conscious friend to you. The present*
> *Sultan is not of the same mind ... You are fools to think you can*
> *frighten us with your fantasies, and that when the ink on our*

recent treaty is barely dry. We are not children without strength or reason. If you think you can start something, do so. If you want to proclaim Orhan as Sultan in Thrace, go ahead. If you want to bring the Hungarians across the Danube, let them come. If you want to recover the places which you lost long since, try this. But know this: you will make no headway in any of these things. All that you will achieve is to lose what little you still have.

Halil had no choice but to inform Mehmed of the Roman 'demand'. The sultan made no display of anger, indicating he would consider the matter at a later time. But Constantine's bluff was called: he won no extra gold, the city's last remaining friend in the court was alienated, and his enemies' hand was strengthened. The letter also gave Mehmed a handy excuse to break his earlier promises of peace and goodwill. The breach was not long in coming.

SEAGULLS ARE CIRCLING ABOVE. The late-afternoon shadows are lengthening and our long walk along the walls is just about done. We dodge some traffic to pass through a gate and find ourselves in a Muslim cemetery. It's an eerie sight, the headstones dusted with a ghostly patina of concrete powder from a nearby building site.

We get lost in some back streets for a few blocks and then we come upon the ruins of the Palace of the Porphyrogenitus, the last building to be constructed in the Blachernae complex. All that remains are some angled slabs of thick, high walls, topped with marbled Byzantine arch windows. Twisted saplings sprout from gaps in the brickwork. The entry portal is stopped up with sheets of corrugated metal.

A steep road leads us down past a school, and the cramped streets open up to the expanse of the Golden Horn. It has taken the better part of a day for us to follow the Theodosian Walls from the Sea of Marmara to here. What would it mean to face an army so large it could form a long, thick line of attack along the entire length of these defences?

The Throat Cutter

IN THE EARLY SPRING of 1452, teams of Ottoman workers and engineers began laying the groundwork for a new fortress on the European side of the Bosphorus, just thirteen kilometres upstream from Constantinople. The sultan had selected the site himself and proposed the design. The Ottomans already possessed a castle known as Anadolu Hisar ('Anatolian Fortress') on the Asian side of the Bosphorus; two strongholds on opposite shores would give Mehmed the power to pinch both sides of the narrow strait and control its shipping lanes. The new fortress could also act as a forward base from which to attack Constantinople.

News of Ottoman activity on the Bosphorus was received in Constantinople with alarm and dismay. The emperor sent an envoy to Mehmed with a polite letter, pointing out that the construction of the new fortress was taking place on Roman territory in violation of their treaty.

Mehmed's reply to the envoys was a blunt statement of political realities:

What Constantinople contains is its own. Beyond the moat it has
no dominion, owns nothing. If I want to build a fortress at the

sacred mouth, it can't forbid me. Go away and tell your Emperor this: 'The Sultan who rules is not like his predecessors. What they couldn't achieve, he can do easily and at once. The things they did not wish to do, he certainly does.'

Mehmed dismissed the envoy with a threat: 'The next man to come here on a mission like this will be flayed alive.'

Mehmed could hardly have made his intentions clearer. Constantine sent another desperate appeal to Venice for help. The Venetians received the letter with some discomfort, wary of damaging their commercial interests with the Ottoman Turks. But the members of the governing council of the Serene Republic couldn't quite bring themselves to openly abandon their Christian brothers and sisters. Their response was sympathetic but noncommittal.

Meanwhile, construction of the new stronghold proceeded rapidly. Mehmed rode out each morning to supervise the work. His three viziers were each given responsibility for the construction of one of the three main towers; in doing so, they competed for his favour. Roman observers standing on the roof of the Hagia Sophia could only look on in helpless wonder at the fortress walls rising in the distance.

Roman farmers in the surrounding countryside were powerless to stop Mehmed's soldiers raiding their fields for grain. The farmers sent urgent requests to the palace for military support against these outrageous acts of theft. Constantine sadly had to refuse; he knew Mehmed was trying to goad him into sending his feeble forces outside the city walls, where Mehmed's soldiers could crush them. Instead the emperor offered to send food to Mehmed's workers if they agreed to leave his fields alone. Mehmed ignored this offer, and encouraged his workers to let their animals graze in the fields. Inevitably, a skirmish broke out between the sorely provoked farmers and the Turkish workers. Mehmed then gave his soldiers orders to slaughter the locals.

Rumeli Hisar, the Throat Cutter.

In response, Constantine ordered the gates of the city be closed, and the few remaining Turks within the city were detained. The Turkish prisoners begged to be allowed to return to the Ottoman lines; otherwise, they said, Mehmed would execute them as traitors. Constantine relented and let the men go. Mehmed would not trade for their lives so there was little point in keeping them.

Constantine was now compelled to acknowledge the hard truth of the situation. He drafted a message of defiance for Mehmed:

Since you have preferred war to peace and I can call you back to peace neither with oaths or pleas, then follow your own will. I take refuge in God. If He has decreed and decided to hand over this city to you, who can contradict Him or prevent it? If He instils the idea of peace in your mind, I would gladly agree.

For the moment, now that you have broken the treaties to which I am bound by oath, let these be dissolved. Henceforth

I will keep the city gates closed. I will fight for the inhabitants
with all my strength.

Mehmed received the message and had the envoys executed, just
as he had promised. His reply to Constantine was blunt: 'Either
surrender the city, or stand and do battle.'

THE NEW FORTRESS was completed after an astonishingly short
four months on 31 August 1452. Its position on the narrowest point of
the strait earned it the nickname of Bogaz Kezen, the Throat Cutter.
It's still there today, an oddly medieval castle on the Bosphorus shore
with round stone towers and parapet walls that run steeply down to
a point on the water's edge.

Mehmed was intrigued by the possibilities of a relatively new
weapon of war, the cannon. He ordered three heavy bronze cannons
to be placed close to the shore of the Throat Cutter. Each of these
wide-barrelled guns was able to thrust a heavy stone ball across
the strait, low enough to shatter the hull of any passing ship. More
cannons were mounted on the Asian shore, so that ships could be
strafed from both sides. Mehmed gave the fortress commander an
order that all ships travelling up and down the strait were to be
stopped and a toll was to be extracted.

IN LATE NOVEMBER, a Venetian trading galley sailed out of the
Black Sea with a cargo of food destined for Constantinople. The
galley slipped into the fast-moving Bosphorus Strait and soon came
within range of the Throat Cutter. The captain, Antonio Rizzo,
impulsively decided to race his ship past the fortress, in the hope that
he could pass before the Ottoman guards could rouse themselves
to open fire. But the Turks were alert and ready for such a test. The

sound of cannon fire boomed out from the shore and a massive stone ball whistled across the surface of the water and smashed into the hull of Rizzo's galley, splintering its timbers. As the shattered ship broke apart in the water, Rizzo and thirty of his crew escaped into a small boat and rowed to shore. The Venetians were picked up by Ottoman soldiers, imprisoned and then hideously executed. Rizzo was impaled on a spike, his body left to rot in the street, unburied.

After that, there were no more ships prepared to test the Throat Cutter. Mehmed declared Constantinople was now under blockade.

Pope Nicholas was horrified by the news of the sultan's new fortress. The kingdoms of France, Germany and Spain were slowly becoming roused to the fact that Constantinople now faced an existential threat, but their rulers were too weakened or distracted by their own internal struggles, or were so far away they couldn't bring themselves to care.

CHAPTER TEN

A Thing Not of This World

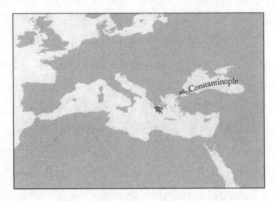

The empire in 1453, at the final siege of Constantinople.

The Book of Animals

MORNING IN SULTANAHMET: shopkeepers are sweeping the footpaths, dragging out postcard stands. Two rug-sellers are sitting on milk crates in the lane between their shops, smoking and sipping at small glasses of apple tea. Joe and I are walking up a narrow street towards the Arasta Bazaar. Joe points to a toy house, like a kennel, next to the stoop of an apartment block. The resident of this little hand-painted house is a smug-looking black-and-white cat, poking its head out to enjoy the winter sunshine.

Cats are everywhere in Istanbul. Their presence seems to take the edge off life in the big city. Each night, from the window of our room, Joe and I have been observing the shopfront of the carpet seller across the street. In his display window is a cardboard box

390

containing a fluffy white cat with her litter of four kittens that hop about and skitter up the fabric of the rug behind them.

Joe keeps a tally of the cats we pass on our walk. He sees them perched on a stone windowsill, sitting on an ancient stairway, yawning at a tram stop, chasing a leaf in front of Topkapi Palace. In Istanbul, a cat will happily leap onto your table and then curl asleep on your lap before your food arrives.

Cats are admired in Islamic tradition because they practise ritual cleanliness. The Prophet himself is said to have outlawed the persecution and the killing of cats. One story has it that Muhammad chose to cut off a sleeve of his gown to go to prayer, rather than wake the cat that was sleeping on it.

In the Middle Ages, an Egyptian scholar named Al-Damiri compiled a wonderful encyclopaedia called the *Book of Animals*, which painstakingly listed all the creatures mentioned in the Qur'an in alphabetical order. Alongside each animal he placed Arab and Persian folktales that related to it. The origin of the cat, he wrote, could be traced back to Noah's Ark. The animals on board the ark were complaining about the mice. So God caused the lion to sneeze, and out popped the first cat.

Cats dogged Joe and me throughout our lunch that day. Our platters of food arrived, and with them came two cats, nagging us for scraps. Three more appeared and all five of them formed a circle of intimidation around Joe, who was greatly amused by the ring of fluffy brazenness around him. One of the cats, a smoky grey kitten with searching black eyes, defected to my side of the table and squeaked out a plaintive noise. I laughed in such a way that could only mean, *No kofte for you, kitty-kat.* I turned back to my meal and the little beast leapt up and clouted me on the hand.

Islam is more ambivalent about dogs; they're regarded as unclean and the term 'dog' is commonly used as an insult. But there are stories in the Qur'an of protective and loyal canines, and again, the Prophet is reported to have said that when a man or woman gives water to a thirsty dog, God will reward that person and he or she will enter paradise.

Rum Papa

THE LATIN CHURCH of Rome was, in those final months, a widely detested institution in Constantinople. *Rum Papa* – 'the Roman Pope' – was a name commonly given to dogs in the city. In the eyes of Orthodox hardliners, the Latin church was an abomination, a perversion of Christianity. Its followers were worse than Muslims.

And yet, as the outlook continued to darken at the end of 1452, Emperor Constantine XI still clung to the hope that the pope might somehow persuade the princes of the west to gather up their armies and come to the rescue of their hard-pressed fellow Christians in Constantinople. The emperor fired off a series of letters to Rome, alerting Pope Nicholas to the imminent destruction of his city.

But the papacy no longer had the power to compel or inspire the kings of Europe into another crusade. Nicholas tried to conceal his weakness and use the crisis to extract a narrow political advantage: he told Constantine he really couldn't do anything to help until the Orthodox church formally agreed to accept his spiritual leadership.

The eastern and western churches had been drifting further apart for centuries. They were like an unhappy couple who had lost sight of whatever it was that had brought them together in the first place. The façade of unity had collapsed back in 1054, when a delegation of papal legates dressed in full ceremonial finery had marched into the Hagia Sophia during High Mass, and slapped a formal bull of excommunication on the altar, in front of the open-mouthed worshippers. The excommunication led to anti-Catholic riots in the city. The patriarch retaliated by burning the document in a public bonfire and by excommunicating the papal officials from *his* church. Despite its dubious legality, this incident had created an enduring rift, a terrible schism between the two churches. As time passed, Rome insisted the schism could only be repaired if the Orthodox church submitted to the authority of the pope.

THE PROSPECT OF submission to the western church was galling and distressing, but for Constantine XI it was a necessary hypocrisy. He sent ambassadors to patch up their remaining differences. Some progress had been made, and there was a degree of goodwill among some of the emperor's bishops, but there was still much bad blood among the flock and within the monasteries. The sack of Constantinople by the Latin Crusaders had implanted a lingering bitterness within the Orthodox faithful. And they were still divided on so many things: on the nature of the Holy Trinity, on whether priests could marry, and on whether the bread they consumed in the Eucharist should be leavened or unleavened. Too many people in Constantinople said they would never accept the Latin church, no matter what the emperor and his bishops said.

The leading voice in Constantinople against the union was a charismatic monk named Gennadius, who was unmoved by those who argued that the union was an unfortunate but necessary business. Submission to the pope, he insisted, would not save the city, but damn it for all time. The Latin church was a heresy and the pope was the anti-Christ; the surrender of the one true church would be so repugnant to God, it would certainly trigger the End of Days, the destruction of the city and the entire world. What did one city matter, he said, when the fate of the world and the immortal soul were at stake?

Many Orthodox Christians preferred the idea of living under a tolerant Muslim ruler to submitting to a Catholic pope. Grand Duke Lucas Notaras distilled this defiance into a popular slogan: 'Better the Sultan's turban than the Pope's cap!' But eventually, even he was forced to accept the political realities of the situation, and he agreed to help his emperor find some middle ground between the chilly demands of Rome and the heated sentiment of Constantinople.

Pope Nicholas was well aware of the narrowness of the path Constantine had to travel. But his reply to the emperor's desperate plea was pompous and bloody-minded:

> If you, with your nobles and the people of Constantinople,
> accept the decree of union, you will find Us and Our venerable
> brothers, the cardinals of the Holy Roman Church, ever eager
> to support your honour and your empire. But if you and
> your people refuse to accept the decree, you will force Us to

*take such measures as are necessary for your salvation and
Our honour.*

Nicholas set the bar high: he insisted the union of the churches would have to be proclaimed in the Hagia Sophia before he could call upon a new Crusade to save the city. Constantine wearily gave his assent, and the pope authorised Cardinal Isidore of Kiev to close the deal and perform the ceremony. When Isidore arrived in the city, he presented Constantine with a gift of two hundred archers for the city's defence, and a chest of gold to pay for the repair of the land walls. This act of goodwill momentarily boosted public support for the union.

A member of the emperor's court, Ducas, was present at the reception of Cardinal Isidore. Ducas saw through the shadowplay:

> *The Emperor received them graciously and paid them due
> honour, after which they settled to a discussion of the Union.
> They found him in favour of it, as were the principal lay
> members of the church. But the majority of the priests and
> monks, the abbots, archimandrites and nuns, were against it.
> The majority, did I say? My mention of the nuns compels me
> to alter my words and make this clear, that not a single one
> of them consented; and the Emperor himself only pretended
> to agree.*

AND SO ON TUESDAY 12 December 1452, the union of the eastern and western churches was officially sealed in a miserable ceremony in the Hagia Sophia. The rite was Catholic rather than Orthodox; the language Latin, not Greek; the bread unleavened. The pope and the absent Patriarch were honoured. Constantine appeared to be subdued and depressed as he sat on his throne under the great dome.

A crowd of distressed anti-unionists gathered at the Monastery of the Pantocrator, calling on Gennadius to instruct them on what to do next. Gennadius refused to leave his room. He scrawled a note and pinned it to the door of his cell: 'O unhappy Romans, why have you forsaken the truth? Why do you not trust in God, instead of in the Italians? In losing your faith you will lose your city.'

The anti-unionist majority felt heartsick and abandoned. Groups of monks wandered about, wailing in anguish. The city's taverns filled up as people drank themselves into a stupor, stumbling into the streets with bowls of wine in their hands, cursing the faithless unionists.

The following morning, Isidore penned an upbeat letter to Rome: the Cardinal was pleased to inform His Holiness that his mission had been accomplished and the two churches were now officially 'united and Catholic'.

It was an empty victory. The Orthodox faithful shunned the Hagia Sophia as if it were a pagan temple. Justinian's great church, which had rung out with the voices of the faithful for nine hundred years, became empty, dark and silent.

Friend of the Infidels

TWO HUNDRED AND FORTY kilometres up the road in Edirne, Mehmed received reports of the religious turmoil in Constantinople with growing excitement. The sultan was restless, obsessive. He lay awake at night in his palace, configuring and reconfiguring in his mind his plans to attack the city. He would often rise from his bed and stride over to his desk to incorporate some new thought into the plan. He spent his days sketching and memorising the walls and outposts, grilling anyone he could find with any knowledge of the city's defences.

Despite the huge disparity in size between the Ottoman and the Roman armies, Mehmed could not hope to succeed unless he brought overwhelming military superiority to the city walls, sustained by strong supply chains. He would also need the full and enthusiastic support of his advisors. The Janissaries Shihabettin and Zaganos were eager, but Halil was still advocating caution and warning of a European backlash. Behind his back, Halil's rivals nicknamed him 'Friend of the Infidels'.

Late one night, Halil was shaken from his sleep by two eunuchs, who told him the sultan required his presence immediately. Fearing the worst, Halil took with him a bowl of gold. He was brought to the sultan's quarters, where he saw Mehmed sitting up in bed. Halil laid the gold at his feet. Mehmed, taken aback, asked what on earth he thought he was doing.

'It is the custom,' replied the vizier, 'that when a nobleman is summoned by the sultan at such an unusual hour, he must not arrive with empty hands.'

'I have no need of your gold,' Mehmed scoffed. 'I want only one thing from you: your help in taking possession of Constantinople.' The sultan gestured to the tangled bedcovers around him. 'Look at my bed, in which I have been tossing and turning from side to side all night.' Then, hinting that he knew of the bribes Halil was receiving, he warned, 'I tell you Halil: do not be softened by gold or silver. We shall fight the Romans bravely, and with Allah's will, we shall take the city.'

BY JANUARY, Mehmed could wait no longer. He called his advisors, and after hearing arguments for and against, announced he would pursue his heart's desire – to lay siege to Constantinople relentlessly, by land and sea, until he could break the city and take the world throne of the Caesars for himself.

He told his advisors he would need to bring overwhelming force to take the city quickly, before the Christian powers in Europe could muster themselves to respond, and before his army could suffer the demoralisation and disease that would inevitably accompany a prolonged siege.

The Blood Tax

AN OLD MILITARY ADAGE has it that amateurs concern themselves with tactics, but professionals worry about logistics. Mehmed's instinctive aggression was tempered by a painstaking attention to detail, and he directed his restless mind into the complex business of mounting an amphibious assault on the world's most heavily fortified city. Workers across his empire gathered timber, iron, hemp, sulphur, tin and scrap bronze, which were fashioned into ships, armour, chain mail, arrows, crossbows and tents. Mehmed mobilised every regiment in his army and cancelled all leave. He put out a call to arms and was promptly answered by the arrival of volunteers from all over the Ottoman lands, inspired by the prospect of glory on the battlefield, and the chance to share in the fabled treasure of the city of the Romans.

At the heart of Mehmed's army were his Janissaries, an elite corps of professional soldiers who served as crossbowmen, musketeers, sappers and engineers. The Janissaries wore distinctive white turbans and blue woollen coats; they marched to military music, lived in barracks and, unlike the *ghazi* volunteers, were paid for their service. All their ranks were taken from the jargon of the kitchen. The commanding officer of each company held the title of çorbaci, 'soup cook', and wore a ladle as his insignia, to symbolise his humility before the sultan. Other ranks were known as 'chief cook', 'baker' and 'pancake maker'. Janissary regiments would gather around a *kazgan*, a heavy cauldron, in which their pilaf was cooked. When they turned mutinous, they would signal their unhappiness by overturning the *kazgan* and beating on it with spoons, creating a great clanging din to indicate their rejection of the sultan's rice.

They were all orphans of a kind, with very few links to anything outside their elite band of brothers; the corps of Janissaries was the only family they knew or cared for. They had all been born into Christian families within the Ottoman empire. Once they reached boyhood, they were taken away from their parents as payment of a 'blood tax', known as the *devsirme*, that was levied by the sultan on his Christian subjects.

The boys were sent to a Muslim home where they were circumcised, indoctrinated into Islam and brought into a daily regime of constant military training. As the memories of their early lives faded away, they received instructions in Turkish, Persian and Arab literature, conversation, horsemanship, javelin throwing, wrestling and archery. Family life was replaced by the comradeship of the barracks. Over time a Janissary would forget his childhood, his family and his home. He would know 'no lord and father other than the Sultan, no will but his, no hope but in his favour'. Mehmed's second vizier, Zaganos Pasha, had himself been taken from a Christian family in the Balkans as a boy.

This process of rigorous training and indoctrination moulded the boys into disciplined, dedicated warriors. On reaching adulthood, they were inducted into the most professional corps of soldiers in Europe. A Janissary would always officially retain the status of *kapukulu*, 'slave of the Sultan'. But they were well treated and highly prized by their sultan. In battle, their role was often decisive. Initial fighting would typically be carried forward by the *ghazis*, the regular soldiers. Janissaries would be held back until the critical moment, when they would charge into the attack with overwhelming force.

Drawing of a fifteenth-century Janissary by Gentile Bellini.

BY THE SPRING OF 1453, Mehmed's preparations were complete and his 60,000-strong force of Janissaries, infantry and cavalry set out from Edirne towards Constantinople, followed by a retinue of cooks, blacksmiths, carpenters and holy men who offered prayers for the journey.

Somewhere within that vast marching mass of soldiers was the sultan's secret weapon: an artillery device so immensely huge and heavy that a team of sixty oxen and two hundred men were required to haul it along the muddy track on a train of wagons. The sultan's soldiers caught glimpses of it as they passed; it was the bronze barrel of a cannon, the biggest the world had ever seen.

The Great Bombard

THE BRONZE CANNON was the creation of an ingenious Hungarian metalsmith named Urban, who had been wandering around Europe offering his expertise to anyone who could afford his services. The year before, he had arrived in Constantinople and met with the emperor. Urban offered to help the emperor's engineers cast super-large, single-piece bronze cannons. Constantine agreed to pay him a small retainer, but the sad truth was the imperial treasury was nearly empty – there was no money to develop new bronze cannon pieces, not enough to even keep up with Urban's wages. The Hungarian was running out of money and food, so he left the city.

Soon afterwards he appeared in Mehmed's palace in Edirne where he was welcomed warmly and given food and clothes.

Urban was brought before the sultan, who asked him, 'Can you cast a cannon that is able to hurl a stone ball large enough to smash the walls at Constantinople?'

'If you wish, Sire,' he replied, 'I can cast a bronze cannon of the size you require. I have examined the walls of the city in great detail. I can shatter to dust not only these walls with the stones from my gun, but the very walls of Babylon itself.'

Mehmed was pleased and excited by this answer, and so Urban went to work at the sultan's foundry. Urban's first large gun was hauled over to the newly built fortress on the Bosphorus, the Throat Cutter; it was this cannon that fired the stone ball that sank Antonio Rizzo's galley. Mehmed was delighted, and ordered Urban to produce a much larger cannon, twice the size of the first one.

Urban returned to the sultan's foundry. Workers laboured for weeks in dangerous and hellish conditions. The cannon shaft that emerged was immense. The barrel, more than eight metres long, was big enough for a man to crawl inside.

Mehmed requested a test firing and the Great Bombard, as the cannon came to be called, was hauled into position outside the palace. A warning was sent out to the people of Edirne 'to pay attention, and not to allow the noise and the thunderous roar to terrify uninformed people who might become speechless and cause pregnant women to miscarry'. A black stone ball weighing more than half a ton was hoisted and loaded into the cannon's gaping muzzle. The taper was lit, igniting the gunpowder, and with a great shuddering boom, the ball was shot out of the barrel. It soared through the air for well over a mile, before landing with a thud, burying itself into the soft earth.

News of the super-cannon soon reached Constantinople, only intensifying the dread and despair in the city, just as the sultan intended. Mehmed, well pleased with the test firing, ordered the creation of more bronze cannon pieces, but none would be so large as the Great Bombard. The size and destructive power of the cannon encouraged people to reach for superlatives. In Constantinople it was named the Royal Gun and the Romans wondered whether this time, their legendary walls could withstand such a monstrous new weapon.

The Theodosian Walls were the ultimate expression of everything the Romans had learnt about the protection of their cities against arrows, catapults and trebuchets. The slow advance of technology in the Middle Ages had left these principles unchallenged for a thousand years. Gunpowder, invented in China and carried into Europe along the silk roads, threatened the logic of brittle stone walls. The arrival of the Great Bombard would shatter it.

The Genoese

CONSTANTINE paid a high price for bringing his church into the Catholic fold; the effort evidently pained and humiliated him, but it was done and now he and his advisors hoped they would soon see some ships and soldiers from the west. But Venice dithered – there was little appetite for a new Crusade. Embarrassed by the lack of response, the pope sent three Genoese ships to Constantinople, at his own expense, laden with arms and food.

The Italian city-state of Genoa was torn by the crisis. Genoa, like Venice, was a rich maritime republic with a powerful navy. The plight of Constantinople roused their Christian sympathies, but Genoa's leaders were attempting to maintain a pragmatic posture of neutrality between Constantinople and the Ottoman empire.

The situation was further complicated by the position of the colony of Galata: the small Genoese settlement that sat directly across the Golden Horn from Constantinople. If Constantinople fell, would Galata fall too? And if Genoa gave conspicuous aid to Constantine and the city fell anyway, would that poison their trade with the powerful new empire of the Ottomans?

The governor of Galata appealed to his fellow Genoese for help anyway, and in January 1453 a wealthy soldier of fortune named Giovanni Giustiniani Longo answered the call. Giustiniani, on his own initiative, recruited and equipped some seven hundred soldiers, and arranged for two large galleons to carry them from Genoa to Constantinople at his own expense.

Giustiniani was charismatic, brave and experienced in siege warfare. He and his men were warmly welcomed by a greatly relieved emperor. Constantine instantly appointed Giustiniani general-in-chief and gave him command of the Theodosian Walls at its most vulnerable, central point. Minotto, the Venetian bailey in Constantinople, placed whatever resources he had in the city at the service of the emperor, as did Prince Orhan, the pretender to Mehmed's throne. Other soldiers arrived in dribs and drabs from elsewhere in Europe, but that was it. George Sphrantzes, Constantine's closest advisor, remarked with some bitterness that they had received as much help from the pope as they did from the Sultan of Egypt.

IN LATE MARCH Constantine ordered Sphrantzes to conduct a headcount of able-bodied fighting men in the city and an inventory of weapons: crossbows, shields and cannon. Sphrantzes quietly went about his task and reported the terrible news back to his emperor: there were just under eight thousand men in the city, many completely untrained in warfare. The numbers were far fewer than Constantine had expected, and he asked Sphrantzes to keep the figure a secret. He was outnumbered more than ten to one. How was he going to defend his city against so many with so few?

Constantine shored up his defences and sealed off the Golden Horn. The great chain was dragged across the mouth of the waterway. Ten powerful ships – nine from Italy, one from Constantinople – formed a defensive line behind the chain and waited for Mehmed's navy to arrive.

The Doctor

AS THE SENSE of crisis mounted in the city, a Venetian named Niccolò Barbaro sat down at his desk and wrote in his diary: 'On the fifth of the month of April: one hour after daybreak, Sultan Mehmed came before Constantinople with about a hundred and sixty thousand men. They camped about two-and-a-half miles from the walls of the city.'

Barbaro was a ship's surgeon stranded in Constantinople. Constantine had confiscated his merchant galley for the city's defence, making Barbaro a virtual prisoner of the siege. In early

April, he began to write daily entries in his diary, recording the steady advance of the Ottoman army as it marched up to the Theodosian Walls. Barbaro would be one of the most reliable witnesses of the coming cataclysm.

THE SULTAN'S FORCES stopped 400 metres short of the city, and spread out along the entire length of the walls. Mehmed's red-and-gold tent was erected in front of the vulnerable middle segment, between the St Romanus Gate and the Charisian Gate. His Anatolian army was camped to his right, his European army to his left. The white-turbaned Janissaries were amassed behind him.

The process of hauling the three great cannons up to the line, hoisting them off their ox-carts and laying them into position was agonisingly slow. Meanwhile, Mehmed ordered soldiers to clear the land in front of the walls in preparation for a major assault. Platoons of men scurried up to the empty moat, filling it in as best they could, tipping boulders, timber and soil into the ditch. Coming under heavy fire from the walls above, they made little progress.

Sappers set to work digging tunnels under the walls, but Mehmed paid little attention. His mind was focused on the imminent firing of his new cannons. The Great Bombard was placed in the centre of the Ottoman line, in front of Mehmed's tent, so he could observe its impact on the outer wall.

ON 11 APRIL Mehmed gave the order to commence firing. Tapers were lit, the ground shuddered, and the air was punctured by dozens of blasts along the entire length of the Theodosian Walls. The Great Bombard sent a black marble stone half as tall as a man hurtling through the air. The ball crashed into the wall and sent bricks and shrapnel flying, killing those on the wall who happened to be nearby.

For the defenders it was an awesome and terrifying spectacle, but for Mehmed, progress was slower than expected. The Great Bombard took three hours to prepare, load and fire. After firing it had to be cooled down carefully, by pouring hot oil into the muzzle, otherwise the barrel would crack. In the meantime, the defenders threw up a protective wooden palisade and repaired the damaged wall segments, stuffing the gaps with wool, branches and soil, which were better able to absorb the shock of the cannonballs.

The bombardment continued for a week, day and night. Several groups of Janissaries came forward to skirmish at the foot of the walls, but were shot down. The defenders were unsettled by the devotion of the Janissaries to these fallen comrades. Barbaro records that they would come forward and take away their dead, 'carrying them on their shoulders as one would a pig, without caring how near they came to the city walls'. Then the rescuers too were shot down with crossbows and muskets, and yet even more would come forward to take *them* away.

In mid-April, Mehmed launched an assault on the broken central section of the wall. At two in the morning, with a blast of percussion and horns, a battalion of heavy infantry charged across the moat. Coming under heavy fire, the attackers attempted to set fire to the gate, but Giustiniani and his Genoese archers put out the flames. The Ottoman spearmen tried to tear down the improvised stockade with grappling hooks fixed onto their javelins, but were quickly cut down.

At dawn, the sultan called off the attack. Giustiniani and his defenders had taken down a great many Ottoman soldiers, but had not suffered a single casualty themselves. Frustrated on land, Mehmed turned his attention to delivering a full-scale naval attack on the city.

The Four Against the Hundred

ON 12 APRIL AT AROUND one in the afternoon, the Turkish fleet was sighted in the Sea of Marmara. Watchers on the sea walls saw an armada of 145 low-slung galleys rowing steadily towards the city. The sultan's fleet paused ominously for a few hours on the Asian side of the Bosphorus, then skirted around the entrance to the Golden Horn and resumed its northward journey. The fleet came to anchor two miles upstream at a place known as the Double Columns, today the inner-city suburb of Beşiktaş. The Ottoman sailors filled the air with their war cries and the hammering of their drums and cymbals. The commotion could be heard two miles away in the city.

A few tense, watchful days passed on the water as the Italian galleons lined up at the great chain and waited for the inevitable attack. On 18 April, after his setback at the land walls, Mehmed called for the admiral of his fleet, Baltoglu, and ordered him to use his superior numbers to attack the chain, destroy the big Italian ships, and then occupy the Golden Horn. Taking the harbour would deny the Romans an important food source, and force Constantine to defend his northern sea wall, stretching his meagre forces at the land walls even thinner.

The Ottoman fleet set out from the Double Columns, rounded the corner into the Golden Horn in good order and charged at the ships in front of the chain, firing volleys of arrows and fireballs. But the Italian ships had the height advantage: the high decks created an elevated platform from which their battle-hardened seamen could fire down onto the Turkish galleys with arrows, stones and javelins. The overconfident Turks were shocked by the fury of the defence. Then one of the Italian ships swung out a wrecking ball, attached by a rope to the mast. The stone swung back and forth, smashing into Turkish ships, splintering their hulls and sending mangled sailors flying into the undertow of the Bosphorus, where they drowned in the current.

Roman observers on the walls cheered and howled. Mehmed, apoplectic with rage, watched helplessly from the shore. And still the swarm of Turkish boats pressed their attack against the European galleons, again and again. After four hours, the attack was called off, and Baltoglu sailed with his battered fleet back to the Double Columns.

TWO DAYS LATER, another hopeful sign for the beleaguered city: three Genoese galleons were spotted in the Sea of Marmara. These were the ships that had been sent by the pope, laden with weapons and food. The three ships were joined by one more: a large imperial transport ship loaded with corn. The report of the four ships was greeted in the city with cheers.

Mehmed saw the ships too, and resolved that they must not reach the safety of the Golden Horn. His orders to Baltoglu were simple: 'take these four ships. Sink them if you have to ... or don't come back alive'.

That afternoon, observers on the sea walls saw more than a hundred Ottoman galleys bearing down on the four trading ships. The Christian ships were absurdly outnumbered, but still had the advantage of greater height, bulk and momentum. A stiff southerly breeze filled their sails and carried them forward towards the safety of the Golden Horn. Then, just as they began to round Acropolis Point, the wind completely died away. The sails slackened and fell. The four trading ships drifted helplessly towards Mehmed's army on the Galata shore.

Baltoglu made his move. He ordered his own flagship to row forward at full speed, ramming the prow of his ship into the stern of the imperial transport. The listless Genoese galleons were stuck, dead in the water, as the Ottoman galleys swarmed around them. Desperate Turkish soldiers attempted to grapple onto the tall ships and climb on board, but as they pulled themselves up to the deck walls, Genoese sailors brought their axes down, lopping off heads and hands. Italian crossbowmen fired bolts from the crow's nest. Great tubs of water were tipped onto the Ottoman galleys. Again the heavy stone wrecking balls were swung out on cranes from the high masts of the Italian ships into the Turkish ships.

For three hours the battle raged, filling the water with blood, the dead and the drowning wounded. Eventually, through all the killing, 'blaspheming, scolding, threatening and groaning', the relentless Turkish attack began to wear down the four Italian ships. Mehmed, watching from the shore, rode his horse into the water, shouting hysterical instructions to his men.

Then, at last, a fresh southerly wind picked up, and the luck of the defenders changed again. The big sails billowed out and the four ships pushed through their attackers and into the safety of the Golden Horn. Cheering broke out along the city walls. Mehmed, watching in disbelief, screamed and cursed at his sailors, tearing at his clothes in fury. Again, his fleet was humiliated. He rode away from the shore in silence.

THE NEXT DAY Mehmed summoned Baltoglu. Still bleeding from a wound to his eye, Baltoglu was exposed to the full force of Mehmed's rage and frustration.

'You are a fool and a coward,' he spat. 'How is it possible that this great fleet I have placed into your command has been defeated by a pathetically small clutch of merchant galleons?'

Baltoglu offered no answer.

Mehmed rose from his chair and declared he would cut off

Baltoglu's head with his own sword. The admiral's officers rushed forward to intervene, begging Mehmed to be merciful. Baltoglu pointed to the wound in his eye as proof that he had fought hard and honourably. Mehmed relented, but he stripped Baltoglu of his high office and private possessions, and ordered that he receive a hundred lashes in front of his men.

Land Ships

AFTER TWO UNEXPECTED defeats, Mehmed's navy had not only failed to intimidate the city, it had boosted the defenders' confidence that they might, somehow, survive this siege after all.

The key, Mehmed realised, was the great chain. If he could somehow get his ships past the chain and into the Golden Horn, then Constantine would be forced to stretch his tiny forces even further to defend the northern sea wall. Mehmed rode up from his base on the Bosphorus shore into the forested hill behind it. He studied the landscape to the rear of the walled settlement of Galata, and then rode down to the north shore of the Golden Horn. Returning to the Double Columns, Mehmed summoned his advisors and proposed a radical plan, a masterstroke that would shift the initiative back to him. The sultan said that if he couldn't attack the chain head-on, he would bypass it.

Teams of workers were sent to clear a path behind the Double Columns. They laid down a track of rollers, made from tree trunks greased with fat, running from the shore of the Bosphorus, up the hill and back down to the Golden Horn, to a point on the water's edge known as the Valley of the Springs, well behind the great chain.

The track was laid within a couple of days, and on Sunday 22 April, a crew of Ottoman sailors waded into the Bosphorus and guided a small galley into a wheeled cradle. The cradle was dragged ashore by teams of oxen, supported by workers and crewmen, straining on ropes and pulleys. Then the creaking galley was slowly hauled onto the greased rollers, and pushed all the way up the hill, and then carefully eased back down the slope to the Valley of the Springs, where the ship splashed into the waters of the Golden Horn. Mehmed now had his first ship behind the chain.

The first galley was followed by another, and another. The exciting and weird spectacle of 'ships being carried over land instead of sea' inspired an Ottoman crew to climb aboard their galley and playfully assume their positions on deck. The sails were hoisted, the oarsmen took their positions, and on command, they began to row in the air, amid laughter and whoops of joy. Roman soldiers on the sea walls looked on helplessly.

The defenders now realised the Golden Horn was no longer a sanctuary. By the end of the day, sixty-seven Ottoman ships were behind the chain. Mehmed ordered several guns to be mounted on the shoreline to protect them.

Constantine's hopes were now fixed on Venice sending a fleet to break the blockade. Minotto, the chief Venetian official in the city, had sent an appeal three months earlier, but there was still no sign of a relief fleet. Just before midnight on 3 May, a Venetian ship, disguising itself as a Turkish vessel, slipped out of the Golden Horn. It returned twenty days later with crushing news: they had scouted the Dardanelles and the Aegean and seen no sign of a Venetian fleet. The men had nonetheless decided to return to Constantinople to report the news, even though it meant they would probably share the city's doom. Constantine tearfully thanked each one of the crew for their service.

*

JOE AND I DECIDED TO WALK the same path as Mehmed's land ships and up the same hill, which is now part of Istanbul's Beyoglu district. On the map it looked like a pleasant stroll. On the ground it's an exhausting, sweaty hike up a chain of steep, cobblestoned streets.

We get off at a tram stop on the Bosphorus shore, at the point where the Double Columns once stood, then trudge up a very steep incline towards Taksim Square. Five minutes in, I'm peeling off my coat and breathing heavily.

'I guess you're pretty old, Dad,' Joe says, smiling.

'Just middle-aged. Shut your mouth.'

'Ottoman soldiers managed to get up this hill and they did it carrying a ship. Do you think you could manage a ship?'

'I thought I told you to shut up.'

'Can I get a cold drink?'

'No,' I wheeze, spitefully.

'You told me you were never a smoker. Are you sure you were never a smoker, Dad?'

From a window just above us, an old woman hears us; she leans out and gestures for me to give her a cigarette.

Khym and I find it galling that our kids recognise no such way-station as 'middle-aged' on the great journey of life. They lump us into the same age bracket as their grandparents, which is simply 'old'. They've seen pictures of Khym and me as newlyweds, in our twenties, and it amuses them we are no longer quite so lithe and fresh-faced. It's as though we weren't paying attention one day and stupidly left our youth on a bus.

Joe is getting older too. At fourteen he's accelerating rapidly out of boyhood into adolescence, a process I watch, like most fathers, with pride but also with a tinge of grief. I know I'm losing a part of him to adolescence soon. His properly proportioned fourteen-year-old physiognomy is starting to elongate and become absurdly gangly, an untidy tangle of knees and elbows. When he reclines on the couch in front of the TV he resembles a heap of discarded chicken wings. His feet – almost as big as mine – are too big. The sweet choirboy voicemail message he recorded on his phone in January sounds nothing like the honking baritone of December. I can't quite gather him up and hold him like I could when he was little. Now I embrace him awkwardly, like a brother or a friend.

We get to the top of the hill and find our way into Taksim Square. There are no signs at all of the anti-government protests that had filled the square a week previously. I scan the skyline for the Galata Tower but we're too far back from the water to see it.

'Hey, Joe,' I sputter, 'how about we get a cab back to Sultanahmet?'

'Sure, Dad,' he grins. 'If that's what you need to do.'

Tunnels and Towers

WHILE MEHMED'S FORCES were fighting on land and sea, his sappers had been burrowing underground from the Ottoman base. Shielded from view by ramparts of earth, they dug a long tunnel from their camp towards the St Romanus Gate. The sappers were experienced silver miners from Germany. They dug by torchlight, inserting timber frames at each stage to hold up the earthworks. Their orders were to burrow under the walls, then set fire to the props and watch the wall collapse into the hole.

By 16 May, the sappers had dug a half-mile long tunnel right up to the outer wall, but their work was detected by sentries who were astonished to hear the sounds of digging and muffled voices coming from beneath their feet.

The emperor and Lucas Notaras were notified at once. A military engineer was found among Giustiniani's mercenaries, a Scotsman named John Grant, who oversaw the digging of a deep mine, leading crossways into the Turkish tunnel. The defenders burrowed their way into the Turkish mine and set fire to the timbers, sending the earthworks crashing down on the heads of the sappers inside. Thereafter the defenders kept large drums of water near the walls; a tremor on the water's surface would indicate excavation work below.

ON THE MORNING OF 19 MAY, the defenders awoke to a shocking and terrible sight: in the course of a single night, the sultan's men had built an enormous siege tower right on the edge of the ditch, just ten metres from the outer wall. The tower was a veritable skyscraper of timber scaffolding, looming higher than the walls. The defenders were at a loss to explain how it had been constructed so quickly, and put in place so stealthily. The emperor and his court were alerted and they came up to the ramparts to see the behemoth for themselves. Just as startlingly, they saw the Turks had ingeniously constructed a protected pathway behind the tower, covered with animal hides, which led back to their camp. This allowed soldiers to rush back and forth to the tower in safety.

The tower was constructed with heavy timber beams and protected by a skin of camel hides to shield the men within from crossbow bolts. The lower half was filled with earth to absorb artillery fire.

Inside the protected tower, the Turks were digging up earth and using it to fill in a section of the ditch, which would allow their soldiers and siege towers to move right up to the walls. There seemed to be nothing the defenders could do to stop the earthworks, so they looked on helplessly all day, as the tower inched closer to the outer wall. Barbaro noted that the Turks 'shot a great number of arrows into the city from the place where the tower was, firing them, it seemed, from sheer high spirits, while our men were all very sad and fearful'.

That night, in desperation, the defenders prepared barrels of gunpowder, lit the fuses and rolled them towards the tower. There was a pause, followed by a sequence of explosions, sending men, timber and earth flying up into the air. The wooden frame of the tower caught fire and completely collapsed. Up on the walls, the defenders poured boiling pitch onto the wounded survivors. Once more, the Turks had to withdraw.

AS THE MONTH OF MAY came to a close, both defenders and attackers were exhausted and dispirited. Giustiniani and his men on the walls were stuck in an endless daily routine: pushing back the enemy by day, patching up the shattered brickwork by night. Some men deserted their posts and returned to their families in the city. Soldiers began to openly curse the emperor's name.

Mehmed sent an envoy into the city under a banner of truce to make the offer required of him by Islamic protocol. Constantine received the envoy and heard his message: 'Surrender now,' the envoy advised, 'and you will be saved from slavery.'

Constantine tried to make a siege seem more trouble for Mehmed than it was worth: 'I am prepared to pay tribute,' he told the envoy, 'but I will not surrender the city. To defend it, every one of us is prepared to die.'

Constantine could not surrender and Mehmed would not withdraw. Holy men in both camps read and reread their respective books of prophecies and looked to the skies for signs that God was pleased or angered with their work. They were not long in coming.

View from a tower on the inner wall.

Big Black Drops

ON THE NIGHT OF 22 MAY, a peculiar moon rose in the sky. A full moon had been expected, but on this night it was shrouded by a partial eclipse, which left the city darkened and troubled. Ominously, the eclipse transfigured the moon into a crescent, the symbol of Islam, the same crescent the Romans could see on the banners of the sultan's army. Priests in the city unhappily recalled a prophecy that predicted that Constantinople would not fall until the full moon should give a sign.

That night the Turks held a celebration, but within Constantinople, morale was sinking. To lift the city's spirits, the emperor decreed that the city's most precious icon, the Virgin Hodegetria, should be paraded through the city the following day.

The Hodegetria, 'She Who Shows the Way', was Constantinople's most powerful talisman, an image of the infant Jesus held tenderly by his mother, the Virgin Mary. The Hodegetria was believed to be impregnated with all kinds of miraculous powers. Priests dabbed at the icon with swabs of cotton wool, hoping to soak up a drop of the holy oil that was thought to seep out from it. But it was the identity of the painter that made this icon so incalculably precious: the artist was believed to be Luke the Evangelist himself, the author of the third gospel. If St Luke was the painter, it was reasoned, then the portrait of the infant Christ must have been taken from life.

Late the next morning, the solemn procession of the Hodegetria filed out of the monastery. Black-robed priests led a train of clerics in a deep, sonorous chant. The icon bearers hoisted the Hodegetria high so the crowd could all see the Virgin. The procession made its way through the streets, and then ... the icon slipped from its bearers and fell face-down onto the ground with a splat. Bystanders rushed to rescue it, but no amount of straining, it seemed, could lift it from the mud.

Eventually the icon was hoisted up, and the badly rattled priests staggered forward again. Then, at noon a violent thunderstorm suddenly broke over Constantinople. A Russian observer recorded that 'the air suddenly thickened and, in a moaning way, it hovered above the city. Then, big black drops of rain, as large as the eye of a buffalo, began to fall'. The storm flash-flooded the streets, and the marchers were lashed with rain and hail. The procession broke up in distress and confusion. The Orthodox faithful retreated to their homes, gripped by a palpable sense of doom.

The people of Constantinople woke up to a new terror the next morning. Looking out their windows, they saw the city was blanketed in fog – no one had ever seen such thick fog at that time of year. The haze hung over the city all day. Perhaps this was proof that Gennadius had been right all along: their capitulation to the Latin church had driven God to abandon the city, for it was said that 'the Divinity conceals itself in cloud, and appears and again disappears'.

The atmospheric weirdness came to a climax of sorts that night. At dusk, witnesses in the city looked up and saw an unearthly band of red light glowing around the upper levels of the Hagia Sophia. The weird light rose up from the windows of the great church onto the copper dome, rode up to the tip, and then it just ... winked out. In the street someone wailed, 'The light itself has gone up to heaven!'

Outside the walls in the Ottoman camp, Mehmed saw the strange lights too, and wondered what they portended for him. He called for his astrologers, who were quick to assure him that the lights were surely an excellent omen: they said it meant the light of Islam would soon be coming to the city.

More strange lights were seen that night emanating from the countryside behind the Turkish camp. The defenders on the walls hoped the flashes might indicate the arrival of a rescuing army, but no such army appeared.

THE LIKELY CULPRIT behind these strange portents in the sky lay 15,000 kilometres to the east, on the far side of the world. Sometime in 1452, the year before the siege, a volcanic island in the Pacific Ocean exploded. The island of Kuwae, in the Vanuatu archipelago, erupted with a force equivalent to two million Hiroshima-type bombs, throwing up forty cubic kilometres of rock and dust into the sky.

The massive eruption rates as one of the biggest volcanic events in human history, and the spreading plume of atmospheric dust affected weather all over the world, spoiling crops in China and Europe. Most likely the strange lights reported in May 1453 were either a manifestation of St Elmo's Fire or an optical illusion, a reflection of an 'intensely red twilight glow by clouds of volcanic ash high in the atmosphere'.

The Romans had no knowledge of such things.

The volatile weather, the fog, the ghostly electricity, the awful spectacle of the Virgin hurling herself into the mud – all of this blighted the already weak morale of the city, and ruined its spiritual confidence. The people of Constantinople were without, it seemed, a single friend in Heaven or on Earth.

THE EMPEROR, despite the pressures, remained resolute. His closest friend, George Sphrantzes, came to him with a delegation of ministers and begged him to leave, to save himself from the coming cataclysm. Constantine, overcome with emotion and exhaustion, heard their pleas and fainted. When he recovered he declared he would stay. The emperor would fight and die with his people.

Two Days Before

ON 27 MAY, the middle section of the walls was pounded all day by cannon fire, giving the defenders almost no opportunity to repair the damage. Parts of the ancient outer wall began to crumble.

The endgame of the siege was almost upon them. Mehmed summoned his officers and told them to prepare for one final push. A general attack by land and sea would begin in two days. They were going to push wave after wave of men at the heavily damaged central section of the walls. At some point, he said, the hammer blows would open a crack in the defensive lines and they would break into the city. The siege was about to end for them, in death or glory.

Great fires were lit right along the line of the Ottoman camps that night. Mehmed's soldiers shouted and sang around the flames. The Turkish tumult was heard within the city. Soft cries of *kyrie eleison*, *kyrie eleison* were raised up from the city's churches to the night sky. *Lord have mercy. Lord have mercy.*

The Day Before

IN THE MORNING, thousands of Ottoman soldiers moved forwards to fill in the empty moat with earth, rocks and branches. The sultan's cannoniers hauled the artillery into position. Hundreds of long ladders were brought up to the frontline.

At dusk, rain began to fall. The sultan mounted his white horse and galloped along the entire length of the Theodosian Walls, inspecting his troops. Mehmed had been advised that an appeal to their *jihadi* spirit would fall flat, so he enticed them with visions of the treasures of that awaited them.

'Here is the great and populous capital of the ancient Romans,' he said, gesturing to the walls behind him. 'A city which has reached the very pinnacle of good fortune and glory … the head of the whole inhabited globe. I give it now to you for spoil and plunder. Unlimited wealth, men, women, children, all the other adornments and arrangements. All these you will enjoy like a brilliant banquet.'

Mehmed reminded them that if they broke through they would be entitled to three days of plunder, in accordance with medieval custom.

'Take whatever property you can find,' he offered. 'But remember, the buildings belong to *me*.'

But the city's fabled treasures were long gone, stolen two-and-a-half centuries ago, spirited away to faraway Venice and France. However, Mehmed's soldiers weren't to know that, and so, despite their weariness, they went about their preparations with renewed energy.

Inside a guard tower.

THE MEN ON THE WALLS were hungry, sore and exhausted. The defenders were a mix of local men, Genoese archers, Venetian marines and a band of Turks. Prince Orhan, the pretender to the sultan's throne, and his men had no choice but to fight to the death for Constantinople. They faced the coming struggle with no illusions, aware that the final battle would be upon them within a few hours.

Church bells rang out across the city. Inside the Blachernae Palace, Constantine XI gathered his commanders and advisors and delivered a passionate speech. He singled out each faction – the Genoese, the Venetians and his own troops – for praise, and called on them to put aside their differences, and be willing to die in defence of their God, their families and their emperor.

Neither Constantine nor Mehmed could be confident of the outcome. The final onslaught would certainly be fierce and terrible, but both rulers were aware the defenders on the walls might still somehow find it within themselves to hold off the Ottomans. For them, it was a matter of life and death: if the assault failed, Mehmed would be forced to call off the siege and trek back to Edirne, where he would almost certainly be assassinated. Constantine, for his part, knew he was hours away from either a martyr's death or eternal fame as the emperor who saved the city – but only if his men could somehow hold the line at the walls for one more night.

At sunset, as the shadows lengthened across the city, people came out of their homes spontaneously, and converged on the Hagia Sophia for vespers. The church, darkened for nearly five months, was again ablaze with golden light. Old hatreds were put aside as Orthodox and Catholic bishops sang the liturgy together. Constantine arrived late for the service, entering the narthex through the Imperial Gate. Trembling with emotion, he took the holy sacrament, fell to his knees and begged God for forgiveness for his sins. The emperor then drew himself up, bowed respectfully to everyone present, and strode out of the church. As he departed, a terrible cry of anguish went up from the congregation.

The Night Before

AS NIGHT FELL ACROSS the fearful city, the men on the walls saw thousands of fires light up along the Ottoman lines, giving their camps a hellish appearance. Then a great and terrible noise erupted into the night sky, a combination of wild shouting, cymbals, drums and cannon fire.

Then, at midnight, the Turkish camp fell ominously silent.

1.30 am, 29 May: The First Wave

AN HOUR AND A HALF after midnight, Mehmed gave the order and a blast of noise erupted from the Ottoman camp. The sultan's artillery opened up a bombardment; heavy marble balls whistled through the air and crashed into the battered walls and towers. Inside the city, church bells rang out, signalling the final battle had begun. Women rushed to the walls through the darkness, carrying heavy stones for the artillery and water for the thirsty men.

With a tremendous cry, the Ottoman line of attack pressed forward along the full five-and-a-half kilometre length of the land walls, forcing the city's defenders to space their meagre numbers further apart. The heaviest assault was directed at the weakest section in the centre, at the St Romanus Gate.

Peering into the darkness, the defenders on the walls caught flashing glimpses of soldiers rushing forward, briefly illuminated by the flare of cannon fire. These were the sultan's Irregulars, his shock troops: a mix of Christian Slavs, Germans and Greeks from Mehmed's lands, bound to him by the medieval code of vassalage. The Irregulars charged forward, dodging missiles, bearing tall siege ladders and whatever weapons they had brought with them from their homelands. They ran at the wall in a huge, terrified mass, driven forward by the sultan's military police, who lashed out at waverers with rawhide whips and iron rods.

At their rear stood a line of Janissaries with scimitars, ready to behead deserters. The defenders high up on the battlements fired arrows, rocks and missiles, knocking down hundreds of the Irregulars before they could get close to the walls. Giustiniani's men were amazed by the ease with which they shot down the enemy, even as they were appalled by the carnage.

The first Irregulars to survive the onslaught arrived at the foot of the outer wall; they planted their long scaling ladders in the soft earth and began to climb. The shattered brickwork of the outer wall had been replaced by a heavy stockade of timber beams, bundles of vine-branches, and barrels stuffed with earth, which the Irregulars clawed at as they scaled their ladders.

The defenders blasted the invaders with muskets and culverins, dropped heavy stones on their heads, or simply pushed the ladders back, sending stacks of men crashing to the ground. The Ottomans' greater numbers proved to be no advantage at all as the Irregulars fell over each other, clawing and scrambling for position. Pressed between certain death from the front and Janissary swords at their rear, Mehmed's Irregulars howled in agony and anguish as the dead and wounded began to pile up in the darkness below. Then Constantine was seen on the battlements, goading his men on. And still the waves of Irregulars kept coming and crashing to the ground in a broken heap.

After two-and-a-half hours of mass slaughter, Mehmed called back his Irregulars. They had failed to break through anywhere along the line. Nonetheless they had served their grim purpose, which was to wear down the defenders before the real fighting began.

4 am: The Second Wave

AS MEHMED'S irregulars pulled back, Giustiniani's men lowered themselves onto the stockades for another frantic round of repairs. They had just set to work when they heard, in the distant darkness, the clanking of metal and the thumping tread of thousands of marching feet, announcing the arrival of the Anatolian army. These were the sultan's Muslim troops: heavily armoured, well fed and more disciplined than the Irregulars.

The columns of Anatolians marched into position in the Lycus Valley, and then wheeled around to face the walls. With another blast of horns and percussion, and a cry of *Allahu Akbar!* the Anatolians charged at the wall, as the repair workers scurried back up to the battlements.

Again, crossbow bolts and small artillery fire from the walls easily cut down the sultan's men. The defenders dropped boulders and poured vats of boiling black oil on their heads. The Anatolians reeled back, and pushed forward once more. The heap of dead at the base of the walls piled higher. Mehmed rode his horse back and forth along the line, shouting encouragement above the terrible din of battle.

An Ottoman cannon let loose a missile that smashed into the stockade. Rubble tumbled out, leaving a gaping hole in the outer wall. Hundreds of Anatolian soldiers rushed forward into the gap, but with nowhere to go, they soon found themselves pressed against each other, trapped between the two walls. The defenders fired down upon the trapped Anatolians from all directions until every one of them was dead.

In the final hour of darkness the decimated Anatolian army pulled back. After four hours of fighting, Mehmed had expended the better part of two armies and he was still outside the city. The men on the walls were exhausted, but elated. Mehmed had just one more card to play – his most precious military corps, the dreaded Janissaries.

5 am: The Third Wave

MEHMED GAVE the order to attack immediately, to give the defenders no time to rest and repair the damage. The Janissaries, in their pristine white turbans, presented an impressive spectacle as they marched forward with deadly precision and began to dismantle the timbers and barrels of the stockade with grappling hooks.

Inside the city, the church bells sounded the alarm once more. Again, priests, women and children hauled heavy rocks up to the battlements, and threw bricks at the invaders. Giustiniani's men hacked at the climbing Janissaries with javelins and axes. Constantine appeared again on the wall, striding back and forth with his advisors;

by one account, the emperor drew his sword and personally cut down several of the sultan's men as they attempted to climb the stockade.

Barbaro recorded that the Janissaries fought like 'lions', spurred on by shouts and crashing percussion that sounded like 'a thing not of this world'. The roar of the cannon fire created such a din, 'the very air seemed to be split apart'. Then, as the fading morning star signalled the approach of dawn, the Janissaries began to falter. Constantine sensed a change in the dynamic of the battle and shouted encouragement to his troops. For one dizzying moment, it appeared the defenders had saved their city after all.

AND THEN THE SMALLEST act of carelessness opened a crack in the city's defence. Hidden in a fold of the walls around Blachernae was a small portal known as the *kerkoporta*, or the Gate of the Wooden Circus. The defence of the walls above the gate was led by the Bocchiardi brothers from Genoa. The brothers were unlikely to have been aware of a prophecy uttered nearly eight hundred years earlier, in the *Apocalypse of Pseudo-Methodius*, which predicted the city would meet its doom from the Muslims at this very gate: *Woe to you, city of Byzantium, because Ishmael overtakes you. For every horse of Ishmael will pass through. And the first among them will pitch his tent before you, and will break down the Gate of the Wooden Circus.*

The brothers had been using the *kerkoporta* to slip out and launch surprise attacks on the Ottoman flank. But on this critical morning, someone had forgotten to bar the gate. A group of Turkish soldiers pressed against it and crashed through. Fifty of the sultan's men rushed into the enclosure between the walls and began to climb the stairs up to the battlements. The defenders, seeing the Ottoman troops rush in, turned to fire down on the enemy charging up the stone steps. The invaders were isolated and killed, but in the melee, one Ottoman soldier fought his way up a tower, where he tore down the standards of the emperor and of the Lion of St Mark, and replaced them with the Ottoman banner. In the hazy dawn light, the first crescent flag of Islam could be seen fluttering on the walls.

FURTHER DOWN the line, a second critical blow was struck. Giustiniani, strained and exhausted beyond belief, was shot, either by a crossbow bolt, or by a lead ball fired from a culverin. Accounts differ, but the terrible pain finally broke his spirit.

Giustiniani's men rushed to him. Bleeding badly, he asked them to carry him down to his ship. One of his Genoese then dashed to the emperor to ask him for the key to a gate on the inner wall. Constantine, alerted to the danger, was horrified, and begged his commander not to leave. Giustiniani feebly promised to return once his wound was treated, and so the emperor ruefully handed over the key. Giustiniani's bodyguard carried him out the gate into the city. The other Genoese fighters, observing their fallen leader leaving his post, broke and ran to the open gate, following their comrades down to their ship on the Golden Horn. Constantine and his dwindling band of Romans were now alone on the wall.

THE EMPEROR ordered his men to spread out further and fill the gaps left by the departing Italians. Mehmed, watching from below, could see that something was up, that the line of defence was buckling.

'Friends!' he cried, wild with excitement, 'we have the city! Just one more effort and the city is ours!'

Another wave of Janissaries charged forward. Mehmed was offering a prize to the first man to break through the stockade, and a giant warrior named Hasan was set on claiming it. Hasan charged up the stockade with the Ottoman flag in one hand, as he covered his head with his shield. He clambered to the top, pushed aside the confused defenders, and stood atop the stockade, defiantly flying the flag of Islam over the city walls.

The Janissaries, thrilled by the spectacle, rushed forward and found more gaps in the Roman line. The Roman defenders recovered, pounded Hasan with heavy rocks, and then hacked him to death with swords and spears.

But the line had broken. Dozens, and then hundreds, of Janissaries pressed forward, invading the narrow space between the walls. A group of Roman soldiers suddenly found themselves pushed back into a ditch against the inner wall, where they were slaughtered. More Janissaries now raced up to the battlements atop the high inner wall, where they could see the Ottoman flag now over the *kerkoporta*.

A great roar of victory went up along the line: *The city is ours! The city is ours!*

THE EMPEROR DASHED back and forth, desperately trying to rally his fleeing soldiers, but the frantic Romans fell over each other in a panic, fighting to get out the small gate with the enemy almost on top of them. The crush of Roman soldiers blocked up the doorway, trapping the rest inside the killing zone. The horn blasts, cheers and screams were deafening now. Constantine, seeing that his city was lost, resolved not to flee, but to die at the walls.

THERE ARE NO eyewitness accounts of the emperor's last stand, only a mess of contradictory secondhand reports. One account records that the emperor tore off his imperial insignia, drew his sword, ran into the melee and was never seen again. Another less heroic account reports that Constantine and his colleagues were cut down by the wave of advancing Janissaries, who mistook him for a common soldier. Either way, Constantine's long struggle was over. The last of the Roman emperors was dead.

The King under the Mountain

THERE WAS ONCE a young herdsman who lived in the north of England, near the Roman wall of Hadrian, where he tended his goats. One day he realised one of his goats was missing. As he searched the hills for his lost animal, he stepped on some bracken, which snapped under his feet, and he fell into the hidden entrance of a cave.

The young man found his way through a dark tunnel into a large chamber illuminated with a strange golden glow. There he was astonished to see a dozen knights, dressed in chain mail, standing solemnly around a catafalque. Upon the catafalque lay the body of a man with a crown upon his head, holding a shining sword. His eyes were closed and his beard was very long, so long that it trailed onto the cavern floor. Into the timbers of the catafalque was carved the legend: Hic iacet Arthurus, rex quondam, rexque futurus. Here lies Arthur, the once and future king.

The herdsman swallowed his fear and asked the knights who they were and what they were doing.

'We keep watch over the once and future king,' they said. 'He is King Arthur of the Britons, who was struck down in battle many, many years ago.'

'How can he be the future king if he is dead?' asked the herdsman.

'He is not dead,' they said. 'He is asleep.'

'When will he awake?'

'He will awaken in Britain's darkest hour, when he will take up Excalibur once more and save Britain from her enemies.'

When the herdsman emerged from the cave, he saw that his beard had turned white and his body had become stooped and he had somehow become an old man.

The legend of the sleeping King Arthur is the one of many 'King in the Mountain' folktales. The stories all follow the same contours: the heroic leader is struck down in battle by his enemies, but is carried away at the moment of death to a hidden place, under the earth, where he lies sleeping, awaiting the call to save his people once again. Charlemagne was said to be resting underground somewhere near Salzburg. Frederick Barbarossa was believed to be asleep under the Kyffhäuser Mountains. Such legends are comforting to a people grieving over a lost leader, or the passing of a golden age.

INEVITABLY, a similar legend grew up around the tragic end of Constantine XI, like briars around a crypt. It was said among the exiled Romans of Constantinople that in the moment of his death, the doomed emperor was turned into marble by a merciful angel, and then sealed up within a secret underground tomb somewhere underneath the Golden Gate.

And there he lies in suspended animation, awaiting the call to return in glory, resume his ancient throne and restore the lost city to his people.

The Artifice of Eternity

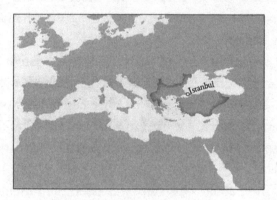

The Ottoman Empire, 30 May 1453.

8 am

THOUSANDS OF OTTOMAN soldiers now stormed through the gaps in the walls while their comrades atop the towers cheered them on, giddy with victory.

Like the Crusaders 250 years before them, Mehmed's soldiers trod through the streets of the outer suburbs warily, until they realised there was no one left to oppose them. Weeks of pent-up frustration exploded from these men, creating a shockwave of violence that rippled out onto the city. The locals had taunted and cursed the Ottomans for weeks from the safety of the land walls. Now, to their horror, they found the invaders at their door, wild with greed and hungry for vengeance.

Each house was, in turn, ransacked and stripped of its gold, jewellery and tapestries. Women and men who fought back were the first to be cut down, followed by small children and the elderly, who were of no use to the invaders. Old men were dragged by their white hair into the street, where their throats were cut. Nuns were taken from their convents and raped or sold into slavery. Fist-fights broke out among the invaders for the most beautiful girls. Some women chose to hurl themselves into wells, rather than fall into the hands of the enemy.

Guttural screams of naked panic rang out through the streets. The men posted to the sea walls heard the strange, awful din and ran to their homes to find their families either dead or abducted. Prince Orhan the pretender tried to pass himself off at the harbour as a Greek-speaking local, but was recognised by a Turkish soldier and beheaded.

Barbaro, from aboard his ship, witnessed the unfolding horror: 'The blood flowed in the city like rainwater in the gutters after a sudden storm, and the corpses of Turks and Christians were thrown into the Dardanelles, where they floated out to sea like melons along a canal.'

He escaped the maelstrom of violence just in time; after several agonising delays, his galleon was able to slip past the Ottoman navy into the Sea of Marmara, bound for home. Giacomo Tetaldi, a Florentine merchant, threw off his clothes, leapt into the water, swam out to a Venetian ship and, to his great relief, was hauled on board. The departure of the Italian galleons was of no interest to the sultan's navy anyway; the Turkish sailors were rushing to the shore to claim their share of the loot.

As the sultan's men plundered their way through the outer suburbs, the cry went up along the Mese that the city was lost. People who had slept through the night ran out to see what the commotion was about, only to run into the blades of Ottoman soldiers. Frantic citizens bolted from their homes with children in their arms, and streamed down to the harbour, hoping to find passage on a ship. But the gates of the sea walls had been locked and barred by the emperor's men in a futile attempt to compel citizens to stay and fight.

A GREAT MANY FAMILIES, remembering the apocalyptic prophecies, fled to the Hagia Sophia for sanctuary. It was foretold that in the End of Days, before the return of Christ, the demonic hordes would swarm into God's city, but they would be stopped short outside the great church by an Angel of the Lord, who would strike down the unbelievers with a blazing sword. Thousands of panic-stricken citizens now grasped at this slender thread of hope, and so within an hour, every part of the Hagia Sophia was filled and the doors barred shut. As the rays of the morning sun streamed through the upper windows, the priests began to intone a matins service; men, women and children sang and offered their most urgent prayers for one last time inside that candle-lit, incense-clouded space. How many of them truly expected to be delivered by God's Avenging Angel, we cannot know.

A party of Janissaries were the first of the invaders to reach the Hagia Sophia. They ran hard, believing that untold riches awaited them inside. The turbaned warriors charged into the courtyard, up through the outer narthex and began to hack at the heavy doors with axes, each blow eliciting a scream of terror from the worshippers inside. The door timbers cracked, splintered and crashed, and the Janissaries rushed inside, ready to snatch every treasure they could find.

The slaughter was minimal; by now the bloodlust of the conquerors had been overtaken by a pragmatic scramble for plunder. The chalice, the candelabras and the emperor's chair were all quickly seized. Soldiers began to hack apart the altar screen for its precious metals.

The next treasures to be seized were the worshippers themselves. Again, the sultan's men fought each other for the most beautiful women. The old and infirm were put to the sword; the rest gathered up as slaves or hostages. Some groups were led back to the Ottoman camps outside the walls. Others were brought down to the Golden Horn, to be shipped off to the slave markets of Cairo.

In less than an hour, every item of value in the Hagia Sophia that could be carried or dismantled was extracted from the church. A group of Janissaries found the tomb of Enrico Dandolo and ransacked it for treasure. Finding nothing valuable, they threw the Doge's bones onto the streets for the dogs.

Midday

MEHMED THE CONQUEROR did not immediately follow his men into the city, waiting outside the walls until he received confirmation that the emperor was dead. At noon the sultan mounted his white stallion, followed by his entourage. He passed through the Charisian Gate onto the blood-streaked streets of the conquered city.

Mehmed was in a sombre mood, seemingly humbled by his victory. He led his entourage down the Mese, witnessing pitiful scenes of dead and dying people. Ottoman banners hung from many windows, to indicate the house and its property had been claimed. The sultan rode into the Forum of Constantine, where the toppled colossus of the city's founding emperor lay impassively. At the end of the Mese, the great hulking form of the Hagia Sophia came into view. Mehmed dismounted and bowed down before the church, sprinkling a handful of dirt over his turban as a sign of humility before God.

Inside the church, he saw one of his men hacking away at the marble floor. Enraged, Mehmed struck at the soldier with the flat of his sword.

'Content yourself with the loot and the prisoners!' he shouted at the scurrying soldier. 'The buildings belong to me!'

Mehmed looked up at the great dome, spun around, and then directed his imam to climb into the pulpit and proclaim the Muslim creed: *There is no God but Allah, and Muhammad is his Prophet.*

Stepping out of the ravaged church, Mehmed crossed the Augustaeum to the ruined Great Palace of the Caesars. It was a forlorn sight, long since uninhabitable. As the sultan wandered through the ruined chambers, he quoted the melancholic lines of an unknown Persian poet:

The spider weaves the curtains in the Palace of the Caesars;
The owl calls the watches in the towers of Afrasiab.

And with that, the Roman empire was gone forever.

Megadux and Grand Vizier

THE GRAND DUKE Lucas Notaras was held under guard in his home. Soon enough the sultan came to see him. Mehmed bluntly told Notaras that he and Constantine must accept the moral responsibility for the mass slaughter, because they had refused to surrender the city to him.

'Sire,' Notaras replied, 'neither I nor the emperor had the power to make the people of this city surrender. And why should we want to give up, when we have been receiving letters from your people, urging us to fight on?'

Mehmed knew at once that Notaras was talking about Halil Pasha.

Three days later, the grand vizier was thrown into a dungeon, and then executed as a traitor. Halil's money was confiscated by the treasury and his friends were forbidden to mourn for him.

Mehmed considered bringing Lucas Notaras into his court to govern Constantinople, but thought better of it, and had him executed, along with his family.

MEHMED RETURNED temporarily to the comforts of his palace in Edirne to plan the rebuilding of his conquered city. By the time he left, almost the entire Christian population of Constantinople was gone, either enslaved or in exile. For six whole months, the once-great metropolis lay quiet, an empty vessel. Ducas, a Byzantine historian, captured the eerie bleakness: 'The city was desolate, lying dead, naked, soundless, having neither form nor beauty.'

Then Mehmed sent his labourers to repair the city. The walls were restored, and the Hagia Sophia was reconsecrated as a mosque and renamed the Ayasofya. Tall minaret towers sprouted up from its four corner points, which only enhanced its majesty. The mosaics and frescoes inside were mostly covered in whitewash.

Constantinople was renamed Istanbul. It's not clear where the name comes from; it could be a rough reworking of 'Constantinople', or it could derive from a Turkish interpretation of the Greek phrase *eis ten polin*, 'to the city', a common response to the question 'where are you going?'

If the city was to recover and thrive under Ottoman rule, then it needed to maintain something of its multicultural flavour. Mehmed appointed the anti-unionist monk Gennadius as Patriarch of Constantinople, and established a Jewish grand rabbi in the city. Genoese traders were encouraged to return to Galata. Muslim and

Christian subjects of the sultanate were relocated from the Balkans and Anatolia to repopulate the city. Mehmed's Christian slaves were settled in a neighbourhood named Fener, near Blachernae, where a tiny population of Orthodox 'Romans' endures to this day.

Old trading routes were reopened and Istanbul began to recover its wealth and confidence. Mehmed established a university, and invited Arab scientists, architects and artists to live and work in the city. The shape of the skyline changed and sharpened as dozens of tall minarets poked up into the sky. In 1478 a census recorded a population of eighty thousand in the city. At the end of the century, Constantinople was again the biggest city in Europe.

Russians vs Ottomans

ON OUR LAST full day in Istanbul, Joe and I catch a tram to the Grand Bazaar to buy trinkets for home. The air is filled with the sounds of spruikers and the scent of spice and ground coffee. We see countless shops selling necklaces, rings and bracelets with evil eyes to ward off bad luck, a tradition that has endured in the city since Roman times. An aged black cat curls around my leg; her back leg performs a little arthritic kick when she walks. Her coat is glossy but when I pat her, I feel the bony skeleton underneath.

In a shop window I spy a set of chess pieces on a marbled board. It's the most beautiful chess set I have ever seen, so I buy it. The hand-painted pieces are styled as Orthodox Russians and Ottoman Turks. The Russian castle piece is a little crimson Kremlin; for the Turks it's a cream-and-caramel campaign tent.

Outside the Bazaar, a cold drizzle has settled in, so Joe and I go to a café to wait it out. I order a Turkish coffee, Joe has a small glass of apple tea. I can't resist the urge to pull out the chess pieces to study their intricate details more closely. Then I set up the chessboard on the table for a game. Joe likes the look of the Ottoman pieces so I get to be the Russians. I win the first two games. In the third I make a few dumb moves and he checkmates me. He looks at me quizzically, suspecting I've thrown the match, but I haven't. I never do. A few years back I bought the board game Risk at his urging. I won the first few games, and then Joe began winning and hasn't lost a game since. At first he was a bad winner, crowing to his mother and his friends; then as he racked up bigger and bigger victories, he became more generous and advised me on where I'd gone wrong.

The Burnt Column, Istanbul.

It's really pouring down now and shoppers outside are dashing into the luxury brand-name shops of Divanyolu Street for shelter. Joe is hunched over the board, his eyes darting about, trying to compute all the permutations of his next move. His apple tea is getting cold.

I stare out the window, and a little further along the way, I see what appears to be an ugly industrial chimney mounted on a crude pedestal of stone bricks. I check my street map and realise it is no such thing.

'You see that tower?' I say, excitedly.

'Yep,' Joe seems glad for the distraction.

'The Turks call it the Burnt Column. But do you know what it *really* is?'

He just looks at me patiently. He's getting used to my rhetorical tricks.

'That, Joe, is the Column of Constantine.'

THE COLUMN IS AS OLD as the imperial city, unveiled the very same day that Constantine's New Rome was founded seventeen centuries ago. If Constantinople has a birthplace, it is here, at the base of this burnt tower. Once among the city's most impressive monuments, today it's a blackened ruin of its former self, like a tree trunk after a forest fire.

Yet it is still upright, still on its feet.

Local shoppers and tourists stream past it like they would a homeless man, ignoring its still, spectral presence.

Joe glances at the column and back at me.

'You know,' I say, suddenly enthused, 'if we could somehow burrow our way under that column's pedestal, we *might* find the most precious Roman talisman of all ... an object of incredible mythic power. You could write the plot of an Indiana Jones movie around it.'

'Oh yeah? What is it?'

'It's a little wooden statue called the Palladium.'

✳

Palladium

THE PALLADIUM WAS a metre-long wooden effigy of the Greek goddess Pallas. According to Greek mythology, the statue was carved by a sorrowful Athena, full of regret for having killed Pallas, her stepmother. Zeus picked up the statue and hurled it down to Earth as a gift for the people of Troy.

The Trojans revered the Palladium, and came to believe this little statue would keep their city safe, so long as it remained inside Troy. But one night, at the climax of the Trojan Wars, two Greek warriors crept into the Trojan citadel and stole the Palladium, leaving the city unprotected and open to attack. Only then was it possible for the Greeks to take the city through the famous ruse of the Trojan Horse.

Sometime after the fall of Troy, it was said that the Palladium was smuggled into the fledgling city of Rome, where it was safeguarded for centuries in the Temple of Vesta. The Palladium worked the same protective magic on the city of Rome, keeping it inviolate and free to extend its dominion over the whole world. It bolstered Rome's self-assurance and its belief in its exceptional destiny. When Constantine the Great made plans for his new capital in the east, he wanted to transfuse something of that prestige into Constantinople's bloodstream.

ON MONDAY 4 NOVEMBER 328, Constantine led a procession through the streets of New Rome into an oval-shaped forum named in his honour. The transformation of Byzantium into an imperial capital had been rushed to meet Constantine's deadlines, and so the new city had all the cracks and imperfections of a shoddy renovation. But within this ceremonial space the emperor could survey the scene with satisfaction: the new Forum of Constantine was splendid to the eye, paved with marble and ringed with elegant colonnades and beautiful classical statues.

The centrepiece of the forum was an impressively tall column supporting a colossal statue of – who else? – Constantine himself. Creating this monument had been no small task. Since a suitable column could not be found anywhere nearby, the emperor's workers improvised by constructing a tall stone tower and cladding it with curved bands of porphyry, the purpled marble associated with imperial authority. The colossus of Constantine at the apex of the column, splendid as it was, was also a bit of a mish-mash. There was no time to build it up from scratch, so a suitably gigantic statue of Apollo was located elsewhere and the head lopped off, replaced by a newly carved likeness of the emperor, crowned by a nimbus of golden metal spikes that caught the radiance of the late-afternoon sun.

Constantine formally dedicated the city as the new Roman capital with a mix of pagan and Christian rites. At the emperor's side was Praetextus, the high priest of Rome, who had brought with him, at Constantine's request, the Palladium. At a particularly auspicious moment the wooden effigy was buried at the foot of Constantine's column where it could not be easily stolen. Precious Christian relics – twelve baskets of crumbs left over from the miracle of the loaves and fishes, and the legendary axe used by Noah to construct his Ark – were also buried under the column for safekeeping.

A pious inscription at the base of the monument bound the might of Rome to the God of the Christians: *O Christ, ruler and master of the world, to You now I dedicate this subject city, and these sceptres and the might of Rome.*

THE COLUMN OF CONSTANTINE remained in place for centuries, the statue at the top and the Palladium buried underneath like a dirty, pagan secret. But as the eastern Roman empire entered its long decline, the column began to deteriorate correspondingly.

In 1106, a severe storm toppled the statue of Constantine, sending it crashing into the forum below. Emperor Manuel Comnenus, who may have felt uncomfortable with its pagan overtones, replaced the statue with a simple, pious cross.

In 1204, the rampaging Crusaders tore away the bronze bands that held the porphyry outer shell in place. After the Ottoman conquest, Mehmed had the cross taken down, but the monument was otherwise left alone. A fire in 1779 left the column blackened and scorched.

For all we know, that little wooden totem is still buried at the foot of the burnt column, under that rocky pedestal, in the heart of downtown Istanbul.

The Third Rome

MEHMED'S DREAM was not so very different from that of a Roman emperor: to establish a universal empire under one rule and one faith. He adopted the title of 'Fetih', conqueror, and as his court settled into their new imperial capital of Istanbul, they abandoned the simple, egalitarian habits they had maintained from their days as nomadic warriors. As Mehmed grew older, he was transfigured from a lean warrior into a fattened, bejewelled monarch, increasingly distant from his subjects. He became more reliant on a large bureaucracy, which inevitably adopted longstanding Roman habits of administration.

In 1480 Mehmed commissioned a portrait from the Venetian painter Gentile Bellini. In it, his lips are pursed, his eyes vague and unfocused. He looks like a man who has attained his heart's desire and is still unhappy.

Portrait of Mehmed the Conqueror in his later years, by Gentile Bellini.

The Sultan was pleased to award himself another new title: 'Kayser-i Rûm', Caesar of the Romans. Soon enough there would be other claimants for the title of Kaysar, Kaiser or Czar.

ZOE PALAEOLOGUS, the niece of the last emperor, was only a child when Constantinople fell. Her family brought her to Corfu and then Rome, where she came under the pope's protection. Zoe was educated as a Catholic and her name was Latinised to Sophia.

In 1472, Pope Paul II, hoping to improve his influence with the Russian Orthodox church, arranged a marriage between Sophia and the Grand Prince of Moscow, Ivan III. The marriage was performed by proxy in St Peter's Basilica, with an ambassador standing in for the prince.

The next day Sophia embarked on the long journey to meet her new husband. Accompanied by a large entourage, she travelled

443

north through Italy and Germany to the port of Lübeck, where a ship carried her across the Baltic Sea to Tallinn. From there she was transported overland to Novgorod, and then at last to Moscow, where she arrived in time for the first winter snow.

Sophia was warmly received by Ivan, who dedicated several palaces and gardens to her, and she soon settled into her new life in Russia. The pope's ambitions were thwarted; Sophia walked away from Catholicism and returned to her Orthodox roots. Like other transplanted Byzantine princesses before her, Sophia brought a touch of sophistication to her new palace. She introduced elaborate Roman ceremonies to Ivan's court, and encouraged her husband to think of himself as the rightful successor to the Roman throne. There was a certain logic to it: Ivan was now the most powerful Orthodox ruler in the world, married to the last emperor's niece.

An Orthodox monk later sent a letter to Sophia's son, Vasilli II, which began with a dramatic flourish: 'Two Romes have fallen. The third stands. And there will be no fourth. No one shall replace your Christian Czardom.' Ivan's successors would thereafter adopt the imperial title of Czar of Muscovy: the Third Rome.

The Immortal City of the Imagination

THE LONG STORY of the Roman empire comes to a close with those two elegiac lines of Persian poetry uttered by Mehmed in the Great Palace. A doctor might have said the patient suffered a violent death, at the end of an unnaturally long life and a painful decline. But the disembodied presence of Byzantium haunted the world it left behind; it became a ghost empire, still influencing the course of events, like an impulse from the subconscious.

In Constantinople's final, turbulent century, even as its leaders drove the empire to extinction, somehow, heroically, the city experienced a resurgence of culture and ideas, like a final burst of light from a dying star. As the outside world became too horrible to contemplate, the Orthodox church turned inward, venturing deeper into mysticism. Priests adopted an intense style of prayer known as hesychasm, taken from a Greek word meaning 'to keep stillness'. Hesychasm was not unlike Buddhist meditation; it required breath control and constant repetition of a mantra, the Jesus prayer – 'Lord Jesus Christ have mercy on me, the sinner' – to help the worshipper withdraw from the noise and clutter of the outside world. Then, once a state of utter stillness had been reached, the mind would be opened to the uncreated light of God. In such moments, the worshipper might be flooded with ecstasy, although the church cautioned against seeking ecstasy for its own sake. This was an undeniably powerful form of *theosis*, union with the divine, realised in the most personal manner possible.

MEANWHILE, in other corners of the city during that last desperate century, scholars were marching steadily in the other direction, away from mysticism and towards a revival of reason, inspired by the writings of Aristotle and by other ancient texts. These scholars were no less Christian for all their love of pagan wisdom, believing enlightenment could be arrived at through rational thought. In the past, the term *hellene* had been used to describe the ancient Greek pagans, to hold them slightly at a distance from their own identity as Christian Romans. But in these last decades, there was a greater willingness among scholars in Constantinople to embrace their Hellenic heritage.

The classic works of ancient Greece had always been present in Constantinople, never quite forgotten, not even in its Dark Age, when the city was fighting for its life against the Persians and the armies of the Prophet. The torch of classical culture kept burning in Constantinople; its statues adorned its public places, and its manuscripts were kept safe in the city's monasteries and universities.

As the empire began to recover in the ninth century, the classics enjoyed a resurgence. Anyone pursuing higher education in Constantinople was taught to read ancient Greek and instructed in the works of the classical historians, poets and philosophers. In the *Alexiad*, Anna Comnena refers to Homer simply as 'the Poet', and just assumes her readers are as well acquainted with his work as she is.

Orthodox scholars struggled to reconcile the knowledge of the ancient world with their faith. Christian thought was more precious to them than pagan wisdom, but still, the elegance and insight of classical writing kept tugging at their sleeves. It was easy enough, then, to divide Christian and pagan wisdom into two distinct spheres. Pagan wisdom was deemed to be 'Outer Learning', the stuff of the created world, such as geometry, mathematics and history – paganism could do no harm here. Christian wisdom was the 'Inner Learning', the place reserved for the contemplation of the eternal. Pagan logic was excluded from this inner sanctum of thought. The only aspects of God that could be known were those that had been revealed through the scriptures. Anything beyond that was deemed to be profoundly mysterious, and beyond human comprehension.

Then, as the empire slid into its final decline, the church was convulsed in a bitter dispute over hesychasm. In 1337, an astronomer and a mathematician named Barlaam publicly ridiculed the Hesychasts as 'navel-gazers' (*omphalopsychoi*), for their practice of focusing on their navels during meditation. Barlaam argued that the presence of God could never be directly encountered, as the hesychasts claimed, but could only be deduced by our God-given powers of reason.

Barlaam's argument was attacked by a hesychast from Mount Athos named Gregory of Palamas, who insisted that Barlaam had it backwards: to him, trying to grapple with the uncreated light of God through the crude and puny tool of reason was absurd, like a spider attempting to capture the sun in its web. God, he said, could be experienced through prayer and meditation, but He could never be 'understood'.

The church came down hard on Gregory's side and Barlaam the rationalist monk was condemned as a heretic. Realising there was no longer any place for him in Constantinople, he left the city for the court of Robert the Wise in Naples, where a rebirth of interest in classical wisdom was already underway.

Italian and Byzantine scholars were already tentatively reaching out towards each other. Europeans were slowly rediscovering the works of Homer, Plato, Aristotle, Aeschylus, Sophocles, Herodotus and Thucydides, and they soon realised the only place that still held these invaluable Greek manuscripts was Constantinople. The Byzantines, for their part, could see the empire crumbling away under their feet, and that the Orthodox church was turning its back on Outer Wisdom. They began to understand that a better life might be waiting for them in the vibrant, humanist courts of Florence, Venice and Rome.

In Italy, Barlaam converted to Catholicism, and befriended three scholars who would go on to become the key literary instigators of the Italian Renaissance: Paul of Perugia, Boccaccio and the poet Petrarch. All three were very anxious to be introduced to the ancient Greek works that Barlaam knew so intimately.

WHEN CONSTANTINOPLE fell in 1453, another wave of influential scholars stuffed their bags with classical manuscripts and fled the city forever. As they infiltrated the Italian courts, the educated easterners taught their willing hosts how to read Greek, and helped translate the classics into Latin or into the Italian vernacular. By 1487, the Byzantine population of Venice was said to number close to four thousand, which led the local cardinal to remark that Venice had become 'almost another Byzantium'.

While it's not quite true that the Renaissance was ignited by Byzantine exiles, it's certainly true that the partnership between Italian and Byzantine scholars gave fuel to a flickering fire, and stoked it into a roaring blaze.

THE FALL OF CONSTANTINOPLE changed the world in other ways that could hardly have been foreseen at the time. Ottoman control of the region disrupted the spice trade between western Europe and Asia. Although the Turks were prepared to tolerate Christian traders, it was deemed in the west that the overland route was now too dangerous and difficult. And so Portuguese navigators began to search for a new sea route to India and China.

In 1486, Bartholomew Diaz sailed south, down the west African coast, and rounded the Cape of Good Hope, bringing a European-made galleon into the Indian Ocean for the first time. In 1497, Vasco de Gama sailed all the way from Lisbon to Calcutta, completely bypassing the Ottoman world.

Thirty-three years after the fall of Constantinople, a Genoese explorer named Cristoforo Colombo appeared before the Spanish court, asking for financial support to find another route to Japan and China by sailing west, across the unknown waters of the Atlantic. In this way, the death of Constantinople was a catalyst for the European Age of Exploration, and for the conquest of the Americas.

THE REPUTATION OF the eastern Roman empire suffered in the centuries after its death. Enthusiastic scholars of the Enlightenment had little interest in the history of a dead medieval theocracy. Edward Gibbon disdained the 'Byzantine Empire' as effete and superstitious, unworthy of the Roman name. The hostility persisted into the nineteenth century, leading one historian – in a book titled, unpromisingly, *A History of European Morals from Augustus to Charlemagne* – to pompously dismiss eleven centuries of Byzantine civilisation:

> *The universal verdict of history is that it constitutes, without*
> *a single exception, the most thoroughly base and despicable*
> *form that civilisation has yet assumed. There has been no other*
> *enduring civilisation so absolutely destitute of all forms and*
> *elements of greatness, and none to which the epithet 'mean'*
> *may be so emphatically applied ... The history of the empire is a*
> *monotonous story of the intrigues of priests, eunuchs and women,*
> *of poisonings, of conspiracies, of uniform ingratitude.*

European interest in Byzantium revived in the twentieth century, but historians knew they were cutting across the grain of centuries of western prejudice.

William Butler Yeats, a poet well attuned to Byzantine mysticism, dreamt of visiting the ghost empire of Constantinople. With two sublime poems, 'Byzantium' and 'Sailing to Byzantium', he invited the English-speaking world to see the empire afresh, uncluttered by western European prejudice. 'Sailing to Byzantium' was written when Yeats was sixty-eight and feeling like 'a tattered coat upon a stick'. To him, the dream of Byzantium seemed to promise entry into an immortal realm of shimmering mosaics, clockwork birds and drowsy emperors:

And therefore I have sailed the seas and come
To the holy city of Byzantium.
O sages standing in God's holy fire
As in the gold mosaic of a wall,
Come from the holy fire, perne in a gyre,
And be the singing-masters of my soul.
Consume my heart away; sick with desire
And fastened to a dying animal
It knows not what it is; and gather me
Into the artifice of eternity.

As an Irishman living outside the borders of the British empire, Yeats was perhaps better able to see past the martial music of the ancient Romans and appreciate the lustre of distant Constantinople. Speaking of the poem in a BBC broadcast, Yeats reminded listeners that, 'When Irishmen were illuminating the Book of Kells, and making the jewelled croziers in the National Museum, Byzantium was the centre of European civilisation and the source of its spiritual philosophy.'

IN 2004, THE METROPOLITAN MUSEUM of New York launched a blockbuster show titled *Byzantium: Faith and Power 1261–1557*, which displayed countless gilded icons, frescoes, silks, manuscripts, caskets and amulets from the final centuries of the eastern Roman empire. In a metropolis driven by steroidal capitalism, the still, sacred aura of Byzantine art left visitors dazzled and unsettled.

The exhibition's catalogue was prefaced with a blessing from Bartholomew I, the Ecumenical Patriarch of Constantinople, who noted the atmosphere of 'bright sadness' that pervades the art of the empire's final years. He concluded with a prayer that people 'may find faith in higher values and ideals than those that are being offered by the world marketplace'.

'Fat chance,' wrote the *New Yorker* critic. 'I came away,' he wrote, 'with a chilly sense of having been warned.'

TODAY BARTHOLOMEW lives in a walled compound in the district of Fener in Istanbul. The Turkish government doesn't recognise his title of Ecumenical Patriarch, only acknowledging him as the leader of the ethnic Greek minority known as the *Rum* or 'Romans' that once dominated this precinct of the city. As Turkey becomes increasingly torn between modernity and Islamism, more and more Greeks have chosen to pack up and leave Fener. The multi-ethnic flavour of the city that prevailed through the Ottoman era is fast disappearing. More families leave every year and Istanbul's 'Roman' population is now close to extinction.

AT THE AIRPORT, Joe and I queue to check our bags in, surrounded by backlit billboards for tech companies and financial services offering 'innovative solutions'. 'Innovation' has been a popular buzzword since the internet boom of the nineties. In the western world it's seen as a positive good, promising creativity, novelty and disruption. To the Byzantines, an innovation was a paltry thing, an embarrassment, like a cheap modern extension to a grand old house. Innovation, to them, was the enemy of the eternal, the perfect. In the struggle for and against icons in the eighth and ninth centuries, each side accused the other of introducing a shameful innovation to religious life. They maintained their aversion to innovation right up until the Turks dragged a giant cannon to their walls.

August 2015

IT IS A YEAR-AND-A-HALF since Joe and I journeyed to Istanbul. My son is now a lanky sixteen-year-old and he's as tall as me. He has a guitar. He's into the Pixies and the Strokes and Nirvana and Japanese noodles and Chinese barbecue duck and comedians on YouTube. He doesn't smoke dope because it's lame. He's learning to speak Mandarin and receives praise for his accent. He still wants to be an architect.

This month I have had to leave my family in Australia to make a radio series in Iceland. On my way home, I take a two-day stopover in Paris. I'm alone, and lonely, so I wander around the city aimlessly, allowing myself to be drawn down any street on a whim. On this warm summer evening I find myself outside the entrance of a modest Orthodox church on the Rue Jean de Beauvais. I assume it will be closed or deserted on a Thursday evening, but as I push open the door my senses are confronted with light, music and incense.

Inside I see twenty to thirty worshippers. Most are kneeling on the long carpets that run from the altar to the back of the room. The women wear headscarves and the men prostrate themselves on the floor towards the altar. It would be easy to mistake this place for a mosque if it weren't for all the Christian imagery. I feel like I've intruded on the rituals of a secret society.

I stand at the back, trying to observe unobtrusively. Then I notice the room is divided along gender lines and I am on the women's side. I shift over to the other side as surreptitiously as I can manage. No one is paying me the slightest attention anyway; the congregation are intensely focused on their worship.

Three aged priests, bent under the weight of their heavy robes, lead the service. Their rich voices are joined by two cantors in plain clothes at the side of the altar. The liturgy is entirely musical. The voices of the cantors soar up and swoop down through the eastern scales with assurance. One cantor, dressed in a jogging suit, looks bored, like he's only here to please his mother. The other cantor wears a crisp, white shirt; he seems more devoted to the music.

Here there is both *taxis* and *theosis*. I entered the church feeling footsore and irritable. After ten minutes or so I am cool and calm, and I begin to daydream. My eyes wander down to the floor and there it is, emblazoned on the carpet runner: the insignia of the double-headed eagle under a single crown. One talon clutches a sword, the other holds a globe. After all these years, the ghost empire still makes its claim, even here, to dominion over the upstart land of the Franks. The double-headed eagle, representing the unity of the eastern and western empires, still awaits its resurrection in Constantinople, the capital of a universal empire.

Acknowledgements

I would like to thank my wife Khym and daughter Emma for their patience with a heavily distracted father and husband; Kári Gíslason, who at times had a better idea of what this book should be than I did; the extraordinarily erudite Scott Stephens, editor of the ABC's Religion & Ethics online portal for his insights into early Christian history and theology; Pam O'Brien and Elizabeth Troyeur for their sound advice and warm encouragement; Brigitta Doyle, Lachlan McLaine, Foong Ling Kong and the people at ABC Books and HarperCollins for their editorial wisdom and guidance, and for engaging so enthusiastically with the idea; the great Liz Gilbert, who knows how to write a book for a single person that everyone wants to read; Simon Winchester, whose relentless curiosity has propelled him to just about all the strange and wonderful places on and under the face of the earth, for his kind words and for his beautiful books; and the State Library of Queensland, so surprisingly well-endowed with otherwise difficult-to-locate texts of Byzantine history. And my deepest thanks to my son Joe, who lay back on the couch listening as I read each passage to him, and who told me everything I needed to know.

Endnotes

Introduction

1   There he would place: *Apocalypse of Pseudo-Methodius*, 14: 2–3.

1   Radiant City

14   A Russian pilgrim: Sherrard, p. 51.

15   In their letter: *Russian Primary Chronicles*, chapter 6.

2   Rome to Byzantium

26   Historians place him: Norwich, *Byzantium*, volume 1, chapter 1.

32   The court historian Lactantius: Grant, p. 21.

35   Diocletian wrote back: Gibbon, 13: 111.

35   The decline and death: Lactantius, chapter 33.

43   Bishop Eusebius of Caesarea: Eusebius, *Constantine*, 9: 4.

44   The emperor expressed: Durant 30: 3.

46   This early version: legacy.fordham.edu/halsall/basis/nicea1.txt

48   Who else could be: www.stnicholascenter.org/pages/who-is-st-nicholas

54   Constantine replied enigmatically: Davies, p. 208.

69   A Roman ambassador: Jordanes, 35: 182.

70   Priscus later recorded: Priscus, *Dinner with Attila*; Gibbon, *The History of the Decline and Fall of the Roman Empire*; Thompson, *A History of Attila and the Huns*.

73   Did the exotic Hunnish prince: Herrin, *We Are All the Children of Byzantium*.

74   St Jerome, writing from: *Letters of St Jerome*, Letter CXXVII.

3   The Deep State

80   Procopius, the court historian: Procopius, *Secret History*, chapter 8.

83   Theodora's famous sexual: Procopius, *Secret History*, chapter 9.

83   Justinian lovingly acknowledged: Quoted in Pazdernik, p. 266.

83   After her death: Ibid., p. 262.

84   'Our subjects are: *Novels*, 43, Preface.

85   One courtier declared: Procopius, *Secret History*, chapter 12.

85   John was, begrudgingly: Ibid., chapter 10.

86   Justinian complained there: *The Digest*, First Preface: 1.

86   Since John was illiterate: Quoted in Rosen, p. 113.

86   Justinian crowed as he: *The Enactments of Justinian, The Code, First Preface*

92   Surely, he wrote: Procopius, *History of the Wars*, 1: 14.

95   Environmental groups led: Kotsev, 2 June 2013.

96   Erdoğan stated bluntly: Quoted in Tabet, 'Turkey and the Deep State.'

97   Some journalists have: Rainsford, '"Deep State" Trial Polarises Turkey'.

100 Theodora now gestured: Procopius, *Secret History*, chapter 24.

105 'It exults in an: Procopius, *On the Buildings*, I.

105 Procopius saw how: Ibid.

107 Once inside the church: Hichens, chapter 6.

108 To the Romans: Procopius, *Buildings*, 1: 30.

109 Then one of the: Isaiah, 6: 6.

115 'So it was: Procopius: *History of the Wars*, 5: 14.

116 'Tell us Lord Pope': *Liber Pontificalis*, 60: 8.

118 Narses presented Belisarius: Ibid., 6: 7.

119 'As for John: Ibid., 6: 16.

122 He was, Procopius records: Ibid., 7: 30.

124 Procopius records sympathetically: Procopius, *Secret History*, chapter 4.

125 Procopius records that: *History of the Wars*, 4: 14.

125 At sea, there were: John of Ephesus, p. 75.

127 Inevitably, they too: John of Ephesus, p. 74.

128 John of Ephesus reports: Ibid., p. 75.

128 Workplaces fell silent: Ibid., p. 88.

129 Within the space: Rosen, p. 187.

131 'For a few weeks: Oman, p. 95.

138 Pliny estimated that: Pliny the Elder, *Natural History*, Book 11.

4   Persian Nightmares

152 Tiberius ruled for: Norwich, *Byzantium*, volume 1, p. 272.

154 Historian Edward Gibbon: Gibbon, 4: 46: 49.

156 Persian campfires were visible: Norwich, volume 1, p. 284.

156 Heraclius was handsome: Quoted in Kaegi, p. 31.

159 Ambassadors were sent: Kaegi, p. 85.

159 Revelling in his: Davies, p. 245.

166 Instead his guards: Nikephoros, p. 63.

166 News of Khusrau's: Quoted in Sarris, p. 118.

168 Princess Anna Comnena: *Alexiad*, 12:6.

171 According to Muslim tradition: www.cyberistan.org/islamic/letters.html

172 A German historian: Heck, *The Burden of Hitler's Legacy*, p. 259.

174 Procopius had written: Procopius, *The Wars of Justinian: Book II*, chapter 18.

177 George of Pisidia: George of Pisidia, *On the Vain Life*, 10.215–25, quoted in Kaegi, pp. 322–23.

178 The annihilation of Carthage: penelope.uchicago.edu/Thayer/E/Roman/Texts/Polybius/38*

5   Children of Ishmael

183 'Superstition riveted their chains: Gibbon, chapter 48.

183 Voltaire was similarly: Quoted in Harrison, p. 46.

187 The revelations were: Quoted in Armstrong, p. 5.

188 There is only one: Qur'an 82:1.

189 An anonymous Muslim: Sizgorich, pp. 1–2.

190 The document notes: *Letter of John of Sedra*.

190 Another clue can be: Sebeos, chapter 30.

196 Pliny the Elder wrote: Pliny 34: 18.

198 Spiced wines were: Liutprand of Cremona, *Report of his Mission to Constantinople*

205 The three sages: en.wikisource.org/wiki/Khazar_Correspondence

208 As the boat rolled: Bury, p. 359.

214 The author of Revelation: Revelation 20: 7–10.

215 They wretched creatures ate: *The Greek Alexander Romance, supplement J*.

217 In the next phase: *Apocalypse of Pseudo-Methodius*, 13: 9.

218 With Gog and Magog: Ibid., 14: 2–3.

227 According to these sources, Leo's correspondence: Theophanes, *The Chronicle of Theophanes*

6   Uncreated Light

237 Muslims accused the Christians: Exodus 20: 4–5.

237 Theodore, the abbot: MacCulloch, p. 451.

247 The envoys of: *Russian Primary Chronicles*, chapter 6.

258 Constantine, in Christ: *De Administrando Imperio*, p. 45.

263 Liutprand recorded his impressions: Liutprand, p. 443.

264 The adulation of the emperor: Ibid., pp. 446–47.

264 He bade Constantinople: Liutprand, *Report of his Mission to Constantinople*.

270 A German chronicler: Thietmar, p. 158.

276 The witch-wife was feeding: *Helmskringla*, 84.

277 The runestones are carved: www.worldlibrary.org/articles/greece_runestones

282 John Scylitzes, a contemporary historian: Quoted in Norwich, volume 2, p. 356.

7 The Starlit Golden Bough

286 She begins by: *Alexiad*, Preface I.

289 The night before battle: *Alexiad*, 7: 5.

294 Anna, the emperor's daughter: *Alexiad*, 13: 10.

297 In any event: Freising: *The Legend of Prester John*, pp. 334–5.

298 It began with: Silverberg, p. 2.

299 India was known: De Rachewiltz, p. 22.

300 Yelü Dashi's victory: Ibid., p. 34.

305 Irene was renowned: *Irene*, chapter 3.

315 He was physically powerful: Choniates, s. 141.

318 Andronicus laid down: Ibid., s. 139.

321 Unburdened by any: Ibid., s. 323.

8 The Fourth Crusade

328 The merchants of Venice: Gleeson-White, *Double Entry*, pp.6–7.

331 The congregation was hushed: Villehardouin, s. 7.

334 Dandolo climbed into: Villehardouin, s. 16–17.

335 I will not in: Clari, p. 44.

339 Simon of Monfort: Tyerman, p. 529.

340 Villehardouin recorded the awe: Villehardouin, s. 31.

344 The Roman soldiers: Villehardouin, s. 43.

346 Isaac heard him: Ibid., s. 47.

347 You stupid boy: Clari, chapter 6.

351 The conflagration ran: Villehardouin, s. 64.

356 One historian observed: Southern, *The Making of the Middle Ages*, p. 61.

9 End of Days

362 Théophile Gautier: Gautier, p. 214.

369 To such a degree: Vasiliev, p. 680.

371 'I, sinful Stephen of Novgorod: Majeska, p. 28.

371 His advice reads: Ibid., p. 44.

371 Stephen of Novgorod: Ibid., p. 237.

373 As he wandered: Tafur, *Travels and Adventures*, p. 17.

373 It was a thrilling: Ibid.

377 But the chief advisor: Sphrantzes, quoted in Philippides, p. 360.

378 Gurani taught Mehmed: rasoolurrahmah.wordpress.com/2014/05/29

380 With the murder: Ibid., p. 66.

383 Halil's reply to: Quoted in Nicol, p. 52.

385 Mehmed's reply to the envoys: Doukas, quoted in Crowley, p. 59.

387 He drafted a message: Doukas, quoted in Philippides, p. 409.

10 A Thing Not of this World

392 *Rum Papa*: Crowley, p. 68.

394 Pope Nicholas was well: Runciman, Steven, *The Fall of Constantinople*, pp. 63–64

395 Ducas saw through: Quoted in Geanakoplos, *Byzantium: Church, Society, and Civilization Seen Through Contemporary Eyes*, p. 225

396 He scrawled a note: Gibbon, VII, 176.

397 Then, hinting that: Babinger, p. 81.

399 He would know: Quoted in Babinger p. 7.

402 A warning was sent out: Doukas, quoted in Philippides, p. 423.

404 As the sense of crisis: Barbaro, 5 7 April.

405 The ball crashed: Kritovoulos, 1: 136.

408 His orders to Baltoglu: Kritovoulos, 1: 162.

409 Eventually, through all: Ibid., 1: 166.

415 Barbaro noted that: Barbaro, 19 May.

417 A Russian observer: Iskander, p. 59.

417 Perhaps this was proof: Kritovoulos, 1: 185.

418 In the street: Philippides, p. 222.

418 Most likely the strange lights: www.jpl.nasa.gov/releases/93/release_1993_1543.html.

426 The roar of the cannon: Barbaro, 29 May.

426 The brothers were unlikely: *Apocalypse of Pseudo-Methodius*, 13: 9.

11 The Artifice of Eternity

432 Barbaro, from aboard his ship: Barbaro, 29 May.

445 Priests adopted an intense: McCulloch, p. 487.

446 Christian wisdom was: Runciman, *The Last Byzantine Renaissance*, p. 28.

448 By 1487, the Byzantine: Harris, *Byzantines in Renaissance Italy*.

450 Speaking of the poem: Yeats, *The Major Works*, p. 502.

450 The exhibition's catalogue: *Byzantium: Faith & Power*, p. vii.

451 Fat chance: Schjeldahl, *Striking Gold*.

Bibliography

Ancient and Medieval Sources

Accounts of Medieval Constantinople, The Patria, trans. Albrecht Berger, Dumbarton Oaks Medieval Library, 2013

Al-Tabari, *The History of Al-Tabari Vol. 30: The 'Abbasid Caliphate in Equilibrium,* trans. C.E. Bosworth, State University of New York Press, 1989

Ambrose, *The Death of Theodosius,* trans. Roy J. Deferrari, Fathers of the Church, 1953

Ammianus, Marcellinus, *The Later Roman Empire,* trans. Walter Hamilton, Penguin, 2004

Anonymus Valesianus, penelope.uchicago.edu/Thayer/E/Roman/Texts/ Excerpta_Valesiana/2*

Barbaro, Nicolo, *Diary of the Siege of Constantinople*

Choniates, Nicetas, *O City of Byzantium: Annals of Niketas Choniates,* trans. Harry J. Magoulias, Wayne State University Press, 1984

Comnena, Anna, *The Alexiad,* trans. Elizabeth A. Dawes, Fordham University Medieval Sourcebook, legacy.fordham.edu/Halsall/basis/ AnnaComnena-Alexiad.asp

Constantine Porphyrogenitus, *De Administrando Imperio,* trans. R.J.H. Jenkins, Dumbarton Oaks, 1967

Constas, Nicholas, *Proclus of Constantinople and the Cult of the Virgin in Late Antiquity,* Brill, 2003

De Clari, Robert, *The Capture of Constantinople,* Fordham University Medieval Sourcebook, legacy.fordham.edu/halsall/source/clari1.asp

De Villehardouin, Geoffroi, *Memoirs, or Chronicle of the Fourth Crusade,* trans. Frank Marzials, J.M. Dent 1908

The Enactments of Justinian: The Digest, or Pandects, www.constitution.
org/sps/sps02_j2-01.htm

Eusebius of Caesarea, *The History of the Church*, trans. Arthur Cushman
McGiffert, Acheron Press, 2012

Eusebius of Caesarea, *Life of Constantine*, trans. Ernest Cushing
Richardson, Heraklion Press, 2014

Eusebius of Caesarea *Martyrs of Palestine*, people.ucalgary.ca/~vandersp/
Courses/texts/eusebius/eusempaf.html

The Greek Alexander Romance, trans. Richard Stoneman, Penguin
Classics, 1991

Evagrius Scholasticus, *Ecclesiastical History (AD431–594)*, trans. by E.
Walford, 1846, www.tertullian.org/fathers/evagrius_4_book4.htm

Gyllius, Petrus, *The Antiquities of Constantinople*, 1729, trans. John Ball,
from digitised copy of original 1729 translation, hdl.handle.net/2027/
njp.32101075990547

Harrison Frederic, *Byzantine History in the Early Middle Ages*,
Macmillian, 1900

The Holy Bible, English Standard Version, EPUB edition

Jerome, *The Letters of St. Jerome*, Christian Classics Ethereal Library,
www.ccel.org/ccel/schaff/npnf206.v.CXXVII.html

John of Ephesus, *Pseudo-Dionysius of Tel-Maḥrē: Chronicle of Zuqnin,
Part III*, trans. Witold Witakowski, Liverpool University Press,
1996

John of Sedra, *The Letter of John of Sedra*, trans. Dr. Abdul-Massih Saadi,
published in *Karmo Magazine*, Mar Aphram Institute, Vol. 1 No. 2,
1999, www.chaldeansonline.org/Banipal/English/karmo2.html

Jordanes, *The Origins and Deeds of the Goths*, trans: Charles C. Mierow,
people.ucalgary.ca/~vandersp/Courses/texts/jordgeti.html

Justinian, *The Enactments of Justinian, The Code, First Preface*, trans. S.P.
Scott, 1932., droitromain.upmf-grenoble.fr/Anglica/codjust_pre1_
Scott.htm

The Koran, trans. N.J. Dawood, Penguin, 1974

Kritovoulos, *History of Mehmed the Conqueror*, trans. Charles T. Riggs, 1970, www.promacedonia.org/en/kmc/index.htm

Lactantius, *On the Manner in which the Persecutors Died*, www. newadvent.org/fathers/0705.htm

Leo the Deacon, *Historiae Libri X*, ed. C. B. Hase, 1828, www. paulstephenson.info/trans/leo3.html

Liber Pontificalis, archive.org/details/bookofpopesliber00loom

Life of Saint Irene Abbess of Chrysobalanton: A Critical Edition with Introduction, Notes and Indices, trans. Jan Olof Rosenqvist, Acta University Upsaliensis, Studia Byzantina Upsaliensis, Almqvist & Wiksall, 1986, 3–113, legacy.fordham.edu/halsall/basis/irene-chrysobalanton.asp

Liutprand of Cremona, *Report of his Mission to Constantinople*, Medieval Sourcebook, Fordham University, legacy.fordham.edu/Halsall/source/liudprand1.asp

Mango, Cyril, *The Art of the Byzantine Empire 312–1453: Sources and Documents*, University of Toronto Press, 1986

Medieval Tales from Byzantium, trans. Alice-Mary Talbot & Scott Fitzgerald Johnson, Dumbarton Oaks Medieval Library, 2012

Nestor-Iskander, *The Fall of Constantinople*, wps.pearsoncustom.com/wps/media/objects/2427/2486120/chap_assets/documents/doc9_4.html

Nikephoros, *Nikephoros, Patriarch of Constantinople, Short History*, trans. Cyril Mango, Dumbarton Oaks Texts, 1990

Novels of Justinian, www.uwyo.edu/lawlib/justinian-novels

Otto of Freisling, *Chronicon*, ed. G.H. Pertz, Hanover, Hahn, 1867, VII, 33, (pp. 334–35), translated by James Brundage, *The Crusades: A Documentary History*, Marquette University Press, 1962: *The Legend of Prester John*, Fordham University, Medieval Sourcebook, legacy.fordham.edu/halsall/source/otto-prester.asp

Pliny the Elder, *Natural History*, trans. H. Rackham, Loeb Classical Library, 1938

Procopius, *The Secret History/The Wars of Justinian*, Halcyon Classics
    eBook, 2009
The Buildings, Loeb Classical Library, 1940
Prudentius, *The Reply to Symmachus*, trans. H.J. Thompson, Loeb
    Classical Library, 1955
Psellus, Michael, *Fourteen Byzantine Rulers*, trans. E.R.A. Sewter,
    Penguin, 1966
Psellus, Michael, *Historia Syntomos*, trans. W. De Gruyter, Milan Savić, 1998
Pseudo-Methodius, *Apocalypse*, An Alexandrian World Chronicle, trans.
    Benjamin Garstad, Dumbarton Oaks Medieval Library, 2012
Russian Primary Chronicles, pages.uoregon.edu/kimball/chronicle.htm
Sebeos, *The History of Sebeos*, trans. Robert Bedrosian, 1985, rbedrosian.
    com/seb1.htm
Skylitzes, John, *A Synopsis of Byzantine History, 811–1057*, trans. John
    Wortley, Cambridge University Press, 2010
Sphrantzes, George, *The Siege of Constantinople, 1453, According to
    George Sphrantzes*
Strabo, *The Geography of Strabo*, trans. Horace Leonard Jones, 1917,
    penelope.uchicago.edu/Thayer/E/Roman/Texts/Strabo/home.html
Sturluson, Snorri, *Heimskringla*, trans. Samuel Laing, John. C. Nimmo,
    1889, www.wisdomlib.org/scandinavia/book/heimskringla/d/
    doc5732.html
Tafur, Pero, *Pero Tafur: Travels and Adventures (1435–1439)*, trans.
    Malcolm Letts, Harper & Brothers, 1926
Theophanes, *The Chronicle of Theophanes*, trans. Harry Turtledove,
    University of Pennsylvania Press, 1982
Theophylact Simocatta, *The History of Theophylact Simocatta*, trans.
    Michael and Mary Whitby, Oxford University Press, 1986
*Three Byzantine Saints: Contemporary Biographies of St. Daniel the
    Stylite, St. Theodore of Sykeon and St. John the Almsgiver*, trans.
    Elizabeth Dawes, Blackwell, 1948, legacy.fordham.edu/halsall/basis/
    dan-stylite.asp

Thietmar of Merseberg, *Ottonian Germany: The Chronicon of Thietmar of Merseburg*, trans. David A. Warner, Manchester University Press, 2001

Vitalis, Orderic, *The Ecclesiastical History of Orderic Vitalis*, trans. Thomas Forrester 1853, https://archive.org/details/ecclesiasticalhi03orde

Modern Sources

Alexander, Paul Julius, *The Byzantine Apocalyptic Tradition*, University of California Press, 1985

Alexander, Paul Julius, 'The Medieval Legend of the Last Roman Emperor and Its Messianic Origin', *Journal of the Warburg and Courtauld Institutes*, Vol. 41, (1978), pp. 1–15, Warburg Institute

Angold, Michael, *The Byzantine Empire, 1025–1204*, Longman, 1997

Armstrong, Karen, *A Short History of Islam*, Modern Library, 2002

Babinger, Franz, *Mehmed the Conqueror and His Time*, Princeton University Press, 1992

Baring-Gould, Sabine, *Curious Myths of the Middle Ages*, Dover Publications, 2005

Brown, Peter, *The World of Late Antiquity*, Folio Society, 2014

Bury, J.B., *A History of the Later Roman Empire: From the Death of Theodosius I to the Death of Justinian Vols. I, II*, Dover Publications 2011

Bury, J.B., *A History of the Later Roman Empire: From the Fall of Irene to the Accession of Basil I*, Dover Publications, 2011

Campo, Juan Eduardo, *Encyclopedia of Islam*, Infobase Publishing, 2009

Cavallo, Guglielmo (ed)., *The Byzantines*, University of Chicago Press, 1997

Connor, Carolyn L., *Women of Byzantium*, Yale University Press, 2004

Crowley, Roger, *Constantinople, the Last Great Siege, 1453*, Faber & Faber, 2005

Curtis, Robert I., 'In Defense of Garum', *The Classical Journal*, Vol. 78, No. 3 (Feb–Mar, 1983), pp. 232–240

Davies, Norman, *Europe: a History,* Pimlico 1998

De Rachewilts, Igor, *Papal Envoys to the Great Khans,* Stanford University Press, 1971

Drake, H.A., *Constantine and the Bishops: The Politics of Intolerance,* Johns Hopkins University Press, 2002

Durant, Will, *The Complete Story of Civilization: Our Oriental Heritage,* Simon & Shuster, 1942

Evans, Helen C. (ed.) *Byzantium: Faith and Power (1261–1557),* Metropolitan Museum of Art, New York, 2004

Evans, Helen C. & Wixom, William D. (eds.), *The Glory of Byzantium: Art and Culture of the Middle Byzantine Era AD 843–1261,* Metropolitan Museum of Art, New York, 1997

Filkins, Dexter, 'The Deep State', *The New Yorker,* Dec. 12, 2012

Fleming, K.E., 'Constantinople: From Christianity to Islam', *The Classical World,* Vol. 97, No. 1 (Autumn, 2003), pp. 69–78, Johns Hopkins University Press

Frankopan, Peter, *The Silk Roads: A New History of the World,* Bloomsbury 2015

Garland, Lynda, *Byzantine Empresses: Women and Power in Byzantium, AD 527–1204,* Routledge, 2011

Gautier, Théophile, *Constantinople,* trans. Robert Howe Gould, Holt, 1875

Geanakoplos, Deno John, *Byzantium: Church, Society, and Civilization Seen Through Contemporary Eyes,* University of Chicago Press, 1984

Geanakoplos, Deno John, *Constantinople and the West,* University of Wisconsin Press, 1989

Gibbon, Edward, *The History of the Decline & Fall of the Roman Empire,* HMDS Press eBook 2015

Gleeson-White, Jane, *Double Entry: How the Merchants of Venice Shaped the Modern World,* Allen & Unwin, 2012

Goldsworthy, Adrian, *The Fall of the West: The Death of the Roman Superpower,* Phoenix, 2009

Grant, Michael, *The Emperor Constantine*, Weidenfeld & Nicholson, 1993

Harris, Jonathan, *The End of Byzantium*, Yale University Press, 2010

Harris, Jonathan, *Byzantines in Renaissance Italy*, Online Reference Book for Medieval Studies, the-orb.arlima.net/encyclop/late/laterbyz/harris-ren.html

Heather, Peter, *The Fall of the Roman Empire: A New History of Rome and the Barbarians*, Oxford University Press, 2006

Heck, Alfons, *The Burden of Hitler's Legacy*, Primer Publishers, 1998

Herrin, Judith, *Byzantium: The Surprising Life of a Medieval Empire*, Penguin, 2007

Herrin, Judith, *We Are All the Children of Byzantium*, 18th Annual Runciman Lecture, 2009, oodegr.co/english/istorika/romi/children_of_byzantium.htm

Hichens, Robert, *The Near East: Dalmatia, Greece and Constantinople*, Hodder & Stoughton, 1913

Holland, Tom, *In the Shadow of the Sword*, Hachette, 2012

Holland, Tom, *Millennium*, Hachette, 2011

Huizinga, Johan, *The Waning of the Middle Ages*, Dover, 1999

Hunt, Patrick, *Byzantine Silk: Smuggling and Espionage in the 6th Century CE*, Stanford University, 2011, altmarius.ning.com/profiles/blogs/byzantine-silk-smuggling-and-espionage-in-the-6th-century-ce

James, Liz (ed.), *A Companion to Byzantium*, John Wiley & Sons, 2010

Kaegi, Walter, *Heraclius Emperor of Byzantium*, Cambridge University Press, 2003

Kaldellis, Anthony, *The Byzantine Republic: People and Power in the New Rome*, Harvard University Press, 2015

Kaldellis, Anthony, *Hellenism in Byzantium*, Cambridge University Press, 2008

Kaya, Serdar, 'The Rise and Decline of the Turkish "Deep State": The Ergenekon Case', *Insight Turkey*, vol. 11 / No. 4 / 2009 pp. 99–113

Lidov, Alexei, *The Flying Hodegetria the Miraculous Icon as Bearer of*

Sacred Space, 2004, archiv.ub.uni-heidelberg.de/artdok/3674/1/Lidov_
The_flying_Hodegetria_2004.pdf

MacCulloch, Diarmaid, *A History of Christianity*, Allen Lane, 2009

Majeska, George P., *Russian Travelers to Constantinople in the Fourteenth
and Fifteenth Centuries*, Dumbarton Oaks Research Library and
Collection, 1984

Mango, Cyril, et al, *The Oxford History of Byzantium*, Oxford University
Press, 2002

Marlowe, Elizabeth, 'Framing the Sun: The Arch of Constantine and the
Roman Cityscape', *The Art Bulletin*, Vol. 88, No. 2, 2006, pp. 223–242

Muthesius, Anna, 'Silk in the Medieval World', *The Cambridge History of
Western Textiles*, Vol. I, ed. T.D. Jenkins, Cambridge University Press,
2003

Nicol, Donald M., *The Immortal Emperor: The Life and Legend of
Constantine Palaiologos, Last Emperor of the Romans*, Cambridge
University Press, 2002

Norwich, John Julius, *A History of Venice*, Viking, 1983

Norwich, John Julius, *Byzantium Vol I: The Early Centuries*, Viking,
1989

Norwich, John Julius, *Byzantium Vol II: The Apogee*, Viking, 1992

Norwich, John Julius, *Byzantium Vol III: The Decline and Fall*,
Viking, 1995

Odahl, Charles Matson, *Constantine and the Christian Empire*,
Routledge, 2004

Oman, Charles William Chadwick, *The Byzantine Empire*, G.P. Putnam,
1892

Pazdernik, Charles, ' "Our Most Pious Consort Given Us by God":
Dissident Reactions to the Partnership of Justinian and Theodora,
AD 525–548', *Classical Antiquity* 13.2 (1994): 256–281

Pamuk, Orhan, *Istanbul: Memories of a City*, Faber & Faber 2005

Pevny, Olenka Z. (ed.), *Perceptions of Byzantium and its Neighbours
(843–1261)*, Metropolitan Museum of Art, New York, 2000

Philippides, Marios & Hanak, Walter, *The Siege and the Fall of Constantinople in 1453: Historiography, Topography, and Military Studies*, Ashgate, 2011

Phillips, Jonathon, *The Fourth Crusade and the Sack of Constantinople*, Jonathan Cape, 2004

Ramirez, Janina, *The Private Lives of the Saints. Power, Passion and Politics in Anglo-Saxon England*, W.H. Allen, 2015

Rosen, William, *Justinian's Flea: Plague Empire and the Birth of Europe*, Pimlico 2008

Runciman, Steven, *The Fall of Constantinople 1453*, Cambridge University Press, 1990

Runciman, Steven, *History of the Crusades, Vol III*, Cambridge University Press, 1987

Runciman, Steven, *The Last Byzantine Renaissance*, Cambridge University Press, 1968

Schjeldahl, Peter, 'Striking Gold', *The New Yorker*, May 17, 2004

Sherrard, Philip, *Constantinople: Iconography of a Sacred City*, Oxford University Press, 1965

Silverberg, Robert, *The Realm of Prester John*, Ohio University Press, 1996

Silverberg, Robert, *The Crusades*, Borgo Press, 2010

Sizgorich, Thomas, *Violence and Belief in Late Antiquity*, University of Pennsylvania Press, 2009

Soulis, George C., 'The Gypsies in the Byzantine Empire and the Balkans in the Late Middle Ages', *Dumbarton Oaks Papers*, Vol. 15 (1961), pp. 141+143–165

Southern, Richard William, *The Making of the Middle Ages*, Yale University Press, 1953

Spier, Jeffrey, 'Medieval Byzantine Magical Amulets and Their Tradition', *Journal of the Warburg and Courtauld Institutes*, Vol. 56, 1993

Stephenson, Paul, *Constantine: Unconquered Emperor, Christian Victor*, Quercus, 2009

Tabet, Jonathon, 'Turkey and the Deep State', *Veche Magazine*, 4 Feb, 2009, University College London, arabsandrussians.blogspot.com. au/2012/01/turkey-and-deep-state.html

Treadgold, Warren, *A History of the Byzantine State and Society*, Stanford University Press 1997

Tyerman, Christopher, *God's War*, Penguin 2007

Vasiliev, Alexander A., *History of the Byzantine Empire, 324–1453*, University of Wisconsin Press, 1958

Wells, Colin, *Sailing from Byzantium: How a Lost Empire Shaped the World*, Random House, 2007

White, Cynthia, *The Emergence of Christianity: Classical Traditions in Contemporary Perspective*, Fortress Press, 2010

Woods, David, 'On the Death of the Empress Fausta', *Greece and Rome*, 2nd Ser., Vol. 45, No. 1, Cambridge University Press, 1998

Yeats, W.B., *The Major Works*, Oxford University Press, 2001

Young, Monica, 'A Universe from Nothing', *Radcliffe Magazine*, 2013, www.radcliffe.harvard.edu/news/radcliffe-magazine/universe-nothing

Image Credits

Index